THE
BOOK OF MATTHEW

the Smart Guide to the Bible™ series

Dewey and Rebecca Bertolini

Larry Richards, General Editor

THOMAS NELSON
Since 1798

NASHVILLE   DALLAS   MEXICO CITY   RIO DE JANEIRO   BEIJING

The Book of Matthew
The Smart Guide to the Bible™ series
© 2008 by GRQ, Inc.

Published in Nashville, Tennessee, by Thomas Nelson. Thomas Nelson is a trademark of Thomas Nelson, Inc.

Originally published by Starburst Publishers under the title *Matthew: God's Word for the Biblically-Inept.* Now revised and updated.

Thomas Nelson, Inc. titles may be purchased in bulk for educational, business, fundraising, or sales promotional use. For information, please e-mail SpecialMarkets@ThomasNelson.com.

General Editor: Larry Richards
Managing Editor: Lila Empson
Scripture Editor: Deborah Wiseman
Assistant Editor: Amy Clark
Design: Diane Whisner

ISBN 13: 978-1-4185-1006-0

Printed in the United States of America
10 11 RRD 9 8 7 6 5 4 3

Introduction

Welcome to *The Book of Matthew—The Smart Guide to the Bible™*. The moment you picked up this book, you embarked on an incredible journey of discovery. Like a modern-day time traveler, you are about to enter an amazing world—the land of Israel—at a unique time in its storied history, the dawning of the first century AD. As we break the seal on the New Testament, we'll walk the stony streets and dusty paths that Jesus walked, climb hills, descend into a desert wilderness, sail through a storm on the Sea of Galilee and live to tell about it, encounter many of the people whom Jesus met, watch as angels minister to him and demons flee from him, marvel at his miracles, and listen in rapt attention to his teaching. This study of Matthew certainly changed our lives; we have no doubt that it will change yours as well.

If the key to the value of a piece of property is "location, location, location," then the key to the value of good Bible teaching is "make it clear, make it clear, make it clear." That's exactly what we've tried to do in *The Book of Matthew—The Smart Guide to the Bible™*, make the Bible clear.

Someone once lamented, "No one has ever reasoned me out of my faith. But I've nearly been bored out of my faith many times." Know the feeling? Unfortunately, too many people greet the Bible with a yawn. To them, the Bible is nothing more than a drab, dreary, dusty old book that doesn't even begin to relate to the problems and pressures of their everyday lives. How sad. One thing's for sure—you won't be bored out of your faith reading this book. Quite the contrary: From the very first verse of the first chapter, you'll discover a vibrant, living, breathing verbal video of the most amazing man who ever lived. *The Book of Matthew—The Smart Guide to the Bible™* is sure to ignite the flames of your imagination as it touches your life and challenges your thinking in ways that you cannot even begin to anticipate.

Who Wrote Matthew?

Every effort has been made to resuscitate (figuratively, of course) our dear friend Matthew just long enough to plop him down in an easy chair in your living room or position him bedside in your bedroom and allow him to tell you his amazing story. It's a twisting, turning tale of intrigue and inspiration, tender love and volcanic hatred, passionate devotion and brutal betrayal, sky-high hopes and dashed dreams. It's all here for public consumption. Matthew is perfectly positioned to tell it.

Before he met Jesus, Matthew held the despicable position of a turncoat tax collector, considered to be the dregs of that society, lower even than a prostitute. Why? Because as a Jew, Matthew sold out his own people when he decided to hold hands with the Romans, overtax his own countrymen, and pocket the profits for himself. "Scum of the earth" is too nice to capture what people felt about him. But when Jesus called him to "follow Me" (Matthew 9:9 NKJV), Matthew couldn't resist. Right on the spot he gave up everything and never looked back. From that moment on until the day he died, Matthew was a faithful follower of Jesus—a disciple, one of twelve apostles who would go on literally to change the world.

Our Qualified Guide!

Through Matthew's eyes, we will view vast vistas of landscape—the towering slopes of Mount Hermon where the Transfiguration likely took place (Matthew 17) to the plummeting depths of the Jordan rift valley where Jesus was baptized (Matthew 3). We'll go with Jesus from the desert oasis of Jericho, the oldest known, continuously inhabited city[1] (Matthew 20) to the mountaintop grandeur of Jerusalem, the crowned jewel of the Middle East, the place where God chose to touch the earth, where his radiant glory flashed and flamed in the blessed Jewish Temple. It is an epic journey that begins in a cradle and ends (apparently) on a cross.

We'll stand helplessly beside that cross as Jesus attends to one last need before he dies—the care of his anguished mother. We'll wake up the next morning after a fitful night of sleep with that hollow cavity of doubt in our guts because we've given up everything—everything—to follow a dead man. We'll make one last visit to his grave...only to find it empty!

Matthew was there to experience it all. And even though he is long gone, his words still live. Through his eyes, his ears, his heart, we will live it too. Matthew will be our qualified guide on this life-changing journey.

Where Does Matthew Fit in the Bible?

The Bible is divided into two large sections: the Old and New Testaments. The simplest way to distinguish between them is to remember that the Old Testament was written before the birth of Jesus Christ and prepares the reader for that defining moment of history. The New Testament was written after Jesus's death, burial, and resurrection, and reminds the reader of what happened during those monumental events and how we should now live our lives in light of Jesus's ministry and message.

Here's a neat memory peg for you: The words *Old* and *New* contain but three letters each, while Testament boasts a full complement of nine letters. Put the three and nine together, and what do you get? The thirty-nine books of the Old Testament (Genesis through Malachi) loudly proclaim, "Jesus is coming; Jesus is coming." A little multiplication—three times nine—and the twenty-seven books of the New Testament systematically explain why he came—to save you and me from our sins. As far as the twenty-seven New Testament books are concerned, Matthew is the grand-marshal of the parade.

Why Four and No More (Or Less)

In the book of Revelation, John recorded a most amazing sight: "Before the throne there was a sea of glass, like crystal. And in the midst of the throne, and around the throne, were four living creatures full of eyes in front and in back. The first living creature was like a lion, the second living creature like a calf, the third living creature had a face like a man, and the fourth living creature was like a flying eagle" (Revelation 4:6–7 NKJV). These four living creatures "give glory and honor and thanks to Him who sits on the throne, who lives forever and ever" (Revelation 4:9 NKJV). As they lavish continuous praise upon Jesus, these mysterious creatures actually reflect the fourfold nature of Jesus's person, a four-part composite of his character, exactly like the four Gospels do:

1. *Lion* (the king of the beasts)—Matthew presents Jesus as the King of kings, the only one who can rightfully proclaim, "All authority has been given to Me in heaven and on earth" (Matthew 28:18 NKJV).

2. *Calf*—Mark, who wrote a fast-paced, out-of-breath Gospel, has Jesus running (never walking) hither and yon as he tirelessly teaches, heals, encourages, and encounters all sorts of people—a selfless servant who "did not come to be served, but to serve" (Mark 10:45 NKJV).

3. *Man* (a human being)—Luke introduces us to a fully human Jesus: "The Son of Man has come to seek and to save that which was lost" (Luke 19:10 NKJV).

4. *Eagle* (the ruler of the skies)—From the get-go, John describes Jesus as "the Word [who] was God" (John 1:1 NKJV).

If Jesus is a melody, the Gospel writers sing it in four-part harmony. Jesus is the King who serves, the man who is God.

The Four Gospels Side by Side

	Matthew	Mark	Luke	John
Author	Tax Collector Turned Disciple	Close Associate of Peter	Medical Doctor/Close Associate of Paul	"The Disciple Whom Jesus Loved" (21:20).
Likely Date	AD 58–68	AD 55–65	AD 60–68	AD 80–90
Theme	Prophesied King	Obedient Servant	Perfect Man	Divine Son
Original Readers	Jews	Romans	Greeks	Everyone
Portrait of Christ (Revelation 4:6–7)	Lion	Calf	Man	Eagle
Key Word	*Fulfilled*	*Immediately*	*Son of Man*	*Believe*
Notable Content	Sermons or Discourses	Miracles	Parables	Signs

Why Study Matthew?

Matthew appears first in the New Testament, rightly so. Here's why we study this Gospel masterpiece called Matthew:

1. *Matthew is the regal Gospel.* It is the authoritative presentation of Jesus as the "King of the Jews" (Matthew 2:2 NKJV).

- Matthew is the only Gospel written by a Jew to the Jews about their Jewish Messiah, the King of the Jews.[2]

- Matthew alone records the genealogy of the King.

- Matthew alone describes the adoration of the King (by the wise men).

- Matthew alone includes the five discourses of the King to his subjects (the words of Jesus make up over 60 percent of Matthew).

- Matthew alone demonstrates the authority of the King (over every aspect of his kingdom through no less than twenty miracles).

- Matthew alone repeats the formal presentation of the kingdom (the phrase "the kingdom of heaven" occurs thirty-three times in Matthew, but nowhere else in the entire New Testament).

- Matthew alone reveals a people's total, final, and absolute rejection of their King.

- Matthew alone alludes to or directly quotes nearly 130 Old Testament prophecies of the King (fulfilled only by Jesus).

- Matthew uniquely explains the Crucifixion—"They put up over His head the accusation written against Him: THIS IS JESUS THE KING OF THE JEWS" (Matthew 27:37 NKJV)—and the climax of the King—"All authority has been given to Me in heaven and on earth" (Matthew 28:18 NKJV).

2. *Matthew is a truthful Gospel.* A God-inspired record of Matthew's eyewitness accounts, Matthew tells the truth about:

- God (his love for his people)

- You and me (our sinfulness before our Holy God)

- Jesus (who he is and what he does)

- The devil (we'll encounter this character a dozen or so times before we're done)

- Heaven (mentioned seventy times in Matthew)

- Hell (referenced in ten of Matthew's twenty-eight chapters)

- The Church ("The gates of Hades shall not prevail against it");

- Salvation—the opening message of Matthew—Jesus came to "save His people from their sins" (1:21 NKJV).

With so many voices clamoring for our attention today, we desperately need a source of truth we can trust. The Bible in general and Matthew in particular are books by which we can live our lives, make our choices, lead our families, establish our relationships, and determine our destinies.

3. *Matthew is a timeless Gospel.* From its opening verses, you will recognize that Matthew is as relevant today as the day in which Matthew composed his masterpiece. Early on in our study together, we will establish an unbreakable link to the people of Jesus's day. We will come to view them as human beings just like us, with the same struggles, emotions, passions, joys, sorrows, delights, fears, dreams, and disappointments that we experience every day. And as we watch God penetrate their world and touch their lives, we will learn just how he is penetrating our world and touching our lives today.

A Word About Words

As you read *The Book of Matthew—The Smart Guide to the Bible*™, you'll notice some interchangeable words: *Scripture, Scriptures, Word, Word of God, God's Word*, etc. All of these terms mean the same thing and come under the broad heading of "The Bible."

Likewise, *Jesus Christ, Jesus, Christ, the Christ, Messiah, Lord, Lord Jesus Christ, Son of God*, and *Son of Man* all refer to the same person. We will use different names or titles at different times in order to emphasize different aspects of who Christ is or what Christ does. The meanings of the names and titles will be explained as needed.

One Final Tip

In Matthew 13:15, Jesus gave an ominous warning to his disciples: "For the hearts of this people have grown dull. Their ears are hard of hearing, and their eyes they have closed, lest they should see with their eyes and hear with their ears, lest they should understand with their hearts and turn, so that I should heal them" (NKJV). The same thing can happen to us. We can become hard-hearted, too. Let me urge you, then, to begin your study of Matthew each day by sincerely asking God to help you see his truth with your eyes, hear his truth with your ears, and obey his truth with your heart. Let the blessings begin!

About the Author

To say that Dewey and Rebecca Bertoloni love the Scriptures would be the height of understatement. They have devoted their adult lives to teaching the Bible with a total commitment to scriptural accuracy and biblical integrity. Rebecca specializes in making the Bible come alive before the watching and wondering eyes of children; Dewey has taught in churches, seminaries, and Christian colleges. They live in the majestic Pacific Northwest along with their son, David, and daughter, Ashley.

About the General Editor

Dr. Larry Richards is a native of Michigan who now lives in Raleigh, North Carolina. He was converted while in the Navy in the 1950s. Larry has taught and written Sunday school curriculum for every age group, from nursery through adult. He has published more than two hundred books, and his books have been translated into some twenty-six languages. His wife, Sue, is also an author. They both enjoy teaching Bible studies as well as fishing and playing golf.

Understanding the Bible Is Easy with These Tools

To understand God's Word you need easy-to-use study tools right where you need them—at your fingertips. The Smart Guide to the Bible™ series puts valuable resources adjacent to the text to save you both time and effort.

Every page features handy sidebars filled with icons and helpful information: cross references for additional insights, definitions of key words and concepts, brief commentaries from experts on the topic, points to ponder, evidence of God at work, the big picture of how passages fit into the context of the entire Bible, practical tips for applying biblical truths to every area of your life, and plenty of maps, charts, and illustrations. A wrap-up of each passage, combined with study questions, concludes each chapter.

These helpful tools show you what to watch for. Look them over to become familiar with them, and then turn to Chapter 1 with complete confidence: You are about to increase your knowledge of God's Word!

Study Helps

The thought-bubble icon alerts you to commentary you might find particularly thought-provoking, challenging, or encouraging. You'll want to take a moment to reflect on it and consider the implications for your life.

Don't miss this point! The exclamation-point icon draws your attention to a key point in the text and emphasizes important biblical truths and facts.

death on the cross
Colossians 1:21–22

Many see Boaz as a type of Jesus Christ. To win back what we human beings lost through sin and spiritual death, Jesus had to become human (i.e., he had to become a true kinsman), and he had to be willing to pay the penalty for our sins. With his <u>death on the cross</u>, Jesus paid the penalty and won freedom and eternal life for us.

The additional Bible verses add scriptural support for the passage you just read and help you better understand the <u>underlined text</u>. (Think of it as an instant reference resource!)

How does what you just read apply to your life? The heart icon indicates that you're about to find out! These practical tips speak to your mind, heart, body, and soul, and offer clear guidelines for living a righteous and joy-filled life, establishing priorities, maintaining healthy relationships, persevering through challenges, and more.

This icon reveals how God is truly all-knowing and all-powerful. The hourglass icon points to a specific example of the prediction of an event or the fulfillment of a prediction. See how some of what God has said would come to pass already has!

What are some of the great things God has done? The traffic-sign icon shows you how God has used miracles, special acts, promises, and covenants throughout history to draw people to him.

Does the story or event you just read about appear elsewhere in the Gospels? The cross icon points you to those instances where the same story appears in other Gospel locations—further proof of the accuracy and truth of Jesus' life, death, and resurrection.

Since God created marriage, there's no better person to turn to for advice. The double-ring icon points out biblical insights and tips for strengthening your marriage.

The Bible is filled with wisdom about raising a godly family and enjoying your spiritual family in Christ. The family icon gives you ideas for building up your home and helping your family grow close and strong.

Isle of Patmos
a small island in the
Mediterranean Sea

something significant had occurred, he wrote down the substance of what he saw. This is the practice John followed when he recorded Revelation on the **Isle of Patmos.**

What does that word really mean, especially as it relates to this passage? Important, misunderstood, or infrequently used words are set in **bold type** in your text so you can immediately glance at the margin for definitions. This valuable feature lets you better understand the meaning of the entire passage without having to stop to check other references.

the big picture

Joshua
Led by Joshua, the Israelites crossed the Jordan River and invaded Canaan (see Illustration #8). In a series of military campaigns the Israelites defeated several coalition armies raised by the inhabitants of Canaan. With organized resistance put down, Joshua divided the land among the twelve Israelite

How does what you read fit in with the greater biblical story? The highlighted big picture summarizes the passage under discussion.

what others say

David Breese
Nothing is clearer in the Word of God than the fact that God wants us to understand himself and his working in the lives of men.[5]

It can be helpful to know what others say on the topic, and the highlighted quotation introduces another voice in the discussion. This resource enables you to read other opinions and perspectives.

Maps, charts, and illustrations pictorially represent ancient artifacts and show where and how stories and events took place. They enable you to better understand important empires, learn your way around villages and temples, see where major battles occurred, and follow the journeys of God's people. You'll find these graphics let you do more than study God's Word—they let you *experience* it.

Chapters at a Glance

Part One
Focus on Israel

Let's Get Started

The population of our little "Third Rock from the Sun" now exceeds six billion people. If you stop and think about it, every single one of us billions got here exactly the same way. The biological function of human reproduction has not changed since Adam and Eve gave <u>birth</u> to their son, Cain, and later his brother, Abel. Animal cloning notwithstanding, the mathematics of making babies—1 seed (from the dad) + 1 egg (from the mom) = 1 baby (the pride and joy of both) has never been violated. Except once.

birth
Genesis 4:1

One Zinger of a Statement

Pretend you're Matthew, an individual skilled at the use (and abuse, as we'll see in chapter 9) of money, but with very little training as a writer. You've been told, "You've got to reach out and grab your readers by the throat, thump 'em on the head, shake 'em to their bones, get their attention." With that in mind, you sit down and proceed to compose an absolutely killer opening sentence guaranteed to do all of the above. What do you come up with? "The book of the genealogy of Jesus Christ" (Matthew 1:1 NKJV). Oh, boy!

Forgive me for pointing out the obvious. But if "shake 'em to their bones" is the goal here, Matthew's first line utterly and completely failed to hit the mark. Or did it? Maybe there's something here not so obvious to our untrained eyes. If the truth be told, Matthew's opening eight words were guaranteed to produce in his readers his desired effect.

Promises, Promises

MATTHEW 1:1 *The book of the genealogy of Jesus Christ, the son of David, the son of Abraham:* (NKJV)

go to

divided
Joshua 13:7

property
Ruth 4:9–10

Abrahamic
Genesis 12:1–3

Davidic
2 Samuel 7:5–16

Isaac
Genesis 21: 3,12

Ishmael
Genesis 16:15

throne
2 Samuel 7:16;
Luke 1:30–32

covenants
sacred promises
between God and
his people

Abrahamic
covenant between
God and Abraham

Davidic
covenant between
God and David

Isaac
Abraham's son with
Sarah

Ishmael
Abraham's son with
Sarah's maid Hagar

During biblical times the Jewish people were mad about their genealogies—and for good reason. If, for example, you had been alive when Joshua <u>divided</u> the land, the place you eventually settled was determined by your family line. During the time of Judges, the transfer of <u>property</u> depended upon who was related to whom.

The fulfillment of the two most important **covenants** in the Bible—the **Abrahamic** and **Davidic** covenants—hung upon the branches of a family tree. The hope of the fulfillment of both these divine promises burned brightly in the hearts of every Jew of Jesus's day. It still does today. Jesus came to fulfill both of these covenants as the God-promised and long-awaited Jewish Messiah. But did he qualify to do so? It all depended upon his genealogy.

In his covenant with Abraham, God promised to send a Savior to the world through whom "all the nations of the earth shall be blessed" (Genesis 22:18 NKJV). Furthermore, God made it clear that the Messiah would have to be a descendant of Abraham through his son **Isaac**, *not* through his son **Ishmael**. Though this may seem like a trivial detail to some, try telling that to our Jewish or Muslim friends, and you'll quickly find out just how untrivial this is! To Abraham, it wasn't trivial at all. This was huge.

Here's the point: In order to qualify as the Jewish Messiah and the Savior of the world, Jesus had to be Jewish. He had to be a direct descendant of Abraham through Isaac. Was he? Check the genealogy. He was indeed! A very Jewish Jesus.

Two for Two

So far, so good. Jesus is one for one. But what about the Davidic covenant? There, God promised Israel's King David that the Messiah would rule the earth from David's <u>throne</u> forever. In order to qualify as the King of the Jews, Jesus had to be in the kingly line going back to David. Was he? Once again, check the genealogy. It reads, "David, the son of David." Jesus is two for two!

Do you think Matthew had a captive audience of those who read the first verse of his Gospel? Did his opening sentence grab them? You'd better believe it! In just one verse, three short phrases,

Matthew both declared and defended his theme: Jesus is the King of the Jews and the Savior of the world. He will now devote twenty-eight chapters to proving it.

Tamar
Genesis 38:6

Canaanite
person from Canaan, Israel's enemy

> **what others say**
>
> **Ronald A. Beers**
>
> This genealogy was one of the most interesting ways Matthew could begin a book for a Jewish audience. Because a person's family line proved his or her standing as one of God's chosen people, Matthew begins by showing that Jesus was a descendant of Abraham, the father of all the Jews, and a direct descendant of King David, fulfilling Old Testament prophecies about the Messiah's line. The facts of this ancestry were carefully preserved. This is the first of many proofs recorded by Matthew to show that Jesus is the true Messiah.[1]

Four Notorious Women

> **the big picture**
>
> **Matthew 1:2–17**
>
> Matthew lists a staggering forty-six names in Jesus's family line, beginning with Abraham, moving through David, and ending with Joseph. The details of the lives of many of these individuals have become obscured by the passage of time, while the stories of several others have been well documented by the biblical writers. Taken together, these many names underscore one undeniable fact: Jesus is the Messiah.

The inclusion of women in Jesus's genealogy is most curious. Generally speaking, legal documents of this sort only included men. Let's break out our zoom lenses for a moment and focus upon these four women—Tamar, Rahab, Ruth, and Bathsheba—to figure out why Matthew broke with tradition.

We'll begin with <u>Tamar</u>, the **Canaanite** daughter-in-law of Judah. Hers is a sad and sordid tale. So wicked were her husband and brother-in-law that God struck them dead. Judah took this young widow into his home and promised her his third son in marriage. When he broke his promise, Tamar was understandably devastated. She disguised herself as a prostitute, seduced her own father-in-law, and conceived twins by that encounter. And so we read, "Judah

go to

Rahab
Joshua 2:1

faith
Joshua 2:11

spared
Joshua 6:22–25

Ruth
Ruth 1:4

Moab
Genesis 19:37

curse
Deuteronomy 23:3

accepted
Ruth 1:16

Bathsheba
2 Samuel 11:3

Hittite
2 Samuel 11:6

murder
2 Samuel 11:14–15

Gentile
non-Jew

begot Perez and Zerah by Tamar" (Matthew 1:3 NKJV). Yes, it's true. Jesus was the product of an incestuous relationship between a broken, bitter woman and her deceptively immoral father-in-law.

If Tamar desperately turned to prostitution in her bitter frustration, the second Canaanite woman, Rahab, did so willingly as her chosen profession. This lady of the night plied her trade within the walls of wicked Jericho. When Joshua sent two of his men to spy out the city, Rahab put her life on the line and hid the spies from Jericho's murderous king. Because of this **Gentile**'s faith in the God of Israel, God spared her life and the lives of her family when the walls of Jericho came a-tumblin' down. Not only that, but God enshrined her forever in our Lord's genealogy when he wrote, "Salmon begot Boaz by Rahab" (Matthew 1:5 NKJV).

Ruth is the third Gentile woman to be mentioned in this Jewish genealogy. Ruth came from Moab, a tribe of people descended from Lot and his incestuous relations with his two unmarried daughters.

Moab became one of Israel's most treacherous enemies, so evil in their intentions that the entire nation fell under a curse. Yet, despite her people's hostility toward God and his people, Ruth broke ranks and accepted the God of Israel as her own God and the people of God as her own people. God thus immortalized Ruth with, "Boaz begot Obed by Ruth" (Matthew 1:5 NKJV).

Bathsheba rounds out our quartet of confused and conflicted young ladies, she the adulterous wife of Uriah the Hittite. On a night that has lived long in infamy, Bathsheba violated her marriage vows by agreeing to have an affair with King David. Thus began David's moral and spiritual free fall that saw him attempt to cover up his sin and even concoct a plan that would result in the murder of Uriah.

If you've been tempted to think that because Matthew is the "Jewish Gospel" it has nothing to say to a non-Jewish reader, think again. Matthew begins by illustrating God's grace to four non-Jewish women of the world. He ends his Gospel with Jesus's command to take his gospel to all the people of the world. The Jesus of Matthew's Gospel is equally the King of the Jews and the Savior of the world.

A Motley Crew

go to

risk
Genesis 12:13; 20:2

deceiver
Genesis 25:29–34

concubines
1 Kings 11:3

The men were (as my daughter might say) no basket of fruit themselves. We've already detailed some of David's doings. But how about these paragons of male virtue? Abraham—liar, adulterer, doubter—put his own wife at <u>risk</u> twice to save his sorry hide. Jacob was a world-class schemer and <u>deceiver</u>. Tamar might have posed as a prostitute, but it was Judah who hustled her. With seven hundred wives and three hundred **concubines**, Solomon was a world-class womanizer who eventually turned away from God. And then there's the story of Jeconiah and his brothers (Matthew 1:12).

concubines
members of a king's harem

Remember that in order to qualify to occupy his throne, Jesus had to be directly descended from King David. Jeconiah was such an evil king that God pronounced this judgment against him: "None of his descendants shall prosper, sitting on the throne of David" (Jeremiah 22:30 NKJV). Hmmm. Jesus is directly related to David through Jeconiah. How, then, can he occupy David's throne as the Jewish Messiah when the curse clearly prohibited Jeconiah's offspring from doing just that?

Matthew's amazing statement, "And Jacob begot Joseph the husband of Mary, of whom was born Jesus who is called Christ" (Matthew 1:16 NKJV), answers the question. Do you see it there? Jesus is not Joseph's son by *blood*. Jesus is Joseph's son by *adoption* since Jesus was virgin-born. Since Jesus was not a physical descendant of Jeconiah, the curse miraculously passed him by.

You might be wondering, "If Jesus is not the physical descendant of David, how does he qualify to sit upon David's throne?" Check out Luke 3:23–28. There you will read Jesus's genealogy through Mary. It's a bit confusing because Luke mentions no women in his genealogy, not even Mary. Jesus is "the son of Joseph, the son of Heli" (Luke 3:23 NKJV), but only by marriage since Joseph was likely the son-in-law of Heli.[2] Thus, through Mary, Jesus is the physical descendant of David through another branch on the family tree, a totally different branch from the one upon which Jeconiah hangs. Thus, Jesus possessed the legal right (through Abraham) and the regal right (through David) to sit on David's throne.

The following chart shows how Jesus was descended from David through both Joseph and Mary, his mother.

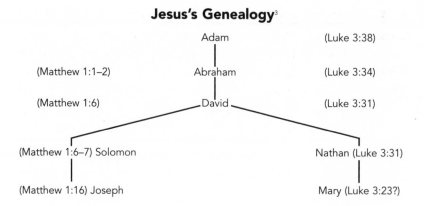

Jesus's Genealogy³

	Adam	(Luke 3:38)
(Matthew 1:1–2)	Abraham	(Luke 3:34)
(Matthew 1:6)	David	(Luke 3:31)

(Matthew 1:6–7) Solomon — Nathan (Luke 3:31)

(Matthew 1:16) Joseph — Mary (Luke 3:23?)

There is a fifth woman in the genealogy. Her name is Mary. Since the Bible does not reveal anything improper regarding Mary's personal life, some conclude that she was immaculately conceived—or conceived without a sin nature—and worthy of our worship. Such a conclusion overlooks Mary's own admission about herself when she exclaimed, "My soul magnifies the Lord, and my spirit has rejoiced in God my Savior" (Luke 1:46–47 NKJV). As wonderful a woman as Mary was, she still needed a Savior.

A Birth Unlike Any Other

> MATTHEW 1:18–19 *Now the birth of Jesus Christ was as follows: After His mother Mary was betrothed to Joseph, before they came together, she was found with child of the* **Holy Spirit***. Then Joseph her husband, being a just man, and not wanting to make her a public example, was minded to put her away secretly.* (NKJV)

Here's a bolt out of the blue for you: Virgin women don't have babies. Going all the way back to Eve, no woman has ever conceived a child apart from her intimate relations with a man . . . except one. There is no denying that the conception of Jesus within the womb of a virgin was nothing short of miraculous. On the fact of the virgin birth, the reliability of the Bible and the credibility of Christianity stands or falls.

Farther along in his Gospel, Matthew will record one of the many confrontations between Jesus and a hostile group of religious leaders. Jesus will ask them, "What do you think about the Christ? Whose Son is He?" (Matthew 22:42 NKJV). That is the central question, isn't it? For if Jesus is the son of Joseph, or any other man for that matter, he would be nothing more than the natural product of the physical union of two human parents, and, alas, a mere mortal himself. But Matthew's statement is clear: "Before they came together, she was found with child of the Holy Spirit" (Matthew 1:18 NKJV).

Matthew used no dramatic language to embellish the event, as if a virgin birth needed embellishment. He suggested no proof nor offered any evidence. He allowed the record of the virgin birth to stand as its own proof:

- Listen to Mary's own words regarding her own pregnancy as recorded by Luke, a <u>medical doctor</u>: "How can this be, since I do not know a man?" (Luke 1:34 NKJV).

- Observe Joseph's initial reaction to the news of Mary's pregnancy— he decided to "put her away secretly" (Matthew 1:19 NKJV).

- Note the ridicule of Jesus's enemies: "We were not born of fornication" (John 8:41 NKJV). These words were shouted as a bitter attack upon Jesus, yet they ironically punctuated the point that Jesus was indeed virgin-born. For throughout his entire lifetime no one ever came forward, nor was anyone ever identified, as Jesus's earthly father. This cheap shot, completely baseless in its insinuation, is ironic in that it is only Jesus who can rightfully claim, "We have one Father—God" (John 8:41 NKJV).

- Watch the things Jesus did. No mere mortal can rebuke the wind and <u>calm</u> a storm, touch a **leper** and make him <u>clean</u>, speak a command and <u>drive out</u> a **demon**, touch blind eyes and make them <u>see</u>, or grasp a dead girl's hand and <u>raise</u> her to life.

Observe Joseph's reaction to the news of Mary's pregnancy. He decided to "put her away secretly." Why? Because he knew that he was not the father.

Isn't it striking how simply Matthew stated the sublime, the majestic? Matthew offered no lavish explanations, as if a miracle of the magnitude of the virgin birth could be explained. If a miracle could be explained, it would cease to be a miracle. No, Matthew did not need to prove the virgin birth. The virgin birth proved itself.

medical doctor
Colossians 4:14

calm
Matthew 8:26

clean
Matthew 8:3

drive out
Matthew 8:31–32

see
Matthew 9:29–30

raise
Matthew 9:25

leper
one with leprosy, a dreaded skin disease

demon
angel who rebelled against God

A Most Engaging Couple

For all the press that they have received over the years—deservedly so, we might add—we actually know very little about Joseph and Mary. What we do know about Joseph is this:

- Joseph was a just or righteous man (Matthew 1:19).
- Joseph was of the family line of David (Luke 2:4).
- Joseph was a worker in wood and/or stone, most likely a village carpenter (Matthew 13:55).
- Joseph loved Mary deeply, even in the face of apparent betrayal (Matthew 1:19).
- Joseph likely died some time after Jesus turned twelve (Luke 2:42), but possibly before his first miracle at a wedding in Cana (John 2:1), and certainly before Jesus's death (John 19:27).

Concerning Mary, we know these things:

- Mary was young; women were typically married in their early teens.[5]
- Mary was a native of Nazareth (Luke 1:26).
- Mary was a woman of moral excellence (Luke 1:34).
- Mary had a humble reverence, thankfulness, and love for God (Luke 1:46–49).

Of them both, we know the following:

- Joseph and Mary were poor (Luke 2:24; Leviticus 12:8).
- Joseph and Mary were pledged, or betrothed, to one another (Matthew 1:18).

That's about it. Most of the above is self-explanatory. But this betrothal thing deserves a bit of a discussion.

The easiest way to describe betrothal is to think of it like our custom of engagement with some added features. Specifically, a marriage was almost always arranged by the families of the bride and groom. A contract was made, then sealed with the payment of a dowry by the groom or his family to the father of the bride.

Now here's the tricky part: Once the dowry was paid, the contract was legally binding; the couple was considered legally married, even though no ceremony had taken place, nor had the marriage been consummated. The betrothal period could last as long as one year, during which time the husband prepared a house for his bride and the bride proved her fidelity to her husband. (This explains why Joseph responded to Mary's apparent infidelity by deciding to divorce her even though the wedding ceremony had not yet taken place.[6])

Pharaoh
Genesis 41:1

Nebuchadnezzar
Daniel 2:1

Sweet Dreams

> MATTHEW 1:20a *But while he thought about these things, behold, an angel of the LORD appeared to him in a dream, saying,...* (NKJV)

On extremely rare occasions in biblical history, God revealed his plan to individuals through dreams. So rare were such dreams that when one did occur, everyone who heard about it knew immediately that God was going to do something dramatic. For example, think about Joseph of Genesis fame who saved a nation from the iron grip of a prolonged famine because its coming was revealed to <u>Pharaoh</u> in advance through his dreams. Or how about <u>Nebuchadnezzar</u>, whose dream revealed God's future plan for the nations? These kinds of divine dreams were anything but the norm.

As if to underscore the fact that with the birth of Jesus the world was about to enter an entirely new period of human history, Matthew records five such dreams (Matthew 1:20; 2:12, 13, 19, 22).

What a Difference a Night Makes

> MATTHEW 1:20b–21 *Joseph, son of David, do not be afraid to take to you Mary your wife, for that which is conceived in her is of the Holy Spirit. And she will bring forth a Son, and you shall call His name JESUS, for He will save His people from their sins.* (NKJV)

go to

death
Deuteronomy
22:23–24;
John 8:5

angel
God's heavenly mes-
senger or servant

original sin
inclination to do
wrong things, inher-
ited from Adam

Joseph's heart must have been broken by the news that Mary, his betrothed wife, was pregnant. Of course, he assumed that she had had relations with another man. If so, he had every right to divorce her and break their betrothal. As a man of principle and knowing that he was not the father of the child, he concluded that the best possible course of action for all concerned was to end their engagement.

Joseph weighed his options. If he divorced her, he ran the risk of exposing Mary to public humiliation. Even though he also would be open to scorn and ridicule when his friends learned of his wife's unfaithfulness to him, Joseph's first thought—his immediate instinct—was to protect her reputation at all costs. Joseph truly loved Mary. The fact that the law of the land back then provided for Joseph to demand Mary's <u>death</u> for such an offense only amplifies how great a love he had for her. He sought to divorce her, but "secretly" (Matthew 1:19 NKJV).

You've heard the old line "What a difference a day makes"? In this case, what a difference a night makes! God dispatched an **angel** to speak to Joseph in a dream. The angel assured Joseph that:

- Mary had not lost her virtue.
- Plans for the wedding must go forward "full steam ahead."
- The child in her womb was the long-awaited Messiah. (No wonder God spoke to Joseph in a dream. If Joseph had been awake, he might have dropped dead on the spot.)
- They were to name their son Jesus, *Jeshua* in Hebrew, meaning "Jehovah is salvation; Jehovah is the Savior."[7]

Matthew 1:21 contains the clearest possible declaration that Jesus is God.

key point

what others say

Herbert Lockyer

Because He was conceived of the Holy Spirit, His substance was pure and immaculate and without **original sin**. To save sinners, it was imperative for Him to be sinless; hence, the necessity of a virgin birth.[8]

<u>O Come, O Come, Immanuel</u>

MATTHEW 1:22–23 *So all this was done that it might be ful-filled which was spoken by the Lord through the prophet, saying:*

"Behold, the virgin shall be with child, and bear a Son, and they shall call His name Immanuel," which is translated, "God with us." (NKJV)

Matthew will now establish a pattern that he will follow throughout the remainder of his great Gospel: state a fact, then prove the fact through Old Testament prophecy. Remember that he was writing to a largely Jewish audience with the purpose of establishing in their minds, beyond the shadow of any doubt, that Jesus truly is who he claimed to be—God—the promised and long-awaited Messiah.

Matthew anchored his arguments in the ancient predictions of a coming Messiah. For any Jew to deny the credibility of Jesus was to deny the authority of his religious founding fathers. Matthew begins with one of the most amazing prophecies of all—that of a virgin giving birth to a baby.

The **skeptics** among us would be quick to gleefully point out that the Hebrew word *almah* can be translated either "virgin" or "young woman," thus disemboweling this prophecy from the get-go. Nice try. While their claim is technically true, when deciding the proper meaning of a word, the careful Bible student must always consider the **context** of the word in question.

Obviously, in this case, the definition of *almah* can only be "virgin." Isaiah wrote, "The Lord Himself will give you a sign: Behold, the virgin shall conceive and bear a Son, and shall call His name Immanuel" (Isaiah 7:14 NKJV), the same verse quoted by Matthew. If *almah* means "young woman," what kind of a sign is that? Take a stroll through your local maternity ward and what will you see? Babies are born to young women every minute of every day. If you ever find a *virgin* who gives birth to a baby, *that* would be a sign.

what others say

Josh McDowell

The apostles throughout the New Testament appealed to two areas of Christ's life to establish His Messiahship. One was the resurrection and the other fulfilled messianic prophecy. The Old Testament written over a 1500-year period contains several hundred references to the coming Messiah. All of these were fulfilled in Christ and they establish a solid confirmation of His credentials as the Messiah.[9]

brothers and sisters
Matthew 12:46;
13:55–56

pilgrimage
journey of religious
significance

Passover
one of three Jewish
pilgrimage festivals

Over seven hundred years before the fact, Isaiah predicted that Jesus would be a virgin-born son named Immanuel (Isaiah 7:14).

Isaiah was not the first biblical writer to predict a virgin-born Savior. The very first hint of the virgin birth can be found way back in the beginning, in the book of Genesis. Immediately following the first-ever sin by Adam and Eve, God made this prediction to the slippery serpent who tempted Eve: "And I will put enmity between you and the woman, and between your seed and her Seed" (Genesis 3:15 NKJV). Where is the virgin birth in that statement, you might ask? How about a little Basic Biology 101: Women don't have seeds. The seed is provided only by the man. Unless, of course, God himself does the providing!

Trust and Obey

MATTHEW 1:24–25 *Then Joseph, being aroused from sleep, did as the angel of the Lord commanded him and took to him his wife, and did not know her till she had brought forth her firstborn Son. And he called His name JESUS. (NKJV)*

Kudos to Joseph! Here was a man who trusted God completely and obeyed him immediately. He woke up from his dream, took Mary as his wife, and kept her a virgin until the birth of the child. (Matthew will mention later that Jesus had younger brothers and sisters, thus dispelling any notion of the perpetual virginity of Mary.)

Little else is revealed in the Bible about this extraordinary man:

- Joseph takes the infant Jesus to the Temple for his dedication (Luke 2:22–33).

- Joseph, Mary, and Jesus run for their lives down to Egypt (Matthew 2:13–23).

- When Jesus is twelve, Joseph and his family make a **pilgrimage** to Jerusalem for **Passover** (Luke 2:42–52).

- As mentioned earlier, Joseph apparently died some time during Jesus's adolescence.

This chapter closes with one last act of obedience and faith on Joseph's part: "And he called His name JESUS" (Matthew 1:25 NKJV). He didn't name the baby after himself or some other male relative, as was the usual custom of the day. Naming the baby was an act of obedience because God told him to do so. It was an expres-

sion of faith because Joseph gave him the name that means, "He will save His people from their sins" (Matthew 1:21 NKJV). That's why he came. That's why Jesus was born, and that's why he died. Jesus truly is the virgin-born King of the Jews and Savior of the world. Jesus is truly the virgin-born Savior-King.

Chapter Wrap-Up

- As the "son of Abraham," through Abraham's son Isaac, Jesus fulfilled the promise God made to Abraham that through him "all the nations of the earth shall be blessed." (Matthew 1:1; Genesis 12:1–3)

- As the "son of David," Jesus is qualified to sit on the throne of King David forever, just as God promised in the Davidic covenant. (2 Samuel 7:5–16)

- Jesus's genealogy establishes Jesus's legal right through Abraham and his regal right through David to be the King of the Jews. (Matthew 1:1)

- Four Gentile, non-Jewish women were included in Jesus's genealogy, something that was rare in those days. (Matthew 1:3, 5–6)

- Each of the men and women in the genealogy reveals a God of grace who sent his Son to be the King of the Jews and the Savior of the world. (Matthew 1:21)

- Joseph and Mary were betrothed, a legally binding relationship somewhat similar to what we would call engagement, that required a certificate of divorce to break. (Matthew 1:19)

- Matthew states categorically, just as Isaiah indicates prophetically, that "before [Mary and Joseph] came together, she was found with child of the Holy Spirit." (Matthew 1:18 NKJV; Isaiah 7:14)

- Five times in the opening two chapters of his Gospel, Matthew states that God communicated to Joseph and the wise men through his dreams, a most unusual occurrence. (Matthew 1:20; 2:12–13, 19, 22)

- Joseph named his newborn son Jesus, a name that means "Savior," because Jesus "will save His people from their sins." (Matthew 1:21 NKJV)

Study Questions

1. What is the theme of Matthew?

2. How important were genealogies in the culture into which Jesus was born?

3. What does the genealogy of Jesus prove?

4. What are the two most important covenants in the Bible?

5. Why did Joseph consider divorcing Mary?

6. How does the record establish that Jesus's birth was miraculous?

7. Why is Matthew's evidence irrefutable?

8. What is the meaning of Jesus's name?

Matthew 2: Child Born King

Chapter Highlights:
- The Worshiping Wise Men
- For Whom the Bell Tolls
- Herod Meets His Maker

Let's Get Started

One might assume that as an innocent young newlywed couple, Joseph and Mary were wonderfully happy. If so, they were rudely awakened out of their newly wedded bliss by the deadly **decree** of Caesar Augustus that forced them to brace themselves against a tidal wave of **tribulation** that would push any family to its limit.

Though the four Gospels are strangely silent about Jesus's infancy and adolescence, Matthew gives us a few intriguing glimpses into a turbulent childhood. Before he concludes his second chapter, Matthew will escort us through many months and thousands of miles of travel on a wide-ranging itinerary that includes five faraway locations—Persia, Jerusalem, Bethlehem, Egypt, and Nazareth (see Map of Israel, Appendix A).

You've probably seen their pictures colorfully printed on countless Christmas cards—a trio of travelers, their **ruddy** faces cooked by the Middle Eastern sun, bearing exotic gifts befitting a king, huddling in awestruck silence and wide-eyed wonder around a newborn baby cooing quietly in his manger. A well-meaning drama director seeking to re-create this **manger** scene as the centerpiece of his Christmas pageant might scribble in the margins of his script, "Wise men enter stage right." But that would be inaccurate, for reasons that might surprise you.

The Worshiping Wise Men

MATTHEW 2:1 *Now after Jesus was born in Bethlehem of Judea in the days of Herod the king, behold, wise men from the East came to Jerusalem, . . .* (NKJV)

The mythology of the **Middle Ages** boldly asserts that there were exactly three wise men, based on the observation that they presented <u>three gifts</u> to Jesus, and that their names were Casper, Balthazar, and Melchior.[1] A twelfth-century bishop of Cologne even claimed that he had found their skulls![2] But mythology aside, most scholars agree

---

go to

three gifts
Matthew 2:11

decree
orders given by a king

tribulation
intensely painful circumstances

ruddy
rosy, slightly sun-bronzed glow

manger
animal's feeding trough, usually hewn out of stone

Middle Ages
roughly AD 476 to 1450

go to

regal
Psalm 89:4

throne
2 Samuel 7:5,
12–13, 16;
Psalm 132:11

astronomy
study of the stars
and planets

astrology
fortune-telling using
the positions of the
stars and planets

occult
secret knowledge
and use of super-
normal powers

Persia
parts of modern-day
Iran, Afghanistan,
and Pakistan

Babylon
region of present-
day Baghdad

Julius Caesar
Roman ruler from 55
BC–44 BC

prefect
civil or military
official

Galilee
region in the
north of Israel

that the visitors were learned (hence, "wise") men schooled in the knowledge of **astronomy**, **astrology**, agriculture, mathematics, history, and the **occult** who traveled to Jerusalem from their native **Persia**, or possibly **Babylon**.

> **what others say**
>
> **Henry H. Halley**
>
> They were men of high standing, for they had access to Herod. They are commonly spoken of as the "Three Wise Men." But the Scripture does not say how many. There were probably more, or at least they were with an entourage of scores or hundreds, for it would not be safe for a small group to travel a thousand miles over desert wastes that were infested with bandits.[3]

Some two years would pass between the birth of Jesus at the end of Matthew 1 and the arrival of the wise men at the beginning of chapter 2. The following facts confirm this conclusion:

1. Herod ordered the executions of all boys in Bethlehem who were "two years old and under" (Matthew 2:16 NKJV).

2. Jesus and his family had moved from a cave or stable with a manger (Luke 2:7) to a house (Matthew 2:11).

3. Matthew described Jesus as a child (Matthew 2:11), and not as a baby.

The Late, Great Herod

"Herod the Great," as he is often known, is the first of several Herods mentioned in the New Testament. Herod's rise to prominence began years earlier after his father, Antipater, was propelled into power by none other than **Julius Caesar** of "Et tu, Brute?"[4] fame. Daddy used his influence in Rome to secure for his son the prestigious position of **prefect** over **Galilee**. Over time, Herod would manipulate his superiors into conferring upon him the mother of all job titles: "Herod, King of the Jews."

Never mind that Herod was not a descendant of King David, had no place in the kingly line, and lacked the <u>regal</u> right to rule from David's <u>throne</u>. Never mind that Herod was not a descendant of

Abraham, therefore not Jewish, and thus had no <u>legal</u> right to the title "King of the Jews." Never mind that immediately upon ascending the Jewish throne and proclaiming himself the Jewish king, Herod savagely butchered forty-five of the seventy members of the **Sanhedrin** and confiscated their properties in the process.[5] Make no mistake about it. By 37 BC, buttressed by the full fury of the Roman military machine, Herod basked in the brilliance of his unrivaled power as the self-proclaimed "King of the Jews" . . . until the wise men showed up.

One of the reasons that we can study the Bible with great confidence is that its stories are anchored in history and geography. Matthew sets the scene for this visit of the wise men by telling us when it happened—after Jesus's birth, but during Herod's reign— and where it happened—Bethlehem in Judea. The history of Herod is well documented in multiple sources outside of the Bible.

go to

legal
Galatians 3:16
birth
Luke 2:1–20

Sanhedrin
Jewish council of supreme authority

ashen
gray from fear

anomaly
something strange, abnormal, not easily explained

Twinkle, Twinkle Little Star

MATTHEW 2:2 . . . *saying, "Where is He who has been born King of the Jews? For we have seen His star in the East and have come to worship Him." (NKJV)*

The extraordinary events surrounding the <u>birth</u> of Christ must have been a marvel to behold. Try as we might, we can't begin to imagine it all—the angelic announcement that Jesus had been born; the lowly shepherds now quaking in fear, scared out of their sandals by their unexpected heavenly guests, the skies above them exploding in a pyrotechnic display of galactic proportions; the ear-splitting sound of heavenly voices praising in unison their almighty God. It gives me chills just thinking about it.

But that's not all. In the east, far away from Bethlehem, something else happened that has remained a mystery for over two thousand years. A group of men who studied the stars must have shivered in the chilly night air and squinted as they stared in the direction of the setting sun. They saw something high up in the sky that they had never seen before. Many months and several hundred miles later, while standing before an **ashen** Herod, the wise men's learned vocabulary must have failed them, for they referred to this astronomical **anomaly** simply as a "star."

go to

Shekinah
Luke 2:9

pillar of fire
Exodus 13:21

stars
Job 38:7

appearance
Matthew 28:3

announced
Luke 2:10–11

supernova
exploding star,
sometimes bright
enough to be seen
during the day

Shekinah
presence of God
manifested in
brilliant light

How I Wonder What You Are

Exactly what was the so-called Christmas star? No one knows for sure. Here are your options:

- A star of unrivaled brilliance, possibly a **supernova**. A nova appeared in the skies above the Middle East in March/April 5 BC.

- A bright comet—though comets were usually considered omens of evil, not as divine signs marking the birth of a king.

- An exceedingly rare and eye-catching triple conjunction of Jupiter and Saturn occurring on May 22, October 5, and December 1, 7 BC, appearing just before sunrise in the constellation Pisces.

- The conjunction of Jupiter and Venus, the two brightest planets in the night sky, occurring on the western horizon (the direction of Jerusalem) just after sunset on June 17, 2 BC, appearing so close together that they would have been seen as one dazzling star.

- The lunar eclipse of January 9, 1 BC, when the earth's shadow nibbled at and eventually swallowed the full moon, eerily turning it into a coppery red glow.

- The <u>Shekinah</u> glory of God, similar to the <u>pillar of fire</u> that led the Israelites from their bondage in Egypt to their Promised Land. Might the wise men have referred to this as a "star"?

- An angel sent by God to lead the wise men to the Christ child. The Bible sometimes refers to the angels as <u>stars</u> because of their luminescent <u>appearance</u>. This explanation seems plausible given that an angel <u>announced</u> the birth of Christ to the shepherds.

For Whom the Bell Tolls

MATTHEW 2:3 *When Herod the king heard this, he was troubled, and all Jerusalem with him. (NKJV)*

Herod regarded himself, and only himself, as the King of the Jews. Suddenly, like a bolt out of the blue, Herod faced an unidentifiable force that threatened to shatter his stranglehold on his empire. This became the most unsettling thing of all: His newly discovered archenemy was—had he heard them right?—a mere "Child" (verse 8 NKJV). This fiendishly wicked ruler had good reasons to be disturbed. From the moment this thug dug his fingernails into the arm-rests of his throne, Herod had held on to his power with all of the military might he could muster. Was someone else now destined to occupy his throne, not by military might but by divine right? Had he been forced into the ring to face an opponent he could not beat? Herod weighed his options.

Anyone who has any knowledge of Herod the Great and his role in history can understand the meaning of the biblical report that records Herod's mental state. When Herod wasn't happy, the whole city shuddered in fearful anticipation of what this madman might do. The people knew only too well of what he was capable whenever he flew into one of his legendary rages over any disruption of his per-verted plans.[6]

polarization
division into two opposites

what others say

Jim Fleming

If we read the birth narratives carefully we find in them the lit-erary device of **polarization**. The Gospel writers contrast Jesus with Herod the Great: A) King by Might vs. King by Right—Herod came to power only by force as an usurper king; Jesus, from the lineage of David, is the rightful king. B) King of Pride vs. King of Humility—Herod the proud builds palaces for himself all over the country; Jesus came from such a humble background that he is born in a stable. C) King Who Takes People's Lives vs. King Who Gives His Life—Herod is responsible for the deaths of the children in Bethlehem; Jesus laid down his life for others.[7]

Check the Record

MATTHEW 2:4–8 *And when he had gathered all the chief priests and scribes of the people together, he inquired of them where the Christ was to be born. So they said to him, "In Bethlehem of Judea, for thus it is written by the prophet:*

'But you, Bethlehem, in the land of Judah,
Are not the least among the rulers of Judah;
For out of you shall come a Ruler
Who will shepherd My people Israel.'"

Then Herod, when he had secretly called the wise men, deter-mined from them what time the star appeared. And he sent them to Bethlehem and said, "Go and search carefully for the young Child, and when you have found Him, bring back word to me, that I may come and worship Him also." (NKJV)

little
Micah 5:2

chief priests
religious leaders
who served in the
Jewish Temple

teachers of the law
scholars who taught
the Old Testament

A panic-stricken Herod turned to the **chief priests** and **teachers of the law** in order to determine where the Christ was to be born. They knew immediately where to turn for the requested information—to the writings of the prophet Micah. Yet, these religious leaders seemed weirdly indifferent to the wise men's mission or their own prophet's prediction.

Herod was anything but indifferent. His diabolical mind settled upon a plan. Based upon the wise men's testimony regarding the first appearance of the star, Herod concluded that this interloper, this threat to his throne, could be no older than two years of age. Herod the Great then set his trap by voicing a deceptive desire to join the wise men in their worship of the child-born-King.

A full seven centuries before Herod's day, the prophet Micah predicted with crystal clarity and pinpoint accuracy that Jesus would be born in the <u>little</u> town of Bethlehem (Micah 5:2).

Bethlehem means "House of Bread," most likely because of the fertile fields that surround it. Bread was viewed as a staple of life in biblical times, much as it is today. The "breaking of bread" (Acts 2:42 NKJV) symbolized the common bond of friendship and fellowship shared between people. Jesus is (1) "The bread [or source] of life" (John 6:35 NKJV), and (2) the one through whom we have "peace [or fellowship] with God" (Romans 5:1 NKJV). Could it be that of all places, God chose Bethlehem as the birthplace of his Son in order to convey to the world this dual object lesson, as if to say to every person on this planet, "I long to wrap my arms around you and have an intimate relationship with you"?

what others say

J. Vernon McGee

He's being as subtle as an old serpent and that's exactly what Herod was. Suppose he had said, "I'll tell you that if there's a king born around here, I'm going to do something about it," and then had sent soldiers down to Bethlehem. I can assure you, he would never have found the child. He would have been hidden. He knew that the clever way and the best way was to let the wise men go down and find the child and then come back and tell him. He said he wanted to go down and worship Him, but of course what he really wanted to do was to kill Him.[8]

History has immortalized him as "Herod the Great"—not because of who he was, but only because of what he built. "The colossal building projects of Herod the Great, fabled late first century **BCE** ruler of Judea, earned him fame throughout the world....His fondest ambition was to bring coveted international standing to himself and, moreover, announce to all the world the importance of his kingdom's relationship to Rome."[9] On that level, Herod achieved his goal. But as a man, he was both hated and hunted.

go to

nobility
1 Kings 10:10

presence
Exodus 30:7–9

prayers
Psalm 141:2

perfume
Psalm 45:8

Bearing Gifts We Traverse Afar

MATTHEW 2:9–13 *When they heard the king, they departed; and behold, the star which they had seen in the East went before them, till it came and stood over where the young Child was. When they saw the star, they rejoiced with exceedingly great joy. And when they had come into the house, they saw the young Child with Mary His mother, and fell down and worshiped Him. And when they had opened their treasures, they presented gifts to Him: gold, frankincense, and myrrh. Then, being divinely warned in a dream that they should not return to Herod, they departed for their own country another way.*

Now when they had departed, behold, an angel of the Lord appeared to Joseph in a dream, saying, "Arise, take the young Child and His mother, flee to Egypt, and stay there until I bring you word; for Herod will seek the young Child to destroy Him." (NKJV)

BCE
Before the Common Era; equal to BC

The contrasting reactions to the Christ child are striking in the extreme. First, note the responses of the wise men. The respect the wise men felt for Jesus is clearly seen in the worship they offered and the gifts they presented. "It's the thought that counts" clearly didn't apply in this situation. The wise men carefully chose their gifts and presented treasures of great significance:

Gold: Mentioned in forty-three books of the Bible; a precious metal used throughout history as a currency standard; symbol of nobility and royalty; a measure of a person's character or an object's worth—"As good as gold."

Frankincense: An expensive type of incense with a beautiful aroma; used to signify the holiness of the presence of our God and the sweetness of our prayers as they rise to God.

Myrrh: A common perfume, but with an ominous undertone to its

burial
John 19:39

deity
Jesus is God

sweetness. Myrrh was also used to prepare a body for <u>burial</u>, including the body of Jesus.[10]

Thus, the wise men gave Jesus three extremely significant and telling gifts: gold, to emphasize Christ's royalty; frankincense, to emphasize his **deity**; and myrrh, to emphasis Jesus's humanity and mortality. In short, these learned men presented to Jesus gifts fit only for a king.

Gifts Fit for a King

Gift	Significance	Scripture
Gold	Precious metal; symbol of nobility and royalty	1 Kings 10:10
Incense	Symbolizes God's presence and the sweetness of our prayers rising to God	Exodus 30:7–9; Psalm 141:2
Myrrh	Perfume; used to prepare a body for burial	John 19:39

It is interesting to note that gold and frankincense were expensive gifts. Myrrh was quite common and thus relatively inexpensive. Jesus had equal respect for all three. His parents, I'm sure, received them with equal gratitude. So did Jesus.

Look now at Herod. Did he truly intend to *worship* Jesus as he promised (Matthew 2:8)? Not on your life. He determined to "seek the young Child to destroy Him" (Matthew 2:13 NKJV). No wonder this hateful Herod was always looking over his shoulder. God knew his murderous plan and used dreams to warn the wise men as well as Joseph to steer clear of this maniacal madman.

A Plaintive Wail

MATTHEW 2:14–18 *When he arose, he took the young Child and His mother by night and departed for Egypt, and was there until the death of Herod, that it might be fulfilled which was spoken by the Lord through the prophet, saying, "Out of Egypt I called My Son."*

Then Herod, when he saw that he was deceived by the wise men, was exceedingly angry; and he sent forth and put to death all the male children who were in Bethlehem and in all its districts, from two years old and under, according to the time which he had determined from the wise men. Then was fulfilled what was spoken by Jeremiah the prophet, saying:

"A voice was heard in Ramah,
Lamentation, weeping, and great mourning,

Rachel weeping for her children,
Refusing to be comforted,
Because they are no more." (NKJV)

kingdom
Luke 18:16

Herod put his plot into action. Every child living in the immediate vicinity of Bethlehem and its environs was hunted down and summarily executed by Herod's henchmen. Joseph, Mary, and their son escaped Herod's hatchet by literally running for their lives down to Egypt (see Illustration #1).

Upon the execution of Herod's order, the loud wail of women weeping could be heard throughout the region, thus fulfilling a prediction made centuries earlier by the prophet Jeremiah. Two elements in his prophecy are most significant:

1. *Ramah:* In Jeremiah's day this little town just north of Jerusalem was the place from which captive Jews were taken hostage into Babylon. Jeremiah's prophecy served as a grim reminder that as the Jews were under a Babylonian bondage then, they were equally under a Roman yoke now (Jeremiah 40:1).

2. *Rachel:* This wife of Jacob cried out in anguish, "Give me children, or else I die!" (Genesis 30:1 NKJV). Rachel epitomized the heartfelt desire of every young Jewish woman to marry and bear children. Tragically and yet ironically, Rachel died while giving birth to her son Benjamin. She "was buried on the way to Ephrath (that is, Bethlehem)" (Genesis 35:19 NKJV). Thus, "Rachel weeping for her children" (Matthew 2:18 NKJV) referenced the collective heartrending anguish felt by every Bethlehem mother as they watched in helpless horror as their loved and longed-for children were brutally butchered on that infamous day of Herod's holocaust.

Hosea predicted that Jesus would be called out of Egypt (Hosea 11:1). Jeremiah predicted the slaughter of the innocents in Bethlehem (Jeremiah 31:15).

prophecy

something to ponder

If it doesn't seem fair to you that these infants should senselessly die through no fault of their own, you're absolutely right. But there is a silver lining to this dark cloud. Those infants were immediately transported into God's protective presence where they will dwell in his heavenly <u>kingdom</u> forever.

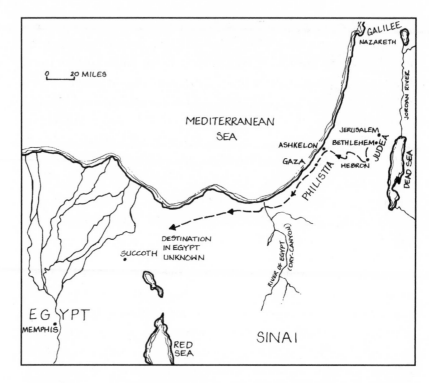

Rachel's tomb is literally a stone's throw from Bethlehem. (Today, whenever we hear of rock-throwing violence just outside of Bethlehem, it almost always takes place right in front of Rachel's tomb.) Since biblical times, Rachel's tomb has been a place of pilgrimage, largely for Israeli women who go there to pray that God will open their wombs and bless them with children.

Herod Meets His Maker

> MATTHEW 2:19–23 *Now when Herod was dead, behold, an angel of the Lord appeared in a dream to Joseph in Egypt, saying, "Arise, take the young Child and His mother, and go to the land of Israel, for those who sought the young Child's life are dead." Then he arose, took the young Child and His mother, and came into the land of Israel. But when he heard that Archelaus was reigning over Judea instead of his father Herod, he was afraid to go there. And being warned by God in a dream, he turned aside into the region of Galilee. And he came and dwelt in a city called Nazareth, that it might be fulfilled which was spoken by the prophets, "He shall be called a Nazarene." (NKJV)*

"When Herod was dead" (Matthew 2:19 NKJV) is a telling statement. Herod died of a horribly wretched disease described by Josephus as "an intolerable itching over all the surface of his body, and continual pains in his colon, and dropsical tumors about his feet, and an inflammation of the abdomen, and a putrefaction of his privy member, that produced worms. Besides which he had a difficulty of breathing upon him, and could not breathe but when he sat upright, and had a convulsion of all his members."[11] One is tempted to think of Herod's torments as a fitting way for this tormentor to die slowly.

Herod's death signaled the opportunity for Joseph, Mary, and Jesus to begin their much anticipated journey home. But there was a problem.

Herod's demise led to the three-way division of his kingdom between his sons: Antipas, Philip II, and Archelaus. Herod Antipas, who would later <u>murder</u> John the Baptist, was given Galilee and Perea. Herod Philip II got the areas northeast of the Sea of Galilee, including Caesarea Philippi, which he humbly named after himself and Caesar, with whom he curried favor. Herod Archelaus received Idumea, Samaria, and Judah, including Bethlehem.

Archelaus wasted no time establishing his reputation as a "chip off the ol' block." When he visited the Temple and observed the excitement of the Jews over the death of his dad, he exploded. Passover was in full swing. Crowds were pouring into Jerusalem. The atmosphere was charged. So he called out his troops and squeezed the people firmly in his iron grasp. The crowds reacted.

Archelaus overreacted. He called in more troops and smugly watched over the massacre of three thousand Jews.[12]

We can understand why, when Joseph "heard that Archelaus was reigning over Judea instead of his father Herod, he was afraid to go there" (Matthew 2:22 NKJV). He and Mary heeded yet another dreamland warning and settled with their son some sixty miles north of Bethlehem in the tiny town of Nazareth, where this child-born-King would live and <u>grow</u> to adulthood just like every other little boy in town.

Isaiah predicted that the Messiah would live in Nazareth, the boyhood home of Jesus (Isaiah 11:1).

murder
Matthew 14:10

grow
Luke 2:52

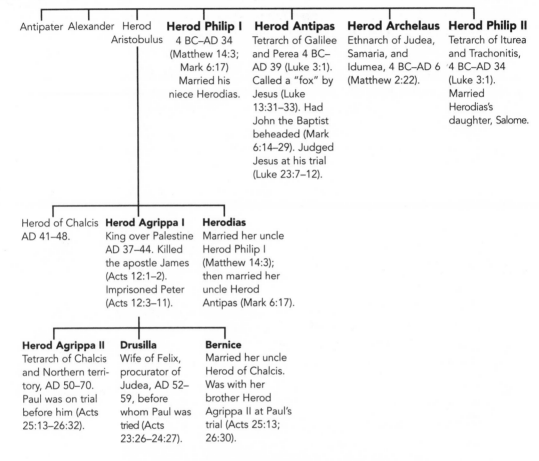

Herod the Great
King of the Jews, 37BC–4 BC (Luke 1:5)
Killed the baby boys of Bethlehem

Antipater Alexander Herod Aristobulus

Herod Philip I
4 BC–AD 34
(Matthew 14:3;
Mark 6:17)
Married his
niece Herodias.

Herod Antipas
Tetrarch of Galilee
and Perea 4 BC–
AD 39 (Luke 3:1).
Called a "fox" by
Jesus (Luke
13:31–33). Had
John the Baptist
beheaded (Mark
6:14–29). Judged
Jesus at his trial
(Luke 23:7–12).

Herod Archelaus
Ethnarch of Judea,
Samaria, and
Idumea, 4 BC–AD 6
(Matthew 2:22).

Herod Philip II
Tetrarch of Iturea
and Trachonitis,
4 BC–AD 34
(Luke 3:1).
Married
Herodias's
daughter, Salome.

Herod of Chalcis
AD 41–48.

Herod Agrippa I
King over Palestine
AD 37–44. Killed
the apostle James
(Acts 12:1–2).
Imprisoned Peter
(Acts 12:3–11).

Herodias
Married her uncle
Herod Philip I
(Matthew 14:3);
then married her
uncle Herod
Antipas (Mark 6:17).

Herod Agrippa II
Tetrarch of Chalcis
and Northern terri-
tory, AD 50–70.
Paul was on trial
before him (Acts
25:13–26:32).

Drusilla
Wife of Felix,
procurator of
Judea, AD 52–
59, before
whom Paul was
tried (Acts
23:26–24:27).

Bernice
Married her uncle
Herod of Chalcis.
Was with her
brother Herod
Agrippa II at Paul's
trial (Acts 25:13;
26:30).

Like Father, like Sons. The Ungodly Line of Herod the Great
(Names in boldface appear in the New Testament)

God often chooses obscure, out-of-the-way, off-the-beaten-path places of preparation for his choice servants. Jesus grew up in the place of ridicule called Nazareth. Moses labored <u>forty</u> years on the back side of a desert. David tended <u>sheep</u> long before he ruled people. Paul was dispatched to Arabia and later Damascus to study and prepare for <u>three</u> years. The pattern is clear.

You may be tempted to think that you are stuck in a no-account backwater of a place of virtually zero influence. But think again. God may use you right where you are to touch the lives of those around you, and through them to touch the world.

go to

forty
Acts 7:30

sheep
1 Samuel 17:15

three
Galatians 1:18

Nazareth was an utterly insignificant town that rested at the bottom of what you might think of as a donut hole since it was completely surrounded by a circle of hills. "Nazareth" comes from the Hebrew word for "branch," a term mentioned in Isaiah's <u>prophecy</u> of Jesus's boyhood home. So backward was this place that the mere mention of Nazareth spawned snickers of derision. Nathanael had it right when he asked, "Can anything good come out of Nazareth?" (John 1:46 NKJV). The fact is, something very good came from there.

prophecy
Isaiah 11:1

Chapter Wrap-Up

- Joseph and Mary lived in the midst of political oppression that literally threatened their lives, and that of the newborn Son. (Matthew 2:1)

- A group of learned men—Magi—traveled a long distance to pay their respects to Jesus, who by this time was perhaps two years of age. (Matthew 2:1)

- Herod the Great, the self-appointed "King of the Jews," viewed Jesus as a threat and put into motion a diabolical plan to murder the child. (Matthew 2:8)

- A "star," very possibly an angel, led the "wise men" to the house in Bethlehem where Jesus, Mary, and Joseph were living. (Matthew 2:10)

- The Magi gave to Jesus gifts fit for a king. Together the three gifts painted a picture of Jesus as a King, as God, and as a human who would one day die. (Matthew 2:11)

- Every Bethlehem baby boy two years of age and younger was senselessly murdered by Herod in his attempt to remove Jesus as a threat to his throne. (Matthew 2:16)

- Herod the Great was referred to as such, not because he was a great man, but because he was a great builder.

- When Herod the Great died, Jesus and his family settled in Nazareth, having been warned in a dream about Herod's son Archelaus, who inherited the region around Jerusalem and Bethlehem. (Matthew 2:23)

Study Questions

1. Who were the wise men and were they a part of Jesus's birth narrative?

2. Why is it inaccurate to include the wise men in the manger scene?

3. What is the significance of the gifts the wise men presented?

4. What was the word on the street regarding Herod the Great?

5. What was the difference between Herod as the "King of the Jews," and Jesus as the "King of the Jews"?

6. Why did Herod the Great build so many fortresses throughout the little land of Israel?

7. Who were the "chief priests" and "teachers of the law"?

8. What is the meaning of "Bethlehem," and what might its significance be?

9. Why did Jeremiah's prophecy concerning Herod's slaughter of the innocents include a reference to Rachel?

Matthew 3: King's Herald

Chapter Highlights:
- John the Baptizer
- Preparing the Way
- A Brood of Vipers
- A Merciful Messiah
- This Is My Son

Let's Get Started

His name was simply John. But there was nothing simple about this mysterious man of the desert.

He must have been quite a sight when he suddenly burst on the scene. His eyes were ablaze with the fire of conviction as he peered out from behind his uncut hair and unkempt beard; he probably looked like he was hiding in some sort of wild bush.[1] He wore a single garment of woven camel's hair bound with a leather belt. His strangely strict diet guaranteed that he would remain slim and trim. By anybody's standards, this guy looked weird. Yet, there was nothing weird about his words. When he spoke, the people trembled.

John the Baptizer

> MATTHEW 3:1 *In those days John the Baptist came preaching in the wilderness of Judea, . . . (NKJV)*

Three full decades would pass between the calm conclusion of Matthew 2—a young family settling down to a peaceful life in tranquil Nazareth—and the raucous resumption of the story in Matthew 3 with this wild man of the wilderness thundering on the scene. God <u>sent</u> him. That much we know. Who raised him? That remains a mystery.

Both of John's parents, Zacharias and Elizabeth, were of <u>priestly</u> descent, so we know that John grew up around the Temple with all of its worship traditions and rituals. He came from godly stock as both parents were "righteous before God, walking in all the commandments and ordinances of the Lord blameless" (Luke 1:6 NKJV). They were already <u>advanced</u> in age and without other children when they experienced **divine intervention** to conceive and bear John. He was certainly not virgin-born as was his cousin Jesus. (Elizabeth and Mary were closely <u>related</u>.) The fact that Elizabeth conceived at such an old age, and that Elizabeth's pregnancy was <u>announced</u> by

sent
John 1:6

priestly
Luke 1:5

advanced
Luke 1:18

related
Luke 1:36

announced
Luke 1:11–13

divine intervention
something that
God did

Tetrarchs
governors ruling
over a fourth of a
region

Qumran
community center
of the Essenes,
overlooking the
Dead Sea

Dead Sea Scrolls
collection of ancient
scrolls found in the
caves of Qumran

an angel, left no doubt that God's hand was uniquely upon this child.

The many descriptions and predictions concerning John stagger the imagination. From the announcement of an angel we hear, "Many will rejoice at his birth. . . . He will be great in the sight of the Lord. . . . He will also be filled with the Holy Spirit, even from his mother's womb. . . . He will turn many of the children of Israel to the Lord their God. He will also go before [the Lord] in the spirit and power of Elijah . . . to make ready a people prepared for the Lord" (Luke 1:14–17 NKJV).

His mother said, "You, child, will be called the prophet of the Highest . . . to give knowledge of salvation to His people by the remission of their sins, through the tender mercy of our God...to give light to those who sit in darkness" (Luke 1:76–79 NKJV). Stringy hair and bushy beard notwithstanding, John was going to be quite the man.

But all that glitters is not gold. John's upbringing was not without its challenges. It's entirely possible that Zacharias and Elizabeth both died when John was young. This would explain Luke's otherwise curious comment, "The child...was in the desert till the day of his manifestation to Israel" (Luke 1:80 NKJV). At some point in his childhood, circumstances beyond his control ejected John from the protective womb of his loving home and hurled him headlong into the godforsaken wasteland of the Judean desert.

what others say

G. Campbell Morgan

How important the personality of John was considered, is seen in the manner Luke introduces him. One Roman Emperor, one Roman Governor, three **Tetrarchs** and two High Priests are all made use of to mark the hour in which the Word came to John (Luke 3:1).[2]

A community of men known as the Essenes lived in the desert of Judea at the time of John's birth. Having settled in **Qumran**, the place where the famed **Dead Sea Scrolls** were discovered, these religiously strict, highly disciplined Jews did not marry, but they did adopt children and raise them in their own teachings. Key elements of John's preaching—heralding the coming of the Messiah, calling the people to repentance, and warning of the coming judgment of

God—sounded similar in tone and theme to the writings of the Essenes. It may well be that John grew up as an adopted member of the Essene community, quite possibly at Qumran itself.[3]

A Lean, Mean Baptizing Machine

The Judean desert, as we'll see in chapter 4, was and is an empty, lonely, barren, hot, dry, wind-blown moonscape. John emerged from this hostile terrain and detonated on the scene with the nuclear force of an atomic bomb. He came as a herald, the one appointed by God to prepare the people to receive their Messiah. His voice became a rallying cry, like the blaring of a bugle, the clarion call of a prophet that rumbled across the desolate wasteland, rattling the people to their bones.

He is most often referred to as "John the Baptist" (Matthew 3:1 NKJV), due, frankly, to the common but lazy translation of his title from Greek to English. Matthew, Mark, and Luke refer to him as "John the 'Baptistais'" in Greek no less than fourteen times. (The apostle John refers to him only as "John.") *Baptistais*, commonly translated *Baptist*, refers not to what John was in terms of his **denominational** affiliation (John was not a member of a Baptist church!), but rather to what John did. John baptized people. Properly rendered, John's title is more accurately translated, "John the Baptizer."[4]

John
John 1:15

denominational
local church's national affiliation, such as Baptist, Methodist, Presbyterian

> ### what others say
>
> **William Barclay**
>
> The emergence of John was like the sudden sounding of the voice of God. At this time the Jews were sadly conscious that the voice of the prophets spoke no more. . . . But in John the prophetic voice spoke again.[5]

The Kingdom Is Coming

MATTHEW 3:2 . . . *and saying, "Repent, for the kingdom of heaven is at hand!"* (NKJV)

John's preaching was straight and to the point. He told the people what to do (repent) and why to do it (the kingdom was coming).

Repent was a commonly used term in New Testament times, but is a tragically misused or underused word today. *Repent* means much more than merely feeling bad or sorry for something. *Repent* means "to change one's mind or purpose" concerning one's sins, and "a complete change of attitude, spiritual and moral, toward God. The primary meaning involves a turning to God, which may indeed make a person sorry for his sins, but that sorrow is a by-product and not the repentance itself."[6] To put it simply, when John told the people to repent, he challenged them to turn away from their sins and to turn toward God.

John the Baptist called on the people to repent. Jesus called on the people to repent (Mark 1:15). The disciples called on the people to repent (Mark 6:12). Peter called on the people to repent (Acts 2:38). Paul called on the people to repent (Acts 17:30). The apostle John called on the people to repent (Revelation 2:5). The angels rejoice in heaven when even one sinner repents (Luke 15:7). Jesus meant it when he said, "I tell you...unless you repent you will all likewise perish" (Luke 13:3 NKJV). The writers of the New Testament use the word *repent* or a form of that word a full fifty-two times.

Matthew uses the phrase "kingdom of heaven" thirty-three times, and he's the only Gospel writer who uses it. Mark, Luke, and John use the phrase "kingdom of God" (Mark 1:15; Luke 4:43; and John 3:3 NKJV). There is no distinction in meaning, as the two phrases refer to the same thing. In fact, at times they are used interchangeably (Matthew 19:14; Mark 10:14; Luke 18:16). There is only a distinction in emphasis. Matthew prefers the phrase "kingdom of heaven" in deference to his Jewish readers, who were extremely skittish about speaking, let alone writing, God's name. Often they would substitute the word *heaven* for *God* in their daily speech.[9]

Jesus
Matthew 16:14

Preparing the Way

MATTHEW 3:3 *For this is he who was spoken of by the prophet Isaiah, saying:*
"The voice of one crying in the wilderness:
'Prepare the way of the LORD;
Make His paths straight.'" (NKJV)

The Old Testament closed with this promise: "I will send you Elijah the prophet before the coming of the great and dreadful day of the LORD" (Malachi 4:5 NKJV). Imagine it. Elijah would live again. Not literally, though many people took it that way. Some even thought that <u>Jesus</u> was the reincarnation of Elijah!

prophecy

Four centuries later, the New Testament opened with the fulfillment of that promise. Elijah did indeed return, figuratively, in the person of John the Baptist. Jesus himself confirmed this when he said, "If you are willing to receive it, [John the Baptist] is Elijah who is to come" (Matthew 11:14 NKJV). Does this seem a tad confusing? Consider this:

Elijah and John the Baptist

Comparisons	Elijah	John the Baptist
Both were children of the desert.	1 Kings 17:3	Matthew 3:1
Both withdrew and lived apart from mainstream society.	1 Kings 17:5	Luke 1:80
Both wore the clothing of the desert.	2 Kings 1:8	Matthew 3:4
Both shattered the prophetic silence of many years and spoke to the masses on behalf of God.	1 Kings 18:21	Matthew 3:5
Both had fiery personalities and an explosive intensity.	1 Kings 18:8	Matthew 3:7
Both fearlessly confronted the religious leaders of their day.	1 Kings 18:25	Matthew 3:7

Enoch
Genesis 5:24

Comparisons	Elijah	John the Baptist
Both put their lives on the line by confronting the political leaders of their day.	1 Kings 18:18	Matthew 14:4
Both condemned the sins of a wicked and hard-hearted people.	1 Kings 18:21	Luke 1:17
Both turned the hearts of many away from their sins and toward their God.	1 Kings 18:37	Luke 1:16
Both fell into despair and briefly doubted their missions and masters.	1 Kings 19:4	Matthew 11:3

John the Baptist was not the reincarnation of Elijah; he was a carbon copy of Elijah. The baton was passed from the Old Testament prophet Elijah to the New Testament prophet John. And carry the baton well, he did.

John's task was clear—to call a sinful nation back to God, thus fulfilling his mandate to "prepare the way of the LORD" by making "His paths straight" (Matthew 3:3 NKJV). This wording perfectly pictures a road crew busily removing rocks and debris, filling in any potholes, and otherwise clearing the road of any other obstacles or hazards in advance of the arrival of a monarch. In a spiritual sense, that's exactly what John was doing, with some measure of success as we'll soon see.

John fulfilled to a T the predicted description of the Messiah's herald in Isaiah 40:3.

Interestingly enough, Elijah never actually died. In 2 Kings 2:1 Elijah was taken up to heaven in a whirlwind, becoming the second of only two people in the Bible who did not die. Enoch was the first. This has led some to believe that Enoch and Elijah are the two witnesses who appear in Revelation 11. Since the two witnesses are not specifically identified by name, we cannot know for sure. What we do know is that John the Baptist will be executed in Matthew 14 and never come back, while Elijah will come back on the Mount of Transfiguration in Matthew 17.

Dieter's Delight

MATTHEW 3:4–6 *Now John himself was clothed in camel's hair, with a leather belt around his waist; and his food was locusts and wild honey. Then Jerusalem, all Judea, and all the region around the Jordan went out to him and were baptized by him in the Jordan, confessing their sins.* (NKJV)

kosher
conforming to
Jewish dietary laws

John's dress and diet might seem strange to us. But it wouldn't seem strange at all if we lived in the harsh environs of a Middle Eastern wilderness.

John's camel's hair garment, complete with leather belt, was the essence of simplicity and practicality, perfectly suited to life in the desert with its searing heat, skin-cracking dryness, and continuously blowing sand. There are places in the Judean desert where the temperatures can soar to a sizzling 130 degrees. Certain parcels of parched earth, ever praying for a reprieve from the relentlessly blazing sun, might be rewarded with but one good cloudburst of rain in a decade. Under such challenging conditions, fashion and style are not high on one's list of priorities when it comes to choosing a wardrobe. When survival is the name of the game, clothing is nothing more than a simple, durable, functional protective covering, a shield against the life-threatening elements of the barren wilderness.

John ate with equal simplicity and practicality. The Old Testament describes Israel as a land "flowing with milk and honey" (Exodus 3:8 NKJV). The sugars of honey provided John with life-sustaining energy. Protein-rich locusts were equally plentiful and were a **kosher** food dating back to the early days of Leviticus 11:22.

People from the populated areas surrounding the desert poured out to hear this prophet preach. John's message obviously had an immediate impact; scores of people confessed their sins and submitted to his baptism in the chilly waters of the Jordan River.

what others say

D. Larry Miller

John the Baptist was named that because his ministry was to call people to repentance and then baptize them. The baptism itself did not save them from their sins, but their repentance did.[10]

A Brood of Vipers

MATTHEW 3:7–10 *But when he saw many of the Pharisees and Sadducees coming to his baptism, he said to them, "Brood of vipers! Who warned you to flee from the wrath to come? Therefore bear fruits worthy of repentance, and do not think to say to yourselves, 'We have Abraham as our father.' For I say to you that God is able to raise up children to Abraham from these*

stones. And even now the ax is laid to the root of the trees.
Therefore every tree which does not bear good fruit is cut down
and thrown into the fire. (NKJV)

At last we meet the famous, or should we say infamous, Pharisees and Sadducees. We'll get to know them all too well before this voyage is over. They hounded, harassed, and otherwise made life miserable for Jesus until the day he died.

The Pharisees were smug, proud, self-righteous, self-centered, intolerant, judgmental extremists—the very worst of the worst of what a hostile media today might cruelly call the radical religious right. They forgot that there was only one God and that they were not him. The religious leaders rebuffed John's preaching and did not repent.

The Sadducees were no better. Of priestly descent, they used religion solely as a means of societal advancement. The Temple (see Illustration #8, page 265) was their social and business club. They went there to ink a deal, make a buck, and turn a quick profit. They arrogantly determined for themselves what portions of the Bible applied to them and readily rejected anything God said that they did not like.

Now here they were—two mortal enemies, two fierce competitors for the allegiance of the people—standing on the riverbank, for the first time ever united as one in their common hatred of Jesus and his faithful forerunner. The minute he saw them, John appropriately exploded with righteous indignation, his anger motivated not by their defiant rejection of him, but by their brazen rebellion against God. These self-appointed religious leaders misused their positions of power to abuse the very people they were called to serve. John knew it, and he called them on it.

Vipers were small, slithery, deadly desert snakes. When lying still they looked like harmless twigs or small sticks. Pick one up, and you die. That's exactly what the Pharisees and Sadducees were—small men who proclaimed themselves to be big; baby-faced assassins who looked harmless on the outside while planning and plotting their sinister deeds on the inside; slithery men whose walk contradicted their talk; men of death who proclaimed themselves to be sources of life. John questioned their character, heralded their hypocrisy, and warned them to flee God's wrath. John hit his bull's-eye with pinpoint accuracy. True repentance, the kind that John demanded of these people, had nothing to do with what they said or how they felt; true repentance had everything to do with how they lived.

If, as they say, "The proof of the pudding is in the eating," then the proof of true repentance is in the walking. Their walk proved beyond the shadow of a doubt that their talk was cheap, their lives were lies, their very existence a shameless sham. None of those who refused to repent were baptized.

go to

fruit
Galatians 5:22–23

Herculean
extraordinary

what others say

Lehman Strauss

In the spiritual realm, fruit can never be the results of human exertion and self-effort in order to obtain holiness. The fruit of the Spirit is the outward expression of God's power working in us. The lust of the flesh manifests itself in works.

The Holy Spirit manifests his presence and power in his fruit. Any one of us may be theologically correct in the doctrine of the Holy Spirit, yet live a life that does not display the Spirit's fruit.[11]

A Humble Herald

MATTHEW 3:11–12 *I indeed baptize you with water unto repentance, but He who is coming after me is mightier than I, whose sandals I am not worthy to carry. He will baptize you with the Holy Spirit and fire. His winnowing fan is in His hand, and He will thoroughly clean out His threshing floor, and gather His wheat into the barn; but He will burn up the chaff with unquenchable fire." (NKJV)*

John knew his place. He understood his role. There aren't many people these days who are content being number two. Vice presidents aspire to be presidents. But John was different. A genuinely humble man, he fulfilled his role as a perpetual number two without a murmur of complaint. As the people gathered to hear him speak and watch him baptize, he consistently and passionately directed their attention to the one place where it belonged—their promised Messiah, their coming King, their only Savior, Jesus Christ.

John possessed the perfect blend of humility mixed with intensity. His meekness did not translate into weakness. Humble in his personality, John was **Herculean** in his power. What a balance! The man who was not worthy personally to untie Jesus's sandal was all too willing publicly to stomp on the religious leaders' toes.

go to

anticipation
Luke 2:25

pour
Joel 2:28

water
Ezekiel 36:25

spirit
Ezekiel 36:26

A Merciful Messiah

As severe as John's warnings sound, he also sings a high note of hope. John played off the word *baptize*. "Baptize" was a common term in New Testament times. It simply meant to dip or immerse, as one would immerse a garment into a vat of dye or dip a ladle into a bowl of soup.[13] John "dipped" people into water; his was what we would call today "water baptism." But when the Messiah arrived, John warned, he would offer a dual baptism—one of blessing or one of cursing; one of salvation or one of damnation; one a baptism "with the Holy Spirit" and the other a baptism with "fire" (Matthew 3:11 NKJV). The people knew exactly what he meant.

Here's the meaning of baptism with the Holy Spirit: Faithful students of the Old Testament Scriptures lived in eager <u>anticipation</u> of the day when God would <u>pour</u> out his Spirit on all people, sprinkle clean <u>water</u> on them, cleanse them from all of their impurities, put a new <u>spirit</u> within them, remove their hard hearts, and replace them with tender hearts. With the prophets using terms like "pour" and "cleanse," you can understand why John's use of "baptize" was, as our British friends might say, "spot-on." The day of the fulfillment of the prophets' predictions had finally come. That's the good news.

Here's the meaning of baptism with fire: God's promises can be rebuffed. The Messiah can be rejected. Jesus would not then, and will not now, drag people kicking and screaming into his kingdom against their will. So, said John, a baptism with the fire of God's judgment awaits those who demand to live in rebellion against him. That's the bad news.

John illustrated baptism "with fire" by using a common cultural comparison. In biblical times a wheat farmer would pile his harvested wheat onto a large, flat surface, usually on the top of a hill or rise, where a breeze could blow across it. This was called the "threshing floor." He would then use a pitchfork-like object, called a "winnowing fork," to hurl the straw into the air (see Illustration #2). The breeze would blow through it, carrying away the chaff while leaving the heavier kernels of wheat to fall to the floor.

In the same way, John warned, the Messiah will separate the "chaff" (those who rebel) from the "wheat" (those who repent). The repentant will be gathered into God's "barn" where they will live with him in bliss and blessing forever. The rebellious will be burned up, much like **chaff** when tossed into a flame.

no sins
2 Corinthians 5:21

chaff
straw

Illustration #2
Winnowing Fork—
Farmers used a winnowing fork such as this to throw the grain into the air. The lightweight chaff would blow away while the heavier kernel of grain would fall down.

This Is My Son

MATTHEW 3:13–17 *Then Jesus came from Galilee to John at the Jordan to be baptized by him. And John tried to prevent Him, saying, "I need to be baptized by You, and are You coming to me?" But Jesus answered and said to him, "Permit it to be so now, for thus it is fitting for us to fulfill all righteousness." Then he allowed Him. When He had been baptized, Jesus came up immediately from the water; and behold, the heavens were opened to Him, and He saw the Spirit of God descending like a dove and alighting upon Him. And suddenly a voice came from heaven, saying, "This is My beloved Son, in whom I am well pleased." (NKJV)*

John baptized those people who approached him with an attitude of genuine, heartfelt repentance. What was he thinking when Jesus got into the line of people to be baptized? Jesus had no sins for which he needed to repent. When John declared, "I need to be baptized by You, and are You coming to me?" (Matthew 3:14 NKJV), he

Moses
Exodus 34:9

Nehemiah
Nehemiah 1:6

Daniel
Daniel 9:6

seminal
original

Trinitarian
referring to the
Trinity

affirmed both his own sinfulness and Jesus's sinlessness. Even in that statement of bewilderment, John was fulfilling his role as the herald of the King by proclaiming the perfection of the sinless Son of God.

So why in the world did the sinless Savior need to be baptized? Here are five possible reasons:

- Jesus identified himself with the sins of his people, much as <u>Moses</u>, <u>Nehemiah</u>, and <u>Daniel</u> had done.

- Jesus validated John's ministry in front of the crowds.

- Jesus marked the official beginning of his public ministry.

- Jesus aligned himself with the tenderhearted masses who were also baptized, rather than with the hard-hearted Pharisees and Sadducees who refused to be baptized.

- Jesus illustrated his death, burial, and resurrection since water baptism symbolizes a person's dying to his old life and rising to a new life in Christ.

Which of these five offers the best explanation? Frankly, there's some truth in each of them. But the why of Christ's baptism is not nearly as important as what happened immediately after the baptism. As Jesus came up out of the water, the booming blast of John was replaced by the thundering voice of God.

When God spoke from heaven, he quoted two significant Old Testament verses. He said, "This is My beloved Son" (Matthew 3:17 NKJV, a direct quote from Psalm 2:7), and then added, "in whom I am well pleased" (3:17 NKJV, a clear reference to Isaiah 42:1). Every Jew who heard God's voice that day knew that in Psalm 2 God spoke of the time when his own Son would rule the world as the Messiah. They also knew that in Isaiah 42 God described his presentation of the Messiah to a nation that was spiritually blinded to God's glory and deafened to God's truth. That day now had arrived.

Neither the people nor their leaders could plausibly deny it. Jesus's baptism was a one-two punch of profound importance, the **seminal** event that spotlighted both John's preparing the people for the coming Messiah and God's presenting to the people the Messiah who had now come.

Matthew 3:16–17 is a **Trinitarian** passage. Even though the Bible does not use the word *trinity*, it certainly teaches that our one God consists of three distinct persons united together in one essence (see

Illustration #3). Perhaps a more accurate word to describe God would be *Triunity*, for that is what God is. Thus, right after he was baptized, Jesus looked up into heaven, God the Father spoke from heaven, and the Holy Spirit (in the form of a **dove**) descended from heaven. In the mathematics of the Bible, 1 Father + 1 Son + 1 Holy Spirit = 1 God. From this point on, the fingerprints of the Trinity will be all over Jesus's ministry. Jesus will serve the people in obedience to the Father and in the power of the Holy Spirit.

go to

dove
symbol of innocence and purity

Father

God

Son   Holy Spirit

Fingerprints of the Trinity

Matthew 28:19	"Baptizing them in the name [singular] of the Father and of the Son and of the Holy Spirit" (NKJV).
John 15:26	"But when the Helper comes, whom I shall send to you from the Father, the Spirit of truth who proceeds from the Father, He will testify of Me [Jesus]" (NKJV).
1 Corinthians 12:4–6	"There are diversities of gifts, but the same Spirit. There are differences of ministries, but the same Lord. And there are diversities of activities, but it is the same God who works all in all" (NKJV).
2 Corinthians 13:14	"The grace of the Lord Jesus Christ, and the love of God, and the communion of the Holy Spirit be with you all" (NKJV).
Ephesians 2:18	"For through Him [Jesus] we both have access by one Spirit to the Father" (NKJV).
1 Thessalonians 1:3–5	". . . Remembering without ceasing your work of faith . . . in our Lord Jesus Christ in the sight of our God and Father . . . For our gospel did not come to you in word only, but also in power, and in the Holy Spirit" (NKJV).
1 Peter 1:2	"Elect according to the foreknowledge of God the Father, in sanctification of the Spirit, for obedience and sprinkling of the blood of Jesus Christ" (NKJV).

Illustration #3
The Trinitarian Triangle—Just as an equilateral triangle is one geometrical figure manifesting itself in three distinct, coequal angles, so God manifests himself in three distinct, coequal persons: Father, Son, and Holy Spirit. The Father can send his Son; his Son can pray to his Father; the Holy Spirit can glorify the Son; the Son can perform miracles in obedience to the Father in the power of the Holy Spirit.

Chapter Wrap-Up

- John the Baptist's birth was miraculous, the result of divine intervention, in that his parents—Zechariah and Elizabeth—were both beyond child-bearing age. (Luke 1:7)

- Luke tells us that John lived in the desert, perhaps an indication that his parents died when he was young. Some believe that he was raised by the Essenes, perhaps at Qumran. (Luke 3:2)

- John is referred to often in Scripture as "John the Baptist" because of his ministry of baptism. He should more properly be referred to as "John the Baptizer." (Matthew 3:6)

- John the Baptizer and Elijah have many striking similarities in their respective ministries. In that sense, John was not a reincarnation, but rather a carbon copy of Elijah. (Matthew 11:14)

- John the Baptist's clothing and diet were perfectly suited to the harsh conditions of the barren wilderness from where he came. (Matthew 3:4)

- John the Baptist served as the perfect forerunner of Jesus Christ as he called the people to repentance and announced the coming of their Messiah, Jesus. (Matthew 3:2)

- John the Baptist in a sense formally launched Jesus's ministry by baptizing him in the Jordan River. The earthly ministry of Christ can thus be sandwiched between his baptism and his crucifixion/resurrection. (Matthew 3:13–17)

- At the baptism of Jesus, God revealed himself as the Triune God—as Jesus came up out of the water, God the Father proclaimed his approval of his Son, and the Holy Spirit descended upon him as a dove. (Matthew 3:16–17)

Study Questions

1. Why is John commonly referred to as "the Baptist"?

2. Some believe that John the Baptist was raised by what community? Why do they believe this?

3. What does the term "repent" mean?

4. What is John the Baptist's relationship to Elijah?

5. What is the significance of John the Baptist's diet and clothing?

6. What was the dual baptism that John said would occur now that Jesus was on the scene?

7. Who are the wheat and who are the chaff?

8. What is the Trinity, and how is it seen in Jesus's baptism?

9. Why did a sinless Savior need to be baptized?

Matthew 4: Testing of the King

Let's Get Started

There are times when nature seems to hold her breath. Nothing moves. The breeze stops blowing. The crickets stop chirping. Dogs stop barking. Trees stop rustling. You know that something strange is about to happen. I've lived through three earthquakes, two of them severe. Each time, just before another large aftershock rocked the rink, everything stopped as if in anticipation.

That's exactly what we think happened in Matthew 4. Mortal combat was about to occur. Jesus's archenemy, the devil, crept into the camp. Hitting Jesus with the full fury of his nuclear arsenal, the devil launched a relentless attack with one aim in mind—to destroy forever this King of the Jews. As we learned in Matthew 1, Jesus possessed the legal right (through Abraham) and the regal right (through David) to sit on David's throne. But did he have the moral right to rule? Nature held her breath as she waited to find out.

praises
Luke 2:14

spoke
Psalm 148:2–5

demon
Matthew 7:22

All-Out War

Angels are amazing beings. Did you know that exactly one-half of the books of the Bible, thirty-three books out of sixty-six, specifically mention angels? They undeniably exist. They flit here and fly there, serving God in all sorts of ways. They lit up the sky and filled the heavens with God's <u>praises</u> when Jesus was born.

When God merely <u>spoke</u> the word *angels*, the heavens exploded with "ten thousand times ten thousand, and thousands of thousands" (Revelation 5:11 NKJV) of them, more than anyone could possibly count. Today, the vast majority of angels enjoy the lofty designation "holy angels" (Revelation 14:10 NKJV). But there are many angels who are anything but holy. Their most common designation is "<u>demon</u>." Riding high, ruling the demons from his precarious perch atop this trash heap of spiritual vice and villainy, is the "ruler of the demons" (Matthew 12:24 NKJV), the devil.

go to

created
Ezekiel 28:12–15

Lucifer
Isaiah 14:12

until
Ezekiel 28:15

Satan
Job 1:6

one-third
Revelation 12:4

stood
Revelation 8:2

Lucifer
means "shining one," "morning star," or "son of the dawn"

anointed
set apart for a special purpose

cherub
a type of angel

Most High
God

The Devil Made Me Do It

MATTHEW 4:1 *Then Jesus was led up by the Spirit into the wilderness to be tempted by the devil.* (NKJV)

When God <u>created</u> him, **Lucifer**, as he was called then, was a breathlessly beautiful angel. Some believe that because of his privileged position as God's **anointed cherub**, he was second only to God in both power and authority. He modeled perfection, wisdom, and beauty.

<u>Until</u> . . .

And with that one ominous word, the whole story tragically changes.

There came a day (we don't know when), there came a time (we don't know why), there came a moment forever frozen in history (we don't know how) when Lucifer marched into God's presence, challenged him to his throne, clenched his fists as it were and held them up high, and defiantly declared that he, Lucifer, was now God. Five times Lucifer uttered the two rebellious words "I will" (Isaiah 14:12–14 NKJV). The monster within him reared its ugly head. Perfection became corruption. Rebellion replaced reverence. His beauty turned ugly. This newly named devil turned defiant. He threw down the gauntlet. He set the stakes high—sky-high—when he announced, "I will be like the **Most High**" (Isaiah 14:14 NKJV). The mother of all battles had begun.

By his one mutinous act, Lucifer's position forever changed from one of privilege to one of perversion. The anointed cherub became <u>Satan</u>, the adversary. He sought the allegiance of the other angels, and <u>one-third</u> joined with him in rebellion against God. Imagine it—angels who at one time <u>stood</u> before God now bowed before Satan.

Mark 1:12 tells us that immediately following Jesus's baptism, the Holy Spirit, who mere moments before had descended upon Jesus in the form of a dove, now led him out of the lush bounty of the Jordan River valley into the dank desolation and eerie isolation of the Judean wilderness, where the temperatures soar, the limestone blisters and peels, the rocks stand bare and jagged, the ridges lie warped and twisted, and heaps of dust masquerade as hills.[1] Nowhere in all of Israel could Jesus have felt more isolated, abandoned, or alone.

The devil goes by a variety of names, each underscoring a specific characteristic of his diabolical depravity, as shown in the following chart.

What's in a Name?

Name	Significance	Scriptural Reference
Abaddon/Apollyon	Destroyer; he seeks to destroy everything he touches.	Revelation 9:11
Accuser of Our Brethren	The author of accusations and condemnations. Even though God has forgiven us, he tries to prevent us from forgiving ourselves.	Revelation 12:10
Adversary	The archenemy of God and of his people.	1 Peter 5:8
Angel of Light	Appears so seductively attractive and irresistible.	2 Corinthians 11:14
Anointed Cherub Who Covers	Prior to his rebellion against God, Lucifer enjoyed the privileged position of covering or guarding God's throne.	Ezekiel 28:14
Beelzebub	Philistine deity associated with satanic worship. "The ruler of the demons."	Matthew 12:24
Belial	"Worthless" or "Hopeless Ruin," descriptive of all who follow him in his rebellion against God.	2 Corinthians 6:15
Devil	*Diabollos*, the diabolical defamer who delights in slandering God's holy name. Used 34 times in the Bible.	Matthew 4:1
Dragon	Stresses Satan's cruel, vicious, and violent nature.	Revelation 12:9
Enemy	Hateful or hate-filled; one who hates God, his people, and everything associated with him.	Matthew 13:39
Evil One	The source of all that is evil in the world; a degenerate wickedness; a malignancy on the earth; a cancer of the soul.	John 17:15
Father of All Lies	Dupes people through his deceptions; sower of false doctrines and religions.	John 8:44
God of This Age	Speaks of his pervasive and perverted influence over the values and morals present in our culture today.	2 Corinthians 4:4
Lucifer	Shining one; his radiance prior to his rebellion against God.	Isaiah 14:12
Prince of the Power of the Air	Similar in meaning to the "god of this age"; his influence dominates the milieu in which we live.	Ephesians 2:2

tempted
Mark 1:13

created
Colossians 1:16

Name	Significance	Scriptural Reference
Satan	"Adversary"; one who opposes God's plans, program, and people. Used 54 times in the Bible.	Matthew 4:10
Serpent of Old	A possible reference to the serpent in the Garden of Eden; he slithers up to his prey often unseen and unsuspected; craftiness.	Genesis 3:1; Revelation 12:9
Tempter	One who entices another to sin.	Matthew 4:3
Wicked One	The embodiment of all that is wicked in the world; sower of malice and mischief.	Matthew 13:19

what others say

Pope John Paul II

The devil exists and is a cosmic liar and murderer. . . . [He] has the skill in the world to induce people to deny his existence in the name of rationalism and of every other system of thought which seeks all possible means to avoid recognizing his activity.[2]

C. S. Lewis

There are two equal and opposite errors into which our race can fall about the devil. One is to disbelieve in his existence. The other is to believe, and to feel an excessive and unhealthy interest in him.[3]

The Lust of the Flesh

MATTHEW 4:2–4 *And when He had fasted forty days and forty nights, afterward He was hungry. Now when the tempter came to Him, he said, "If You are the Son of God, command that these stones become bread." But He answered and said, "It is written, 'Man shall not live by bread alone, but by every word that proceeds from the mouth of God.'"* (NKJV)

The forty days immediately after his baptism, Jesus fasted in the desert. Mark tells us that Jesus was <u>tempted</u> throughout that forty-day period. The three temptations recorded by Matthew comprise Satan's final all-out assault.

The temptation to turn stones into bread seems on the surface to be no temptation at all. It's not like Jesus was stealing something that belonged to somebody else; there are plenty of rocks in Israel. For that matter, he <u>created</u> the rocks. In the ultimate sense, he owned them. And he was hungry. So what if he turned a few stones into bread? Who could possibly blame him for that?

Satan is smooth and subtle. He is often most successful in seducing us into sin by tempting us to fulfill legitimate desires in an illegitimate ways.

Satan effectively used doubt to knock Eve off balance. His first words to her in the Garden of Eden were, "Has God indeed said . . . ?" (Genesis 3:1 NKJV). He used the same tactic against Jesus. Before he ever mentioned the rocks or bread, he tried to gain a foothold by getting Jesus to doubt: "If You are the Son of God…" (Matthew 4:3 NKJV). He will do the same to us.

Jesus certainly possessed the power to turn stones into bread. But when he became a man, he willingly <u>relinquished</u> his right to use his power for his own benefit and chose to submit himself fully to the <u>will</u> of his Father. In obedience to his Father, he used his power for other people's benefit, never his own. To use his power for himself would have compromised his mission—Jesus came here to <u>serve</u> others, never to serve himself.

Jesus promptly thwarted the temptation by quoting Deuteronomy 8:3.

go to

relinquished
Philippians 2:7–8

will
Luke 22:42

serve
Matthew 20:28

> ## what others say
>
> ### Max Lucado
>
> I am terribly concerned as I hear more and more about how people flirt with immorality and how people dance with materialism and how they consider themselves invulnerable to Satan. We are not invulnerable to Satan—he's wise, he's crafty…and just as God wishes you to spend forever with him in heaven, Satan wishes you to spend eternity separated from God. Guard your heart![4]

<u>The Pride of Life</u>

MATTHEW 4:5–7 *Then the devil took Him up into the holy city, set Him on the pinnacle of the temple, and said to Him, "If You are the Son of God, throw Yourself down. For it is written:*
  'He shall give His angels charge over you,'
and,
  'In their hands they shall bear you up,
  Lest you dash your foot against a stone.'"
  Jesus said to him, "It is written again, 'You shall not tempt the LORD your God.'" (NKJV)

pinnacle
highest accessible
point

The devil will stop at nothing to get us to compromise our convictions or corrupt our character. So coldly calculating is the devil that he will stoop so low as to misquote Scripture, pervert its meaning, twist its truth, and if possible use our own Bibles against us, all to achieve his diabolical ends. Case in point: He did it to Jesus.

The devil took Jesus up to the **pinnacle** of the Temple in Jerusalem, towering some 450 feet above the hustling, bustling shopping center that lined the street below. He told Jesus to jump, if you can believe it, and then misquoted Psalm 91:11–12 to make it sound as if angels would catch Jesus in midair, much to the pomp and circumstance and fanfare of the crowds below. A careful comparison of Matthew 4:6 and Psalm 91:11–12 will reveal that Satan cleverly omitted the key phrase, "to keep you in all your ways." That phrase assures us that every moment of every day we are surrounded by God's holy angels who protect us from anything happening to us outside of God's permissive will. It was never the psalmist's intent to convey the mistaken notion that we can take foolhardy risks or accept foolhardy dares and expect the angels to protect us from our foolhardy choices.

Had Jesus jumped, he would have died—not a death on the cross as payment for our sins, but an untimely death of no consequence except to Jesus himself. Satan hoped that by appealing to Jesus's pride he could get him to make a deadly decision. But Jesus didn't take the bait. Jesus resisted this temptation by correctly quoting Deuteronomy 6:16: "You shall not tempt the LORD your God." This was the perfect biblical response to thwart this temptation dead in its tracks.

The Lust of the Eyes

> MATTHEW 4:8–11 *Again, the devil took Him up on an exceedingly high mountain, and showed Him all the kingdoms of the world and their glory. And he said to Him, "All these things I will give You if You will fall down and worship me." Then Jesus said to him, "Away with you, Satan! For it is written, 'You shall worship the LORD your God, and Him only you shall serve.'" Then the devil left Him, and behold, angels came and ministered to Him. (NKJV)*

To the west of the Dead Sea, a bald mountain towers over lush and green Jericho, the one oasis in an otherwise barren desert.

Climb to the top of this mountain and what will you see? When you look to the north, you'll be peering into Lebanon; to the northeast, Syria; directly east, you'll get a breathtaking view of the mountains of Jordan; to the south lies Egypt; and to the west, up and over the top of the Mount of Olives and beyond Jerusalem sparkles the Mediterranean Sea, gateway to Europe. If Jesus did a ballerina's pirouette and turned a 360, he would have "all the kingdoms of the world" (Matthew 4:8 NKJV) laid out before his wonder-filled eyes like some spectacular panoramic picture. All of this was his for the taking if he would simply bow down and worship the devil.

Did Satan make Jesus a legitimate offer? Were the kingdoms of the world his to dangle before Jesus's eyes? Jesus referred to Satan in the present tense as "the ruler of this world" (John 12:31 NKJV). God the Father will one day establish Jesus firmly upon the throne of David, giving him the nations as his "inheritance." But this is future tense. This hasn't happened yet. Jesus has not yet been given "the ends of the earth [as his] possession" (Psalm 2:8 NKJV). Many Bible teachers have therefore concluded that yes, this was a legitimate offer; yes, Satan did have the authority to offer Jesus the kingdoms of the world; yes, Satan offered Jesus a crown without the cross.

Jesus knew that before he would wear his crown of glory he would first wear his crown of thorns. Satan offered him an easy way out. Tempting as it was, Jesus loved his Father and he loves you and me too much to take it. He didn't have to die for our sins; he chose to. So rather than bow, Jesus bellowed, "Away with you, Satan!" (Matthew 4:10 NKJV). And, according to Luke's account, Satan "departed from Him until an opportune time" (Luke 4:13 NKJV). It would be three more years until the devil was finally and completely crushed by the Cross.

go to

inheritance
Psalm 2:8

crown
John 19:2

> ## what others say
>
> ### Larry Richards
>
> Jesus' response to the tempter spotlights resources that you and I can draw on to overcome. In each case, Jesus went back to the Word of God and found a principle by which He chose to live.

lust
craving or
intense desire

> This is important. It is not simply "The Word" that is our resource. It is the commitment to live by the Word. It is resting the full weight of our confidence on what God says, and choosing in each situation to do that which is in harmony with His revealed will.[5]

The devil possesses a limited, but highly effective arsenal of three weapons—"the lust of the flesh, the lust of the eyes, and the pride of life" (1 John 2:16 NKJV). When the devil attempted to get a starving Jesus to turn stones into bread, he appealed to the **lust** of the flesh. When Satan showed Jesus all the kingdoms of the world laid out before him, he appealed to the lust of his eyes. When the tempter told Jesus to jump off the Temple Mount in full view of the crowds below, he appealed to Jesus's human sense of pride.

Satan tempts us using his favorite three tricks. Be on guard by asking these three questions: (1) Am I fulfilling any legitimate bodily appetites in an illegitimate way? (2) Am I allowing myself to look upon things that I know I shouldn't have? (3) Am I making compromising choices because I seek the applause of people more than the approval of God? If the answer to any of these three questions is yes, then we have fallen prey to the devil's schemes. Turn to 1 John 1:9 and confess the sins to God. Receive his cleansing and forgiveness, and begin to make the right choices in place of our wrong choices.

Setting Up Shop

MATTHEW 4:12–16 *Now when Jesus heard that John had been put in prison, He departed to Galilee. And leaving Nazareth, He came and dwelt in Capernaum, which is by the sea, in the regions of Zebulun and Naphtali, that it might be fulfilled which was spoken by Isaiah the prophet, saying:*
"The land of Zebulun and the land of Naphtali,
By the way of the sea, beyond the Jordan,
Galilee of the Gentiles:
The people who sat in darkness have seen a great light,
And upon those who sat in the region and shadow of death
Light has dawned." (NKJV)

Jesus received some heartbreaking news that no doubt shook him to the very core of his being. his cousin and our old friend, John the Baptizer, was imprisoned. The news of John's incarceration occasioned Jesus's move from Nazareth, his tiny boyhood hometown, to Capernaum, the bustling Roman metropolis that was to become Jesus's headquarters for the remainder of his ministry.

Nearly a year would elapse between Matthew 4:11 and 12. The events of that year are recorded in John 1:19–4:42. Matthew omits any discussion of this period of Jesus's ministry, most likely because it doesn't relate directly to Matthew's theme: Jesus, the King of the Jews. He chooses instead to exercise his editorial prerogative and take us immediately into Galilee where Jesus will establish his ministry headquarters.

go to

tribes
Joshua 19:10–39

Canaanites
Judges 1:32–33

Assyrians
2 Kings 15:29

Canaanites
pagans whose religion included ritual sex, child sacrifice, and witchcraft

An Improbable Prediction

On one level Jesus's selection of Capernaum as his ministry headquarters makes perfect sense. On another level his choice seems puzzling.

The Upper Galilee, which includes the Sea of Galilee, measures some sixty miles long by thirty miles wide. This region was heavily populated in Jesus's day, with some estimates running as high as two million people. That people would settle there is understandable when you consider that the soil is fertile, the rainfall abundant, and the lake provides ample fresh water for irrigation and drinking along with a seemingly endless supply of delectable fish readily available for public consumption. "Zebulun" and "Naphtali," along with Asher, were the tribes to whom God gave the area of the Galilee, which included Capernaum.

At the time of the conquest, going back to the book of Joshua, and in direct violation of the will of God, these two <u>tribes</u> refused to expel all of the **Canaanites** from their territories. Instead, they intermarried and over time adopted the Canaanite culture. In the eighth century BC, the <u>Assyrians</u> rumbled through the region and captured most of its inhabitants. From that point on, the entire area literally became the "Galilee of the Gentiles" (Matthew 4:15 NKJV). Over the intervening centuries Jews had slowly returned to Galilee. By the time Jesus came on the scene, these Galilean Jews lived in a culture weak in both biblical and traditional Jewish heritage.

Jerusalem's religious aristocracy despised the Galilean Jews, portraying them as compromisers. This explains why Jerusalem's religious elite reacted with such shock at the notion that their Messiah should come from <u>Galilee</u>.

Prophecy

More than seven hundred years before Christ's birth, Isaiah made the improbable prediction that the Messiah would settle in the regions of Zebulun and Naphtali, the "Galilee of the Gentiles" (Isaiah 9:1 NKJV).

The Sea of Galilee is the largest body of fresh water in Israel (see map in Appendix A) and figures prominently in Jesus's life and ministry. Measuring some thirteen miles long by seven miles at its widest point, it is nestled on the bottom of the Jordan rift some seven hundred feet below sea level. This lake is also referred to in the Bible as the Sea of <u>Chinnereth</u>, from the Hebrew word that means "harp," a reference to its shape, and the Sea of <u>Tiberias</u>, a reference to what was at the time the seaside capital city of the entire Galilee region. Up in the northern-most tip of the sea, just west of the inlet of the Jordan River, lies the city of Capernaum.

Capernaum means "village of Nahum," quite possibly a reference to the Old Testament prophet Nahum. "Nahum" means "compassion." Isn't it fascinating that Jesus, who himself embodied compassion, made the "village of compassion" his new mailing address, so much so that Matthew will later refer to Capernaum as Jesus's "own city" (Matthew 9:1 NKJV)?

go to

Galilee
John 7:41, 52

Chinnereth
Numbers 34:11

Tiberias
John 21:1

tax office
Matthew 9:9

centurion
Matthew 8:5

synagogue
Luke 7:5

Capernaum was perfectly positioned along major trade routes of the time—the King's Highway, which linked with the "Via Maris" or "Way of the Sea"—right on the border between the kingdoms of two of the late Herod the Great's sons, Herod Antipas and Philip.[6] Caravans traveling from Egypt in the south along the Mediterranean coast (hence the name, the "Way of the Sea") up to Damascus to the northeast, and back again, went through Capernaum. This port town therefore boasted its own <u>tax office</u> where Matthew used to hang out before he met Jesus. It also housed a Roman garrison led by a **centurion** to ensure the peace. The Jewish population of this Roman city evidently struggled financially, indicated by their need for a Gentile to provide the funds for their **synagogue**.[7]

Capernaum was thus a place of profound influence comprised of a population of hurting people. Jesus did not randomly choose

centurion
Roman army captain who commands one hundred soldiers

synagogue
Jewish house of worship

Capernaum as his home base of operations. News about what He did and what he taught would spread far and wide along those trade routes. And as we will soon see, Jesus daily encountered plenty of people facing a whole variety of personal needs. For someone whose stated mission was "to seek and to save that which was lost" (Luke 19:10 NKJV), Jesus picked a prime location.

Following Jesus's example, it is perfectly appropriate for Christians today to seek places and positions of high visibility or influence, with this one caution: We are to be honestly motivated as Jesus was by a humble, heartfelt desire to have our Christian witness touch the lives of hurting people. Any selfish ambition motivated by the pursuit of personal pleasure, power, fame, or fortune for our benefit rather than the **glory** of God and the good of <u>others</u> is not from God and will not enjoy his blessing.

apply it

Let There Be Light

MATTHEW 4:17 *From that time Jesus began to preach and to say, "Repent, for the kingdom of heaven is at hand." (NKJV)*

The preaching ministry of Jesus now begins in earnest. Picking up where John the Baptist left off, Jesus continued to call sinners to repentance. As Isaiah had predicted, a dense fog of spiritual darkness had settled upon the land (verse 16). The land of the living had become enshrouded in the darkness of the dying. Jesus showed up and promptly ignited his blazing beacon of truth.

Fishermen or Fishers of Men?

MATTHEW 4:18–22 *And Jesus, walking by the Sea of Galilee, saw two brothers, Simon called Peter, and Andrew his brother,*

go to

glory
1 Corinthians 10:31

others
Philippians 2:3–4

glory
praise, honor

simple
Acts 4:13

millstones
Matthew 18:6

millstones
large, heavy stones
used for milling
wheat

*casting a net into the sea; for they were fishermen. Then He said
to them, "Follow Me, and I will make you fishers of men." They
immediately left their nets and followed Him. Going on from
there, He saw two other brothers, James the son of Zebedee, and
John his brother, in the boat with Zebedee their father, mending
their nets. He called them, and immediately they left the boat
and their father, and followed Him. (NKJV)*

Talk about a ragtag team of players, Jesus assembled a cast of characters that seemed, on the surface anyway, the least likely troupe to
turn the world on its ear. Jesus's first disciples were simple,
untrained, uneducated, tough, crusty fishermen. Fishing was one of
the top two industries around the Sea of Galilee. The other one was
the manufacture and export of **millstones** (see Illustration #7, page
235). According to Josephus, there could be as many as 240 fishing
boats regularly bobbing atop the sparkling ripples of Lake Galilee.9
From the hundreds of men who worked those waters, Jesus chose
four. He committed himself to training his team. Jesus chose his raw
materials. He would now begin a three-year period of preparation,
patiently mentoring his men into the world changers they would
become.

To their credit when Jesus called out, "Follow Me" (Matthew
4:19 NKJV), the fishermen responded with obedience and left their
life's work "immediately" (Matthew 4:20 NKJV). Jesus sees today
what people can become tomorrow. He places a premium on preparing people, no matter how much time and effort the period of
preparation may require. He cuts his servants a ton of slack and
never gives up on us. Let us follow his example and never give up on
one another, or on ourselves.

what others say

Dallas Willard

The word "disciple" occurs 269 times in the New Testament.
"Christian" is found three times, and was first introduced to
refer precisely to the disciples.[10]

The disciples gave up more to follow Jesus than we might imagine. People often assume that these men were poor, struggling desperately to eke out a meager existence. So, the reasoning goes, when
Jesus called them to toss aside their nets and follow him, they didn't
have much to lose.

Yet, while the Bible doesn't specifically say that some of these men were wealthy, there are a few hints to that effect. For instance, James and John not only left fishing as a career, they left their father's fishing franchise. We know from Mark's account that James, John, and their father, Zebedee, had <u>hired</u> men working with him.

Peter <u>owned</u> his own boat, meaning that he could subcontract it out to other fishermen and potentially have his boat producing a twenty-four-hour-a-day income. And there's a very good probability that Peter's <u>house</u> has been excavated.[11] It's perched on a prime piece of real estate immediately adjacent to the shore of the sea with a spectacular, commanding view of the entire lake and its surrounding hillsides. It was a rather large house for its day and bespeaks of personal wealth. When the disciples <u>left everything</u> to follow Jesus, they may have given up much more than we ever imagined.

hired
Mark 1:20

owned
Luke 5:3

house
Matthew 8:14

left everything
Matthew 19:27

too many
John 21:25

Is There a Doctor in the House?

> **MATTHEW 4:23–25** *And Jesus went about all Galilee, teaching in their synagogues, preaching the gospel of the kingdom, and healing all kinds of sickness and all kinds of disease among the people. Then His fame went throughout all Syria; and they brought to Him all sick people who were afflicted with various diseases and torments, and those who were demon-possessed, epileptics, and paralytics; and He healed them. Great multitudes followed Him—from Galilee, and from Decapolis, Jerusalem, Judea, and beyond the Jordan. (NKJV)*

The Gospel writers never intended to record all of Jesus's miracles. They couldn't have done so, even if they had wanted to. There were just <u>too many</u> to write down. They had to make editorial choices. John, for example, selected miracles that demonstrated beyond the shadow of any doubt that Jesus is God. Matthew handpicked from his palette of possible signs and wonders those miracles that proved his point that Jesus is the Messiah who exercises kingly authority over "all kinds of sickness and all kinds of disease among the people" (Matthew 4:23 NKJV). Starting in Matthew 8, he gives us detailed accounts of specific, individual miracles. Here in Matthew 4:23–25, he provides us with a general outline of both the methods and scope of Jesus's ministry.

go to

repent
Matthew 4:17

validated
Hebrews 2:3–4

demon possession
Matthew 12:22

demon possession
being controlled by
a demon

Jesus's ministry style included three basic methodologies:

1. *Teaching*—Jesus communicated the truth to people in a clear, concise, and understandable way.

2. *Preaching*—Jesus challenged the people to "<u>repent</u>" of their sins and to live their lives with love and compassion for others. He offered to the nation of Israel the good news that his long-awaited kingdom had finally come. How the nation of Israel responded to that offer is the subject of much of the remainder of Matthew's Gospel.

3. *Healing*—Jesus <u>validated</u> the truth by basically banishing disease from the villages he visited.[12]

Jesus's ministry scope was huge. He touched everyone everywhere about everything:

- *Everyone*—"Great multitudes" (Matthew 4:25 NKJV) dogged his every step.

- *Everywhere*—The news about Jesus ricocheted through the countryside with lightning speed. People poured into Galilee from locales throughout the entire region—"Syria," to the northeast; "Galilee," the region just west of and encompassing the Sea of Galilee; "Decapolis," the territory of ten cities (*Deca* = ten; *Polis* = city) to the east and southeast of the sea; "Jerusalem," south of Capernaum some eighty miles as the crow flies; "Judea," the large area immediately to the south and west of Jerusalem; and "the region across the Jordan (River)," the area of Perea, just south of the Decapolis and east of Judea. The hordes of people who followed Jesus literally came from everywhere.

- *Everything*—Jesus healed the people of "various diseases" (Matthew 4:24 NKJV), a reference to the many maladies represented in the masses, and "torments," the symptoms of those maladies.

The variety of people's ailments fell into three broad categories:

1. *Spiritual*—Jesus healed those whose diseases were caused by **demon possession**.

2. *Emotional*—Jesus healed "epileptics," who suffered from a disease of the central nervous system.

3. *Physical*—Jesus healed "paralytics," a general term referring to people suffering a broad range of crippling and debilitating handicaps.

The Old Testament prophets predicted that the Messiah would heal people of their diseases when he came (Isaiah 35:5–6).

prophecy

The King's authority over every kind of spiritual, emotional, and physical infirmity was absolute and undeniable. Disease and symptom alike bowed before his healing power in humble submission and utter defeat. Jesus affirmed his kingly authority again and again in the changed lives of those touched by the King.

Chapter Wrap-Up

- Before His ministry formally began, Jesus did hand-to-hand combat with the devil. (Matthew 4:3)

- Jesus was tempted over a forty-day period, the climax of which included the three temptations recorded by Matthew. (Matthew 4:2)

- Lucifer, an "anointed cherub," rebelled against God and became an evil angel who goes by the names of Satan, the Devil, the Tempter, Destroyer, Liar, Deceiver, and a whole host of other names. (Isaiah 14:12–14; Ezekiel 28:14)

- The devil followed the pattern explained in 1 John 2:16 by tempting Jesus in the areas of the "lust of the flesh, lust of the eyes, and the pride of life."

- When Jesus received the devastating news that his cousin, John the Baptist, had been imprisoned, Jesus relocated to Capernaum and made his Galilean headquarters there. (Matthew 4:13)

- Capernaum was situated along the major trade route that linked Egypt with Syria and beyond, and was thus a place of tremendous influence.

- Some of the disciples may have been quite wealthy. Consequently, when they left everything to follow Christ, they may well have given up a lot. (Matthew 4:20)

- Jesus's ministry was characterized by teaching, preaching, and healing. (Matthew 4:23–24)

Study Questions

1. How prominent are angels in the Bible?

2. What are some of the names of the devil?

3. What did Lucifer say that changed his role and set him at odds with God and God's purposes forever?

4. What are the three areas, according to 1 John 2:16, in which we are vulnerable to temptation?

5. How did Jesus resist the onslaught of temptation that he faced from the devil?

6. Why did Jesus choose to relocate to Capernaum?

7. What are the indications that some of the disciples might have left a lot more to follow Jesus than we might have previously realized?

8. What is significant about Jesus establishing his earthly headquarters in the Galilee region?

9. What three methodologies characterized the style of Jesus's ministry?

Matthew 5: Sermon on the Mount, Part One

Chapter Highlights:
- Developing a Be-Attitude Attitude
- Cause and Effect
- Our Firm Foundation
- Righteousness from the Inside Out

Let's Get Started

He didn't own a palace; the hills and valleys became his home. He had no throne from which to make his pronouncements; he probably perched himself on a rock. He wore no regal robes. His hands displayed no royal rings. He had none of the trappings of an earthly king.

homiletic
related to the art of preaching

On a hilltop plateau that day, Jesus delivered something of which other kings could only dream—a message of majesty infused with heavenly authority. As he concluded his inspired and inspiring remarks, "the people were astonished at His teaching" (Matthew 7:28 NKJV). No one before him had ever preached like Jesus.

Developing a Be-Attitude Attitude

MATTHEW 5:1–2 *And seeing the multitudes, He went up on a mountain, and when He was seated His disciples came to Him. Then He opened His mouth and taught them, saying: (NKJV)*

The Sermon on the Mount (Matthew 5–7) is a **homiletic** masterpiece. From the moment Jesus sat down and began to teach, the crowds fell silent, spellbound and mesmerized by his words. As a skilled oral communicator, Jesus stated his theme early and clearly: "Unless your righteousness exceeds the righteousness of the scribes and Pharisees, you will by no means enter the kingdom of heaven" (Matthew 5:20 NKJV).

He illustrated his theme amply and superbly, peppering his sermon with common illustrations and examples with which every listener would immediately identify. He applied his theme compellingly and dramatically, calling the crowds to obey the standards this King established for the citizens of his kingdom. When he was done the crowds walked away "astonished" (Matthew 7:28 NKJV), with these stinging words ringing in their ears: "Not everyone who says to Me, 'Lord, Lord,' shall enter the kingdom of heaven, but he who does the will of My Father in heaven" (Matthew 7:21 NKJV). Ouch!

Jesus threw down the gauntlet. In one sweeping sermon, he essentially consigned the religious leaders in all of their hypocrisy to **hades** while inviting to the party the very masses these leaders sought to intimidate and control. Everyone seated on that grassy slope knew exactly what he meant. After we dissect Jesus's discourse, so will we.

On the northern shore of the Sea of Galilee, immediately to the west of and overlooking Capernaum, rises the "Mount of the Beatitudes" on which, according to tradition, Jesus preached the Sermon on the Mount. Though no hard archeological evidence establishes this as the actual site, the **topography** of the land gives mute testimony to its likely authenticity.

The gentle slope descending from the top of this particular plateau forms a natural amphitheater that could easily accommodate masses of people in relative comfort. The acoustics are such that a single man without the aid of modern-day amplification could easily address a large crowd and be heard and seen. No other area around the circumference of the lake possesses these particular characteristics.

Though the other Gospel writers—most notably Luke—included snippets of this sermon, only Matthew recorded these landmark lessons in their entirety. This makes perfect sense, given Matthew's theme and purpose for writing his Gospel. As Jesus began his sermon, he "was seated" (Matthew 5:1 NKJV), a symbol of a **rabbi's** teaching authority and a signal to the people that the very first statement out of his mouth should be memorized.[1] Of the four Gospel writers, Matthew alone develops the single most compelling scriptural snapshot of a king addressing the citizens of his kingdom.

Matthew's Gospel is arranged thematically, not chronologically. For a linear, birth-to-death presentation of the life of Christ, Luke is our man. Matthew decided to organize his Gospel around carefully crafted themes—the birth of the King, the testing of the King, or later, the power of the King, the parables of the King, and so forth. Here, in the Sermon on the Mount, we will study the proclamation of the King.

key point

The Be-Attitudes

MATTHEW 5:3–12
Blessed are the poor in spirit,

For theirs is the kingdom of heaven.
Blessed are those who mourn,
For they shall be comforted.
Blessed are the meek,
For they shall inherit the earth.
Blessed are those who hunger and thirst for righteousness,
For they shall be filled.
Blessed are the merciful,
For they shall obtain mercy.
Blessed are the pure in heart,
For they shall see God.
Blessed are the peacemakers,
For they shall be called sons of God.
Blessed are those who are persecuted for righteousness' sake,
For theirs is the kingdom of heaven.
Blessed are you when they revile and persecute you, and say all
kinds of evil against you falsely for My sake. Rejoice and be
exceedingly glad, for great is your reward in heaven, for so
they persecuted the prophets who were before you. (NKJV)

The lives of the common people of Jesus's day revolved around two oppressive and often opposing forces: (1) the pompous pronouncements of their Jewish religious leaders who controlled everything they believed, and (2) the imperial power of their Roman political leaders who controlled everything they did. This was a people beaten down, intimidated, thrashed at every turn, and made to feel utterly hopeless by their priests and woefully helpless by the soldiers.

So when Jesus said that it's not the religiously self-righteous but rather "the poor in spirit" (Matthew 5:3 NKJV) who will inherit the kingdom of heaven, or that it's not the militarily mighty but rather the "meek [who] shall inherit the earth" (Matthew 5:5 NKJV), the people couldn't believe their ears. They had never heard anything like this before. Forgive our sometimes-overused metaphor, but Jesus's words gushed forth like a fountain of refreshing, life-giving water, quenching the thirst of those who with parched throats and cracked lips hopelessly and helplessly stumbled through a spiritual wasteland.

From the first syllable to fall from his lips, Jesus listed the essential characteristics of the genuine citizens of his promised kingdom. We call them the Beatitudes. Think of them as attitudes that we ought to be—character qualities that true citizens of Christ's kingdom

parable
story illustrating a
spiritual principle

aspire to build into their lives as followers of the King. We'll therefore devote a significant amount of time and energy into gaining an understanding of the Beatitudes, the hub around which the entire Sermon on the Mount revolves.

Each of the eight Beatitudes begins with the word *blessed*. Sometimes inadequately translated "happy," the word really expresses a much deeper, inward condition of peace, joy, and rest.[2] To be blessed means to have a true and lasting contentment based not upon the fickle-finger-of-fate kinds of circumstances that can change in a heartbeat, but rather a contentment resulting from one's walk with God through those circumstances, be they trying or triumphant. In today's turbulent, stressful, out-of-control world, who can possibly achieve such a "blessed" life? Jesus's answer may surprise you; it stands in stark contrast to the things we are told should make us happy.

> **what others say**
>
> ### G. Campbell Morgan
>
> "Happy" is the first word of the Manifesto. It is a word full of sunshine, thrilling with music, brimming over with just what man is seeking after in a thousand false ways. . . . That was the first word of the King as He sat upon the mountain, surrounded by His disciples. But ah! His own heart was unhappy, wrung with a great anguish, moved with an infinite compassion. But why His sorrow, why His unhappiness, why the melting, moving, thrilling compassion? Because He saw all the tragedy of human sorrow. From the centre of that sorrow He said, "Happy;" and thus revealed the Divine purpose for men.[3]

Happy Days Are Here Again!

As we consider each of these eight "Beatitudes," we'll view them through the lens of several biblical examples that illustrate each one.

1. *Poor in Spirit.* Jesus raised more than a few eyebrows in Luke 18 when he told a **parable** about a fine, upstanding Pharisee and a lowly, bottom-of-the-barrel, turncoat tax collector. He posed the question, Which of these two would end up in heaven? The smart money was on the Pharisee. The tax collector? Not a chance. As far as the Pharisees were concerned, they would have happily

grabbed the bellows and fanned the flames of Dante's *Inferno* in eager anticipation of the tax collector's arrival. The Pharisee in Jesus's story pompously prayed, "God, I thank You that I am not like...this tax collector. I fast twice a week; I give tithes of all that I possess" (Luke 18:11–12 NKJV). The lowly tax collector stood off in a corner. Recognizing his unworthiness, he "would not so much as raise his eyes to heaven, but beat his breast, saying, 'God, be merciful to me a sinner!'" (Luke 18:13 NKJV).

adultery
2 Samuel 11:4

Who in this story do you think was welcomed into heaven? Who strutted his stuff on the slippery slope into hell? Jesus said, "I tell you, this man [the tax collector] went down to his house justified rather than the other [the Pharisee]" (Luke 18:14 NKJV). The notion that a tax collector would be invited into the kingdom while the heavenly security guard gave the Pharisee the boot blew people's minds.

What was the difference between the two? The Pharisee who thought he had a lock on the kingdom was proud in spirit. The tax collector who recognized and acknowledged his sin and need to his holy God was "poor in spirit." He was poverty-stricken of soul, spiritually empty-handed, someone who may not have fully understood, but nevertheless experienced God's "amazing grace, how sweet the sound, that saved a wretch like me." This story causes one to ask, "With which attitude did I come to Jesus Christ?" If we came with the self-righteous attitude of the Pharisee, thinking that we sure did God a favor by jumping on the Jesus bandwagon, or that God was sure wise when he picked us for his team, we're in serious need of a beatitude attitude check. If, however, we came with the attitude of the tax collector, Jesus promised that ours "is the kingdom of heaven" (Matthew 5:3 NKJV).

2. *Those Who Mourn.* David committed <u>adultery</u> with Bathsheba. He then conspired to have her husband, Uriah, murdered. While David lived in total denial over what he had done, God dispatched Nathan the prophet to confront him about his sin. Nathan looked David in the eyes, wagged a fully extended index finger in his direction, and uttered the four devastating words, "You are the man!" (2 Samuel 12:7 NKJV).

David shuddered in his sandals. The full weight of his grievous sins knocked him to the mat. And he mourned.

fish
Jonah 1:17

Imagine the sight: The king of a nation humbling himself in genuine brokenness over his sins before the King of heaven. He experienced what the apostle Paul described as a *"godly sorrow [that] produces repentance leading to salvation, not to be regretted"* (2 Corinthians 7:10 NKJV). "Not to be regretted" in that godly sorrow is a good thing, even though our mourning over our sins feels like a bad thing. The pain of our brokenness becomes a powerful motivator for us to change our sinful behavior, and a compelling reminder to us of how much pain our sins cause God.

We have this assurance. Jesus promises that peace, joy, contentment, and rest for our souls come to us who are genuinely broken over our sins, for he will comfort us. When was the last time we mourned for our sins like that? There is a silver, no, platinum lining to this dark cloud. Mourners of the moment unite! Jesus promised that we "shall be comforted" (Matthew 5:4 NKJV).

3. *The Meek.* Meekness is a little tougher to illustrate, largely because we often equate meekness with weakness. Let's lampoon that faulty notion right from the get-go. In reality, meekness and weakness are polar opposites, as a trio of test cases—Jonah, Paul, and Jesus—will reveal.

God called Jonah to preach a message of salvation to the Ninevites. Nineveh was the capital city of Assyria. The Assyrians were the barbarians who kidnapped or killed Jonah's kinsmen, the Jews. Nineveh was the last place Jonah wanted to go. The Assyrians were the last people Jonah wanted God to save. So Jonah, prophet of God, chose to rebel.

When he defied God, Jonah was anything but meek. Jonah placed his agenda ahead of God's and refused to obey him. After sitting down to a sumptuous fish-an'-chips meal that he would never forget—only in this case, the <u>fish</u> ate the chips, and Jonah was the chips!—Jonah had a complete change of heart. He recalibrated his moral compass. "Jonah prayed to the LORD his God from the fish's belly. And he said: . . . 'I will sacrifice to You with the voice of thanksgiving; I will pay what I have vowed'" (Jonah 2:1–2, 9 NKJV). With those words, Jonah placed God's interests ahead of his own, and in obedience preached repentance to the Ninevites. Some have defined "meekness" as "power under control." If so, Jonah controlled his personal power and focused it like a laser beam squarely on the bull's-eye of God's will. That is meekness.

Let's consider the second of our triad of test cases: The apostle Paul. When the high priest ordered guards to strike Paul on the mouth, Paul lashed out, "God will strike you, you whitewashed wall!" (Acts 23:3 NKJV). May we suggest that in this particularly embarrassing circumstance, Paul reacted with power out of control, the opposite of meekness? However, to Paul's credit, as soon as someone pointed out to him that he had just insulted the high priest, Paul <u>apologized</u> for his rash remark. Paul admitted that he was wrong, and did so to someone who wronged him. That is meekness.

Paul got angry on another occasion. When he took a stroll through the marketplace in beautiful downtown Athens, Paul beheld a city that sold its soul to false gods of every conceivable variety. "His spirit was provoked within him" (Acts 17:16 NKJV), a phrase that means he became "angry"[4] because of the deities displayed before him. His anger constituted the appropriate, "meek" response. Unlike the previous example, Paul wasn't reacting to an attack upon himself; he reacted to an assault upon his God. God's cause became his cause. God's concerns became his concerns. He viewed the situation in the city the way God did. Something in Paul's sensibilities would have gone seriously awry if he hadn't flashed his fury in the face of wholesale idolatry. That is meekness.

Jesus, our third study in contrasts, committed no crime, yet died a criminal's death. He could have retaliated against his accusers. He could have called in legions of <u>angels</u> to smite his executioners and rip him free from the cross. But he did nothing of the kind. Instead, when he became the object of an unjust act, he placed God the Father's agenda ahead of his own. He actually <u>prayed</u> for his enemies. That is power under control. That is meekness.

When God the Father became the object of attack, however, we see a completely different Jesus spring into action. He never used his power to defend himself. But when his Father's reputation came under assault by those who transformed the Temple from a place of <u>prayer</u> into a <u>marketplace</u> of madness, Jesus took a whip and chased the wolves from their den. His righteous indignation flamed like a controlled burn. That is meekness. For what do we use our power? To further our own self-absorbed agendas, or to further the interests

go to

apologized
Acts 23:5

angels
Matthew 26:53

prayed
Luke 23:34

prayer
Matthew 21:13

marketplace
John 2:16

of the God whom we serve? Perhaps more to the point, What makes us mad? The answer to that question will go a long way into providing us with the insight to determine if ours is a power out of control, or a power under control.

Kay Arthur

Meekness is a sure cure for bitterness. As a matter of fact, if there is any bitterness in your life you can be set free today. What eats at the gut of your soul? What corrodes the beauty of His countenance? What torments you behind those closed-off doors of your mind? It can be done away with today if you will listen carefully to God's Spirit as He speaks to you through His Word.[5]

4. *Those Who Hunger and Thirst.* If "meek" is the most difficult beatitude to understand, this one might be the easiest, as Moses, Nehemiah, and Daniel will attest.

The Israelites rebelled in Moses's absence. He descended from his meeting with God high atop Mount Sinai, only to find his people engaged in wholesale debauchery at the feet of a golden calf. Symbolic of Israel breaking God's Law, Moses shattered the tablets upon which the finger of God had etched the Ten Commandments. He then prayed in his anguish of soul, "If I have found grace in Your sight, show me now Your way, that I may know You and that I may find grace in Your sight" (Exodus 33:13 NKJV). Moses hungered to be a holy man. The people thirsted for something else.

Nehemiah received word that the walls of Jerusalem had been torn down. The crown jewel of the Middle East had been scuffed and scratched perhaps beyond repair. Nehemiah knelt, laid open his heart before God just as the Holy City was now laid open before her enemies, and cried, "I . . . confess the sins of the children of Israel which we have sinned against You. Both my father's house and I have sinned. . . . Let Your ear be attentive to the prayer of Your servant, and to the prayer of Your servants who desire to fear Your name" (Nehemiah 1:6, 11 NKJV). Nehemiah did not regard God's rule in his life as a hindrance to a happy existence; he delighted in doing God's will as his highest privilege and passion. Nehemiah was a hungry man.

72 ——————————— **The Smart Guide to the Bible** ———————————

Daniel "purposed in his heart that he would not defile himself with the portion of the king's delicacies, nor with the wine which he drank" (Daniel 1:8 NKJV). Did he do so grudgingly? Did he whine and complain because of certain things that he could not eat or drink? Did Daniel ask, "How far is too far?" hoping to get as close to the line as possible before trespassing into sin? Don't bet on it. Daniel maintained such an impeccable reputation that when his enemies attempted to dig up dirt on him, these cutthroat political hacks were forced to admit, "We shall not find any charge against this Daniel unless we find it against him concerning the law of his God" (Daniel 6:5 NKJV). Would that such sentiments could be echoed about us! What motivated Daniel's disciplined life of self-restraint? Two words: "my God" (Daniel 6:22 NKJV). Daniel knew God intimately, sought to please him continually, and longed to obey him consistently. Daniel was a thirsty man. Are we?

Cause and Effect

Let's take the remaining four beatitudes, stack them on top of one another, and place this quartet of qualities side by side with the first four beatitudes. Notice that there is a direct one-to-one cause-and-effect correspondence between the first four and the final four beatitudes. Sound confusing?

5. *The Merciful.* Jesus said that "poor in spirit" people are granted the grand privilege of becoming the citizens of his kingdom. Such is the mercy of God. Doesn't it make sense that the recipients of God's mercy ought to be the first to dispense mercy to those who need it?

Consider this example: Who was the one guy to show mercy to Jesus as he hung upon a cross? The answer might surprise some people. One of the two thieves who hung on a cross with him, that's who. Thief One hurled verbal hand grenades at Jesus, literally adding insults to injuries. Thief Two sought to shut him up by shouting, "Do you not even fear God, seeing you are under the same condemnation? And we indeed justly, for we receive the due reward of our deeds; but this Man has done nothing wrong" (Luke 23:40–41 NKJV). Thief Two was "poor in spirit." And wouldn't you

contention
Acts 15:39

useful
2 Timothy 4:11

know, Thief Two was "merciful." He admitted that he was a sinner. He knew that he deserved to be punished for his sins. That thief both gave and received mercy. It was to that thief Jesus said, "Today you will be with Me in Paradise" (Luke 23:43 NKJV).

6. *The Pure in Heart.* God blesses those who "mourn" over their sins by comforting them. He offers to them his mercy, cleansing, and forgiveness. Those who mourn don't hide their sins; they admit them. They do not cover up their sins; they expose them to the searchlight of God's holiness. They do not live in denial about their sins; they confess them. David first had to pray, "Against You…have I sinned" (Psalm 51:4 NKJV) before he could ask God to "create in me a clean heart" (Psalm 51:10 NKJV). Only after he mourned was David transformed, or made pure in his heart—clean, sincere, "honest to God" about his thoughts, words, actions, attitudes and motives.[6] The order here is most significant. First came his confession; then came his cleansing. What was true for David is equally true for us.

7. *The Peacemakers.* Israelis have a common expression that they universally use when greeting one another. They smile, hug, or shake hands, and then say, "Shalom!" The word is commonly translated "peace," but as so often happens, we lose its deeper meaning in the translation. *Shalom* expresses one's heartfelt desire for God to bestow his very best on another.

Our Jewish friends understand that in a world where people are so easily divided from one another, God's people share the common bond of his blessing. Unfortunately, our petty little differences often drive wedges between even the godliest of people. Only the meek—those who put God's agenda ahead of their own—can truly be at peace with each other as they lay their petty differences aside for the greater good of God's cause, and then seek his best in their lives.

Just ask Paul about his knock-down, drag-out <u>contention</u> with Barnabas over including Mark on his ministry team. Only when Paul finally came to his senses, and meekly put God's agenda ahead of his own, did he request Mark's company, heal his divided relationship, and regard Mark as "<u>useful</u>" in the ministry.

8. *Those Who Are Persecuted.* The apostle Paul made a mystifying statement in Colossians 1:24: "I now rejoice in my sufferings" (NKJV). This was written by a guy who earned a Ph.D. in suffering. For starters, he wrote those words in a dark, dank dungeon. Then, in 2 Corinthians 11:24–28, he offered his readers an eye-popping litany of some of his many sufferings. If anyone was qualified to write, "All who desire to live godly in Christ Jesus will suffer persecution" (2 Timothy 3:12 NKJV), it was Paul. We can understand why he suffered, but why he rejoiced is another matter.

Paul explained in Colossians 1:24 that the hatred of his persecutors was not primarily directed at him, but at Jesus. Since Jesus wasn't around anymore, they vented their rage against the next best available target—the followers of Jesus. Paul understood that Jesus hung on a cross in a public place and took the shots that were meant for him. Paul's greatest privilege, then, was to stand in Jesus's place and take the shots that were meant for him. That's our greatest privilege as well. Persecution in one form or another—the mockery of family or friends, unfair treatment at the office, a poor grade from a hostile teacher, the loss of money due to a refusal to fudge the truth about an inferior product—is the promised destiny of all who "hunger and thirst" to live righteously. For the remainder of the Sermon on the Mount, Jesus will tell us exactly what it means to live righteously.

We have now come full circle, ending up where we began. The poor in spirit are blessed because "theirs is the kingdom of heaven" (Matthew 5:3 NKJV). Those who are persecuted are blessed because "theirs is the kingdom of heaven" (Matthew 5:10 NKJV). Sandwiched in between are the six additional qualities that define the character of the true citizens of that kingdom (see Beatitudes chart on page 76), those who strive to have a beatitude attitude.

The Spice of Life

> **MATTHEW 5:13** *You are the salt of the earth; but if the salt loses its flavor, how shall it be seasoned? It is then good for nothing but to be thrown out and trampled underfoot by men. (NKJV)*

Salt does more than add a zesty taste to a gourmet delicacy. Sprinkle a little salt on meat, and an amazing chemical reaction takes place. Salt acts as a preservative that slows or retards the rate of decay.

Jesus used this zesty little metaphor to illustrate the dynamic force we can exert as a preservative retarding the rate of decay in our culture of compromise. By itself, one grain of salt may seem utterly inadequate and woefully insignificant. But grab a saltshaker, sprinkle multiple grains of salt on some food, and voilà! Our tiny taste buds leap for joy at the mouthwatering sensation a little salt can bring. Taken together, we are a force to be reckoned with.

These eight qualities in the following chart define the character of the true citizens of Christ's kingdom.

The Beatitudes

The Beatitudes	Definition	Biblical Example
Poor in Spirit	To approach a holy God as a humble sinner, casting ourselves upon his mercy	Tax collector (Luke 18:13)
Mourn	To be genuinely sorry for and broken over our sin	David (Psalm 51)
Meek	Placing God's purposes above our own; being concerned about the things that concern God	Jesus (John 2:12–17) Paul (Acts 17:16)
Hunger and Thirst	To long to please God in everything we do for righteousness `	Moses (Exodus 33:13) Nehemiah (Nehemiah 1:6) Daniel (Daniel 1:8)
Merciful	Responding to other sinners with the same mercy with which God responded to us	Thief on the cross (Luke 23:40–41)
Pure in Heart	Living in sincerity and honesty before God, who holds us accountable for the choices we make	David (Psalm 51)
Peacemakers	Bringing people together in unity who would otherwise be divided over petty, personal issues	Paul and Timothy (2 Timothy 4:11)
Persecuted	Choosing to suffer for one's beliefs when the pressure is on to compromise	Paul (Colossians 1:24)

what others say

Charles Colson

I think of the old story about the man who tried to save Sodom from destruction. The city's inhabitants ignored him, then asked mockingly, "Why bother everyone? You can't change them."

"Maybe I can't change them," the man replied, "but if I still shout and scream it's to prevent them from changing me!"

So I keep screaming.[7]

You Light Up My Life

MATTHEW 5:14–16 *You are the light of the world. A city that is set on a hill cannot be hidden. Nor do they light a lamp and put it under a basket, but on a lampstand, and it gives light to all who are in the house. Let your light so shine before men, that they may see your good works and glorify your Father in heaven.* (NKJV)

Jesus, the master of the metaphor, compared us to salt—a preservative in a decaying society—and to light—a brilliant beacon of direction and hope to a darkened world of confused and hurting people. If we liken the forces of compromise in our culture to the winds and waves of a raging storm, we serve as lighthouses of truth against the deepening darkness of deceit.

what others say

Oswald Chambers

Light cannot be soiled; you may try to grasp a beam of light with the sootiest hand, but you leave no mark on the light. A sunbeam may shine into the filthiest hovel in the slums of a city, but it cannot be soiled. A merely moral man, or an innocent man, may be soiled in spite of his integrity, but the man who is made pure by the **Holy Ghost** cannot be soiled, he is as light.[8]

Jesus referred to his followers when he said, "You are the light of the world" (Matthew 5:14 NKJV). He referred to himself when he said, "I am the light of the world" (John 8:12 NKJV). Jesus is the source of light. We reflect his light. This is exactly what Paul had in mind when he wrote the church in Philippi, a darkened city in its own right, "that you may become blameless and harmless, children

apply it

discouragement
1 Kings 19:1–5

doubt
Matthew 11:3

of God without fault in the midst of a crooked and perverse generation, among whom you shine as lights in the world" (Philippians 2:15 NKJV).

Our Firm Foundation

> MATTHEW 5:17–18 *Do not think that I came to destroy the Law or the Prophets. I did not come to destroy but to fulfill. For assuredly, I say to you, till heaven and earth pass away, one jot or one tittle will by no means pass from the law till all is fulfilled.* (NKJV)

Jesus paused at this early point in his sermon to underscore this vitally important, foundational fact of the Christian life: The Bible is reliable. We can trust it. We can live our lives by it. We can share its truth with others without fear of contradiction. We can shine its light.

Why did Jesus make this point here? Because at times our salt "loses its flavor" (Matthew 5:13 NKJV), and our blazing beacon of light can falter and flicker and be put "under a basket" (Matthew 5:15 NKJV). Discouragement and doubt can render ineffective the saltiest salt or brightest of lights.

Remember the winds and waves we talked about? After the storms of opposition pummel us relentlessly with their winds of deceit, it's easy to fall into the quicksand of discouragement and doubt. It happened to Elijah. At a time of profound <u>discouragement</u>, he wanted to lie down and die. It happened to our old friend, John the Baptist. In a time of <u>doubt</u>-filled desperation, he needed to have his beliefs affirmed. The same thing can, and probably will, happen to us.

Jesus knew it would. So he provided the surefire antidote to such attacks of the enemy. The next time we are tempted to doubt the Bible, we can call to memory Jesus's absolute and unequivocal affirmation of the Bible.

Jesus clearly affirmed what theologians call "The Inerrancy of the Bible." When Jesus said, "For assuredly, I say to you, till heaven and earth pass away, one jot or one tittle will by no means pass from the law till all is fulfilled" (Matthew 5:18 NKJV), he affirmed the accuracy of the original writings down to the smallest letter or part of a letter. It was Jesus's way of assuring us that when our world starts collapsing down around us, when the winds of persecution begin to blow, when we don't know where to turn, we can rely totally and completely on the truth of God's Word to sustain us even during our most desperate hours. We can trust the Bible; we can trust the God of the Bible!

hated
John 11:53

what others say

Charles H. Spurgeon

Let those give up the inspiration of the Bible who can afford to do so, but you and I cannot. Let those cast away the sure promise of God who have got something else to comfort them, who can go to their philosophy or turn to their self-conceit. But as for you and for me, it is a desperate matter for us if this book be not true....Oh, brethren, it were better to die, that book being true, than to live, that book being false.[9]

Setting the Standard

MATTHEW 5:19–20 *Whoever therefore breaks one of the least of these commandments, and teaches men so, shall be called least in the kingdom of heaven; but whoever does and teaches them, he shall be called great in the kingdom of heaven. For I say to you, that unless your righteousness exceeds the righteousness of the scribes and Pharisees, you will by no means enter the kingdom of heaven. (NKJV)*

"Unless your righteousness exceeds the righteousness of the scribes and Pharisees, you will by no means enter the kingdom of heaven" (Matthew 5:20 NKJV). How's that for throwing down the gauntlet? Jesus took a meat cleaver and cut that crowd in two—the religious leaders on one side, the common folk on the other.

"Don't be like your leaders," Jesus told them. "I'm calling you to a different standard. Don't be proud in spirit like your leaders, but be poor in spirit. Don't be haughty about how holy you are, but mourn how sinful you are. Don't put your interests ahead of God's, but put God's interests ahead of your own. Don't hunger and thirst for power over people, but hunger and thirst to make right choices before your God." This was the righteousness Jesus was talking about. These were the characteristics of the true citizens of the kingdom. The Beatitudes set the standard to which he was calling the people. No wonder the people were amazed by him. No wonder their leaders <u>hated</u> him.

Righteousness from the Inside Out

Ready to turn a corner? The tone and tenor of the Sermon on the Mount now change dramatically. Matthew 5:20 is the thematic statement of the sermon. It also serves as a transition, a bridge, linking the introduction with the body or main section of the sermon. Between his intriguing introduction and his compelling conclusion, Jesus offers his audience example after example of just how their righteousness must surpass that "of the scribes and Pharisees" (5:20 NKJV) and become a righteousness of motives and deeds and not just words.

Jesus carefully crafted several illustrations to demonstrate that if we have truly made a genuine commitment to Christ, that commitment will be shown not merely by our words but by our works, not just by our talk but by our walk, not only by our platitudes but by the be-attitudes that influence our daily choices. Don't think of these illustrations as points of an outline, but rather as movements of his message. Jesus sprints from one illustration to the next in rapid-fire, machine-gun succession.

Like a skilled cardiologist, Jesus cuts through the thin veneer of religious hypocrisy to get to the heart of the matter. Jesus is looking for behavior based upon belief, character (how we live) that is determined by our convictions (what we believe), an obedient lifestyle that flows from the inside out. Please keep in mind that Jesus is not demanding perfection in the lives of his followers, but he is rather looking at the direction of our lives. True citizens of his kingdom purpose, strive, seek, and set as a passionate goal to live in obedience to the standards that Jesus establishes here.

Of course, sincere followers of Jesus fall short of living up to his standards every day. How should we react when we do? He's already told us: Humbly approach God (poor in spirit) with a genuine brokenness over our sin (mourn) as we place God's purposes above our own (meek) while desiring to make right choices (hunger and thirst for righteousness) for his glory. Get the point? Jesus never gave this sermon a title, but an appropriate one might be "Righteousness from the Inside Out."

Fools Rush In

MATTHEW 5:21–26 *You have heard that it was said to those of old, 'You shall not murder, and whoever murders will be in danger of the judgment.' But I say to you that whoever is angry with his brother without a cause shall be in danger of the judgment. And whoever says to his brother, 'Raca!' shall be in danger of the council. But whoever says, 'You fool!' shall be in danger of hell fire. Therefore if you bring your gift to the altar, and there remember that your brother has something against you, leave your gift there before the altar, and go your way. First be reconciled to your brother, and then come and offer your gift. Agree with your adversary quickly, while you are on the way with him, lest your adversary deliver you to the judge, the judge hand you over to the officer, and you be thrown into prison. Assuredly, I say to you, you will by no means get out of there till you have paid the last penny. (NKJV)*

Jews
John 5:18

Pharisees
John 8:5

heathen
godless people

Throughout the main body of his sermon, Jesus introduces his illustrations with this couplet: "You have heard that it was said" (a reference to what their religious leaders taught them) and "But I say to you" (the standards of righteousness that Jesus decrees for the true citizens of his kingdom).

In each case, Jesus takes an outward act (murder, adultery, stealing, etc.) and turns it inward (hate, lust, envy). First example of the "righteousness of the scribes and Pharisees"? Murder. There wasn't a scribe or Pharisee within miles of the scene of this sermon who thought himself guilty of murder. The religious leaders boasted that they were holy men because they valued human life. They committed no acts of murder like the **heathen** did. Yet all the while these leaders of the Jews plotted, planned, and purposed to kill Jesus at their first opportunity. They were the ones who systematically turned the people against their own Messiah. How hypocritical.

You might remember when the Pharisees brought to Jesus a woman caught in the act of adultery and wanted to stone her to death. They weren't interested in justice. If they were, they would have exposed the man as well. (After all, she was caught "in the very act," wasn't she?) Where was their compassion? Where was their grace? Where was their mercy? Did not their demand for her execution unmask a deep-seated hatred for a woman whom they considered worthless, a throwaway, a thing rather than a person?

Jesus entered the fray and exposed the hypocrisy of people and priests alike when he said that anyone who harbored hatred in his heart toward another was guilty of murder. This king issued his decree. This monarch set his standard. The citizens of his kingdom were not to hate other people.

Jesus used some interesting imagery in Matthew 5:22. Why would someone who calls someone else a "fool" be in danger of "hell fire" (NKJV)? Seems a bit extreme, doesn't it? The specific term that Jesus chose is a slanderous, injurious word that is often translated in secular Greek literature as "godless."[10] "Raca" was a then-common and highly offensive epithet. Only a hate-filled person would say that. One does not have to murder on the outside to harbor hatred on the inside. We may not use weapons to murder a body, but we may use words to mortally wound a soul. Neither is acceptable to God.

As the model of consistency, Jesus followed this same inside-out motif throughout his remaining illustrations.

Does Jesus's message mean that if we swear at someone in anger we are in danger of hell? Not necessarily. It does mean that if we are not humbled by it (poor in spirit), broken by it (mourning), seeking God's and the person's forgiveness for it (meekness), and wanting to respond rightly to it (hungering for righteousness), we have good reason to wonder if we truly are citizens of God's kingdom.

Remember, Jesus is not as concerned with the *perfection* of our lives as he is the *direction* of our lives.

apply it

If Looks Could Kill

MATTHEW 5:27–32 *"You have heard that it was said to those of old, 'You shall not commit adultery.' But I say to you that whoever looks at a woman to lust for her has already committed adultery with her in his heart. If your right eye causes you to sin, pluck it out and cast it from you; for it is more profitable for you that one of your members perish, than for your whole body to be cast into hell. And if your right hand causes you to sin, cut it off and cast it from you; for it is more profitable for you that one of your members perish, than for your whole body to be cast into hell.*

"Furthermore it has been said, 'Whoever divorces his wife, let him give her a certificate of divorce.' But I say to you that whoever divorces his wife for any reason except sexual immorality causes her to commit adultery; and whoever marries a woman who is divorced commits adultery. (NKJV)

As with murder, the outward act of adultery begins on the inside with an uncontrollable lust for someone whom we know we should not have. As with every inward/outward issue that Jesus raised in this sermon, lust left uncontained can follow a predictable progression to a regrettable end as outlined in James 1:14–15, "But each one is tempted when he is drawn away by his own desires and enticed. Then, when desire has conceived, it gives birth to sin; and sin, when it is full-grown, brings forth death" (NKJV). Sow a lustful thought, reap a lustful action. Sow a lustful action, reap a lustful lifestyle. Sow a lustful lifestyle, reap the regrettable destruction of a relationship, marriage, family, career, ministry. All the result of what began as a seemingly innocent thought.

Jesus uses hyperbole—a purposeful exaggeration to make his point—to underscore the seriousness of this issue. Obviously, Jesus never intended for his hearers to maim themselves by gouging out their eyes or cutting off their hands in their battles with their lust. Jesus did not advocate self-mutilation. He did, however, use this vivid imagery to convey to us the seriousness of lust left unchecked. While we ought not cut off our hands to deal with our lust, perhaps we should shut off our computers, disconnect our satellite dishes, or cancel our subscriptions to certain magazines—whatever it takes to "flee [our] youthful lusts" (2 Timothy 2:22 NKJV) rather than feed our youthful lusts.

what others say

J. Oswald Sanders

The mind of man is the battleground on which every moral and spiritual battle is fought.[11]

Vance Havner

Our defeat or victory begins with what we think, and if we guard our thoughts we shall not have much trouble anywhere else along the line.[12]

Truth or Consequences

MATTHEW 5:33–37 *"Again you have heard that it was said to those of old, 'You shall not swear falsely, but shall perform your oaths to the Lord.' But I say to you, do not swear at all: neither by heaven, for it is God's throne; nor by the earth, for it is His footstool; nor by Jerusalem, for it is the city of the great King. Nor shall you swear by your head, because you cannot make one hair white or black. But let your 'Yes' be 'Yes,' and your 'No,' 'No.' For whatever is more than these is from the evil one. (NKJV)*

go to

Pharisees
John 8:13

admonition
Exodus 21:24

Citizens of the kingdom should tell the truth. As the saying goes, our word should be our bond. When a true citizen of Christ's kingdom says something, people should be able to take it to the bank. Jesus said our yes should mean yes and our no should mean no.

The "evil one," of course, is a reference to the devil. Jesus described him in John 8:44 in rather unflattering language when he said to the dreaded <u>Pharisees</u>, "You are of your father the devil, and the desires of your father you want to do. He was a murderer from the beginning, and does not stand in the truth, because there is no truth in him. When he speaks a lie, he speaks from his own resources, for he is a liar and the father of it" (NKJV).

In stark contrast, true citizens of Christ's kingdom speak the truth in love and do not lie (Ephesians 4:15, 25). Our reputations for telling the truth should be so beyond question that we need never to punctuate our words with oaths in order to be trusted.

---

what others say

Max Lucado

Is there a situation in which you have not been honest? Admit to God that you have sinned and ask for his forgiveness. Then seek the forgiveness of the person you have deceived and take steps to make things right. Pray that God would keep you honest.[13]

An Eye for an Eye

---

the big picture

Matthew 5:38–48

Jesus gives instructions for dealing with enemies, saying that his followers should love even those who persecute them. He tells them to be perfect as God is perfect.

The Old Testament <u>admonition</u>, "An eye for an eye, and a tooth for a tooth" (Matthew 5:38 NKJV), established the principle that a person's punishment should fit his crime. Some misuse this verse to legitimize a vigilante mentality wherein people take justice into their own hands and seek revenge, an interpretation that God never intended. Jesus told the people to turn the other cheek, and then explained what he meant.

Contrary to the teaching of some, Jesus did not attach virtue to pacifism, or condemn our taking self-defensive measures against an aggressor who puts us or our loved ones at risk. His point in this passage can be summed up with the words "Love your enemies."

execute
2 Timothy 4:6–8

If, for example, "anyone wants to sue you and take away your tunic, let him have your cloak also" (Matthew 5:40 NKJV). In other words, Jesus essentially said, If someone, even an enemy, even a courtroom opponent, asks us for something that meets a sincere and serious need in his life, we should not close our hearts to that individual and "turn away" (verse 42) from meeting his need.

The apostle Paul gave us good commentary on this passage when he wrote the Christians in Rome, the same Rome that killed Jesus and would eventually <u>execute</u> him, "Beloved, do not avenge yourselves, but rather give place to wrath; for it is written, 'Vengeance is Mine, I will repay,' says the Lord. 'Therefore If your enemy is hungry, feed him; if he is thirsty, give him a drink; for in so doing you will heap coals of fire on his head.' Do not be overcome by evil, but overcome evil with good." (Romans 12:19–21 NKJV).

This is a sky-high ethic. One that might prompt us to think, "Just let them wrong me and get away with it?" No, they won't get away with it. When citizens of Christ's kingdom respond to their enemies tangibly, sacrificially, and compassionately—with a beatitude attitude—we fulfill our responsibilities and allow God to fulfill his.

Don't get depressed and give up. If you are thinking, "Whoa! I'd have to be perfect to live like that all the time," you are right where Jesus wants you. No matter how hard we try, we cannot be perfect enough to be accepted by a perfect God. That's why we need Jesus. That's why he died on the cross for us. That's why he paid the penalty of our sins. That's why we come to him empty-handed and cry out for his mercy. That's why he began this sermon with the words "Blessed are the poor in spirit, for theirs is the kingdom of heaven" (Matthew 5:3 NKJV). The moment we say to ourselves, "I can't do it. The standard is just too high," we have become "poor in spirit." The moment we cry out to him in desperation to save us, we are assured that (ours) "is the kingdom of heaven."

Chapter Wrap-Up

- Jesus preached what many scholars regard as a sermonic masterpiece, the so-called "Sermon on the Mount." (Matthew 5–7)

- The other Gospel writers—most notably Luke—include snippets of this sermon in their Gospels, while only Matthew records this sermon in its entirety. (Luke 6:20–23; 11:2–4)

- Jesus began his "Sermon on the Mount" by defining eight characteristics—typically referred to as the Beatitudes—that should mark the lives of true citizens of Christ's kingdom. (Matthew 5:3–10)

- Jesus unequivocally endorsed the inerrancy of Scripture when he pointed out that the Bible is accurate down to the individual letters and parts of letters of each word. (Matthew 5:18)

- Jesus gave the theme of the Sermon on the Mount in Matthew 5:20 when he said, "For I say to you, that unless your righteousness exceeds the righteousness of the scribes and Pharisees, you will by no means enter the kingdom of heaven" (NKJV).

- Jesus defined righteousness as coming from the inside out; in other words, true righteousness goes deeper than outward actions to the inner motives of the heart. (Matthew 5:21–22, 27–28, 31–32, 33–34, 38–39, 43–44)

- Every follower of Jesus, including you and me, falls short of the standards of the Sermon on the Mount. And that's just the point. We need a Savior. (Matthew 5:48)

Study Questions

1. How does Jesus begin his "Sermon on the Mount"?

2. What two oppressive and opposing forces held the people of Jesus's day in their firm grasp?

3. What did Jesus mean when he said that we should be "poor in spirit"?

4. Is meekness the same as weakness?

5. What cause and effect can be found between the first four and the last four beatitudes?

6. Why did Jesus compare his followers to salt?

7. What is the doctrine of inerrancy?

8. How did Jesus take the outward actions of murder and adultery and turn them inward as attitudes of the heart?

9. How can anyone be as perfect as God?

Matthew 6–7: Sermon on the Mount, Part Two

Let's Get Started

If you think of the Sermon on the Mount as a tide pool of truth, then in the previous chapter we barely got our toes wet. Though the entire sermon—from its inspirational introduction to confrontational conclusion—consists of only 107 verses, you've got to admit that there's a lot here for us to chew on and digest.

salvation
dealing with matters of heaven and hell

This is a **salvation** sermon in that it shows us our need for a savior. Jesus is setting the standard by which people must measure their lives. True citizens of Christ's kingdom approach God humbly ("poor in spirit"), confess their sins sorrowfully ("mourn"), place his agenda ahead of their own willingly ("meek"), and "hunger and thirst for righteousness" continuously.

It's What's Inside That Counts

MATTHEW 6:1–4 *"Take heed that you do not do your charitable deeds before men, to be seen by them. Otherwise you have no reward from your Father in heaven. Therefore, when you do a charitable deed, do not sound a trumpet before you as the hypocrites do in the synagogues and in the streets, that they may have glory from men. Assuredly, I say to you, they have their reward. But when you do a charitable deed, do not let your left hand know what your right hand is doing, that your charitable deed may be in secret; and your Father who sees in secret will Himself reward you openly.* (NKJV)

The Pharisees often convened what we might think of as the first-century equivalent of the modern-day press conference. With cameras rolling and tape decks recording, these pompous religious leaders blasted their bugles, huffed and puffed and blew on their horns, and announced to the world that they were about to place their money in the offering plate. How arrogant! How phony! How contradictory to anything even resembling a "beatitude attitude." Jesus soundly and roundly condemned such actions for what they were: the unabashed

prayer
Matthew 26:42

hypocrisy of very small men who pretended to be large men. Why did they do it? So that they would "have glory from men" (Matthew 6:2 NKJV).

In contrast, Jesus is looking for quiet devotion—people who go about their business performing good deeds for the benefit of others. They do so as such a normal and natural part of their lives.

> **what others say**
>
> **Oswald Chambers**
>
> Humility and holiness always go together. Whenever hardness and harshness begin to creep into the personal attitude toward another, we may be certain we are swerving from the light.[1]
>
> **Treblinka Nazi Concentration Camp Survivor**
>
> In our group we shared everything, and the moment one of the group ate something without sharing it, we knew it was the beginning of the end for him.[2]

The Lord's Prayer

The Bible makes this promise: "The effective, fervent prayer of a righteous man avails much" (James 5:16 NKJV). Now 'fess up. Aren't there times when your prayer life seems to be anything but powerful and effective?

Jesus understands our frustration. His prayer in the Garden of Gethsemane seemed to go unanswered. He is therefore perfectly positioned to address this apparent problem. Jesus provided a pattern, a template, a verbal diagram, an instructive manual guaranteed to get us logged on to the hotline to heaven.

> **what others say**
>
> **Samuel Chadwick**
>
> One concern of the devil is to keep Christians from praying. He fears nothing from prayerless studies, prayerless work, prayerless religion. He laughs at our toil, mocks at our wisdom, but trembles when we pray.[3]

Altar-Ego

MATTHEW 6:5–8 *"And when you pray, you shall not be like the hypocrites. For they love to pray standing in the synagogues and on the corners of the streets, that they may be seen by men.*

Nothing is more important for our spiritual success than prayer. Before laying out his blueprint for prayer, Jesus taught his audience three prerequisite "do's" and one equally important "don't" regarding this most important dynamic of victorious kingdom living:

- Do pray in private.

- Do not pray using meaningless repetitions. The Greek word Jesus selected, *batalegéo*, is a compound word. *Bata* is an **onomatopoetic** prefix; *legéo* is the Greek verb translated "to speak." Put 'em together and Jesus basically said, "When you pray, don't talk to God like this: *bata, bata, bata*." Meaningless gibberish is just that—a repetition of "babbling or chattering…a repetition of meaningless sounds."[4]

- Do use this prayer as a pattern to follow faithfully rather than as a litany of phrases to repeat mindlessly. Please note that Jesus said, "*In this manner*, therefore, pray" (Matthew 6:9 NKJV, emphasis added), not "This is what you should pray."

- Do approach God intimately and respectfully. Jesus beautifully blended two equally true but apparently opposing aspects of the nature and character of God. On the one hand, God is our "Father" (Abba), a term of intense intimacy between a child and an adoring, loving, protective, providing, caring mommy or daddy. But he is also our heavenly Father—great, awesome, worthy of our complete devotion, worship, and praise.

onomatopoetic
word that makes the sound it describes, like "bang" or "whoosh"

---

what others say

Corrie ten Boom

A little girl cried because her very old doll was broken. Her father said, "Bring me your doll." Then he repaired it. Why did that grown-up man give his time to mend such a worthless, ugly doll? He saw the doll through the eyes of the little one, because he loved his little daughter. So God sees your problems through your eyes because He loves you….Father, what a joy it is to know that we are Your children and live within Your constant care.[5]

The Pattern of Our Prayers

MATTHEW 6:9–15 *In this manner, therefore, pray:*
Our Father in heaven,
Hallowed be Your name.
Your kingdom come.
Your will be done
On earth as it is in heaven.
Give us this day our daily bread.
And forgive us our debts,
As we forgive our debtors.
And do not lead us into temptation,
But deliver us from the evil one.
For Yours is the kingdom and the power and the glory forever. Amen.
For if you forgive men their trespasses, your heavenly Father
will also forgive you. But if you do not forgive men their tres-
passes, neither will your Father forgive your trespasses. (NKJV)

So much for the hors d'oeuvres, let's get to the main course. What do the individual phrases of the Lord's Prayer actually mean? We'll consider them one by one.

1. *"Hallowed be Your name."* This request literally asks God to set apart his name as holy—in our lives, families, neighborhoods, nation, world. Effective and powerful prayer begins with an all-consuming desire to see our God honored and respected as the holy God he is.

Did you know that the angels in heaven "do not rest day or night, saying: 'Holy, holy, holy, Lord God Almighty'" (Revelation 4:8 NKJV)? Unfortunately, you and I don't live in a "heaven on earth." God does not receive the honor or respect that he deserves. Scores of people thumb their noses at God's holiness every day. It's painful to watch. It's painful to hear. It's painful to experience. We do the right thing, we begin at the right place, we pray with the right motives when we express to God our passionate, heartfelt, all-consuming desire to "set him apart" in our lives as holy. We might call this the "motivation" of prayer.

James, our Lord's half brother, understood the importance of praying with the proper motivation. He wrote, "You ask and do not receive, because you ask amiss, that you may spend it on your pleasures" (James 4:3 NKJV). Could it be that some of our prayers go unanswered because we ask amiss, praying with the wrong motives?

Prayer is not about us; it's all about God. That realization is the prerequisite to an effective prayer life.

go to

salvation
Romans 10:9

what others say
Oswald Chambers
Watch your motive before God; have no other motive in prayer than to know Him. The statements of Jesus about prayer which are so familiar to us are revolutionary. Call a halt one moment and ask yourself—"Why do I pray? What is my motive?"[6]

2. "*Your kingdom come.*" Jesus offered himself to people as a literal king ready and willing to rule over a literal kingdom. But as we'll see later in Matthew, as a nation Israel rejected him as their king. Their own religious leaders shouted, "We have no king but Caesar!" (John 19:15 NKJV). People continue to reject Jesus today.

So Jesus exhorts us to pray that our friends and loved ones who do not honor Jesus as King will submit to him as their King. Notice the progression here. First, we pray that Jesus will be lifted up high as holy. We then pray that as he is, people will see their sinfulness in contrast to his holiness, and will bow their knees to him as the King or Lord of their lives. The moment they do, salvation from sin is theirs. We might call this the "salvation" of prayer.

3. "*Your will be done.*" This is the pivotal point of this prayer. If there is one aspect of prayer where our understanding has possibly become misguided, it's right here.

Too many people think of prayer in terms of asking and receiving. They approach God with their prayer lists in much the same way as children approach Santa Claus with their Christmas lists. As long as they get what they want, everything is good. God is good. But when God fails to deliver, they become bitterly disappointed with God, doubt his goodness, and become disenchanted with the whole concept of prayer.

The primary purpose of prayer is not to change our circumstances; the primary purpose of prayer is to change us. Prayer is not asking and receiving what we want; prayer is discerning what God wants and asking him for that. Prayer is not our bending God's will to agree with our wills; prayer is bending our wills into agreement with

provision
Matthew 6:31–34

warned
James 4:3

God's will. Prayer is not an exercise in selfish acquisition; prayer is a discipline of selfless submission.

Jesus prayed "O My Father, if it is possible, let this cup pass from Me; nevertheless, not as I will, but as You will" (Matthew 26:39 NKJV). Sound familiar? Jesus practiced what he preached. Prayer accomplished its purpose. Jesus's will was brought into submission to his Father's will.

> **what others say**
>
> **Jerry Falwell**
>
> "Thy will be done" emphasizes the idea that prayer is to bring about the conformity of the will of the believer to the will of God. Prayer is an act of spiritual expression which brings us into conformity to the very nature and purpose of God.[7]

4. *"Give us this day our daily bread."* At this halfway point in the prayer, Jesus brings in the kinds of things that we most often pray about—physical needs, emotional pains, and spiritual battles. Why does he end the prayer with these intensely personal and vitally important concerns rather than begin the prayer with them? The answer should be obvious. Until we pray about God—his character ("Hallowed be Your name"), his kingdom ("Your kingdom come"), his control ("Your will be done")—we are not ready to pray about ourselves.

Regarding our physical needs, Jesus did not speak arbitrarily when he referred to "daily bread." *Daily* indicates a continual attitude of dependence upon God and ongoing gratitude for his faithful provision. Bread, as we have seen, is a basic staple of life that represents our needs versus our wants.

There is a danger lurking when our prayers focus on our wants, one about which James has already warned us. To counteract this tendency, Jesus instructs us to prayer daily for his provision of our daily needs. When we do, we tend to focus on all that we have rather than on all that we want but don't have. Heartfelt gratitude replaces bitter ingratitude. Call this the "provision" of prayer.

> **what others say**
>
> **D. Martyn Lloyd-Jones**
>
> "Give us this day our daily bread." It is a good thing for us at least once a day, but the oftener the better, to remind our-

selves that our times, our health, and our very existence, are in His hands. Our food and all these necessary things come from Him, and we depend upon His grace and mercy for them.[8]

go to

forgive
Matthew 18:22

5. *"Forgive us our debts [sins], as we forgive our debtors [those who have sinned against us]."* We move now from the physical to the emotional. We all have two things in common: (1) We have each been hurt by others; (2) we have each hurt God.

God has forgiven us for the pain we have caused him. If we haven't already, the time has come for us to forgive others for the pain they have caused us. Yet this is so difficult to obey that we need the help of God himself to apply it.

Three stellar examples of men who applied this prayer come to mind. Joseph's brothers sold him as a slave. When the opportunity finally came for Joseph to exact his vengeance on his brothers, this is what he said. "But as for you, you meant evil against me; but God meant it for good, in order to bring it about as it is this day, to save many people alive" (Genesis 50:20 NKJV). Like Joseph, we never experience pain without a purpose.

Before Jesus died on the cross, he had an important piece of business to attend to. He prayed, "Father, forgive them, for they do not know what they do" (Luke 23:34 NKJV). As with those who hurt Jesus, those who hurt us often do not realize all that they are doing. If he so forgave them, ought we not <u>forgive</u> others?

Here's the point: Forgiven people should be forgiving people. As we confess, he forgives. And as he forgives, we, too, should forgive.

apply it

Jesus's warning—"If you do not forgive men their trespasses, neither will your Father forgive your trespasses" (Matthew 6:15 NKJV)—indicates that people who remain absolutely unwilling to forgive others may not be true citizens of his kingdom. It may be difficult to forgive someone. It may take time, but we who drink from God's fountain of forgiveness should at least be willing to let God change our hearts from bitterness to forgiveness. We'll call this the "confession" of prayer.

6. *"Deliver us from the evil one."* First Peter 5:8 warns us that our adversary, the devil, prowls around like a roaring lion seeking to devour us. He stalks us relentlessly. Though we cannot see or hear him, he pursues us continuously. We need God's protection, and at this point in the prayer, we ask for it. This, then, becomes the "protection" of prayer.

We have now come full circle in this model prayer. For as God protects us from the evil one, we lift his name up as holy.

Template for a Triumphant Prayer Life

Request	Significance	Cross Reference
"Hallowed be Your name";	Motivation of Prayer: Asking God to set his name apart in our lives and in our world as holy.	James 4:3; Revelation 4:8
"Your kingdom come";	Salvation of Prayer: Asking God to bring our friends and loved ones who don't know him as King to receive him as King.	Romans 10:9
"Your will be done";	Submission of Prayer: Asking God to bring our wills into submission to his will.	Matthew 26:39
"Give us this day our daily bread";	Provision of Prayer: Asking God to provide for our daily needs.	Matthew 6:31–34; Proverbs 30:8
"Forgive us our debts";	Confession of Prayer: Asking God to give us the grace to forgive those who have hurt us, just as God has forgiven those who have hurt him.	Matthew 18:22
"Do not lead us into temptation, but deliver us from the evil one."	Protection of Prayer: Asking God to protect us from the onslaught of the enemy, who seeks to pull us away from God.	1 Peter 5:8; John 17:15
"For Yours is the kingdom and the power and the glory forever. Amen."		

Meals, Money, and Things That Matter

the big picture

Matthew 6:16–7:6

Jesus uses four more powerful examples to further illustrate his point that his "righteousness exceeds the righteousness of the scribes and Pharisees" (Matthew 5:20 NKJV). He demands a righteousness from the inside out. Jesus refers to fasting, saving money, worrying, and judging others to explain his point.

Thirteen of the sixty-six books in the Bible mention fasting as a dynamic of godly living. Some people believe that fasting is

- something we do on a regular basis, such as one day or one meal each week,

- a way to get God's attention,

- a way to add special power to our prayers, or

- a way to evoke people's sympathy or engender their praise.

The religious leaders of Jesus's day grabbed onto this beautiful and meaningful practice and corrupted it for their own personal gain. Let's briefly consider one classic biblical example of fasting, and then compare it to the Pharisees' twisted and self-serving version of Fasting 101.

Whenever the Pharisees skipped a meal, they let the whole world know about it. They sucked in their cheeks. They rumpled their hair and disfigured their faces. They moaned and groaned from the pangs of hunger. That's not biblical fasting; that's a "see-food diet" in that they wanted everyone to see that they were fasting and to conclude that they were spiritual just because they forfeited a meal. Like every other example that Jesus used, theirs was a phony righteousness from the outside in. The people might have been impressed, but Jesus wasn't.

> **what others say**
>
> **H. A. Ironside**
> Let him who is abstaining from food or other things, in order to have more time with God, cultivate a cheerful manner as becomes one who enjoys communion with the Father.[9]

Put Your Money Where Your Heart Is

Proverbs, often regarded as the book of God's "one-liners," makes this intriguing observation: "The ants are a people not strong, yet they prepare their food in the summer" (Proverbs 30:25 NKJV). God praises the wise saving or setting aside of money, as we might say, "for a rainy day." As we'll learn in Matthew 25, Jesus told a story about servants who used their money to make more money, and condemned the servant who failed to do so. God praises the wise, careful investing of money. So when Jesus preached, "Do not lay up

go to

attitude
1 Timothy 6:6–11

mammon
money or material
wealth

for yourselves treasures on earth" (Matthew 6:19 NKJV), he was in no way contradicting the clear teaching of the Bible.

The key to interpreting this passage lies in verse 24: "No one can serve two masters. . . . You cannot serve God and **mammon**" (NKJV). Money is a wonderful servant, but a terrible master. The issue here is not the amount of money someone has, but rather his <u>attitude</u> toward money—how he or she gets it, why he wants it, and how he uses it.

> **what others say**
>
> **Allan Emery**
>
> My parents consistently taught us that all we had must be held in an open hand, that when we closed our fingers tightly over anything placed in our trust, we lost the joy and the blessing. Things acquired as an end in themselves became idols and possessed us.[9]

Don't Sweat the Small Stuff

True citizens of Christ's kingdom have nothing to worry about. Sounds too good to be true, but Jesus makes this promise: "Do not worry, saying, 'What shall we eat?' or 'What shall we drink?' or 'What shall we wear?'...Your heavenly Father knows that you need all these things. But seek first the kingdom of God and His righteousness, and all these things shall be added to you" (Matthew 6:31–33 NKJV).

This promise is conditional, but the two conditions are appropriate for God's people: Love God (give him first place in your life) and obey God (live as he wants you to). When we do that, he will provide for our needs as faithfully as he cares for "the birds of the air" (Matthew 6:26 NKJV) and "the lilies of the field" (Matthew 6:28 NKJV).

> **what others say**
>
> **D. Martyn Lloyd-Jones**
>
> Here we are worrying about food and drink and clothing! The trouble with us is that we do not realize that we are children of our heavenly Father. If only we realized that, we should never worry again. If only we had some dim, vague conception of the purposes of God with respect to us, worry would be impossible.[11]

The Friendship Factor

Jesus warned, "Why do you look at the speck in your brother's eye, but do not consider the plank in your own eye?" (Matthew 7:3 NKJV). The "speck" and the "plank" are the same issue, just a different perspective. Hold a plank at arm's length and it looks like a speck; bring a speck up to our eyes and it looks like a plank!

People's criticisms can leave indelible scars that last a lifetime. However, there is a priceless principle to be found in Matthew 7:1–6. Paraphrased, it goes like this: When someone unfairly criticizes or condemns us, we can be sure that that person is saying about us exactly what he or she believes about himself.

When someone tries to inflict mental or emotional pain on us, it's most likely because they themselves have deep, unresolved pain in their own lives.

When someone rejects us because of our relationship with the King, we are not responsible for the breakdown of that relationship. It's not us they are rejecting; ultimately, they are rejecting the God whom we love and serve. When they do, they are essentially treating something sacred by trampling it "under their feet" (Matthew 7:6 NKJV).

The Grand Finale

MATTHEW 7:7–12 *"Ask, and it will be given to you; seek, and you will find; knock, and it will be opened to you. For everyone who asks receives, and he who seeks finds, and to him who knocks*

go to

salvation
Ephesians 1:3–14

it will be opened. Or what man is there among you who, if his son asks for bread, will give him a stone? Or if he asks for a fish, will he give him a serpent? If you then, being ~~evil,~~ know how to give good gifts to your children, how much more will your Father who is in heaven give good things to those who ask Him! Therefore, whatever you want men to do to you, do also to them, for this is the Law and the Prophets. (NKJV)

In the same way that Matthew 5:17 is a transition between the introduction and the body of the Sermon on the Mount, Matthew 7:7 marks the transition from the body to the rousing climax and conclusion.

If at this point in the sermon you're feeling woefully inadequate as a human being, an utter failure when compared to the standards Jesus set, then I've got great news for you. Jesus said that if we "ask," "seek," and "knock," terms referring to our prayers, our loving Father will give "good things to those who ask Him!" (Matthew 7:7, 11 NKJV). The "good things" to which he referred are our <u>salvation</u> and everything that comes with it.

Two Roads

> MATTHEW 7:13–14 *"Enter by the narrow gate; for wide is the gate and broad is the way that leads to destruction, and there are many who go in by it. Because narrow is the gate and difficult is the way which leads to life, and there are few who find it.* (NKJV)

At some point in his or her life, every person must answer the question, What will I do with Jesus? We have two options: receive him or reject him. The contrast couldn't be clearer, especially given the following examples.

Jesus referred to two roads that lead to two different destinies. The wide road leads to destruction and there are many people on it. The narrow road leads to eternal life and there are tragically few people on it. The followers of Jesus have always been and always will be in the minority. The implied question that Jesus posed to his audience is this: "On which road are you?"

Two Trees

> MATTHEW 7:15–20 *"Beware of false prophets, who come to you in sheep's clothing, but inwardly they are ravenous wolves. You*

will know them by their fruits. Do men gather grapes from thornbushes or figs from thistles? Even so, every good tree bears good fruit, but a bad tree bears bad fruit. A good tree cannot bear bad fruit, nor can a bad tree bear good fruit. Every tree that does not bear good fruit is cut down and thrown into the fire. Therefore by their fruits you will know them. (NKJV)

Jesus no doubt had the hypocritical Pharisees and deceptive teachers of the law in mind when he talked about "false prophets." Their words might have sounded fine, but one's salvation is never validated by one's lips, but only by one's lifestyle. The plant that Jesus picked to illustrate this truth would have been familiar to his audience. They did not need a lecture in horticulture to know that grapes did not come from thornbushes nor figs from thistles. A false prophet cannot live a godly life any more than a weed can produce fruit.

Two Responses

MATTHEW 7:21–23 *"Not everyone who says to Me, 'Lord, Lord,' shall enter the kingdom of heaven, but he who does the will of My Father in heaven. Many will say to Me in that day, 'Lord, Lord, have we not prophesied in Your name, cast out demons in Your name, and done many wonders in Your name?' And then I will declare to them, 'I never knew you; depart from Me, you who practice lawlessness!'* (NKJV)

Jesus is not interested in lip service, but in lifestyle. Throughout the history of the church there have been those who have done things that appeared supernatural or miraculous. They knew the lingo. They put on a good act.

Simon the sorcerer amazed people with his magic. People concluded that he had divine power. But Peter exposed him as a phony, "poisoned by bitterness and bound by iniquity" (Acts 8:23 NKJV). Words mean nothing. Tricks might impress people, but they don't impress God. People may say, "Lord, Lord," with their lips but "practice lawlessness" in their lives. Salvation is not a matter of saying, but of doing "the will of My Father" (Matthew 7:21 NKJV).

Two Builders

MATTHEW 7:24–27 *"Therefore whoever hears these sayings of Mine, and does them, I will liken him to a wise man who built*

*his house on the rock: and the rain descended, the floods came,
and the winds blew and beat on that house; and it did not fall,
for it was founded on the rock. But everyone who hears these sayings of Mine, and does not do them, will be like a foolish man
who built his house on the sand: and the rain descended, the
floods came, and the winds blew and beat on that house; and it
fell. And great was its fall."* (NKJV)

The wise man builds his life on a solid foundation of rock, while
the foolish man builds on an unstable foundation of shifting sand.
What is the solid foundation of rock? "Whoever hears these sayings
of Mine, and does them, I will liken him to a wise man"; but those
who reject Christ and rebel against his teaching are like the foolish
man. Once again, the implied question is crystal clear: On which
foundation are we building our lives?

what others say

Kay Arthur

The essential character of the believer is obedience. The
Sermon on the Mount irrevocably links obedience to faith.
They cannot be separated. This is why Jesus says in Matthew
7:24, "Everyone who hears these words of Mine, and acts
upon them." It is not just hearing, but also acting.[14]

Deuces Wild

Two Roads	The broad road on which many travel; the narrow road on which few travel.	Matthew 7:13–14
Two Trees	Good trees that bear good fruit; bad trees that bear bad fruit.	Matthew 7:15–20
Two Responses	Those whose faith is phony—nothing more than empty words; those whose faith is genuine—confirmed by their obedience.	Matthew 7:21–23
Two Builders	The wise man who builds his life on God's Word; the foolish man who builds his life on the shifting sand of rebellion to God's Word.	Matthew 7:24–27
Two Destinies	Destruction to those who practice lawlessness; life to those who do the will of their heavenly Father.	Matthew 7:21, 24

As One Who Had Authority

MATTHEW 7:28–29 *And so it was, when Jesus had ended these
sayings, that the people were astonished at His teaching, for He*

taught them as one having authority, and not as the scribes. (NKJV)

The people had never heard teaching like this before. Understandably, they walked away amazed. Every person in that crowd now faced these choices: On which road would they choose to walk—wide or narrow? Which teaching would they now believe—false or true? How would they respond to Jesus—with lip service or lifestyle? on which foundation would they build their lives—the unshakable truth of the Word of God or the shifting sands of error and deception? If we had been sitting on that hillside that day, how would we have answered those questions? Would we have acted on Jesus's words or carried On with our lives in the same old way? The crowds who gathered on that hillside that day had to make a choice. Now, so do we.

Chapter Wrap-Up

- Throughout the Sermon on the Mount Jesus demonstrates that none of us can live up to his standards of kingdom living. (Matthew 5–7)

- Jesus condemned the religious leaders for seeking the applause of men rather than the approval of God. (Matthew 6:2)

- The Lord's Prayer consists of six basic categories around which we can organize our own prayers, making it a perfect pattern to follow for our own prayers to God. (Matthew 6:9–13)

- In the introduction to the Lord's Prayer, Jesus taught that we are to approach our heavenly Father with the balance of daddy-like intimacy and awe-filled respect. (Matthew 6:9)

- The motivation of our prayers ought to focus on seeing God's name exalted as the holy God whom he is. (Matthew 6:9)

- Having addressed the motivation of prayer, Jesus then addresses the salvation, submission, provision, confession, and protection of prayer. (Matthew 6:10–13)

- Fasting was never intended to be a way to earn God's favor by missing a meal. When people sincerely fast, it's not because they choose not to eat, but rather because they are so overcome with a desire to be in God's presence, and so distraught over the circumstances driving them to God that they cannot eat. (Matthew 6:16–18)

- Jesus promises us that if we seek to serve him and live a righteous life, he will provide us with all of our needs. (Matthew 6:33)

- Jesus warned his hearers that not everyone who claims to be a Christian truly is, but only those who do the will of his Father. (Matthew 7:21)

Study Questions

1. In contrast to the hypocrisy of "small" men pretending to be "big" men, what is Jesus really looking for? If I were to please him with my life, what would I be doing?

2. What are four prerequisites for effective prayer?

3. What ought to be the proper motivation of our prayers, and why is this so important?

4. What did Jesus mean when he told us to pray for the kingdom to come?

5. Can you cite an example from Jesus's life when he submitted his will to his Father's?

6. What is the significance of praying for God to supply our daily bread?

7. Is it wrong for Christians to save money?

8. What are the two conditions to Jesus's promise that he will take care of the "big stuff" in our lives (as surely as he cares for the birds and flowers)?

9. What's the difference between the speck and the plank in one's eyes?

10. When faced with Jesus Christ, what two options does an individual have?

Matthew 8:1–9:34: Credentials of the King

Chapter Highlights:
- Reaching Out
- Taking Charge
- An Awesome God
- Giving Back
- Of Sights and Sounds

Let's Get Started

Matthew 5:1 states that Jesus "went up on a mountain" (NKJV). As Matthew 8 begins, Jesus "had come down from the mountain" (verse 1 NKJV). Sandwiched in between is the Sermon on the Mount, or what we might call the King's Creed.

During his earthly ministry, Jesus performed more **miracles** than the biblical writers could possibly record or even count! Matthew strategically selected ten miracles to establish graphically and undeniably Jesus's authority over virtually every realm of human existence. If you think of them as pieces of evidence presented in a court of law, taken together they paint a portrait of Jesus as the King of kings, a verdict that no unbiased, open-minded, honest juror could possibly deny. Jesus claimed to be God; miracles prove him to be so.

go to

miracles
John 21:25

miracles
unusual acts
of God

ganglions
moments of
great change
or connection

> **what others say**
>
> ### C. S. Lewis
>
> God does not shake miracles into Nature at random as if from a pepper-caster. They come on great occasions: they are found at the great **ganglions** of history—not of political or social history, but of that spiritual history which cannot be fully known by men.[1]

Reaching Out

MATTHEW 8:1–4 *When He had come down from the mountain, great multitudes followed Him. And behold, a leper came and worshiped Him, saying, "Lord, if You are willing, You can make me clean." Then Jesus put out His hand and touched him, saying, "I am willing; be cleansed." Immediately his leprosy was cleansed. And Jesus said to him, "See that you tell no one; but go your way, show yourself to the priest, and offer the gift that Moses commanded, as a testimony to them." (NKJV)*

Jesus touched a leper. There's more to this statement than meets the eye.

forbidden
Leviticus 13:45

During New Testament times, lepers were the outcasts of society. This dread disease was highly contagious and there was no known cure. When a person contracted leprosy, a priest declared him a leper and in so doing literally banished him from his home, his family, and his community. Exiled to a colony of other lepers, he or she died a slow, agonizing, humiliating, torturous death. And yet, Jesus touched him. Jesus could have merely spoken the word and the man would have been healed outwardly. By touching him, Jesus healed him inwardly, the kind of healing that can only come through human contact.

what others say

L. S. Huizenga

[Leprosy] generally begins with pain in certain areas of the body. Numbness follows. Soon the skin in such spots loses its original color. It gets to be thick, glossy, and scaly. . . . As the sickness progresses, the thickened spots become dirty sores and ulcers due to poor blood supply. The skin, especially around the eyes and ears, begins to bunch, with deep furrows between the swellings, so that the face of the afflicted individual begins to resemble that of a lion. Fingers drop off...toes are affected similarly. Eyebrows and eyelashes drop out....The leper emits a very unpleasant odor...the voice acquires a grating quality. His throat becomes hoarse, and you can now not only see, feel, and smell the leper, but you can hear his rasping voice. And if you stay with him for some time, you can even imagine a peculiar taste in your mouth, probably due to the odor.[2]

That this man believed Jesus could heal him was incredible; that he would dare to approach Jesus, something <u>forbidden</u> in Old Testament Law, was remarkable; but that Jesus would actually touch him was utterly unthinkable.

Jesus wasn't some kind of magician who went about the countryside trying to dazzle people with his heavenly bag of tricks. He was, and is, God. Jesus knew that the man needed an emotional healing as well as a physical one. How Jesus healed the leper demonstrated his kingly authority over physical and emotional disease.

what others say

Charles R. Swindoll

God, our Father, is the "God of all comfort" who "comforts us in all our affliction." Our loving Father is never preoccupied or removed when we are enduring sadness and affliction![3]

Long-Distance Healing

centurion
Roman military
officer in command
of one hundred
troops

MATTHEW 8:5–13 *Now when Jesus had entered Capernaum, a centurion came to Him, pleading with Him, saying, "Lord, my servant is lying at home paralyzed, dreadfully tormented." And Jesus said to him, "I will come and heal him." The centurion answered and said, "Lord, I am not worthy that You should come under my roof. But only speak a word, and my servant will be healed. For I also am a man under authority, having soldiers under me. And I say to this one, 'Go,' and he goes; and to another, 'Come,' and he comes; and to my servant, 'Do this,' and he does it." When Jesus heard it, He marveled, and said to those who followed, "Assuredly, I say to you, I have not found such great faith, not even in Israel! And I say to you that many will come from east and west, and sit down with Abraham, Isaac, and Jacob in the kingdom of heaven. But the sons of the kingdom will be cast out into outer darkness. There will be weeping and gnashing of teeth." Then Jesus said to the centurion, "Go your way; and as you have believed, so let it be done for you." And his servant was healed that same hour. (NKJV)*

Capernaum, where this miracle took place, lies between Gamla on the east and the Arbel Cliffs on the west.

Gamla means "camel hump," so named because Gamla is a steep hilltop hideaway perched on a camel-hump-shaped peak high up on the famed Golan Heights. Here, 4,000 Jewish patriots were bludgeoned to death by the Roman legions, and another 5,000 zealots chose to jump to their deaths rather than submit to the slavery of Rome.

The Arbel Cliffs blinked with some prominence on Herod the Great's radar screen. When scores of Jewish resisters, along with their wives and children, hid in the 100 or so caves dotting the face of the cliffs, Herod lowered his forces in baskets to the entrances to those caves. As they shot flaming arrows into the caves, the men, women, and children inside groped toward the entrances of the caves to gasp for air. The Romans then used huge grappling hooks to hurl them to their deaths below.

With this as the backdrop, a **centurion**, a deathly powerful Roman officer, dared to approach Jesus, a humble Jewish rabbi, asking for his help. "Amazing" doesn't quite capture this scene, but other superlatives equally fail to convey just how amazing it was for the

high
Luke 4:38

powerful to approach the powerless, a Roman to approach a rabbi, a Jew to feel anything other than a deep loathing for this centurion.

Having heard of Jesus, and perhaps having even observed him, the centurion reasoned that if his authority over his men caused them to carry out his every command, Jesus's authority over sickness caused disease to obey his every command. As one loyal to the Roman regime responsible for many Jewish deaths, the centurion appropriately admitted, "I am not worthy that You should come under my roof" (Matthew 8:8 NKJV). He then correctly concluded that Jesus needed only "speak a word, and my servant will be healed" (verse 8 NKJV).

At the very moment Jesus uttered the words "As you have believed, so let it be done for you" (Matthew 8:13 NKJV), the centurion's servant was healed.

Peter's Mother-in-Law

MATTHEW 8:14–17 *Now when Jesus had come into Peter's house, He saw his wife's mother lying sick with a fever. So He touched her hand, and the fever left her. And she arose and served them.*

When evening had come, they brought to Him many who were demon-possessed. And He cast out the spirits with a word, and healed all who were sick, that it might be fulfilled which was spoken by Isaiah the prophet, saying:

"He Himself took our infirmities
And bore our sicknesses." (NKJV)

Peter's mother-in-law suffered because of a "fever," a general term that broadly refers to an elevated body temperature characteristic of a whole range of possible disorders. Keeping in mind that as a former tax collector Matthew was primarily a moneyman, we turn to Luke's parallel account to obtain a more precise diagnosis. He attributes the woman's suffering to a "<u>high</u>" fever, a commonly life-threatening condition.

Matthew records that Jesus touched the patient's hand; Luke reports that Jesus rebuked the fever. You'll remember that Jesus healed the leper through contact and the centurion's servant with a command. Here he combined the two and healed her with both his touch and his words.

Matthew 8:16 simply says Jesus "healed all who were sick" (NKJV).

With so many examples from which to choose, why did Matthew select these three particular miracles to record in his Gospel? The culture of the Middle East during New Testament times regarded four groups of people as outcasts of society: lepers, Gentiles, slaves, and women. Whom did Jesus heal? A leper, a Gentile's servant, and a woman. To a corrupted culture that prided itself on excluding people, Jesus included as many as would come. Jesus clearly is a compassionate King whose kingdom is open to all.

Jesus healed everyone who came to him, just as Isaiah 53:4 predicted he would.

prophecy

Interestingly enough, Peter's house has been excavated! This is not one of those "traditional" sites for which there is much talk but very little evidence. This is an actual, authentic site located in an unearthed first-century Capernaum neighborhood, immediately adjacent to the synagogue where Jesus taught. The evidence supporting this site as authentic is quite compelling,[6] and brings to life the story as recounted in Luke's Gospel, "[Jesus] arose from the synagogue and entered Simon's house. But Simon's wife's mother was sick with a high fever" (Luke 4:38 NKJV).

Sticker Shock

MATTHEW 8:18–22 And when Jesus saw great multitudes about Him, He gave a command to depart to the other side. Then a certain scribe came and said to Him, "Teacher, I will follow You wherever You go." And Jesus said to him, "Foxes have holes and birds of the air have nests, but the Son of Man has nowhere to lay His head." Then another of His disciples said to Him, "Lord, let me first go and bury my father." But Jesus said to him, "Follow Me, and let the dead bury their own dead." (NKJV)

Someone once said, "Nothing succeeds like success," and, boy, that sure was true about Jesus. After the word spread about all his miracles, everyone wanted to jump on the Jesus bandwagon. One guy said, "I will follow you wherever you go." He wanted all the privileges, but failed to count the cost. Jesus essentially replied, "You'd better be careful what you ask for. I don't even own a home. The birds live better than me."

Another guy wanted to jump on board, but like so many, his was a spur-of-the-moment, ill-motivated, halfhearted commitment. He wanted to wait until he received his inheritance.[7] He wanted a commitment that demanded no risk.

what others say

William Barclay

Again and again there come to us moments of impulse when we are moved to the higher things; and again and again we let them pass without acting upon them. The tragedy of life is so often the tragedy of the unseized moment....Jesus was saying to this man: ". . . [Follow me] now—or you will never [follow me] at all."[8]

Taking Charge

MATTHEW 8:23–27 Now when He got into a boat, His disciples followed Him. And suddenly a great tempest arose on the sea, so that the boat was covered with the waves. But He was asleep. Then His disciples came to Him and awoke Him, saying, "Lord, save us! We are perishing!" But He said to them, "Why are you fearful, O you of little faith?" Then He arose and rebuked the winds and the sea, and there was a great calm. So the men marveled, saying, "Who can this be, that even the winds and the sea obey Him?" (NKJV)

The fishermen of Jesus's day lived in mortal terror of storms on the Sea of Galilee—normally so calm, so picturesque, so tranquil. In a matter of minutes a placid sea could become a liquid cauldron of convulsions when just the right combination of atmospheric conditions spun the lake like some gigantic blender. Jesus demonstrated his regal authority over the natural realm when he calmed the fierce storm.

Two weather-related dynamics come into play whenever a storm of this magnitude whips up the sea. From the north, cold air blowing over the perpetually snowcapped Mount Hermon rushes ten thousand feet down the southern face of that majestic mountain, warming as it descends into the Jordan River rift. By the time these winds reach the Sea of Galilee, the unstable air spins and twirls not unlike a tornado. In addition, from the west the prevailing winds that blow in off the Mediterranean funnel their way through a huge triangular crack in the hillside that looks down upon the western shore of the sea, accelerating to a dizzying speed as it is squeezed through this natural wind tunnel.

When these two forceful currents of wind collide over the water, the otherwise mirrorlike calmness of the sea explodes into waves boasting a height of some ten to fifteen feet. Fishermen then and now feared this occurrence more than any other. Only God could still a storm like that.

A Pig in a Poke

MATTHEW 8:28–34 *When He had come to the other side, to the country of the Gergesenes, there met Him two demon-possessed men, coming out of the tombs, exceedingly fierce, so that no one could pass that way. And suddenly they cried out, saying, "What have we to do with You, Jesus, You Son of God? Have You come here to torment us before the time?" Now a good way off from them there was a herd of many swine feeding. So the demons begged Him, saying, "If You cast us out, permit us to go away into the herd of swine." And He said to them, "Go." So when they had come out, they went into the herd of swine. And suddenly the whole herd of swine ran violently down the steep place into the sea, and perished in the water. Then those who kept them fled; and they went away into the city and told everything, including what had happened to the demon-possessed men. And behold, the whole city came out to meet Jesus. And when they saw Him, they begged Him to depart from their region.* (NKJV)

go to

Legion
Luke 8:30

two thousand
Mark 5:13

legion
up to six thousand

Whenever you read the words "the other side" in reference to the Sea of Galilee, sit up and take notice. Something bad is about to happen. So it was in this case. Just when the disciples' feet hit terra firma and they were tempted to think that having survived their fateful journey all would now be well, these terrified twelve were accosted by two men possessed by a **legion** of demons. Some days you just can't win.

In this case, Jesus demonstrated his kingly authority over the supernatural realm when he cast a legion of demons out of two men.

The townspeople where this miracle occurred "begged [Jesus] to depart from their region" (Matthew 8:34 NKJV). Why?

- Some say the people were angry because Jesus had just wrecked the economy of the region by commanding a large herd of two thousand pigs to stampede down the hill into the water to their deaths.

- Some believe the people were terrified by what had occurred and wanted Jesus to leave out of sheer panic.

- Others conclude that these heathens wanted nothing to do with the Son of God.

- Most likely, there are some elements of truth in each of these views. For sure, the response of the people indicates the callousness of their hearts and their total lack of compassion. They cared more about their pigs than the man who now sat "at the feet of Jesus, clothed and in his right mind" (Luke 8:35 NKJV). No wonder "they were afraid" (verse 35 NKJV).

Demon possession can take place today, but within these scriptural guidelines:[9]

- If believers in Christ resist the devil, he must flee (James 4:7).

- Believers in Christ cannot be demon-possessed (1 Corinthians 6:19–20).

- Demon possession is indicated by specific, remarkable, and obvious characteristics that include such things as uncontrollable violence, homicidal and suicidal tendencies, phenomenal strength, loud and disturbing cries, nakedness, an obsession with the dead, a recognition of Jesus as God, and a fear of their final destiny (Matthew 8:28; Mark 5:4–5; Luke 8:27–28).

apply it

The best antidote against demonic harassment is to live an obedient life. James 4:7–8 is God's prescription for demonfree living:

"Therefore submit to God. Resist the devil and he will flee from you. Draw near to God and He will draw near to you. Cleanse your hands, you sinners; and purify your hearts, you double-minded" (NKJV).

blasphemy
to speak against or defame God

An Awesome God

MATTHEW 9:1–8 *So He got into a boat, crossed over, and came to His own city. Then behold, they brought to Him a paralytic lying on a bed. When Jesus saw their faith, He said to the paralytic, "Son, be of good cheer; your sins are forgiven you." And at once some of the scribes said within themselves, "This Man blasphemes!" But Jesus, knowing their thoughts, said, "Why do you think evil in your hearts? For which is easier, to say, 'Your sins are forgiven you,' or to say, 'Arise and walk'? But that you may know that the Son of Man has power on earth to forgive sins"— then He said to the paralytic, "Arise, take up your bed, and go to your house." And he arose and departed to his house. Now when the multitudes saw it, they marveled and glorified God, who had given such power to men. (NKJV)*

The scene shifts back across the sea to Capernaum, Jesus's home base of operations.

Jesus promptly declared the paralytic's sins forgiven, which unleashed an explosive verbal assault as the religious leaders accused Jesus of **blasphemy**. He responded to their accusation by asking them this probing question: "Which is easier, to say, 'Your sins are forgiven you,' or to say, 'Arise and walk'?" (Matthew 9:5 NKJV).

It's obviously easier to say, "Your sins are forgiven you," since there is no way to prove whether or not it happened. To say "Arise and walk" is difficult since, if the paralyzed man still could not walk, the speaker would be publicly humiliated and ultimately discredited. But when this man "arose" and walked home, the crowds understandably "marveled" (Matthew 9:7–8 NKJV). Jesus demonstrated his authority over the moral realm by forgiving a man's sins and miraculously healing him to prove it.

Is There a Doctor in the House?

MATTHEW 9:9–13 *As Jesus passed on from there, He saw a man named Matthew sitting at the tax office. And He said to him, "Follow Me." So he arose and followed Him. Now it happened,*

wineskins
leather wine
container

as Jesus sat at the table in the house, that behold, many tax collectors and sinners came and sat down with Him and His disciples. And when the Pharisees saw it, they said to His disciples, "Why does your Teacher eat with tax collectors and sinners?" When Jesus heard that, He said to them, "Those who are well have no need of a physician, but those who are sick. But go and learn what this means: 'I desire mercy and not sacrifice.' For I did not come to call the righteous, but sinners, to repentance." (NKJV)

A pattern to Matthew's presentation of ten stunning miracles has now emerged. Matthew presented a first group of three miracles and then interrupted his discussion with a brief interlude (Matthew 8:18–22). Next came a second grouping of three miracles, followed by a second interlude. This is the second interlude.

Matthew 9:9 is as close as we are going to get to our author's personal testimony of how he became a disciple. By inference, Matthew is perhaps suggesting to his readers that after considering this account of Jesus's power and authority, we should follow him too. Jesus is a doctor to the sick, a King who saves sinners.

Out with the Old; In with the New

MATTHEW 9:14–17 *Then the disciples of John came to Him, saying, "Why do we and the Pharisees fast often, but Your disciples do not fast?" And Jesus said to them, "Can the friends of the bridegroom mourn as long as the bridegroom is with them? But the days will come when the bridegroom will be taken away from them, and then they will fast. No one puts a piece of unshrunk cloth on an old garment; for the patch pulls away from the garment, and the tear is made worse. Nor do they put new wine into old wineskins, or else the wineskins break, the wine is spilled, and the **wineskins** are ruined. But they put new wine into new wineskins, and both are preserved." (NKJV)*

John the Baptizer's disciples asked Jesus why his disciples did not fast. He gave them an answer that seems confusing to us, though simple and straightforward to them.

If you use a new piece of cloth to patch an old garment, the patch will shrink and tear the garment. New wine expands as it ferments and will burst old wineskins that have lost their elasticity. What was Jesus's point in all of this? Simple.

Jesus offered to Israel a new, fresh, exciting, long-awaited, promised, anticipated, longed-for, blessed kingdom that did not include the old rules, regulations, burdens, and intimidations of their religious leaders. Unlike the Pharisees and teachers of the law, Jesus's followers didn't have to put on an act to appear <u>righteous</u>. By choosing to follow Jesus, he made them righteous. He is a "doctor" to the spiritually sick, a Savior of sinners. He gives his kingdom to the <u>poor</u>, comfort to those who <u>mourn</u>, etc. Get the point? A new day had come. The Messiah had come.

Giving Back

MATTHEW 9:18–26 *While He spoke these things to them, behold, a ruler came and worshiped Him, saying, "My daughter has just died, but come and lay Your hand on her and she will live." So Jesus arose and followed him, and so did His disciples. And suddenly, a woman who had a flow of blood for twelve years came from behind and touched the hem of His garment. For she said to herself, "If only I may touch His garment, I shall be made well." But Jesus turned around, and when He saw her He said, "Be of good cheer, daughter; your faith has made you well." And the woman was made well from that hour. When Jesus came into the ruler's house, and saw the flute players and the noisy crowd wailing, He said to them, "Make room, for the girl is not dead, but sleeping." And they ridiculed Him. But when the crowd was put outside, He went in and took her by the hand, and the girl arose. And the report of this went out into all that land.* (NKJV)

<u>Jairus</u>, a ruler of Capernaum's synagogue, approached Jesus out of desperation since his daughter had just died. As Jesus and the disciples made their way to Jairus's house, a woman who had been hemorrhaging for twelve years "touched the hem of His garment"—most likely one of the <u>tassels</u> that hung from the corners of his prayer shawl (see Illustration #4, page 118) commonly worn by orthodox Jews then and now. This woman's affliction left her permanently, ceremonially **<u>unclean</u>**. For twelve long, agonizing years, she was shunned by her friends, separated from her family, and excluded from the synagogue and the Temple. When Jesus stopped the flow of blood, he not only gave her health back; he also gave this poor woman her life back.

By the time they finally arrived at Jairus's home, the funeral was in

go to

righteous
Matthew 5:6

poor
Matthew 5:3

mourn
Matthew 5:4

Jairus
Mark 5:22

tassels
Numbers 15:38–40

unclean
Leviticus 15:25–27

unclean
ritually impure

full swing. The mourners mourned while the musicians played their dirge. They saw the girl as dead; from Jesus's perspective, she only slept. With the laughing mockery of the crowds as the sound track to this story, Jesus "took her by the hand, and the girl arose" (Matthew 9:25 NKJV). Jesus gave Jairus his daughter back. And the news of this miracle rocketed through the region.

Illustration #4
Prayer Shawl—Jews today sometimes wear a prayer shawl with tassels such as the one depicted here.

Of Sights and Sounds

MATTHEW 9:27–33 *When Jesus departed from there, two blind men followed Him, crying out and saying, "Son of David, have mercy on us!" And when He had come into the house, the blind men came to Him. And Jesus said to them, "Do you believe that I am able to do this?" They said to Him, "Yes, Lord." Then He touched their eyes, saying, "According to your faith let it be to you." And their eyes were opened. And Jesus sternly warned them, saying, "See that no one knows it." But when they had departed, they spread the news about Him in all that country.*

As they went out, behold, they brought to Him a man, mute and demon-possessed. And when the demon was cast out, the mute spoke. And the multitudes marveled, saying, "It was never seen like this in Israel!" (NKJV)

Two blind men followed Jesus, calling out to him for his mercy. This is the first time in Matthew's Gospel that Jesus is called "Son of David." By using this term, the blind men showed that they recognized Jesus as their Messiah. Although they were physically blind, their spiritual eyesight was 20/20. They were blind all right, but not for long.

Finally, Matthew rounds out his presentation of ten rapid-fire miracles with the story of yet another demon-possessed man who could not talk. Jesus drove the demon out. Matthew relays this story in such simple terms that you almost get the feeling that Jesus was performing miracles like these every day. He was!

Strike One

MATTHEW 9:34 *But the Pharisees said, "He casts out demons by the ruler of the demons." (NKJV)*

The Pharisees could no longer remain silent. As Jesus skyrocketed in the public opinion polls, the Pharisees' popularity plunged like a proverbial rock. They had to do something to stop the erosion of their power. They released a press report aimed at manipulating the masses into believing that Jesus wasn't all that he was cracked up to be: "He casts out demons by the ruler of the demons."

> **what others say**
>
> **Tim LaHaye**
>
> A good trial lawyer eventually comes to the place where he must finally rest his case—not because he has presented all the evidence available, but because more proof is unnecessary. We have reached that point. Now it is time for you to evaluate the evidence presented and, like a good juror, make your decision. You now have to decide: Is Jesus "The Christ, the Son of God," as He and His followers claimed?[10]

Chapter Wrap-Up

- Jesus reached out to, and in some cases actually touched, those in his society who had profound needs and challenges. (Matthew 8:1–4)

- Peter, and we presume others of the disciples, was a married man, though the New Testament is strangely silent about the disciples' spouses. (Matthew 8:14)

- Storms could arise on the Sea of Galilee in minutes, turning a calm lake into a spinning whirl of water that threatened to sink any boats caught in such a storm. (Matthew 8:24)

- The disciples dreaded going over to the "other side of the sea." It was the equivalent of them traveling to a different, hostile country. Bad things often seemed to happen whenever they went to the other side of the sea. (Matthew 8:28)

- The numbers of people whom Jesus encountered who were demon-possessed indicates the level of spiritual warfare that swirled around him constantly. (Matthew 8:28)

- When Jesus healed a woman with a twelve-year flow of blood, he not only gave her back her health; he gave her back her life. (Matthew 9:22)

- Miracles of healing had become so common by the ninth chapter of Matthew that he begins to refer to them with a notable understatement. (Matthew 9:35)

Study Questions

1. What was significant about the fact that Jesus touched the leper?

2. How did Christ's words to the centurion open up the gospel to the whole world?

3. The first three miracles reached out to what segments of society?

4. The second three miracles demonstrated Christ's power over what areas of influence?

5. Do storms such as the one described by Matthew really occur on the Sea of Galilee?

6. Why did the pig farmers plead with Jesus to leave their region?

7. What were the indications that the two men Jesus encountered on the shore of the sea were demon-possessed?

8. How did the Pharisees attempt to undermine Jesus's ministry and what decision did it force the people to make?

Matthew 9:35–10:42: Mark These Men

Chapter Highlights:
- A Scriptural Snapshot
- Jesus's Band of Merry Men
- Spiritual Boot Camp
- Nothing to Fear but Fear Itself

Let's Get Started

Many people picture Jesus as a celebrity politician surfing the wave of public opinion as he happily **shoots the curl** of enormous popularity. Those who imagine him working the rope lines, smiling and greeting everyone with a whoop and a cheer, and kissing babies while waving to his adoring fans miss the boat completely. Quite to the contrary, Jesus carried the weight of the world on his shoulders. Jesus experienced sadness and sorrow to mind-numbing proportions.

shoots the curl
surfing term, meaning riding the tube of a wave

A Scriptural Snapshot

MATTHEW 9:35–38 *Then Jesus went about all the cities and villages, teaching in their synagogues, preaching the gospel of the kingdom, and healing every sickness and every disease among the people. But when He saw the multitudes, He was moved with compassion for them, because they were weary and scattered, like sheep having no shepherd. Then He said to His disciples, "The harvest truly is plentiful, but the laborers are few. Therefore pray the Lord of the harvest to send out laborers into His harvest." (NKJV)*

The Gospel writers provide us with several scriptural snapshots of Jesus in his quiet, reflective, meditating moments. Jesus's quite sizable heart broke under the heavy burden that he felt for the "weary and scattered" (Matthew 9:36 NKJV). Jesus sadly bemoaned the crowds' confused condition as "sheep having no shepherd." Jesus quietly vocalizes his overwhelming concern that "the harvest truly is plentiful, but the laborers are few" (9:37 NKJV).

Only an exceptional group of men would qualify to formally follow such a big-hearted, yet heavily burdened man. Of the thousands who daily crowded around him, only a handpicked handful of twelve men made the final cut.

Prophecy

Isaiah lamented that the Messiah would be "a Man of sorrows and acquainted with grief" because "He has borne our griefs and carried our sorrows" (Isaiah 53:3–4 NKJV).

Jesus's Band of Merry Men

> MATTHEW 10:1 *And when He had called His twelve disciples to Him, He gave them power over unclean spirits, to cast them out, and to heal all kinds of sickness and all kinds of disease.* (NKJV)

Jesus's twelve disciples fit nicely into three groups of four, which, like three rings of ripples in a pond, represent three levels of closeness to their master.

Jesus had an inner circle: Peter and his brother Andrew, James and his brother John. He had a middle-management level of four disciples: Philip, Bartholomew (or Nathanael), the doubting Thomas, and Matthew (local IRS agent and our illustrious author). He also had a third, more distant rippling ring: James, Thaddaeus, Simon the Zealot, and Judas Iscariot (Jesus's eventual betrayer).

what others say

Max Lucado

We need to remember that the disciples were common men given a compelling task. Before they were the stained-glass saints in the windows of cathedrals, they were somebody's next-door-neighbors trying to make a living and raise a family. They weren't cut from theological cloth or raised on supernatural milk. But they were an ounce more devoted than they were afraid and, as a result, did some extraordinary things.[1]

Peter: The Leader of the Pack

> MATTHEW 10:2–4 *Now the names of the twelve apostles are these: first, Simon, who is called Peter, and Andrew his brother; James the son of Zebedee, and John his brother; Philip and Bartholomew; Thomas and Matthew the tax collector; James the son of Alphaeus, and Lebbaeus, whose surname was Thaddaeus; Simon the Cananite, and Judas Iscariot, who also betrayed Him.* (NKJV)

The four Gospel writers mention Peter by name more often than the other eleven disciples put together. He factored prominently in the unfolding drama of the life of our Lord for several reasons:

- Peter spoke more often than any other disciple.

- Peter got reproved by Jesus more often than any other disciple.

- Peter <u>affirmed</u> Jesus as his Messiah and Lord more boldly than any other disciple.

- Peter <u>denied</u> Jesus as his Messiah and Lord more firmly than any other disciple.

- Peter <u>received</u> Jesus's praise more enthusiastically than any other disciple.

- If you can imagine it, Peter actually <u>rebuked</u> Jesus, literally becoming Satan's mouthpiece in the process.

- Peter displayed greater <u>humility</u> than any other disciple.

- Peter displayed greater <u>arrogance</u> than any other disciple.

Once Jesus entered Peter's life, this rugged, gruff, strong, well-to-do family fisherman became the leader of the pack. Like so many of us, his strengths became his weaknesses, and his weaknesses became his strengths. Peter talked without thinking, boasted without counting the cost, leaped when he should have looked, bragged when he should have bowed. Over time, he became the recognized <u>leader</u> among the disciples, an **evangelist** of explosive <u>power</u> in his preaching, a noteworthy <u>author</u>, and God's chosen apostle to the <u>Jews</u>.

Every one of God's servants, including you and me, carries boatloads of baggage into his or her commitment to Jesus Christ. God uses flawed people in spite of, or sometimes because of, that very baggage. We are responsible to lay our baggage at his feet; he will do the rest.

The Inner Circle: James, John, and Andrew

Our cast of inner-circle characters would not be complete without a consideration of <u>three</u> other significant men: James, John, and Andrew.

JAMES AND JOHN: James and John were kin, blood brothers. They, along with Peter, were destined for apostolic immortality.

go to

affirmed
Matthew 16:16

denied
Matthew 26:74

received
Matthew 16:17

rebuked
Matthew 16:23

humility
Luke 5:8

arrogance
Matthew 26:35

leader
Matthew 10:2

power
Acts 2:41

author
1 and 2 Peter

Jews
Galatians 2:8

three
Acts 1:3

evangelist
someone who challenges people to put their faith in Christ

go to

martyred
Acts 12:2

responsible
John 1:35–42

connived
Mark 10:37

command fire
Luke 9:54

led
John 1:41

Greeks
John 12:20–22

martyred
someone who dies
for his or her faith

While Peter became a great speaker, James became the first **martyred** apostle, and John set his pen to parchment and became a prolific writer—with one Gospel, three letters, and the book of Revelation to his literary credit.

James and John worked for their father along with Peter and Andrew. James was the <u>responsible</u> disciple, staying behind to tend the boats and nets when Peter, John, and Andrew hightailed it down south to hear John the Baptizer. Later, when Jesus went trolling for his disciples, James eagerly jumped on board and never looked back.

Blind ambition got the better of James when he and John <u>connived</u> together for key positions in Jesus's future kingdom. Both had uncontrollable tempers—so much so that Jesus nicknamed them "Sons of Thunder" (Mark 3:17 NKJV). When Jesus entered a village and received less than an enthusiastic welcome, James and John (who, interestingly enough, described himself as "one of His disciples, whom Jesus loved" [John 13:23 NKJV]) asked Jesus for permission to <u>command fire</u> on the unsuspecting hamlet.

ANDREW: Peter and Andrew were brothers too. They hailed from Bethsaida, which means "house of the fisherman," a quiet, unassuming little town nestled peacefully along the western bank of the Jordan River immediately north of the point where it enters the Sea of Galilee. Andrew was the quiet member of the inner circle. That he should be included among the intimates is clear from such passages as Mark 13:3 and Acts 1:13.

It was Andrew who <u>led</u> Peter to Jesus. When Philip met some <u>Greeks</u> who wanted to see Jesus, he first took them to Andrew so that Andrew could lead them to Jesus.

what others say

Howard W. Ferrin

Let us remember that few of us can be Peters, but many of us can be Andrews. We can be missionaries in spirit—telling others that we have found the Christ; sympathetic with others' interests; ready to do small things or to invest a single talent, trusting that the Master will bless even a cup of cold water given in His name; and feeding the many with the few loaves and fishes which we, in one way and another, are instrumental in putting into His hands.[2]

Middle Management

Jesus's second quartet of comrades consisted of Philip, Nathanael (or Bartholomew), Thomas, and Matthew. Some of God's choicest servants quietly do their thing behind the scenes out of the public eye.

PHILIP: In each of the lists of the twelve apostles, Philip is always mentioned at the beginning of the middle group—an indication perhaps that Philip became the leader of this fearsome foursome. In his Gospel, John spilled more ink and devoted more space to <u>Philip</u> than the other three Gospels combined.

Philip was the analytical apostle. To his credit, Philip obviously had a searching mind and an evangelist's heart. That's the good news. The bad news is that he seemed pessimistic, reluctant, insecure, unsure, and skeptical. When Jesus fed the five thousand, for example, Philip questioned Jesus's ability to do it. As mentioned earlier, when some Greeks asked Philip to take them to Jesus, he ran instead to Andrew. When Jesus declared himself to be equal to God the Father, Philip's faith failed to the point where Jesus had to ask him, "Have I been with you so long, and yet you have not known Me?" (John 14:9 NKJV). Ouch!

As with his other flawed followers, Jesus used him. Philip <u>led</u> Nathanael to Jesus. So hope burns eternal even for the faithless among us!

NATHANAEL: Like every one of us, Nathanael had a magnificently marvelous bright side coupled with a menacing dark side. Jesus identified Nathanael as "an Israelite indeed, in whom is no deceit!" (John 1:47 NKJV). Yet, Nathanael was a bigot.

When Philip invited him to meet the Messiah, Nathanael immediately had a revolting knee-jerk reaction: "Can anything good come out of Nazareth?" (John 1:46 NKJV). But once Philip met Jesus, faith trumped prejudice.

MATTHEW: Matthew had a keen understanding of Old Testament prophecy, skillfully crafted a Gospel account based on that understanding, followed Jesus without hesitation when Jesus called him, and opened his home to Jesus and invited his many friends to meet Jesus there. But prior to becoming a disciple, Matthew betrayed his own people by selling himself to Rome as a bottom-feeder (as far as the Jews were concerned) tax collector. Point is, he knew money. Not surprisingly, Matthew wrote more about money—its uses and abuses—than any other biblical writer.

Philip
John 1:43–46; 6:5–7; 12:20–22; 14:8–11

led
John 1:45

THOMAS: Finally, we meet the "I-have-to-see-it-to-believe-it" disciple, Thomas. It might surprise some to learn that Thomas's first name was not "Doubting." When informed by the others that they actually saw Jesus, Thomas characteristically responded, "Unless I see in His hands the print of the nails, and put my finger into the print of the nails, and put my hand into His side, I will not believe" (John 20:25 NKJV).

what others say

Herbert Lockyer

There are many Nathanaels around today who, with all their mental alertness, have their dangers also, the most perilous of which are superficial objections about the Nazarene Himself and about the claims of truth. These objections often block the way to faith, especially when they excite in the prejudiced one an admiration of his own cleverness. Their only cure, and our most effective approach to them, is that which Philip brought to Nathanael, Come and see! When their eyes see the King, the Lord of Hosts, doubts, arguments, prejudices quickly vanish as darkness does at the rising of the sun. Believing, they prove what wonderful good comes out of Nazareth.[3]

The Final Four

James the son of Alphaeus, Thaddaeus, Simon the Zealot, and Judas Iscariot complete our apostolic cast of characters, those positioned on the outer ring of discipledom.

JAMES THE SON OF ALPHAEUS: The Bible reveals one, and only one, clear, unmistakable, undeniable fact about James: his name! That's it. From its rendering in Mark 15:40 (NKJV), he was affectionately known as "James the Less" or more literally, "Little Jimmy." Does his nickname indicate that he was young in years or small in stature? As a basic principle of Bible interpretation, when you have two equally plausible explanations for something, both are likely true. So we might rightly think of James as just an average Joe, young in years and small in stature—the runt of the litter.

Nothing, and we mean absolutely nothing, is mentioned about anything James said, wrote, thought, or did. He lived and died in virtual anonymity, with his one and only claim to fame—admittedly a notable one—his inclusion in the roster of Christ's cadre of committed followers.

THADDAEUS: Like James before him, Thaddaeus—referred to in John 14:22 (NKJV) as "Judas (not Iscariot)"—remained equally enshrouded in obscurity. He did ask one noteworthy question: "Lord, how is it that You will manifest Yourself to us, and not to the world?" (John 14:22 NKJV). We shouldn't read too much into this question, but we can draw at least one conclusion: Like the other apostles, Thaddaeus could not mentally reconcile how his Jewish Messiah could rule the world and <u>leave</u> the world at the same time. It would take a few more weeks before the apostles finally got it. Jesus had to die physically in order for them to live eternally. Jesus would indeed rule the world, but not quite yet.

leave
John 14:19

apple
Zechariah 2:7–8

rejected
John 19:15

SIMON THE ZEALOT: You remember the zealots, the New Testament's answer to our modern-day militia movement. Sit back for a moment, close your eyes, and imagine this: You've got Matthew (who sold his soul to the Romans) and Simon (who dreamed daily of destroying Romans) together within the cozy confines of Christ's turbulent troupe. Their group dynamics in action must have been amazing to behold. If the way to avoid knock-down, drag-out fights is to sidestep any and all discussions of religion or politics, what chance did these two guys have? Jesus positioned himself in the middle of the fray, trying to keep the peace between these two. Kind of makes you look upon him with a little more sympathy, doesn't it? As if that wasn't enough of a headache, ever lurking in the tall weeds was one . . .

JUDAS ISCARIOT: Of him, our favorite Gospel writer says it all: "and Judas Iscariot, who also betrayed Him" (Matthew 10:4 NKJV).

Spiritual Boot Camp

God loves Jews. They were, are, and ever shall be the <u>apple</u> of his eye—his chosen people.

The apostle Paul underscores this when he states, "I am not ashamed of the gospel of Christ, for it is the power of God to salvation for everyone who believes, for the Jew first and also for the Greek" (Romans 1:16 NKJV). Not surprisingly, the very first missionaries followed this "for the Jew first" principle: "It was necessary that the word of God should be spoken to you first" (Acts 13:46 NKJV). Only when the Jews of a city or town <u>rejected</u> the gospel did these missionaries turn to the Gentiles. Jesus established this pattern in Matthew.

Sheep Among Wolves

go to

authenticating
Hebrews 2:4

Sodom
Genesis 19:1–29

judgment
1 Thessalonians
5:1–3

MATTHEW 10:5–13 These twelve Jesus sent out and commanded them, saying: "Do not go into the way of the Gentiles, and do not enter a city of the Samaritans. But go rather to the lost sheep of the house of Israel. And as you go, preach, saying, 'The kingdom of heaven is at hand.' Heal the sick, cleanse the lepers, raise the dead, cast out demons. Freely you have received, freely give. Provide neither gold nor silver nor copper in your money belts, nor bag for your journey, nor two tunics, nor sandals, nor staffs; for a worker is worthy of his food. Now whatever city or town you enter, inquire who in it is worthy, and stay there till you go out. And when you go into a household, greet it. If the household is worthy, let your peace come upon it. But if it is not worthy, let your peace return to you. (NKJV)

Jesus's instructions were clear: The apostles were to present the promised and long-awaited kingdom to Israel. In order to accomplish their assigned task, the apostles were given the authority and power to perform <u>authenticating</u> miracles, including the casting out of demons and the raising of the dead (though there is no record that they raised the dead at this time). Jesus further instructed them not to take any provisions, including money or clothing, but rather to depend upon the willing support of those to whom they ministered.

They had an unenviable task. Jesus knew that the disciples were about to enter a spiritually darkened and hostile environment, much like harmless sheep sent to a pack of ravenous wolves. Some individuals would accept them and respond positively to their message; others would not.

Reeling from Rejection

MATTHEW 10:14–16 "And whoever will not receive you nor hear your words, when you depart from that house or city, shake off the dust from your feet. Assuredly, I say to you, it will be more tolerable for the land of <u>Sodom</u> and Gomorrah in the day of <u>judgment</u> than for that city!

"Behold, I send you out as sheep in the midst of wolves. Therefore be wise as serpents and harmless as doves. (NKJV)

The majority of people who heard the disciples would reject them, hating both them and their message. If a city or town summarily rejected them, the disciples were to shake the dust off their feet and pronounce a solemn judgment against it, saying it would be more tolerable for Sodom and Gomorrah in the day of judgment than for that city.

accusation
Matthew 9:34

MATTHEW 10:17–25 *But beware of men, for they will deliver you up to councils and scourge you in their synagogues. You will be brought before governors and kings for My sake, as a testimony to them and to the Gentiles. But when they deliver you up, do not worry about how or what you should speak. For it will be given to you in that hour what you should speak; for it is not you who speak, but the Spirit of your Father who speaks in you. Now brother will deliver up brother to death, and a father his child; and children will rise up against parents and cause them to be put to death. And you will be hated by all for My name's sake. But he who endures to the end will be saved. When they persecute you in this city, flee to another. For assuredly, I say to you, you will not have gone through the cities of Israel before the Son of Man comes. A disciple is not above his teacher, nor a servant above his master. It is enough for a disciple that he be like his teacher, and a servant like his master. If they have called the master of the house Beelzebub, how much more will they call those of his household! (NKJV)*

The disciples were leaving the cozy confines of their intimate little clan and entering a world much like ours today, one in which "brother will deliver up brother to death, and a father his child; and children will rise up against parents and cause them to be put to death" (Matthew 10:21 NKJV).

Still stinging from the religious leaders' earlier <u>accusation</u> that he was possessed by the devil, Jesus warned his followers to expect the same treatment. Jesus defined for his apostles the central issue with crystal clarity: If his disciples cared more about being popular than being right, they were in the wrong business.

<u>Nothing to Fear but Fear Itself</u>

MATTHEW 10:26–33 *Therefore do not fear them. For there is nothing covered that will not be revealed, and hidden that will not be known.*

"Whatever I tell you in the dark, speak in the light; and what you hear in the ear, preach on the housetops. And do not fear those who kill the body but cannot kill the soul. But rather fear

deny
Matthew 7:21–23

joined
1 John 2:19

Him who is able to destroy both soul and body in hell. Are not two sparrows sold for a copper coin? And not one of them falls to the ground apart from your Father's will. But the very hairs of your head are all numbered. Do not fear therefore; you are of more value than many sparrows.

"Therefore whoever confesses Me before men, him I will also confess before My Father who is in heaven. But whoever denies Me before men, him I will also deny before My Father who is in heaven. (NKJV)

"It is the measure of a man to die well." So says the master of the Western novel, the esteemed Louis L'Amour.[4]

How does a man die well? Jesus answers the question. He says that a man dies well when he gives up his life for the truth of God. Jesus warned his disciples that they might face just such an opportunity.

Jesus told the Twelve not to fear those who could kill the body for they could not touch the soul. It's all a matter of perspective, he assured them. Death for the Christian is not the end but the beginning, an open door to glories unimagined. God takes care of sparrows, Jesus reminded them. Surely he will take care of us. He knows the numbers of hairs upon our heads. Surely he knows when our lives are threatened.

Death cannot touch us apart from his permission. When it does, we will die well for having lived well. We die well for what we believe when we live well by what we believe. Thus, we have his absolute promise, "Whoever confesses Me before men, him I will also confess before My Father who is in heaven" (Matthew 10:32 NKJV).

Jesus warns, "But whoever denies Me before men, him I will also deny before My Father who is in heaven" (Matthew 10:33 NKJV). Is Jesus suggesting here that we may lose our salvation? No, quite the contrary. Those who ultimately, absolutely, and completely "disown" (or "declare that one does not know or have dealings with someone"[5]) God will have no choice but to <u>deny</u> him. The very nature of their denial—final, complete, absolute—stands as indisputable confirmation that they never genuinely <u>joined</u> the family of God.

Counting the Cost

MATTHEW 10:34–42 *"Do not think that I came to bring peace on earth. I did not come to bring peace but a sword. For I have* *come to 'set a man against his father, a daughter against her mother, and a daughter-in-law against her mother-in-law'; and 'a man's enemies will be those of his own household.' He who loves father or mother more than Me is not worthy of Me. And he who loves son or daughter more than Me is not worthy of Me. And he who does not take his cross and follow after Me is not worthy of Me. He who finds his life will lose it, and he who loses his life for My sake will find it.*

"He who receives you receives Me, and he who receives Me receives Him who sent Me. He who receives a prophet in the name of a prophet shall receive a prophet's reward. And he who receives a righteous man in the name of a righteous man shall receive a righteous man's reward. And whoever gives one of these little ones only a cup of cold water in the name of a disciple, assuredly, I say to you, he shall by no means lose his reward." (NKJV)

brothers
John 7:5

Jesus was, and continues to be, a polarizing influence in the world. Paul acknowledged the polarizing power of the gospel of Christ when he said, "The message of the cross is foolishness to those who are perishing, but to us who are being saved it is the power of God" (1 Corinthians 1:18 NKJV). The gospel can literally and sadly divide family members from one another.

Jesus understood this one sad aspect of his gospel message only too well. In life, he endured the shameless rejection of his own <u>brothers</u>; in death, he died alone. They didn't even come to say good-bye.

---

what others say

Sammy Tippit

When a person comes to Jesus in Eastern Europe, he comes with a keen understanding of the demand of discipleship. He knows it may cost his position, his education, or even his family. Perhaps the problem in the West is that we have made the decision an easy one. We need to understand the demands of discipleship.[6]

Dietrich Bonhoeffer

When God calls a man, he bids him come and die.[7]

Chapter Wrap-Up

- Jesus was moved with compassion for the multitudes because they were harassed and helpless, like sheep without a shepherd. (Matthew 9:36)

- Jesus called twelve men to follow him as his disciples. (Matthew 10:1)

- Jesus even included among his twelve men Judas Iscariot, who would eventually betray him. (Matthew 10:4)

- Jesus warned his disciples that many of the towns in which they entered would reject them, and that they were like sheep being sent into a pack of wolves. (Matthew 10:16)

- Jesus assured his men that they need not be worried when they are brought before rulers who would seek them harm. The Holy Spirit would tell them what to say just when they needed his help. (Matthew 10:19)

- Jesus explained to his men that they would suffer persecution for following Jesus because just as the religious leaders hated him, they would also hate them. (Matthew 10:24–26)

- Jesus indicated that he would be a source of division in the world, between those who love God and those who oppose God. (Matthew 10:34–37)

- Jesus challenged his disciples to follow him, even to the death, because "he who finds his life will lose it, and he who loses his life for My sake will find it" (Matthew 10:39 NKJV).

Study Questions

1. Give a scriptural portrait of the demeanor of Jesus while he was on earth.

2. Which of the twelve disciples made up the inner circle of those who were closest to Jesus?

3. Demonstrate how Peter was a man of contrasts. How does this give us hope?

4. Which two disciples were nicknamed the "Sons of Thunder" because of their explosive tempers?

5. Which disciple has the notable distinction of leading Peter to Christ?

6. Who questioned Jesus as the Messiah since he came from Nazareth, a backward town with a poor reputation?

7. What was the price the disciples would pay for following Jesus as their Lord?

8. When Jesus sent his disciples out to do ministry, what primary issue did he try to prepare them to meet?

9. What central comfort could Jesus offer his followers?

Part Two
Focus on the World

Matthew 11: Turning Tide

Chapter Highlights:
- **No Doubt About It**
- **A Tale of Three Cities**
- **Rest for the Weary**

Let's Get Started

As we break the seal on Matthew 11, we find ourselves staring down the barrel of the major turning point in the book. If you think of this Gospel as a teeter-totter, the fulcrum rests in the fast-approaching Matthew 12. On one side sits the popularity of Jesus with the people. On the other sits the opinion of their leaders. Matthew 11, where we are about to take our stroll together, starts the teeter tottering, showing the swing upward of Jesus's popularity and the swing downward of their leaders. The world continues to feel the tectonic shift from Jesus, the Messiah-King, to Jesus, the sin-bearing Savior.

Jesus's opposition, which has been ever-present, though somewhat diluted until now, begins to crystallize in Matthew 11, eventually evolving into the full-blown fury unleashed upon him in Matthew 12. There we will read of a vicious attack upon his identity, and a final rejection of his authority. This changing tide of public opinion affects many of Jesus's followers in understandably and profoundly negative ways. Most notable among them is our old friend, John the Baptizer.

Herod
Matthew 14:1

Herod
Herod Antipas,
ruler of Galilee

No Doubt About It

He's baaack! Only by this time John's thunderous declarations about Jesus being the long-awaited Messiah are but a distant echo. Instead we read of a doubting, insecure, unsure enemy of the state who's languishing in a Roman dungeon and wondering why no kingdom has come.

Much has happened in John's life since the spotlight shifted from him to Jesus back in Matthew 3. We'll learn more about John in Matthew 14. For now, we'll listen to the doubts that settled on this powerful prophet turned condemned criminal, this at the hands of **Herod** the tetrarch.

go to

prison
Matthew 14:3–4

devil
Matthew 9:34

at hand
Matthew 3:2

John's Faltering Faith

MATTHEW 11:1–3 *Now it came to pass, when Jesus finished commanding His twelve disciples, that He departed from there to teach and to preach in their cities. And when John had heard in* <u>prison</u> *about the works of Christ, he sent two of his disciples and said to Him, "Are You the Coming One, or do we look for another?" (NKJV)*

Dare we say it? John the Baptist began to have serious doubts about the true identity of his cousin, Jesus. How can a man of John's caliber, of such glistening credentials, entertain such doubts? Consider the situation and you'll cut him some slack. If you or I were placed in the same circumstance, we'd have doubts as well.

As much as a full year and a half have come and gone between John's baptism of Jesus in Matthew 3 and this rather unsettling scene in Matthew 11.[1] During that time, the kingdom was offered repeatedly, as recently as Matthew 10. But the religious leaders summarily rejected the kingdom and their King each and every time. As the people seemed overawed at the miracles that Jesus regularly performed, the reactions among their leaders grew in intensity and hostility, even to the point where they accused Jesus of being <u>devil</u>-possessed.

When John the Baptizer confronted Herod Antipas about his illicit sexual escapades with his brother's wife, John got himself hauled off to prison. When John tried to balance his anticipation of a kingdom with his unjust incarceration, well, any intellectually honest man would have to conclude that something was radically wrong with this picture. I'm sure that John lay awake many a night, shivering in the bone-chilling cold, squalid conditions of his dank, dark dungeon, haunted by the torturous thought that maybe, just maybe, he had been wrong all along about Jesus.

When John sent his disciples to ask Jesus, "Are You the Coming One, or do we look for another?" (Matthew 11:3 NKJV), his faith was in a free fall. We're not talking about some minor curiosity here. John questioned the very identity and ministry[2] of the One whom he himself had publicly declared to be "the Lamb of God who takes away the sin of the world!" (John 1:29 NKJV), the King whose kingdom was <u>at hand</u>.

Herod Antipas ordered his men to imprison John the Baptist in Machaerus,[5] a seaside fortress originally built by Herod the Great some fifteen miles southeast of the mouth of the Jordan River as it dumps into the Dead Sea, in the wild and desolate hills that overlook the sea from the east.

As we'll read in Matthew 14, John was indeed beheaded at the request of Herodias, Herod Antipas's sister-in-law, with whom he was having an affair.

The Bible Says It, I Believe It, and That Settles It!

MATTHEW 11:4–6 *Jesus answered and said to them, "Go and tell John the things which you hear and see: The blind see and the lame walk; the lepers are cleansed and the deaf hear; the dead are raised up and the poor have the gospel preached to them. And blessed is he who is not offended because of Me."* (NKJV)

What Jesus did not say in response to John's question is almost as instructive as what he did say. As he so often did, Jesus merely quoted Scripture—in this case, the prophet Isaiah's clear and unambiguous description of exactly what the Messiah would do once he arrived on the scene. Jesus fit the blueprint to a T.

What he did not say was any hint of a rebuke, criticism, condemnation, or any other form of reproof. Jesus met John at his point of doubt and reassured him the best way possible. Jesus offered John the biblical proof he needed to stabilize his faith.

Isn't it comforting to know that Jesus will not rebuke us when our faith falters and fails? He understands the weaknesses of human faith and will lovingly and patiently meet us at our points of doubt every time.

Isaiah 35:4–6 and 61:1 accurately predicted that the Messiah would heal the blind, deaf, lame, and mute, and preach good tidings to the poor.

prophecy

Well-Deserved Praise

MATTHEW 11:7–15 *As they departed, Jesus began to say to the multitudes concerning John: "What did you go out into the wilderness to see? A reed shaken by the wind? But what did you go out to see? A man clothed in soft garments? Indeed, those who wear soft clothing are in kings' houses. But what did you go out to see? A prophet? Yes, I say to you, and more than a prophet. For this is he of whom it is written:*
'Behold, I send My messenger before Your face,
Who will prepare Your way before You.'
"Assuredly, I say to you, among those born of women there has not risen one greater than John the Baptist; but he who is least in the kingdom of heaven is greater than he. And from the days of John the Baptist until now the kingdom of heaven suffers violence, and the violent take it by force. For all the prophets and the law prophesied until John. And if you are willing to receive it, he is Elijah who is to come. He who has ears to hear, let him hear! (NKJV)

Not only did Jesus not rebuke his forerunner for his faltering faith, Jesus praised John as the greatest man who ever lived! He then presented the indisputable evidence. Those who heard Jesus had to admit that John was no weak reed shaken by the wind; John stood straight and tall as a man of impeccable integrity who thundered forth his call for repentance. John did not comfort himself with the trappings of the rich; he clothed himself in the rough raiment of the wilderness. John was not just another prophet; he was the Messiah's forerunner.

Jesus quoted Malachi 3:1 in describing John the Baptizer and his role. As great as John was, those of us who share in the future kingdom will be even greater. Why? Because John was, after all, human, "born of women" (Matthew 11:11 NKJV), subject to every human frailty just like us. When we get to heaven, our sin natures will be gone.

We are engaged in a titanic struggle against forces of evil empowered by no less than Satan himself. This is war! (1 Timothy 1:18). Casualties abound. Even today, in many places around the globe, Christians are paying the ultimate price for their faith. And it will continue to be this way until Jesus comes.

Dancing in the Streets

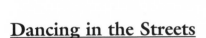

MATTHEW 11:16–19 *"But to what shall I liken this generation? It is like children sitting in the marketplaces and calling to their companions, and saying:*
   'We played the flute for you,
      And you did not dance;
   We mourned to you,
      And you did not lament.'
"For John came neither eating nor drinking, and they say, 'He has a demon.' The Son of Man came eating and drinking, and they say, 'Look, a glutton and a winebibber, a friend of tax collectors and sinners!' But wisdom is justified by her children." (NKJV)

In stark contrast to Jesus's unabashed praise of John, he derisively condemned the Jews of his generation. He compared them to grouchy children being invited by their friends to a wedding celebration. "No," they say. "We hate weddings."

"All right, then," the friends say. "How about a funeral?"

"We hate funerals," they answer.

Like spoiled brats they complained and pouted and used every excuse not to participate: "He has a demon," they said of John (Matthew 11:18 NKJV). "Look, a glutton and a winebibber, a friend of tax collectors and sinners!" they said of Jesus (11:19 NKJV). Much like our own, Jesus's generation elevated excuse-making to an art, and for all of their efforts, ultimately lost the kingdom in the process.

"Wisdom is proved right by her actions." Set a biblical lifestyle next to a rebellious one and compare the results. All things being equal, a biblical lifestyle is superior in terms of the things in life that really matter—peace, fulfillment, joy, abundance.

A Tale of Three Cities

MATTHEW 11:20–24 *Then He began to rebuke the cities in which most of His mighty works had been done, because they did not repent: "Woe to you, Chorazin! Woe to you, Bethsaida! For if the mighty works which were done in you had been done in Tyre and Sidon, they would have repented long ago in sackcloth and ashes. But I say to you, it will be more tolerable for Tyre and Sidon in the day of judgment than for you. And you, Capernaum, who are exalted to heaven, will be brought down to Hades; for if the mighty works which were done in you had been done in Sodom, it would have remained until this day. But I say to you that it shall be more tolerable for the land of Sodom in the day of judgment than for you." (NKJV)*

The cities of Chorazin, Bethsaida, and Capernaum form a triangular parcel of real estate (see Map of Israel, Appendix A) wherein

Jesus spent the lion's share of his time and in which he performed "most of his miracles." Let's quickly review the significance of these three vitally important cities:

- *Chorazin*—Sometimes spelled "Korazin," this small village lay nestled in the hills a mere two and a half miles north of Capernaum and some fifteen hundred feet above the sea. The surrounding vistas afford some of the most breathtaking views of the Sea of Galilee. Jesus visited Chorazin and performed many <u>miracles</u> there.

- *Bethsaida*—"The House of the Fishermen," was a realtor's dream. It boasted riverfront property on the shore of the Jordan River at the point where it enters the sea in the north. Bethsaida could make this claim to fame: Peter, Andrew, and Philip <u>grew</u> up in Bethsaida. If you're a trivia buff, you'll appreciate the fact that other than Jerusalem and Capernaum, Bethsaida is mentioned more times in the Gospels than any other city, village, or town.

- *Capernaum*—"The Village of Nahum" became Jesus's Galilee <u>home</u> and the headquarters of his ministry. Jesus performed more miracles and preached more sermons in this beautiful, prosperous fishing village on the northern shore than in any other place during his entire ministry.

miracles
Luke 10:13

grew
John 1:44; 12:21

home
Matthew 4:13

Tyre
Ezekiel 26–28

Sodom
Genesis 19:24

Tiberias
John 6:1

Yet, Jesus foretold that these cities, near and dear to his rather sizable heart, would suffer a destruction that would eclipse that of <u>Tyre</u> and Sidon, and <u>Sodom</u>. Why? Because the hard-hearted people of these cities, even with Jesus's miracles and teaching staring them in the face, "did not repent" (Matthew 11:20 NKJV).

Today, Capernaum, Bethsaida, and Chorazin lie in ruins. These once prominent and thriving towns are nothing more than piles of rocks, a heaven for an archaeologist, a hell for the former inhabitants of these cities. It's quite striking to note that the nearby city of <u>Tiberias</u> is today a thriving city, yet Jesus never visited Tiberias. One might think that today Capernaum would be the epicenter of commerce, its bustling streets lined with hotels, shops, and souvenir vendors. But no, Tiberias is the civic center. Why? Jesus never cursed Tiberias.

hinted
Matthew 7:13–14

theological
statements relating
to the teachings of
the Bible

doctrine
teaching

remnant
the few who remain
faithful to God

Rest for the Weary

As we look down upon the sweeping panorama of Matthew 11, here's what we see: Jesus is riding the crest of popular opinion. But take out your binoculars and look closer. Beneath the thin veneer of public popularity, the Pharisaic termites are slowly eating away at the foundations of the people's collective perceptions of Jesus. Some cracks can be seen. John the Baptist is in prison; he will soon be martyred for his faith. Jesus has been accused of being devil-possessed. His miracles are said to be the work of Satan. The three cities that had the greatest exposure to Jesus, the populations of which benefited the most from his miracle-working power, have greeted him with unbelieving indifference. The people who have gathered to hear Jesus teach are reeling from the force of his prophecies.

As we turn to the last section of this transitional chapter, we'll see something that will become a fairly common pattern: in contrast to the rejections of the many, Jesus offers comfort to the few who choose to follow him. Ready for some fancy lingo, a little **theological** jargon with which you can impress your friends? For future reference, we'll call this the "**doctrine** of the **remnant**," a subtheme that appears throughout the Bible. Even in the face of a tidal wave of rejection, God will always preserve a remnant—a faithful following of the few who buck the trends and remain true to their commitments to Christ. Jesus has <u>hinted</u> at it in the past. We'll see it demonstrated time and time again in the future. The doctrine of the remnant will factor prominently throughout the remainder of Matthew's Gospel.

Just Say No!

> **MATTHEW 11:25–26** *At that time Jesus answered and said, "I thank You, Father, Lord of heaven and earth, that You have hidden these things from the wise and prudent and have revealed them to babes. Even so, Father, for so it seemed good in Your sight.* (NKJV)

After looking through the lens of predictive prophecy and seeing the destruction that was to come to his adoptive hometown (Capernaum), Jesus must have felt emotionally and spiritually drained. He did what so many of us do during such times of exhaustion, he prayed. More accurately, he praised God. He affirmed that no matter how bleak, hopeless, despairing, irreversible, and unthinkable our circumstances may seem, we can derive much strength from the undeniable fact that God remains ultimately, completely, and totally in control.

The "wise and prudent" (Matthew 11:25 NKJV) in these verses refers to the Pharisees. They bore the responsibility as spiritual leaders to prepare their people for the Messiah's arrival. They failed in their task to the point of demanding that the Romans <u>crucify</u> their King. They were determined from the get-go to harden their hearts against Jesus and to persuade as many as they could to do the same. The "babes" to whom Jesus refers are the few—the remnant—who place their trust in Jesus, much like an infant child places his or her trust in a loving parent.

crucify
Matthew 27:22, 37

Father
John 5:18

If You've Seen One, You've Seen 'Em All

MATTHEW 11:27 *All things have been delivered to Me by My Father, and no one knows the Son except the Father. Nor does anyone know the Father except the Son, and the one to whom the Son wills to reveal Him.* (NKJV)

On its surface, Matthew 11:27 may seem confusing. It was anything but confusing to those who heard Jesus speak. In order to understand what Jesus's statement meant, we must think like a first-century Jew. When Jesus made the astonishing claims that (a) God was his Father, and (b) his Father committed "all things" to him. As far as the religious leaders were concerned, Jesus might have signed his death warrant. Correctly interpreted, Jesus made one of the clearest references to his deity in the Bible. In this one verse, Jesus disclosed the intimate and absolutely unique relationship he shared with his Father, making them essentially one and inseparable.

When Jesus referred to God as "My <u>Father</u>" (Matthew 11:27 NKJV), he claimed equality with him. When Jesus categorically stated that "all things have been delivered to Me by My Father" (11:27 NKJV)—all authority, sovereignty, truth, power—he claimed equality with God.

go to

Illustration #5
Yoke—Farmers used a wooden yoke such as the one shown here to enable two or more oxen to work together. Oxen placed in a yoke could accomplish more and do it more easily than if each worked alone.

An Irresistible Invitation

MATTHEW 11:28–30 *Come to Me, all you who labor and are heavy laden, and I will give you rest. Take My yoke upon you and learn from Me, for I am gentle and lowly in heart, and you will find rest for your souls. For My yoke is easy and My burden is light.*” (NKJV)

Whoever coined the cliché “There’s no rest for the weary” apparently never read Matthew 11:25–30. To those who labor under heavy burdens—the guilt of their sins, the sorrows that are natural to life, the oppression of the religious leaders who “yoked” their people with unattainable demands that they called “Law,” the abuses of a Roman government that oppressed the Jews—Jesus offered rest.

Jesus used a striking and fitting metaphor. A yoke is a heavy wooden harness that fits onto one or more oxen, enabling them to work together to pull a heavy load (see Illustration #5). Such a yoke was a weighty, burdensome thing, giving rise to our common designation of animals who wear such yokes, "beasts of burden."

By contrast, Jesus offers his followers a yoke that is "easy" and a burden that is "light." According to the culture of the times, when a pupil submitted himself to the tutelage of a teacher, or when a disciple committed himself to following a mentor, he was said to come under the "yoke" of his master. Jesus offered the "weary and scattered" (Matthew 9:36 NKJV) Jews of his day a trade-off—their crushing yoke for his light, rewarding, and fulfilling yoke.

There is an inner satisfaction and a blessed rest to our souls that come to every disciple of Christ that is totally foreign to the child of the world who must, by his own choices, bear his burdens alone. Why would anyone turn down such a gracious offer? That question remains to this day one of the timeless mysteries of the universe.

Something to ponder

Chapter Wrap-Up

- John the Baptist was languishing in a dungeon and understandably began to have doubts about Jesus and his mission. (Matthew 11:2–3)

- In spite of the fact that John had significant doubts, Jesus praised him with one of the highest commendations possible, calling him a great man. (Matthew 11:11)

- Jesus pronounced a curse upon three prominent towns because of their lack of faith in the face of the many miracles that he performed in them. (Matthew 11:20–24)

- Jesus invited all who had heavy burdens to come to him, and promised that those who do would be given rest. (Matthew 11:28–30)

Study Questions

1. Where do doubts originate and what do we need to remember about them?

2. Why was John the Baptist imprisoned by Herod Antipas?

3. How did Jesus respond to John's doubts?

4. Contrast Jesus's praise of John the Baptist with his condemnation of "this generation."

5. Why would Chorazin, Bethsaida, and Capernaum suffer a greater judgment? What principle does this affirm?

6. Why was it important for Jesus to restate his authority at the end of this chapter?

7. To whom did Jesus offer a kind invitation?

Matthew 12: D-Day

Chapter Highlights:
- Lawbreaker or Lawmaker?
- What's in a Name?
- Jesus Tells a Fish Story
- It's All in the Family

Let's Get Started

Within the course of one's lifetime there usually come two or three situations where, depending upon how the individual responds to these circumstances, the remainder of his or her life is determined. We typically call these defining moments "turning points." Families and nations also face turning points. For example, where would we be today if the D-Day invasion had failed? No student of history can deny that June 6, 1944, was, in every sense, a turning point.

In Matthew 12 the nation of Israel faces a turning point every bit as vital to its history as D-Day was to our history. Whether you realize it or not, your own life has been indelibly impacted by the events observed and recorded by Matthew. As far as Jesus's plan and program were concerned, things changed—radically and dramatically in Matthew 12. The chart below shows how things changed.

Evidence of Jesus's Turning Point

Before Matthew 12	After Matthew 12
Jesus regularly addressed the crowds.	Jesus increasingly huddled in private with his disciples.
His miracles were public displays of the power of God.	Jesus's miracles were more private acts of compassion on individuals.
Jesus spoke in the present tense about his kingdom.	Jesus spoke in the future tense about his church.
Jesus focused on his mission and message.	Jesus turned his attention to the Crucifixion and the Resurrection.
Jesus spoke in simple and straightforward words.	Jesus taught in parables.

Lawbreaker or Lawmaker?

MATTHEW 12:1–8 *At that time Jesus went through the grainfields on the Sabbath. And His disciples were hungry, and began to pluck heads of grain and to eat. And when the Pharisees saw it, they said to Him, "Look, Your disciples are doing what is not lawful to do on the Sabbath!" But He said to them, "Have you not read what David did when he was hungry, he and those who*

permitted
Deuteronomy 23:25

forbidden
Exodus 34:21

were with him: how he entered the house of God and ate the show-bread which was not lawful for him to eat, nor for those who were with him, but only for the priests? Or have you not read in the law that on the Sabbath the priests in the temple profane the Sabbath, and are blameless? Yet I say to you that in this place there is One greater than the temple. But if you had known what this means, 'I desire mercy and not sacrifice,' you would not have condemned the guiltless. For the Son of Man is Lord even of the Sabbath." (NKJV)

The disciples were hungry. Understandably, they plucked off a few heads of grain. No big deal, right? Wrong. Talk about losing perspective! These legalistic Pharisees were upset not because Peter and company popped a few grains into their mouths, something the Bible clearly <u>permitted</u> them to do, but because they did so on Saturday, the seventh day of the week, the Jewish Sabbath.

According to their traditions, the religious leaders who witnessed this indiscretion equated the plucking of a few heads of grain as equal to a farmer harvesting his entire wheat crop, an act <u>forbidden</u> them on the sacred seventh day. The noted Bible Bible scholar R. C. H. Lenski goes so far as to point out that to pluck the grain could actually warrant a death sentence![1]

These Pharisees had mastered the fine art of putting the people under an unbearable load. No wonder Matthew ended his previous chapter with Jesus's comforting words about his easy yoke.

Lord of the Sabbath

MATTHEW 12:9–14 *Now when He had departed from there, He went into their synagogue. And behold, there was a man who had a withered hand. And they asked Him, saying, "Is it lawful to heal on the Sabbath?"—that they might accuse Him. Then He said to them, "What man is there among you who has one sheep, and if it falls into a pit on the Sabbath, will not lay hold of it and lift it out? Of how much more value then is a man than a sheep? Therefore it is lawful to do good on the Sabbath." Then He said to the man, "Stretch out your hand." And he stretched it out, and it was restored as whole as the other. Then the Pharisees went out and plotted against Him, how they might destroy Him. (NKJV)*

Jesus encountered a man with a withered hand sitting in the synagogue. Mark's account adds a bit of color to this story. First, Jesus asked the man to stand before the entire assembly so that there would be no doubt as to what was said and done. Second, Jesus "looked around at them with anger, being grieved by the hardness of their hearts" (Mark 3:5 NKJV).

Jesus was not trying to pick a fight. Predictably, it was the Pharisees who were looking for any excuse to accuse Jesus; they were the ones who were out gunning for him.

These religious leaders decided to follow an arbitrary tradition that made it unlawful to practice medicine on the Sabbath, except in life-threatening situations. Well, nuts to tradition. The guy was hurting and needed a healing. Jesus performed one and restored his hand. The Pharisees were nearly apoplectic at what they viewed as a flagrant display of disrespect for the Sabbath. From that point on, the religious leaders banded together and obsessed about one all-consuming desire—to kill the King of the Jews.

anathema
hated, detestable, cursed

Only Matthew records the emotional vignette about a sheep falling into the ditch on the Sabbath. Not one person there would hesitate to pull it out. Yet, to restore to a human being the use of his hand on the Sabbath became **anathema** to these guys, even though the law nowhere prohibited the giving of medicine, healing, or any other act of mercy on the Sabbath.

At this point, the Pharisees shifted their strategy, significantly so. Up until now, they merely sought to discredit Jesus by trapping him with their false accusations and carefully crafted questions. Now, they showed their hand clearly and unmistakably. They formed a conspiracy that sought nothing less than Jesus's total destruction.

key point

Mum's the Word

MATTHEW 12:15–21 *But when Jesus knew it, He withdrew from there. And great multitudes followed Him, and He healed them all. Yet He warned them not to make Him known, that it might be fulfilled which was spoken by Isaiah the prophet, saying:*
 "Behold! My Servant whom I have chosen,
 My Beloved in whom My soul is well pleased!
 I will put My Spirit upon Him,
 And He will declare justice to the Gentiles.
 He will not quarrel nor cry out,
 Nor will anyone hear His voice in the streets.
 A bruised reed He will not break,

timing
Galatians 4:4

manner
Hebrews 9:22

focus
Matthew 10:5–7

And smoking flax He will not quench,
Till He sends forth justice to victory;
And in His name Gentiles will trust." (NKJV)

If whodunit novels are your kind of thing, you're going to love this passage. Matthew 12:15–21 contains a clue, a hint, a veiled reference, a subtle indication that Jesus's plan and program are about to change radically and dramatically. Before you read any farther in this commentary, go back and reread the passage and see if anything strikes you as odd or different.

You might have noticed these three curious details:

First, Jesus "withdrew." Prior to this passage, most everything Jesus did was out in the open, in full view of the wondering laypeople and their whining leaders. Not anymore. Jesus shrank from the crowds. He knew that the leaders were plotting his death. At this point Jesus didn't want to incite further the hostilities of these hypocritical men. So he pulled away.

That didn't stop the people from finding him. Drawn to hurting people as he was, even at this personally desperate hour, Jesus took the time, expended the energy, and "healed them all" (Matthew 12:15 NKJV).

Second, Jesus warned those he healed not to reveal who he was. He knew that the <u>timing</u> and <u>manner</u> of his death were just as important as the death itself. He couldn't run the risk of having multitudes of people running around the countryside proclaiming his wondrous acts to others, further enflaming the jealousies of those who sought to kill him.

Added to this, we'll see in Matthew 13 that Jesus will now spend increasing amounts of time alone with the disciples preparing them for his coming demise. The continuous press of the crowds would make this virtually impossible. He needed to withdraw, and he needed to withdraw now.

Finally (and this is huge), this Scripture section ends with a quote from Isaiah: "And in His name Gentiles will trust" (Matthew 12:21 NKJV). Read that again. Do you see that all-important word Gentiles? Up until now, the entire focus of Jesus's message and ministry was on Israel. His sole <u>focus</u> was on the Jews. Gentiles didn't have a seat at the table, as far as Jesus and the disciples were concerned.

Now Jesus is talking about Gentiles—non-Jews, the nations, you and me (assuming you are not Jewish)—turning to him in faith. From this point forward in Matthew's "Jewish" Gospel, Gentiles will factor more and more prominently in Jesus's thinking and teaching.

The nation of Israel is about to make a formal and final rejection of their Messiah, at least as far as the Jews of Jesus's generation are concerned. The kingdom now rejected, Jesus will increasingly turn to the Gentiles and offer to them what Israel declined—salvation in his name.

weak
1 Corinthians
1:26–29

Isaiah predicted this shift in emphasis seven hundred years before Jesus inhaled his first breath. Matthew 12:18–21 contains Matthew's paraphrase of Isaiah 42:1–4. By using images like bruised reeds (musical instruments like flutes, no longer capable of making music because they are "bruised" or cracked) and smoking flax (useless for giving light), Isaiah described the character and conduct of the Jewish Messiah as one who had compassion for the lowliest of the lost, those who in the eyes of others had no value, dignity, or worth. He came not to gather the strong and organize them into a revolutionary force, but rather to show mercy and bring healing to the <u>weak</u>.

What's in a Name?

> MATTHEW 12:22–24 *Then one was brought to Him who was demon-possessed, blind and mute; and He healed him, so that the blind and mute man both spoke and saw. And all the multitudes were amazed and said, "Could this be the Son of David?" Now when the Pharisees heard it they said, "This fellow does not cast out demons except by Beelzebub, the ruler of the demons." (NKJV)*

One of Jesus's lambs suffered from an acute case of demon-possession. As you read the Gospels, it becomes abundantly apparent that demonic activity swirled around Jesus like leaves, dust, and other debris swirl around the eye of a hurricane. In the case of this poor soul, the demon rendered the man blind and mute. Miracles are now becoming so commonplace that Matthew merely states, "[Jesus] healed him" (Matthew 12:22 NKJV). How did the crowds react?

go to

seed
2 Samuel 7:12

Jesus, polarizing force that he was, split the crowd in two along the common fault line of leaders on the one side, and those they led on the other. Look closely at the text, because this shaker was far more than some rolling little tremor; a seismic shift of unprecedented proportions was about to jolt the Jewish nation to the very core of its being.

The people understood, even if their leaders didn't. In a brilliant burst of insight the people in unison asked the rhetorical question: "Could this be the Son of David?" (Matthew 12:23 NKJV). The title "Son of David" of course referred to the Davidic covenant, the promise made to David that his <u>seed</u>, the Jewish Messiah, would sit upon David's throne and rule over his kingdom forever. Why would they draw that conclusion?

Israel was, and is today, an extremely small country with an extremely small population. Times were tough and the Jewish people hung on to one another, literally for dear life. Consequently, everybody knew everybody. Matthew assumes that his readers understand that important dynamic. Thus, when Matthew introduces the key player in this act of the ongoing drama as a man who was "demon-possessed, blind and mute" (Matthew 12:22 NKJV), he assumes that we know everyone in that town, presumably Capernaum, knew this guy personally.

Given his physical limitations, he was no doubt a beggar on the streets. The townspeople passed him every day. Many regularly threw a shekel or two into his outstretched hand so that the guy could eat. When Jesus healed him, this was no mere magician's act using an unknown assistant with smoke and mirrors. This, like all of Jesus's miracles, was undeniable, unmistakable, irrefutable proof that Jesus is God.

Prophecy

Isaiah predicted the miracles Jesus would do: "The eyes of the blind shall be opened, and the ears of the deaf shall be unstopped. Then the lame shall leap like a deer, and the tongue of the dumb sing" (Isaiah 35:5–6 NKJV).

Of all people, the Pharisees should have jumped to the correct conclusion about Jesus and led their people in humble submission to their Messiah. Even in the face of irrefutable biblical evidence and an unmistakable display of the power of God over the spiritual and physical realms, the Pharisees pompously, passionately, and brazenly declared not only that Jesus was not their Messiah but also that he was "Beelzebub, the ruler of the demons" (Matthew 12:24 NKJV).

The Pharisees and all who conclude that Jesus is anyone other than the Messiah have blatantly supressed and rejected the truth. Such suppression is never an act of the mind, but rather an exercise of the will for which God will hold them accountable (Romans 1:18; 2:5–8).

A Lapse of Logic

MATTHEW 12:25–29 *But Jesus knew their thoughts, and said to them: "Every kingdom divided against itself is brought to desolation, and every city or house divided against itself will not stand. If Satan casts out Satan, he is divided against himself. How then will his kingdom stand? And if I cast out demons by Beelzebub, by whom do your sons cast them out? Therefore they shall be your judges. But if I cast out demons by the Spirit of God, surely the kingdom of God has come upon you. Or how can one enter a strong man's house and plunder his goods, unless he first binds the strong man? And then he will plunder his house. (NKJV)*

Jesus responded to the Pharisees' outrageous charge by demonstrating just how utterly outrageous it was. Believing the notion that Satan could or would cast out Satan is as intellectually suicidal as believing that the United States could declare nuclear war on itself and live to talk about it.

The Pharisees did not arrive at this conclusion out of factual deliberation, but rather from willful rebellion. Their logic went something like this: Jesus displayed supernatural power. The Messiah will display supernatural power. This is a problem. We've got a good thing going as far as our own positions of power over the people are concerned. The last thing we want is some Messiah messing it up. They therefore determined that Jesus's power came not from God, but from Satan. Jesus was not God-in-the-flesh, but Satan-in-the-flesh. Jesus was not divine, but demonic. Jesus was not a King; he was the devil.

The Unforgivable Sin

MATTHEW 12:30–32 *He who is not with Me is against Me, and he who does not gather with Me scatters abroad.*

go to

deaf
Isaiah 35:5–6

"Therefore I say to you, every sin and blasphemy will be for-given men, but the blasphemy against the Spirit will not be for-given men. Anyone who speaks a word against the Son of Man, it will be forgiven him; but whoever speaks against the Holy Spirit, it will not be forgiven him, either in this age or in the age to come. (NKJV)

In response, Jesus threw down the gauntlet: "He who is not with Me is against Me, and he who does not gather with Me scatters abroad" (Matthew 12:30 NKJV). Who do you suppose he had in mind? Then he warned them about committing the dreaded unfor-givable sin.

The Pharisees devoted their lives to studying the Old Testament, including the prophecies regarding the coming of their Messiah. When Jesus burst on the scene and fulfilled these predictions in minute detail—including the healing of the <u>deaf</u> and mute man—the Pharisees should have jumped for joy.

By attributing these works to Satan, and thus implying that the ful-fillment of the prophecies of Isaiah and others were a display of the powers of the dark side, the Pharisees committed a sin of grievous proportions. It was so over-the-top wicked, so unthinkable, so beyond the pale, that it's no wonder Jesus warned them that they were about to pass the point of no return in their total, complete, and absolute rejection of Jesus as their Messiah.

Many scholars have debated exactly what constitutes the so-called unforgivable or unpardonable sin. The opinions offered basically fall into one of two camps—those who believe the unforgivable sin can or cannot be committed today.

Those who believe that the unforgivable sin can indeed be com-mitted today point to such warning passages as Proverbs 29:1; Acts 7:51–58; Hebrews 2:1–4; 6:4–6; 10:26–29. Others suggest that it is impossible to commit the unforgivable sin today since it is impossi-ble to duplicate the circumstances in Matthew 12. Specifically, they point out that Jesus is not physically here performing miracles as he was in the Gospels.

We fall squarely in the first camp. Nevertheless, whichever view is correct, the fact remains that the Bible warns us against doing the same thing as the Pharisees. When a person hears the truth about Jesus (that he alone is the one who can save him) and about himself (that he is a sinner who desperately needs to be saved) and becomes convinced of these two facts through the **convicting** ministry of the Holy Spirit, and then rejects that truth in a total, final, absolute act of highhanded willful defiance, there remains nothing else that God can do to save him (Hebrews 10:26–27). It's as if they crucify Jesus all over again (Hebrews 6:6).

convicting
John 16:8

uncharacteristic
John 10:10

convicting
convincing someone
that something is
true

The Convicting Work of the Holy Spirit (John 16:8)

Significance	Cross	References
Sin	That we are sinners; that we have thought, said, and done things, and have had attitudes and motives, that displease the Lord. "For all have sinned and fall short of the glory of God."	Romans 3:23; James 2:10
Righteousness	That through Christ's death on the cross our sins can be forgiven and we can be made righteous. "For He made Him who knew no sin to be sin for us, that we might become the righteousness of God in Him."	2 Corinthians 5:17, 21; 1 John 1:9
Judgment	That if we reject Christ's offer of righteousness, judgment will surely come. "For the wages of sin is death, but the gift of God is eternal life in Christ Jesus our Lord."	Romans 6:23; Hebrews 9:27

Words That Come Back to Bite Us

MATTHEW 12:33–37 *"Either make the tree good and its fruit good, or else make the tree bad and its fruit bad; for a tree is known by its fruit. Brood of vipers! How can you, being evil, speak good things? For out of the abundance of the heart the mouth speaks. A good man out of the good treasure of his heart brings forth good things, and an evil man out of the evil treasure brings forth evil things. But I say to you that for every idle word men may speak, they will give account of it in the day of judgment. For by your words you will be justified, and by your words you will be condemned."* (NKJV)

Jesus used a commonly understood metaphor to drive home his point. Good trees bring forth good fruit. Bad trees produce shriveled, sickly, sour little berries. Nothing as good as the wholesome healing of the impoverished blind and mute man could possibly spring from a sinful source. The quality of life that Jesus restored to the man was something utterly <u>uncharacteristic</u> of anything the devil would do. What Jesus did was characteristic of something that only God would do.

The Pharisees' willfully defiant unbelief, as revealed by their deceptive and damaging claims against Christ, generated some of the strongest language that Jesus used anywhere in the four Gospels. Christ called them a "brood of vipers" (Matthew 12:34 NKJV) or poisonous snakes, hardly terms of endearment. But he was right. These wicked men poisoned the very people they were entrusted to teach, lead, and serve. Their own words, even the casual comments that they uttered day by day, condemned them for what they were—very small but very destructive men in possession of very sick, sour souls.

Charles R. Swindoll

How much hurt, how much damage can be done by chance remarks! Our unguarded tongues can deposit germ-thoughts of hurt, humiliation, and hate into tender minds which fester, become full-blown infections, and ultimately spread disease throughout an adult personality.[2]

As if casting out a demon and healing a blind and mute man weren't convincing enough, the Pharisees had the audacity to ask Jesus for a supernatural sign of his deity. Can you imagine? How could the people keep from snickering at this unbelievably ironic request?

Jesus Tells a Fish Story

MATTHEW 12:38–42 *Then some of the scribes and Pharisees answered, saying, "Teacher, we want to see a sign from You." But He answered and said to them, "An evil and adulterous generation seeks after a sign, and no sign will be given to it except the sign of the prophet Jonah. For as Jonah was three days and three nights in the belly of the great fish, so will the Son of Man be three days and three nights in the heart of the earth. The men of Nineveh will rise up in the judgment with this generation and condemn it, because they repented at the preaching of Jonah; and indeed a greater than Jonah is here. The queen of the South will rise up in the judgment with this generation and condemn it, for she came from the ends of the earth to hear the wisdom of Solomon; and indeed a greater than Solomon is here. (NKJV)*

The religious leaders wanted a sign. Jesus gave them a sign—he essentially made a prediction. They would kill him, bury him, and think they were finally through with him. Three days later, up from the grave he'd arise!

Jesus chose two Old Testament stories to illustrate his point. Just as <u>Jonah</u> spent three days and nights in the belly of a big fish, so Jesus would spend three days and nights in the belly of the grave. When Jonah confronted the people of Nineveh about their sins, these barbaric Assyrians repented of their brutality, something apparently foreign to the Pharisees' thinking. The implication could not have been clearer. When these Assyrian Gentiles walk the golden <u>streets</u> of heaven, guess where these haughty "holy" men will be?

Likewise, the <u>queen</u> of Sheba heard the wisdom of Solomon and bowed in humble submission to his God, something the Jewish leaders of Jesus's day refused to do. Once again, a Gentile positively responded to the truth, while some of God's chosen negatively rejected the truth. Once again they were reminded that when it came to the things of the kingdom, they were on the outside looking in.

Jonah
Jonah 1:17

streets
Revelation 21:21

queen
1 Kings 10:1–13

I Think I Can, I Think I Can

MATTHEW 12:43–45 *"When an unclean spirit goes out of a man, he goes through dry places, seeking rest, and finds none. Then he says, 'I will return to my house from which I came.' And when he comes, he finds it empty, swept, and put in order. Then he goes and takes with him seven other spirits more wicked than himself, and they enter and dwell there; and the last state of that man is worse than the first. So shall it also be with this wicked generation." (NKJV)*

Jesus pulled no punches. He called a spade a spade. These Pharisees, like many "religious" people today, practiced an empty religion, filled with man-made traditions, but utterly devoid of any relationship with the God they professed to know and love. They lived like a guy who pompously thinks that he can get his act together on his own and doesn't need God because he is God, only to end up in worse shape than when he started.

The Christian life is a matter of the will. Jesus defined the hallmark of a Christian as one "who does the will of My Father in heaven"

go to

brothers
Mark 3:31;
Luke 8:19–21;
John 7:3–5

sister
Mark 6:3

(Matthew 7:21 NKJV). He also told his disciples, "If you love Me, keep My commandments" (John 14:15 NKJV). The notion that someone can be a Christian and yet live in continual, willful disobedience is utterly foreign to the Scriptures, and certainly foreign to the final paragraph in Matthew 12.

It's All in the Family

MATTHEW 12:46–50 *While He was still talking to the multitudes, behold, His mother and brothers stood outside, seeking to speak with Him. Then one said to Him, "Look, Your mother and Your brothers are standing outside, seeking to speak with You." But He answered and said to the one who told Him, "Who is My mother and who are My brothers?" And He stretched out His hand toward His disciples and said, "Here are My mother and My brothers! For whoever does the will of My Father in heaven is My brother and sister and mother." (NKJV)*

As Jesus concluded his controversy with the cream of the Pharisaic crop, word came to him that his mother and brothers stood waiting for him, a clear reference to Mary and her younger sons, Jesus's half <u>brothers</u>. Jesus pounced on this as the teachable moment that it was.

"Who is My mother and who are My brothers?" he asked (Matthew 12:48 NKJV). Having piqued their curiosity, he drove home his point with pinpoint accuracy: "Whoever does the will of My Father in heaven is My brother and <u>sister</u> and mother" (Matthew 12:50 NKJV). Coming at the conclusion of this tumultuous chapter, Jesus's otherwise mysterious words emphasized the true nature of biblical Christianity. It's not an external or empty religion, but an internal and intimate relationship with Jesus Christ marked first and foremost by a will to do his will. Fellow believers are Jesus's true spiritual brothers and sisters.

what others say

A. W. Tozer

The Lordship of Jesus is not quite forgotten among Christians, but it has been relegated to the hymnal where all responsibility toward it may be comfortably discharged in a glow of pleasant religious emotion. or if it is taught as a theory in the classroom it is rarely applied to practical living. The idea that the Man Christ Jesus has absolute and final authority over the

Chapter Wrap-Up

- Matthew 12 is the major turning point, both of Matthew's Gospel and of the ministry and message of Jesus.

- Jesus condemned the religious leaders because they were more concerned about keeping every detail of their religious rituals than they were about showing compassion to those in need. (Matthew 12:7)

- The Pharisees plotted to destroy Jesus because he healed a man with a withered hand on the Sabbath. (Matthew 12:9–14)

- Jesus healed a man who was demon-possessed, so that the once blind and mute man could now see and speak. (Matthew 12:22)

- The religious leaders tried to convince the amazed multitudes that Jesus healed the man in the power of Beelzebub, the ruler of the demons. (Matthew 12:24)

- Jesus warned the Pharisees that they were perilously close to committing a sin for which there would be no forgiveness. (Matthew 12:31–32)

- When the religious leaders demanded of Jesus a sign proving his authority—this on the heels of Jesus healing the demon-possessed man—Jesus made a prediction about his resurrection and staked his credibility on that event. (Matthew 12:40)

Study Questions

1. What observable differences did the events of Matthew 12 bring to the ministry and message of Jesus and why?

2. How did the miracle of the demon-possessed man who was blind and mute prove that Jesus was the Messiah?

3. What is the unforgivable sin?

4. Do you believe that it can be committed today?

5. What was the point of the evil spirit and his seven friends' story?

6. According to Jesus, who are his true mother and brothers?

Chapter Highlights:
- Have I Got a Story
- Of Seeds and Weeds
- Losing a Battle While Winning a War
- Hide and Seek
- Hometown Hero?

Matthew 13: I Love to Tell the Story

Let's Get Started

In this chapter King Jesus will present a new and tantalizing subject, constituting nothing less than a redefinition of the nature of the now-rejected kingdom. He will call these stunning disclosures "the mysteries of the kingdom of heaven" (Matthew 13:11 NKJV).

what others say

Bruce Wilkinson and Kenneth Boa

Christ's ministry changes immediately with His new teaching of parables, increased attention given to His disciples, and His repeated statement that His death is now near.[1]

Matthew 13 ranks high among the most difficult chapters in the Bible to interpret. Put three Bible scholars in a room with copies of this chapter and you're likely to get four or more opinions as to the precise meaning of each parable.

The key to unlocking the meaning of these messages lies in an understanding of two key terms: *parables* and *mysteries*.

Have I Got a Story

MATTHEW 13:1–3a *On the same day Jesus went out of the house and sat by the sea. And great multitudes were gathered together to Him, so that He got into a boat and sat; and the whole multitude stood on the shore. Then He spoke many things to them in parables, saying: . . . (NKJV)*

A parable is a carefully crafted story that communicates one basic idea or principle of life. "Parable" combines two Greek words—*para*, which means "alongside," and *bole*, "to throw." So a parable "throws" an unfamiliar idea "alongside" a familiar one. Thus, in its simplest terms, a parable is a story that compares an unknown concept to a known one.[2] The key, then, to interpreting a parable is to

go to

Sermon
Matthew 5:2–7:27

excursion
Matthew 10:5

accusers
Matthew 12:25–45

discover that one basic idea. Fortunately, most of the time, Jesus will tell us that one basic idea.

So much for that term. But what about "mysteries"?

Matthew 13:11 says, "He answered and said to them, 'Because it has been given to you to know the mysteries of the kingdom of heaven, but to them it has not been given'" (NKJV). Mysteries. Intriguing! Jesus was about to reveal truth that had never been revealed before. This marks a radical departure from everything that Jesus had heretofore preached. Now that the nation through the agency of its religious elite had formally and finally rejected the King with his kingdom, Jesus must prepare his men for the unthinkable: his impending execution and the indefinite delay of the manifestation of his kingdom on earth.

Other Gospel writers record some of the parables of Jesus, most notably Luke. Only Matthew arranges the parables in the format found here. This is in keeping with his style and purpose for writing. We have seen the King formally address three groups of people: his subjects in the "Sermon on the Mount," his disciples as he prepared them for their first excursion into the highways and byways of the land, and his accusers. Here, he is huddling in cozy camaraderie with the Twelve.

> **what others say**
>
> **Larry Richards**
>
> There is something very different about the parables recorded in Matthew 13. Rather than illuminating what Jesus said, they almost seem to obscure it!...Jesus later explained to His disciples that the parables were spoken for them (13:16), . . . that they dealt...with those dimensions of the Kingdom which you and I experience today and will experience until, at the return of Christ, the Old Testament's prophesied Kingdom rule is established forever.[3]

We will actually encounter seven parables in this chapter. Jesus followed a three-step pattern to teach these parables to his disciples: (1) the parable itself; (2) a time of reflection during which the disciples either don't have any idea of what Jesus means, or they display their uncanny ability to think logically to an illogical conclusion; and (3) Jesus's explanation.

Of Seeds and Weeds

MATTHEW 13:3b–9; 18–23 *"Behold, a sower went out to sow. And as he sowed, some seed fell by the wayside; and the birds came and devoured them. Some fell on stony places, where they did not have much earth; and they immediately sprang up because they had no depth of earth. But when the sun was up they were scorched, and because they had no root they withered away. And some fell among thorns, and the thorns sprang up and choked them. But others fell on good ground and yielded a crop: some a hundredfold, some sixty, some thirty. He who has ears to hear, let him hear! . . .*

"Therefore hear the parable of the sower: When anyone hears the word of the kingdom, and does not understand it, then the wicked one comes and snatches away what was sown in his heart. This is he who received seed by the wayside. But he who received the seed on stony places, this is he who hears the word and immediately receives it with joy; yet he has no root in himself, but endures only for a while. For when tribulation or persecution arises because of the word, immediately he stumbles. Now he who received seed among the thorns is he who hears the word, and the cares of this world and the deceitfulness of riches choke the word, and he becomes unfruitful. But he who received seed on the good ground is he who hears the word and understands it, who indeed bears fruit and produces: some a hundredfold, some sixty, some thirty." (NKJV)

Just when the disciples thought that they were riding high in the public popularity polls, cruising to a certain overthrow of Rome, Jesus placed his dust-covered foot on the brake pedal of their runaway optimism.

The point of this parable, as summarized in verses 18–23, is this: The preaching of the gospel does not determine the condition of a person's heart; it reveals it. A farmer throws his seeds, symbolic of the "word of the kingdom" (Matthew 13:19 NKJV)—or, to give it a modern-day frame of reference, the message of the gospel—being preached or shared with others. These seeds land on four types of soil:

1. *Hard soil*—Seeds that fall on hard soil cannot and do not take root. These are people whose hearts are so hardened and embittered against God that the devil metaphorically snatches the seed away from them before it takes root and makes any lasting, life-changing impact.

2. *Rocky soil*—The rocky places represent the problems and pressures of life that everyone, Christians included, encounter as a part of living. Added to this is the persecution that Christians often receive at the hands of those who oppose God. These individuals respond to the gospel "with joy" (Matthew 13:20 NKJV), but once the pressures hit, they wilt.

3. *Thorny soil*—The thornbushes or thistles picture the kinds of people who are quickly overcome by the worries of life brought on by the obsessive pursuit of wealth. Once again, they make a commitment to Christ, but they quickly become blinded by their toys and trinkets and distracted from pursuing the things in life that really matter.

4. *Good soil*—The good soil describes those few who hear Jesus's message and truly commit their lives to him, faithfully following him to the end. They will enjoy the fruitfulness of an abundant and fulfilling life.

Four Soils, Four Hearts

Soils	Significance	Scripture References
Hard Soil	People whose hearts are so hardened and embittered toward God that the devil is able to snatch away God's Word before it takes root and makes any lasting, life-changing impact.	You stiff-necked . . . in heart and ears! You always resist the Holy Spirit . . . Whenthey heard these things they were cut to the heart, and they gnashed at him with their teeth. (Acts 7:51, 54–59 NKJV)
Stony Soil	Those who make shallow commitments to Christ that do not last long. Once life's problems and pressures come, they walk away from God, often blaming him for their trials.	Many of His disciples . . . said, "This is a hard saying." . . . From that time many of His disciples...walked with Him no more. (John 6:60, 66 NKJV)
Thorny Soil	Those who are more committed to the pursuit of personal pleasure than they are to pursuing God.	Demas has forsaken me, having loved this present world. (2 Timothy 4:10 NKJV)
Good Soil	Those who hear God's Word, apply it to their lives, and bear the fruit of a life that pleases God.	By this My Father is glorified, that you bear much fruit. (John 15:8 NKJV)

Notice that three out of the four types of people respond positively to the gospel and <u>appear</u> to embrace the message (a veritable bumper crop of pro-Jesus reactions). But only one of the three is genuine (the apparent boom goes bust).

We genuinely become followers of Christ only when we understand and acknowledge that Jesus is God and that we are not. He is our Creator, and we are morally accountable to him. He is holy, and we are sinful. He alone can cleanse and forgive us, and we desperately and helplessly throw ourselves on his mercy for the forgiveness that he died to provide. We seek to live every moment of every day in obedience to his will as revealed in the Bible. To come to Christ for any other reason is to not come to Christ at all.

appear
Matthew 7:22

> **what others say**
>
> **Dietrich Bonhoeffer**
>
> The only man who has the right to say that he is justified by grace alone is the man who has left all to follow Christ. Such a man knows that the call to discipleship is a gift of grace, and that the call is inseparable from grace.[4]

Eyes Wide Shut

MATTHEW 13:10–17 *And the disciples came and said to Him, "Why do You speak to them in parables?" He answered and said to them, "Because it has been given to you to know the mysteries of the kingdom of heaven, but to them it has not been given. For whoever has, to him more will be given, and he will have abundance; but whoever does not have, even what he has will be taken away from him. Therefore I speak to them in parables, because seeing they do not see, and hearing they do not hear, nor do they understand. And in them the prophecy of Isaiah is fulfilled, which says:*

> *'Hearing you will hear and shall not understand,*
> *And seeing you will see and not perceive;*
> *For the hearts of this people have grown dull.*
> *Their ears are hard of hearing,*
> *And their eyes they have closed,*
> *Lest they should see with their eyes and hear with their ears,*
> *Lest they should understand with their hearts and turn,*
> *So that I should heal them.'*

"But blessed are your eyes for they see, and your ears for they hear; for assuredly, I say to you that many prophets and righteous

men desired to see what you see, and did not see it, and to hear what you hear, and did not hear it." (NKJV)

The Bible contains many subthemes, life principles not bound by time or place. One of the most important subthemes is this: Truth ignored results in truth silenced.

You might think of it this way: God doesn't waste his words. Whenever he tells someone something, he expects that person to act upon what he has just been told. If the individual treats the truth with contempt, he or she may forfeit the privilege of receiving any more truth.

Jesus's newly employed teaching style of concealing things to some while revealing things to others should not surprise us. Isaiah 6:9–10 says Jesus would do it this way.

prophecy

The Good, the Bad

MATTHEW 13:24–30 *Another parable He put forth to them, saying: "The kingdom of heaven is like a man who sowed good seed in his field; but while men slept, his enemy came and sowed tares among the wheat and went his way. But when the grain had sprouted and produced a crop, then the tares also appeared. So the servants of the owner came and said to him, 'Sir, did you not sow good seed in your field? How then does it have tares?' He said to them, 'An enemy has done this.' The servants said to him, 'Do you want us then to go and gather them up?' But he said, 'No, lest while you gather up the tares you also uproot the wheat with them. Let both grow together until the harvest, and at the time of harvest I will say to the reapers, "First gather together the tares and bind them in bundles to burn them, but gather the wheat into my barn."''" (NKJV)*

Nobody likes weeds in his or her garden. Weeds can spoil an otherwise bountiful crop. Jesus had this in mind when he told this second parable.

Jesus maintains the image of the sower, a farmer scattering his seed, but this parable has a new twist. An enemy comes along and sows weeds, probably darnel—a grasslike weed. This darnel looks exactly like wheat in its young stages, and only an expert can tell them apart. One nasty side effect of this stuff is its susceptibility to a parasite fungus, which renders the weed poisonous to both man and animals.[5] A farmer cannot pull up the weed once it's fully grown without damaging the wheat. Thus, the farmer gave instructions to the servants to allow the wheat and weeds to grow together until the harvest.

final judgment
Revelation 14:15–19

And the Ugly

MATTHEW 13:36–43 *Then Jesus sent the multitude away and went into the house. And His disciples came to Him, saying, "Explain to us the parable of the tares of the field." He answered and said to them: "He who sows the good seed is the Son of Man. The field is the world, the good seeds are the sons of the kingdom, but the tares are the sons of the wicked one. The enemy who sowed them is the devil, the harvest is the end of the age, and the reapers are the angels. Therefore as the tares are gathered and burned in the fire, so it will be at the end of this age. The Son of Man will send out His angels, and they will gather out of His kingdom all things that offend, and those who practice lawlessness, and will cast them into the furnace of fire. There will be wailing and gnashing of teeth. Then the righteous will shine forth as the sun in the kingdom of their Father. He who has ears to hear, let him hear!" (NKJV)*

When the disciples asked Jesus to interpret the parable for them, he identified the field as the world, the sower as himself, the good seed as the sons of the kingdom, and the weeds as cronies of the devil. The harvest refers to the final judgment at the end of the ages. The harvesters will be God's holy angels. Jesus will elaborate on this final judgment in more detail in Matthew 25:31–46; the metaphor of choice there is the separation not of wheat and weeds, but of sheep and goats. Only at the end of the age will the identities of the true followers of Jesus be revealed.

The implications for the church are quite startling. Some of the fiercest opposition within the cozy confines of a local church may come from some who, by all outward appearances, look and sound just like true Christians. But the reality is that they are fake, phony, counterfeit followers, planted by the evil one in a local congregation to wreak havoc there. They appear righteous on the outside, but on the inside they sow seeds of gossip. They create disunity. They plant in people's minds distrust of or disloyalty to the leaders of the church. They undermine the direction and vision of the church.

They leave in their wake disheartened pastors, divided congregations, and disillusioned believers. And yet all the while, they think they are doing the work of God when in reality they are opposing it.

The contrast of destinies between the blessed and the damned, the sincere followers of Jesus and the phony counterfeits, is stark and frightful. The line separating the two groups, the litmus test, if you will, is the issue of obedience to the Father. The wicked will be judged. The righteous will receive an everlasting reward.

"Those who practice lawlessness" (Matthew 13:41 NKJV) will be cast like chaff into a fiery furnace. Close your eyes and picture dead, dry grass being tossed into a flame and you will know what will happen to the damned. Those who oppose God will weep in their hatred of him and gnash their teeth in their anger at him while being cast like chaff into a flame by him.

> **what others say**
>
> **John F. MacArthur Jr.**
> Hell will not be a place, as some jokingly envision, where the ungodly will continue to do their thing while the godly do theirs in heaven. Hell will have no friendships, no fellowship, no camaraderie, no comfort.[6]

Losing a Battle While Winning a War

The next two parables relate to the way in which the growth of Christ's kingdom will spread throughout the earth. The irony of these stories should not be missed.

In Matthew 13, we are literally standing on the threshold of Jesus's execution in the sense that from then on out Jesus will be preparing his men for his inevitable demise. The die has been cast. The final rejection has been rendered. Christ's crucifixion at the hands of the Romans is assured. His enemies will think they have won the war. But not so fast. Things aren't always as they appear. The irony implied in this next parcel of parables will make that clear for all to hear.

By the way, do you ever feel like we are losing the war? Then be of good cheer. Good news is on the way.

Growing Pains

MATTHEW 13:31–32 *Another parable He put forth to them, saying: "The kingdom of heaven is like a mustard seed, which a man took and sowed in his field, which indeed is the least of all the seeds; but when it is grown it is greater than the herbs and becomes a tree, so that the birds of the air come and nest in its branches." (NKJV)*

Gentiles
Ezekiel 17:23; 31:6;
Daniel 4:21

Time for a little lesson in horticulture. Mustard seeds are small. "The expression 'small as a mustard seed' had become proverbial, and was used not only by our Lord but frequently by the rabbis to indicate the smallest amount, such as the least drop of blood, the least defilement, or the smallest remnant of sunglow in the sky."[7]

Here's the exciting part: The trees these tiny seeds produce can soar to a whopping twelve to fifteen feet tall complete with branches sturdy enough for birds to make these trees their homes.

Image is everything in this parable. The straggling group of twelve men plus their leader was uninspiring by human standards as far as a worldwide movement was concerned. But great things often start from humble beginnings. Jesus predicted that his kingdom would start small but swell to an enormous size with <u>Gentiles</u> (birds) as well as Jews as its inhabitants. Look around the world and you will find ample evidence that Jesus's prediction came true.

The Leaven of Heaven

MATTHEW 13:33–35 *Another parable He spoke to them: "The kingdom of heaven is like leaven, which a woman took and hid in three measures of meal till it was all leavened."*
All these things Jesus spoke to the multitude in parables; and without a parable He did not speak to them, that it might be fulfilled which was spoken by the prophet, saying:
"I will open My mouth in parables;
I will utter things kept secret from the foundation of the world." (NKJV)

The parable of the leaven pictures Christ's kingdom as yeast, multiplying quietly and permeating all that it touches. The image here is identical to that of the mustard seed. From such humble beginnings, the entire world has felt, and will continue to feel, the influence of Jesus's followers. We can only imagine what the world would be like

restrains
2 Thessalonians 2:7

if this influence of love, mercy, compassion, forgiveness, and all that is right was suddenly removed. Hell on earth would surely become a tragic consequence and not just a throwaway cliché.

Some scholars, such as John Walvoord of Dallas Seminary,[8] take an opposing view. They point out, correctly, that leaven is used in the Old Testament as a symbol for evil. Therefore, they say, Jesus illustrated to his disciples that as time moves forward evil will increase in all of its manifestations on the earth, and even permeate the kingdom. However, the context of the chapter, the overriding themes of the other parables (most specifically the parable of the mustard seed), and Jesus's clear declaration that "the kingdom of heaven is like leaven," lead us to conclude that here leaven represents the enormous growth of the kingdom. Indeed, Christ's kingdom, today manifested in the church, has grown from such humble beginnings to a worldwide force for good that holds back or <u>restrains</u> the full manifestation of evil in the world.

Jesus quoted Psalm 78:2 where God's merciful and righteous dealings with Israel were contrasted with the people's rebellion. The psalmist taught by using parables or wise sayings about God's deeds.

Hide and Seek

> MATTHEW 13:44–46 *"Again, the kingdom of heaven is like treasure hidden in a field, which a man found and hid; and for joy over it he goes and sells all that he has and buys that field.*
> *"Again, the kingdom of heaven is like a merchant seeking beautiful pearls, who, when he had found one pearl of great price, went and sold all that he had and bought it. (NKJV)*

These two parables have identical meanings. Salvation is a priceless treasure, a pearl of great price. So precious, in fact, that any sensible, thinking person will exhaust all of his resources—money, time, energy—to find it. When he does, his soul is flooded to overflowing with great "joy."

Some believe that the dual references to the persons in the two parables buying the field or pearl make it impossible to equate them with salvation, since salvation is free. Those who hold this view generally say the field or pearl is the nation of Israel. They cite such verses as Exodus 19:5 and Psalm 135:4, both of which refer to Israel as a "treasure." They explain that since the world today does not regard Israel as a treasure, in a sense Israel is a hidden treasure.

Such an interpretation negates the greater context of the chapter. Our salvation was in fact anything but free. Our salvation from sin cost God the blood of "His only begotten Son" (John 3:16 NKJV), a pretty hefty price tag by anyone's standards. And as many dear martyred believers have discovered, following Jesus could cost us our very <u>lives</u>.

lives
Matthew 10:39

angels
2 Thessalonians
1:7–10

You Should Have Seen the One That Got Away

MATTHEW 13:47–50 *"Again, the kingdom of heaven is like a dragnet that was cast into the sea and gathered some of every kind, which, when it was full, they drew to shore; and they sat down and gathered the good into vessels, but threw the bad away. So it will be at the end of the age. The angels will come forth, separate the wicked from among the just, and cast them into the furnace of fire. There will be wailing and gnashing of teeth." (NKJV)*

The second to last parable, sometimes referred to as the parable of the dragnet, sounds a familiar ring—that of the parable involving the wheat and tares. Here, Jesus compares the kingdom of heaven to a net, described as "the largest kind of net, weighted below and with corks on top, sweeping perhaps a half mile of water."[9]

Due to the sheer size of the net, fishermen used it to collect "some of every kind" (Matthew 13:47 NKJV). Obviously, such an immense collection could not be emptied and sorted in the boat, so the men would draw the net to shore and sort the fish there. Good, edible, salable fish were gathered into vessels to be taken to market; unsuitable fish were cast back into the sea.

Jesus used this familiar operation on the shores of the Sea of Galilee to picture for his disciples the judgment coming at the end of the age.

As King of the future judgment, Jesus described a scene where his <u>angels</u> will separate the wicked from the righteous. They will cast the wicked into "the furnace of fire" where they will weep tears of fury toward God and gnash their teeth in their hatred of God. The angels will invite the righteous into his kingdom where they will enjoy his presence forever.

A. W. Tozer

The vague and **tenuous** hope that God is too kind to punish the ungodly has become a deadly **opiate** for the consciences of millions. It hushes their fears and allows them to practice all pleasant forms of iniquity while death draws every day nearer and the command to repent goes unheeded.[10]

When Yes Means No and No Means Yes

MATTHEW 13:51–52 *Jesus said to them, "Have you understood all these things?" They said to Him, "Yes, Lord." Then He said to them, "Therefore every scribe instructed concerning the kingdom of heaven is like a householder who brings out of his treasure things new and old." (NKJV)*

Matthew gave us no sense of the time involved in Jesus's telling of these parables. When you consider the probability that Matthew did not record a word-for-word transcript of each parable and that Jesus took the time to answer the disciples' questions and explain some of the parables, well, you can see that he must have had a long, drawn-out, and emotionally exhausting day.

Jesus concluded by asking a simple and appropriate question, "Have you understood all these things?" The disciples nodded and said, "Yes." But they didn't have a clue what "all these things" meant. They continued to believe that Jesus would overthrow the Romans, establish his kingdom there and then, assume his place on his eternal throne, and that they would serve in cushy cabinet positions in his new administration.

Jesus knew of their ignorance. He patiently told them that if they truly understood "all these things," they would understand Jesus's shift in focus. Jesus is moving away from the "old" teaching about his kingdom toward the "new" teaching about the church (Matthew 16:18; 18:17), and about his impending death, burial, and resurrection. Sadly, since his offer of a kingdom had been rejected, Jesus was now going to a certain death. His earthly kingdom would now be postponed. This disciples would become hated and hunted men.

Hometown Hero?

MATTHEW 13:53–58 *Now it came to pass, when Jesus had finished these parables, that He departed from there. When He had come to His own country, He taught them in their synagogue, so that they were astonished and said, "Where did this Man get this wisdom and these mighty works? Is this not the carpenter's son? Is not His mother called Mary? And His brothers James, Joses, Simon, and Judas? And His sisters, are they not all with us? Where then did this Man get all these things?" So they were offended at Him. But Jesus said to them, "A prophet is not without honor except in his own country and in his own house." Now He did not do many mighty works there because of their unbelief. (NKJV)*

visit
Luke 4:16–29

Going back to Nazareth was a gutsy move. In his earlier <u>visit</u>, the townspeople, comprising Jesus's childhood friends and perhaps even family members, tried to throw him over a cliff. In this second and last visit to Nazareth, a similar though less violent rejection occurred. They recalled that Jesus was a common carpenter's son, pointed out that Jesus's brothers and sisters still lived in their village, and forced Jesus to concede that he would receive no honor in his boyhood hometown.

There were consequences for their unbelief: "He did not do many mighty works there because of their unbelief" (Matthew 13:58 NKJV). Jesus left Nazareth and would never return to his boyhood hometown again.

Chapter Wrap-Up

- After the religious leaders made their formal rejection of Jesus as their Messiah, he began to teach his disciples using parables. (Matthew 13:1–3)

- Isaiah predicted that when the Messiah came, he would teach in parables. (Isaiah 6:9–10)

- Jesus told his disciples that he was going to reveal to them the mysteries of the kingdom of heaven, something that he was not going to teach the multitudes. (Matthew 13:11)

- Jesus's first parable illustrated how a person's response to the truth when it is preached reveals the true condition of the soil of his or her heart. (Matthew 13:18–23)

- Jesus taught that true followers of Christ and false followers would exist side by side until the judgment to come at the end of the age. (Matthew 13:37–39)

- Jesus compared the salvation he offers to a hidden treasure and a pearl of great price. (Matthew 13:44–46)

- Jesus was sadly rejected when he returned to his boyhood home. (Matthew 13:54–58)

Study Questions

1. What is a parable?

2. What is the point of the parable of the farmer and his seed?

3. What happens when truth is rejected or ignored?

4. What is the lesson to be learned in the parables about the mustard seed and yeast?

5. How did Jesus explain the parable of the wheat and the tares?

6. In Jesus's visit to his hometown of Nazareth, how did his neighbors and acquaintances demonstrate their rejection of him? How did this affect what he could or could not do for them?

Matthew 14: Day in the Life

Let's Get Started

Dead. Such an ominous word. Such finality. Such emptiness, hopelessness, despair. The end of dreams.

Have you ever faced the loss of a loved one? If so, how did you feel when you first received word of your friend's or family member's passing? How long did you grieve? Do you grieve still? Often the overwhelming sense of loss never ends.

We apologize if we have resurrected painful memories. But the remembrance of our feelings puts us in the proper frame of mind to understand something of what Jesus must have felt when he received the word about his cousin, close friend, forerunner, comrade, and colleague—and our old friend—John the Baptizer. We don't know for sure who first broke the news to Jesus that John was dead. But we do know that Jesus was so shaken by this news that he "departed from there by boat to a deserted place" (Matthew 14:13 NKJV). Thus began a dark day in the life of Jesus.

We recently read of a prominent entertainer who checked herself into a hospital, having suffered a "mental, emotional, and physical" breakdown, triggered by seeing a mind-numbing 247 messages on her pager. As mind-boggling as that may seem, with all due respect, she faced nothing in comparison to what Jesus faced daily. You'll see what we mean as we consider one day in the life of this man in demand.

Enemy of the State

Stay tuned for infidelity, incest, a political witch hunt, intrigue, jealousy, spiteful rage, murderous hate, lewdness, lust, and cold-hearted brutality.

Some have rightly referred to the following passage as one of the most tragic and yet triumphant texts in God's Word. Buried within its verses is a life lesson you and I should never forget.

go to

Archelaus
Matthew 2:22

Philip
Luke 3:1

Caesarea Philippi
Matthew 16:13

Herod
Luke 3:1

tetrarch
chief governor

egregious
conspicuously bad

Nabateans
people living in the
southern part of
modern-day Jordan

Like Father, Like Sons

MATTHEW 14:1–2 *At that time Herod the tetrarch heard the report about Jesus and said to his servants, "This is John the Baptist; he is risen from the dead, and therefore these powers are at work in him."* (NKJV)

Herod the **tetrarch** was not having a good day. As the waves of news generated by Jesus flowed through the land, Herod Antipas heard the reports of this miracle man. Guilt over a scandal of massive proportions poisoned Herod's soul and impaired his powers of reason to the point where he mistakenly feared that Jesus was his old nemesis, John the Baptist, raised from the dead. Herod quaked in his boots—and for good reason.

You might remember that upon the death of Herod the Great, the murderous maniac who slew the babies in Matthew 2, his kingdom was divided among his three sons. Archelaus ruled Judea, Samaria, and Idumea; Herod Philip II reigned over the regions north of Galilee, including Caesarea Philippi; and Herod Antipas terrorized Galilee and Perea (see map of Israel, Appendix A).

The Tabloid Tetrarch

MATTHEW 14:3–5 *For Herod had laid hold of John and bound him, and put him in prison for the sake of Herodias, his brother Philip's wife. Because John had said to him, "It is not lawful for you to have her." And although he wanted to put him to death, he feared the multitude, because they counted him as a prophet.* (NKJV)

Time for a flashback. In Matthew 4:12 Jesus returned to Galilee because he "heard that John had been put in prison" (NKJV). Matthew gave us no details then; he merely stated the fact of John's imprisonment. "Why would a man of his character and caliber be imprisoned?" you might wonder. Matthew waited until the account of the baptizer's **egregious** execution to fill in the blanks.

It seems that Herod Antipas's brother Philip had a beautiful wife by the name of Herodias. While on a visit to Rome, Antipas wooed her and seduced her away from her husband. There was one complication. In order to achieve peace with the **Nabateans**, Herod Antipas had married the daughter of their king to seal a political and military alliance. But it was a marriage of convenience, not of love, nor even of lust. In order to marry Herodias, he had to divorce his current wife. But wait—it gets worse.

Herodias was the daughter of Aristobulus, another son of Herod the Great and brother to both Philip and Antipas. When Philip married Herodias, he actually wedded his own niece. Herod Antipas only compounded the incest by seducing her away from her husband and taking her to live with him as his own wife.[1]

John the Baptist, fiery prophet that he was, could not stomach such low-down treachery coming from such high places. So he shook his index finger in Herod's face, as it were, and condemned him as a breaker of God's law. No doubt John had Leviticus 18:16 in mind as the basis of his confrontation: "You shall not uncover the nakedness of your brother's wife; it is your brother's nakedness" (NKJV).

Herod and his illegitimate wife, Herodias, became enraged. Herod sought to have the baptizer executed on the spot, but John had too great a following. So he had him <u>imprisoned</u> instead. Meanwhile Herodias schemed and plotted. She proved herself a most cunning adversary, second in the Bible, perhaps, only to the wildly wicked <u>Jezebel</u>.

We have the Jewish historian Josephus to thank for the specific information concerning the place of John the Baptist's imprisonment and death.[2] John was brought in chains to Machaerus, a plush palace complete with its own underground dungeon, rebuilt and refurbished by—who else!—Herod the Great, and inherited by Herod Antipas. Located some fifteen miles southeast of the mouth of the Jordan, the palace sat nestled in the wild and desolate hills overlooking the Dead Sea. Antipas regarded Machaerus, conveniently located in the direction of Nabatea, as strategically important.[3]

Because of its proximity to Arabia, Herod the Great buttressed the place with the strongest fortifications, making it virtually unassailable. Herod's palace—including rooms, a huge courtyard, an elaborate bath, fragments of mosaics, along with evidences of its fortifications—have been excavated.

Machaerus was a study in contrasts. As plush and palatial as was Herod's hideaway, so dark and dank was John's dungeon. He lan-

imprisoned
Matthew 4:12

Jezebel
1 Kings 18:4

guished for a year or more, isolated in the underground pit where he battled <u>doubts</u> and awaited his tragic end.[4]

Did it ever occur to you that for the first half of Jesus's ministry, he carried the relentless anguish he must have felt over the suffering that his close friend and forerunner had to endure? Did you realize that for the last half of Jesus's ministry, he felt the vacuum of soul created by the untimely and unwarranted demise of this great man? No matter how deeply it runs, how torturous it feels, Jesus understands the pain of any of us who, like him, carry the grief of the loss of a loved one.

what others say

Joni Eareckson Tada

There are times when we want to talk to God...but somehow can't manage it. The hurt goes too deep. Fear locks our thoughts. Confusion scatters our words. Depression grips our emotions.

I'm so glad God can read my heart and understand what's going on even when I am handicapped for words. As it says in Hebrews 4:13, "Nothing . . . is hidden from God's sight. Everything is uncovered and laid bare before the eyes of him to whom we must give account."

Words are not always necessary. When we are in such trouble that we can't even find words—when we can only look toward heaven and groan in our spirit—isn't it good to remember that God knows exactly what's happening? The faintest whisper in our hearts is known to God.[5]

key point

John the Baptist was seized, chained, dumped into a dungeon, and ultimately was beheaded. John the Baptist faithfully fulfilled God's will *for* his life, and paid for his faithfulness *with* his life. If Jesus permitted John to suffer so, why should we expect or demand anything better?

what others say

Richard W. DeHaan

We should anticipate times of hardship, and mentally and spiritually prepare ourselves to meet them. When they occur, it doesn't mean God has forgotten us, or that He no longer loves us. This kind of reaction can only lead to spiritual paralysis and defeat. By realistically viewing ourselves in relation to the world, we won't be taken by surprise.[6]

doubts
Matthew 11:2–3

Surprise Party

MATTHEW 14:6–12 *But when Herod's birthday was celebrated, the daughter of Herodias danced before them and pleased Herod. Therefore he promised with an oath to give her whatever she might ask. So she, having been prompted by her mother, said, "Give me John the Baptist's head here on a platter." And the king was sorry; nevertheless, because of the oaths and because of those who sat with him, he commanded it to be given to her. So he sent and had John beheaded in prison. And his head was brought on a platter and given to the girl, and she brought it to her mother. Then his disciples came and took away the body and buried it, and went and told Jesus.* (NKJV)

When it comes to evil cunning, diabolical treachery, hateful vindictiveness, and unabashed vileness, Herodias is in a class all her own. From the moment John the Baptist confronted her illegitimate husband about their illicit union, Herodias plotted, watched, and waited until just the right moment. On Herod Antipas's birthday the right moment arrived for her to spring her trap.

This mother involved her own daughter by persuading her to dance lewdly and seductively before her stepfather. With the light of his mind dimmed by drunkenness and ravaged by lustful desire, Herod foolishly promised his stepdaughter anything she wanted, up to half of his kingdom. He had jewels, money, and land in abundance. But she wasn't impressed.

The irony of Herod's dilemma should not be missed. He frustrated his wife by his weakness when he imprisoned rather than executed John because "he feared the multitude" (Matthew 14:5 NKJV). Herodias seized upon this cowardly component of his character and used it to her advantage. Using her own daughter to work Herod up into a frenzy, she manipulated him into making a pompous promise in front of a palace full of people.

Although the very thought of John terrorized him, Herod did not want to kill him. But he was trapped. He signed the order to execute. Why? "Because of the oaths and because of those who sat with him" (Matthew 14:9 NKJV). Hate, the volcanic lust for revenge, drives people to do bizarre things. It wasn't enough for Herodias to destroy her nemesis. She added her own perverted relish to the dastardly deed. She instructed her daughter to demand that John's head be presented on a platter, or better translated "charger."[7] Writes one commentator: "Fancy must be gratified; it must be given her in a charger, served up in blood, as a dish of meat at the feast or sauce to all the other dishes; it is reserved for the third course, to come up with the rarities,"[8] thus truly making Herod's birthday feast a meal of the macabre.

what others say

J. Oswald Sanders

John's courageous preaching earned for him the malice of Herod's wife, and issued in the gory but glorious spectacle of his head being presented to Herodias' daughter on a plate. But even death could not silence his convicting voice. When the **craven** Herod heard of the miracles and growing popularity of Jesus, he said: "John the Baptist whom I beheaded is risen from the dead."[9]

John F. MacArthur Jr.

Herod's parties were legendary during New Testament times. Noted for their gluttony, excessive drinking, erotic dancing, sexual orgies, and indulgences of any and every kind imaginable, the phrase "Herod's Birthday" became a cliché for any such shameful gathering.[10]

A Break in the Action

MATTHEW 14:13a *When Jesus heard it, He departed from there by boat to a deserted place by Himself.* (NKJV)

Did you get that? Do me a favor and read the verse above one more time.

There's a choice bit of insight into Jesus's physical and emotional makeup, as well as our own, that ought not be missed: Upon hearing of the demise of his cousin, compatriot, and friend, Jesus "departed . . . to a deserted place by Himself." Mark 6:31 quotes Jesus as saying to his disciples, "Come aside by yourselves to a deserted place and rest a while" (NKJV). The wording suggests that Jesus and the disciples withdrew from the press of the people, found a spot isolated from public view, spent some time together ("come with Me") and then separated for a time of rest and reflection, each man to himself ("by yourselves").

Some commentators suggest that Jesus left the area for fear of meeting the same fate as John.[11] This negates the fact that John showed no fear of Herod; surely Jesus did not fear him either. Keep in mind that Jesus knew he was within months of his crucifixion. He had the timetable for his departure clearly in mind. At the right time, he would travel southward to Jerusalem and lay down his life on the cross. <u>Herod</u> would be a bit player in the overall drama, true. But not yet.

Keep in mind these pertinent facts: Jesus had just received word that his close relative and friend had been executed. The disciples had just <u>returned</u> from an intense time of ministry. The demands of the people pressing in upon them were overwhelming. Jesus bid his disciples to retreat to a private place both for a personal and small group remembrance (of John), reflection (of their ministry just concluded), and most importantly, rest (from the clamor of the crowds).

Read through all four Gospels and note how many times and when Jesus sought privacy so that he could be alone with his disciples or alone with his Father. At specific times in his ministry Jesus just said no to the demands around him. Whenever he pulled back from his punishing schedule, the world didn't stop spinning, planets didn't careen out of control, and life did go on pretty much as usual.

If Jesus needed to take some time off every once in a while to maintain his physical, mental, emotional, and spiritual stability, how much more must we do the same? There's a reason God designed the **Sabbath** to be a day of rest. While we understand that we are no longer bound by Old Testament Jewish Law, nevertheless, the principle behind the Sabbath is a valid one. People need rest.

go to

Herod
Luke 23:7–12

returned
Luke 9:10

Sabbath
the seventh day;
Saturday

something to ponder

what others say

Henry Cloud and John Townsend

Many Christians fear that setting and keeping limits signals rebellion, or disobedience. In religious circles you'll often hear statements such as, "Your unwillingness to go along with our program shows an unresponsive heart." Because of this myth, countless individuals remain trapped in endless activities of no genuine spiritual and emotional value. The truth is life-changing: a lack of boundaries is often a sign of disobedience. People who have shaky limits are often compliant on the outside, but rebellious and resentful on the inside. They would like to be able to say no, but are afraid.[12]

Following Along

MATTHEW 14:13b–14 *But when the multitudes heard it, they followed Him on foot from the cities. And when Jesus went out He saw a great multitude; and He was moved with compassion for them, and healed their sick.* (NKJV)

The people didn't care that Jesus wanted to rest. They still followed him. It is important to note an observation ignored by Matthew but recorded by Luke. After resting a bit with his disciples, Jesus got right back into it. He "spoke to them about the kingdom of God, and healed those who had need of healing" (Luke 9:11 NKJV).

Here's Jesus's day so far. Jesus awoke to the devastating news of his cousin's tragic death. He withdrew to a solitary place for refreshment and reflection. He debriefed his disciples about their recently concluded mission trip, and comforted and encouraged them in the wake of John's execution. He taught a crowd and healed all of the sick who had sought him out. But he still wasn't finished. Even though the sun was starting to set, Jesus had much to do before he could sleep.

A Feast Fit for a King

MATTHEW 14:15–21 *When it was evening, His disciples came to Him, saying, "This is a deserted place, and the hour is already late. Send the multitudes away, that they may go into the villages and buy themselves food." But Jesus said to them, "They do not need to go away. You give them something to eat." And they said to Him, "We have here only five loaves and two fish." He said, "Bring them here to Me." Then He commanded the multitudes to sit down on the grass. And He took the five loaves and the two fish, and looking up to heaven, He blessed and broke and gave the loaves to the disciples; and the disciples gave to the multitudes. So they all ate and were filled, and they took up twelve baskets full of the fragments that remained. Now those who had eaten were about five thousand men, besides women and children.* (NKJV)

Welcome to the only one of Jesus's miracles recorded in all four Gospels. This fact alone tells us something of its significance. The sheer power and majesty of this miracle afforded it a place of prominence in each of the Gospel accounts.

Matthew's account depicts Jesus as the compassionate King who provided for his subjects. <u>Mark</u> emphasizes an exhausted Jesus who despite his fatigue serves those around him who are in need. <u>Luke</u>'s bare-bones account of this miracle gives us the feel of a very *human* Jesus presiding over a very human family meal. In the aftermath of this landmark miracle, John quotes Jesus as applying *God's* unique <u>name</u> to himself when he declares, "I am the bread of life" (John 6:35 NKJV). When we blend or **harmonize** the four accounts,[14] five stunning revelations about the character of Jesus and the nature of miracles emerge.

First, Jesus was a man of <u>compassion</u>. He saw people as shepherd-less sheep. Despite the fact that his world had just been rocked by the loss of his cousin, Jesus focused on the needs of the people by teaching them, healing them, and providing food for them.

Second, Jesus was ever on the lookout for "<u>teachable</u> moments." John gives us this insight: "Jesus lifted up His eyes, and seeing a great multitude coming toward Him, He said to Philip, 'Where shall we buy bread, that these may eat?' But this He said to test him, for He Himself knew what He would do" (John 6:5–6 NKJV). The master teacher set up an impossible scenario by asking the question, forced the disciples to face the impossibility of the situation, led them to a point of curious despair, and set the scene for this most impressive miracle.

Third, Jesus performed an undeniable miracle that marked him as infinitely more than the firstborn son of Mary; Jesus is the Son of God. Note that this miracle was done in the open, before a huge crowd of people. The men in the crowd <u>numbered</u> some five thousand, and this crowd had gathered near the time of **Passover**, meaning that it consisted primarily of families soon to be en route to

go to

Mark
Mark 6:32–44

Luke
Luke 9:10–17

name
Exodus 3:14

compassion
Mark 6:34

teachable
John 6:6

numbered
Matthew 14:21

Passover
John 6:4

harmonize
arrange the four Gospels into one chronological account

Passover
Jewish holy day for which families made pilgrimages to Jerusalem

loaves
Matthew 14:17

small
John 6:9

meet
James 1:27

Moses
Exodus 32:32

Peter
Matthew 26:75

Paul
2 Corinthians 12:7–9

healings
John 6:2

king
John 6:15

food
John 6:26

God
John 6:41–42

Jerusalem.[15] We can safely conclude, therefore, that Jesus used five small barley <u>loaves</u> (made of flour and water, about as thick as your thumb) and two <u>small</u> fish to feed in excess of twenty to twenty-five thousand people.

Fourth, Jesus involved his followers in meeting the needs of the people. Jesus could have turned stones into bread. Instead, he chose to use only that which was freely provided to him—a small boy's lunch. Jesus acted true to form in that even today he continues to <u>meet</u> the needs of people through the hearts and hands of his people.

Fifth, Jesus did with the loaves and fishes what he often does with our lives—he blessed and broke them. Even though the five loaves and two fishes were totally inadequate to meet the needs of this vast throng, Jesus took that which was offered, blessed it, broke it, and used it.

Jesus created food on the spot, something only God can do, making this meal a feast fit for the King of kings.

Jesus took the loaves and fishes in the form they were presented and broke them into a usable form. When we offer our lives to him, he often must break us of—our pride, selfishness, insensitivity, self-sufficiency, abrasiveness—those blindspots of our character that limit God's ability to use us to our full potential. The good news is that we come out of the breaking process better people. The bad news is that God often uses pain to produce the breaking. We are reminded both by direct statement (Romans 5:3–5; 8:28–29; James 1:2–4; 1 Peter 1:6–7) and indirect example (<u>Moses</u>, <u>Peter</u>, <u>Paul</u>) that God uses broken people to touch the lives of broken people.

<u>John's Aside</u>

John adds an epilogue to this miracle in his Gospel: "From that time many of His disciples went back and walked with Him no more" (John 6:66 NKJV). Some people followed Jesus only because of the <u>healings</u> he performed. Others sought freedom from the oppression of Rome and viewed Jesus as a <u>king</u> of convenience rather than a King who commanded their lives. A third group saw Jesus as the embodiment of a meals-on-wheels program, providing free <u>food</u> for those who sought it.

Once Jesus pointed out who he was (Almighty <u>God</u>), why he came (to save people <u>eternally</u> rather than politically), and what it cost to follow him (belief to the point of life commitment), they abandoned him in droves.

eternally
John 6:40

Man Overboard

MATTHEW 14:22–33 *Immediately Jesus made His disciples get into the boat and go before Him to the other side, while He sent the multitudes away. And when He had sent the multitudes away, He went up on the mountain by Himself to pray. Now when evening came, He was alone there. But the boat was now in the middle of the sea, tossed by the waves, for the wind was contrary. Now in the fourth watch of the night Jesus went to them, walking on the sea. And when the disciples saw Him walking on the sea, they were troubled, saying, "It is a ghost!" and they cried out for fear. But immediately Jesus spoke to them, saying, "Be of good cheer! It is I; do not be afraid." And Peter answered Him and said, "Lord, if it is You, command me to come to You on the water." So He said, "Come." And when Peter had come down out of the boat, he walked on the water to go to Jesus. But when he saw that the wind was boisterous, he was afraid; and beginning to sink he cried out, saying, "Lord, save me!" And immediately Jesus stretched out His hand and caught him, and said to him, "O you of little faith, why did you doubt?" And when they got into the boat, the wind ceased. Then those who were in the boat came and worshiped Him, saying, "Truly You are the Son of God." (NKJV)*

Imagine twelve husky men huddled together, quaking in fear, in a twenty-six-foot-long hand-crafted wooden boat.[16] The evening's darkness had long since enveloped the sea. It was between 3:00 and 6:00 a.m. They were exhausted from an unbelievably busy day.

As they headed to that twilight zone known as "the other side of the sea," they were worried. The winds started churning. They looked back from where they had just come. Twelve grown men pointed in fear and screamed in unison: "It's a ghost!"

When Jesus calmed them down and identified himself as their master and friend and not a menace or foe, guess who decided to seize center stage and offer to walk out to him? Our old friend with the foot-shaped mouth, Peter. When he took his eyes off Jesus, Peter began to sink and cried out for Jesus to save him. Jesus hoisted him out of the deep and carried him to the boat. The winds died down, their boat stopped bobbing, and once again all was right with their world.

Staring at Jesus in shocked amazement, the disciples declared with one voice, "Truly You are the Son of God." What a blazing burst of insight! Forgive our cynicism, but they had been living with him for over—what?—a year and a half to two years? Yet, to our own shame, we are compelled to confess that sometimes we face life's challenges as though we have forgotten that Jesus is the Son of God. No wonder Jesus said to them, and sometimes must say to us, "O you of little faith, why did you doubt?" (Matthew 14:31 NKJV).

The disciples' lack of faith has now become a common theme, almost a subtext running throughout the Gospels. If the disciples' faith faltered on occasion, we should not be too shocked when our faith falters as well.

We've Only Just Begun

MATTHEW 14:34–36 *When they had crossed over, they came to the land of Gennesaret. And when the men of that place recognized Him, they sent out into all that surrounding region, brought to Him all who were sick, and begged Him that they might only touch the hem of His garment. And as many as touched it were made perfectly well. (NKJV)*

Jesus's next day almost looks like a carbon copy of the previous one. No sooner had Jesus and the disciples stepped onto the shore, but the throngs came, bringing their sick in tow. As he looked out over this newly gathered crowd, Jesus knew that this day had only just begun.

Chapter Wrap-Up

- Herod Antipas heard the reports about Jesus and thought it was John the Baptist raised from the dead. (Matthew 14:1–2)

- Herod panicked because earlier he had imprisoned John for confronting him about his illicit affair with his brother Philip's wife. (Matthew 14:3)

- During one of his lavish parties, Herod offered to his stepdaughter anything she wanted, up to half of his kingdom. At the behest of her mother, she requested John's head on a platter. (Matthew 14:8)

- When Jesus heard about the death of John the Baptist, he withdrew to a private place to mourn his loss. (Matthew 14:13)

- Jesus miraculously fed over five thousand men, plus their wives and children. (Matthew 14:21)

- Jesus scared the disciples half out of their wits when he walked on the water to join them in a boat halfway across the Sea of Galilee. (Matthew 14:26)

- Jesus healed all who came to him on the other side of the sea. (Matthew 14:34–36)

Study Questions

1. What did you learn about Herod Antipas and his family?

2. What action did Jesus take after John's death before he faced another day of ministry?

3. What can we learn from his example?

4. What differences do the four Gospels include in their accounts of the feeding of the five thousand?

5. What are their similarities in reporting this same miracle?

6. What revelation dawned on the disciples after Jesus showed his power over nature?

7. What should be our response when we observe Christ's power in our lives?

Matthew 15: Lessons on Legalism

Chapter Highlights:
- **You Are What You Eat?**
- **A Man with a Mission**
- **A Simple Case of Déjà Vu?**

Let's Get Started

Welcome to what is in our humble opinion the toughest chapter in Matthew to interpret and understand. The scene takes place some time after Jesus and his men landed on the shore of <u>Gennesaret</u> and were besieged by throngs of needy people.

As the reports of the wild goings-on in Galilee flowed south and then up to Jerusalem, some of the Pharisees decided to exercise their self-righteous and self-serving concern and travel up north to see just what in fact was going on. They were there, ready, waiting, and loaded for bear even before Jesus set foot upon the shore.

Gennesaret
Matthew 14:34

unclean
prohibited from
Jewish worship
ceremony

You Are What You Eat?

MATTHEW 15:1–2 *Then the scribes and Pharisees who were from Jerusalem came to Jesus, saying, "Why do Your disciples transgress the tradition of the elders? For they do not wash their hands when they eat bread." (NKJV)*

The "scribes" were right about one thing. Old Testament Law did have something to say about people ceremonially washing themselves before they ate. Leviticus 22:6 says, "The person who has touched any such thing [referring to things mentioned in verse 5] shall be **unclean** until evening, and shall not eat the holy offerings unless he washes his body with water" (NKJV). But (and it's a great big *but*), to understand that verse we must first ask, "To whom was that instruction given?"

Fortunately, the answer is obvious. The only people who were commanded to ceremonially cleanse themselves before they ate were "of the descendants of Aaron" (Leviticus 22:4 NKJV); that is, priests. Get the point? The Pharisees were not quoting Old Testament Law. They were not faulting the disciples for breaking a commandment of God. They couldn't have cared less about God. By their own admission, they were trying to intimidate the disciples into living in obe-

go to

captivity
2 Kings 24:15

extra-biblical
outside of, or not
contained in, the
Bible

captivity
seventy years of
exile and slavery
beginning in 586 BC

dience to "the tradition of the elders" (Matthew 15:2 NKJV). They were judging, and condemning, them by a standard higher than God's standard, namely, their own traditions.

These man-made traditions formed a body of **extra-biblical** laws that existed in oral form since the time of the Babylonian **captivity**. They weren't formally written down until AD 220, long after Christ had left the scene. This explains why Jesus immediately faulted the Pharisees with this stinging statement: "Why do you also transgress the *commandment* of God because of your tradition?" (Matthew 15:3 NKJV, emphasis mine). The parameters of the debate had now been set—the traditions of men versus the commands of God.

This latest confrontation between Jesus and the religious leaders raises these questions: Do we hold people to a standard higher than God does? Do we want the approval of others more than the approval of God? for example, how many conservative congregations have been torn asunder by divisive arguments over what constitutes "godly" versus "ungodly" music in their worship services? And how many parents have wondered, "What will the people at church think of me if I let my teen pierce his ear or tattoo her ankle?" When we judge the spiritual conditions of people by our preferences or "traditions," we are guilty of the same sin as the Pharisees—legalism. We are the ones whose spiritual vitality is in doubt.

Tradition! Tradition!

MATTHEW 15:3 *He answered and said to them, "Why do you also transgress the commandment of God because of your tradition? (NKJV)*

Let's distinguish between two extremely important terms essential to our understanding of this dramatic dialogue between Jesus and the Pharisees:

1. *Commandment:* A command or commandment of God is by its nature God-given, absolute, binding, not subject to debate, non-negotiable.

2. *Tradition:* Unlike a command of God, a tradition is man-made, and therefore, at least in theory, nonbinding, of limited authority, subject to much debate, and completely negotiable if not thoroughly "ignorable."

Can you see what the Pharisees had done? They pulled off a major-league flip-flop. They treated the commandments of God as though they were traditions—man-made, of limited authority, debatable, negotiable, and "ignorable"—and regarded their traditions as though they were commands of God. Now that's a neat trick if you can get away with it. Until Jesus came along, they did.

The Heart of the Matter

MATTHEW 15:4–9 *For God commanded, saying, 'Honor your father and your mother'; and, 'He who curses father or mother, let him be put to death.' But you say, 'Whoever says to his father or mother, "Whatever profit you might have received from me is a gift to God"—then he need not honor his father or mother.' Thus you have made the commandment of God of no effect by your tradition. Hypocrites! Well did Isaiah prophesy about you, saying:*
> *'These people draw near to Me with their mouth,*
> *And honor Me with their lips,*
> *But their heart is far from Me.*
> *And in vain they worship Me,*
> *Teaching as doctrines the commandments of men.'" (NKJV)*

Jesus was never content to teach in the abstract. He anchored his points with real-life examples. He chose a doozy for this debate.

honor
Exodus 20:12

corban
Mark 7:11

break
Numbers 30:2

encouraged
Romans 1:32

Old Testament Law required sons and daughters to <u>honor</u> their parents. Among other things, this command required grown children to provide for the material needs of their aging parents. The Pharisees, however, found a clever loophole to get around this requirement. It all centered on the Hebrew word *corban*.

Corban literally means "given to God." When an individual vowed to dedicate his money or material possessions to God, thus limiting its use to only sacred purposes, this act of dedication was called "corban." If, for example, a son was personally greedy or became angry with his parents for some reason, he could simply declare his money and property "corban." Since Old Testament Law clearly states that one must never <u>break</u> a vow made to God, that person's money could not be tapped as a resource of financial assistance for his parents. Ebenezer Scrooge would have been pleased by this spiritual sleight of hand.

Jesus, master of the moment that he was, turned the tables on the Pharisees. These guys, so quick to judge Jesus, stood in direct defiance of a clear command of God and couldn't care less. These religious leaders, who not only broke God's law but also <u>encouraged</u> their followers to do the same, stood condemned by the very words of their prized prophet, Isaiah.

Isaiah could have been a cardiac care specialist. In Isaiah 29:13, he perfectly predicted the heart condition of the nation Jesus came to save.

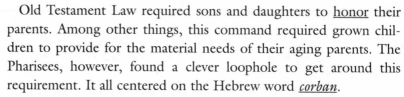

what others say

Lloyd John Ogilvie

Jesus wants us to understand how pride twists and distorts our capacity of self-scrutiny. . . . It's possible to delude ourselves into thinking that we are right with God because of our own accomplishments and goodness.[2]

Was James, our Lord's half brother, thinking of this incident when he confronted those who refused to meet the needs of their loved ones within the framework of the family as having "denied the faith and . . . worse than an unbeliever" (1 Timothy 5:8 NKJV)? James defines "pure" religion as looking after "orphans and widows in their trouble" (James 1:27 NKJV).

Verbal Light Saber

MATTHEW 15:10–12 *When He had called the multitude to Himself, He said to them, "Hear and understand: Not what goes into the mouth defiles a man; but what comes out of the mouth, this defiles a man." Then His disciples came and said to Him, "Do You know that the Pharisees were offended when they heard this saying?" (NKJV)*

Like a laser beam of brilliant insight Jesus honed in on life's central issue. Jesus wasn't afraid to speak his mind in front of a crowd. Earlier he had been talking to the Pharisees. Now he talked about them. And wonder of wonders, they got angry! the disciples scratched their heads. This was no way to run a popular campaign. Didn't Jesus know the Pharisees were the most religiously righteous guys around? When the disciples got Jesus off to the side, they called him on it.

You Are What You Think

MATTHEW 15:13–20 *But He answered and said, "Every plant which My heavenly Father has not planted will be uprooted. Let them alone. They are blind leaders of the blind. And if the blind leads the blind, both will fall into a ditch." Then Peter answered and said to Him, "Explain this parable to us." So Jesus said, "Are you also still without understanding? Do you not yet understand that whatever enters the mouth goes into the stomach and is eliminated? But those things which proceed out of the mouth come from the heart, and they defile a man. For out of the heart proceed ~~evil thoughts, murders, adulteries, fornications, thefts, false witness, blasphemies.~~ These are the things which defile a man, but to eat with unwashed hands does not defile a man." (NKJV)*

As was now often his custom, Jesus used a parable to profess his point. Spokesman Peter wanted more. He asked for an explanation.

Jesus explained that a person could eat something that was not kosher, something that violated Old Testament dietary law, and the consequence was minimal. That person could submit to a ceremonial cleansing. The world of the Pharisees revolved around such trivial pursuits as outward handwashing to the total exclusion of the major pursuits of inward godly character—issues of ~~"evil~~ thoughts,

go to

notorious
Matthew 11:21

hunted
Luke 13:31

plotted
Matthew 12:14

murders, adulteries, fornications, thefts, false witness, blasphemies" (Matthew 15:19 NKJV). The chart below shows how far off they were.

Jesus left no doubt about where the Pharisees stood from a divine perspective. They would "be uprooted" (Matthew 15:13 NKJV). Such is what God thinks of legalistic hypocrites. May we never stumble into their camp.

Food for Thought

What the Pharisees Thought	What Jesus Taught
Narrow and nitpicky concern over matters of outward religious ritual	Wide-ranging concern over matters of inward personal purity
A fascination with food	A quest for character
Judged Jesus for what the disciples did (failed to wash their hands before eating)	Faulted the Pharisees for who they were (hard-hearted hypocrites)
Maximized the need to conform outwardly to man-made customs	Maximized the need to comply inwardly to God-given commands
Worried about defiling themselves ceremonially (short-term consequence)	Warned about those who corrupted themselves morally (long-term consequence)
Lives centered around the symbolism of the ceremony	Teaching centered around the substance of the soul

A Man with a Mission

MATTHEW 15:21 *Then Jesus went out from there and departed to the region of Tyre and Sidon. (NKJV)*

The "region of Tyre and Sidon" lies along the Mediterranean Sea well outside of Israel's borders. These two <u>notorious</u> coastal towns sit several miles beyond the jurisdiction of Herod Antipas, who <u>hunted</u> Jesus, well away from the Jewish religious leaders who <u>plotted</u> against him, and far from the view of the masses of needy people who relentlessly hounded him.

Jesus desperately needed to take a break. In Matthew 14 when

Jesus tried to rest, the crowds found him, followed him, and hounded him all the more. This time, Jesus didn't just leave town; he left the country! He and his men "departed" (Matthew 15:21 NKJV).

Matthew used this term when referring to Jesus's attempts to get away from it all, this time to an **unclean** urban environment up north to which his orthodox Jewish following would hate to travel. That's why Jesus made the journey—he needed a vacation. That's why Matthew and <u>Mark</u> record but one incident from this trip— Jesus didn't go there to minister to people; he went there to rest.

Mark
Mark 7:24–30

Greek
Mark 7:26

unclean
something an orthodox Jew should not touch

Canaan
land of ancestral enemies of the Jews[5]

mercy
undeserved grace

> what others say
>
> ### Richard A. Swenson, M.D.
>
> It is important to understand our emotional reserves. It is important to understand how much we have at the beginning of each day and which influences drain our emotions dry or recharge our batteries. It is important to learn what our limits are, and not to make further withdrawals if we are already maximally depleted. And it is important to respect these limits in others.[4]

Only a Mother's Love

MATTHEW 15:22–24 *And behold, a woman of **Canaan** came from that region and cried out to Him, saying, "Have mercy on me, O Lord, Son of David! My daughter is severely demon-possessed." But He answered her not a word. And His disciples came and urged Him, saying, "Send her away, for she cries out after us." But He answered and said, "I was not sent except to the lost sheep of the house of Israel." (NKJV)*

Jesus's treatment of this woman may sound harsh until we consider his circumstances. He was a man on a mission to the Jews. He no doubt lacked the emotional energy to deal with her. She was a <u>Greek</u>, born in Syria Phoenicia, probably a worshiper of pagan deities that were popular in that region.[6] With her background it is remarkable that she (1) recognized Jesus as her "Lord"; (2) understood that he was the "Son of David," a clear reference to his identity as the Jews' promised Messiah—something the Jewish leaders failed to understand; and (3) acknowledged that she did not deserve, and therefore did not demand, Jesus's healing touch upon her daughter. Instead, she pleaded for his **mercy**.

go to

mission
Matthew 10:6

Is This Any Way to Treat a Lady?

MATTHEW 15:25–28 *Then she came and worshiped Him, saying, "Lord, help me!" But He answered and said, "It is not good to take the children's bread and throw it to the little dogs." And she said, "Yes, Lord, yet even the little dogs eat the crumbs which fall from their masters' table." Then Jesus answered and said to her, "O woman, great is your faith! Let it be to you as you desire." And her daughter was healed from that very hour.* (NKJV)

While our inadequate English translations may not sound compassionate, trust me, Jesus was. "Children's" refers to the Jews, something the woman clearly understood given her identification of Jesus as the "Son of David." But "dogs" is a term of derision, is it not? Usually, but not in this case.

Jesus did not use the more common word for dogs—a term Jews often used to describe Gentiles as filthy, mangy, wild scavengers. Rather, he used an endearing term that referred to a loved family pet. When Jesus replied, "It is not good to take the children's [Jews'] bread and throw it to the little dogs [family pets]" (Matthew 15:26 NKJV), he reaffirmed his Jewish-centered <u>mission</u> and at the same time affirmed his loving care and concern for this non-Jewish woman.

From the Jewish perspective, she might have been an unlovely Gentile, untouchable; from Jesus's perspective, she was a lovable lady whose life he chose to touch. That's why the woman was not offended, but rather felt the freedom to exercise her faith by asking Jesus's permission to eat the "crumbs" that fell from the table—a request Jesus was more than happy to fulfill.

Jesus is never too tired to love the unlovely. Jesus not only healed her daughter but also responded, "O woman, great is your faith!" (Matthew 15:28 NKJV). And now you know why. This one pagan, Gentile woman had greater faith than all the Jewish religious leaders put together.

what others say

Charles H. Spurgeon

May the Holy Spirit, the Comforter, inspire the people of the Lord with fresh faith! . . . God is glorified when His servants trust Him implicitly. We cannot be too much of children with

> our heavenly Father. Our young ones ask no question about our will or our power, but having once received a promise from father, they rejoice in the prospect of its fulfillment, never doubting that it is sure as the sun. May many readers, whom I may never see, discover the duty and delight of such child-like trust in God.[7]

kill
John 5:18

kingdom
Matthew 13:11

anticipation
Luke 9:51

Savior
Luke 19:10

A Simple Case of Déjà Vu?

MATTHEW 15:29–31 *Jesus departed from there, skirted the Sea of Galilee, and went up on the mountain and sat down there. Then great multitudes came to Him, having with them the lame, blind, mute, maimed, and many others; and they laid them down at Jesus' feet, and He healed them. So the multitude marveled when they saw the mute speaking, the maimed made whole, the lame walking, and the blind seeing; and they glorified the God of Israel. (NKJV)*

As we might have expected, no sooner had Jesus returned to Galilee from his coastal vacation near Tyre and Sidon than he was besieged by "great multitudes" of sick people.

Is it my imagination, or does Jesus seem to invest more of his time and energy with Gentiles and less time with the Jews? There are good practical reasons for this not-so-subtle shift of emphasis:

1. The religious leaders now sought to <u>kill</u> him.

2. Having suddenly aborted his plan to establish his <u>kingdom</u>, he gradually altered his manner and message in <u>anticipation</u> of the Cross.

3. He slowly shifted his identity as King of the Jews to <u>Savior</u> of the world—a world that consisted of Jews and Gentiles. Even though Jesus faced a largely non-Jewish crowd, he healed them all, which led to this remarkable response: "And they [the thousands of Gentiles who saw Jesus that day] glorified the God of Israel" (Matthew 15:31 NKJV).

go to

healer
Isaiah 61:1

what others say

W. Phillip Keller

The profound prophetic predictions made in the Old Testament regarding the coming of Christ, cast Him in the role of a <u>healer</u>. He—"The Messiah," "The Anointed One of God," "The Comforter"—would come to bind up the brokenhearted; to mend the bruised; to restore the injured; to raise the sick; to bring healing to the hurt.[8]

What Have You Done for Me Lately?

MATTHEW 15:32–39 *Now Jesus called His disciples to Himself and said, "I have compassion on the multitude, because they have now continued with Me three days and have nothing to eat. And I do not want to send them away hungry, lest they faint on the way." Then His disciples said to Him, "Where could we get enough bread in the wilderness to fill such a great multitude?" Jesus said to them, "How many loaves do you have?" and they said, "Seven, and a few little fish." So He commanded the multitude to sit down on the ground. And He took the seven loaves and the fish and gave thanks, broke them and gave them to His disciples; and the disciples gave to the multitude. So they all ate and were filled, and they took up seven large baskets full of the fragments that were left. Now those who ate were four thousand men, besides women and children. And He sent away the multitude, got into the boat, and came to the region of Magdala. (NKJV)*

We recently watched Jesus create food for his followers as he fed five thousand people plus women and children with a small boy's sack lunch. So why did he repeat this miracle by feeding the four thousand?

Did Matthew get confused? Did he miscount the first time and need to correct himself here? Was it one of those cases of "déjà vu all over again"? Or did Jesus really feed two separate groups of first five then four thousand men on two separate occasions recorded in two separate but consecutive chapters?

Let's place the two stories side by side, compare and contrast them, and draw our conclusions from there. See the chart "Feeding Miracles Compared and Contrasted."

Feeding Miracles Compared and Contrasted

Feeding of the Five Thousand	Feeding of the Four Thousand
In the chronology of Jesus's ministry, this feeding happened first.	In the chronology of Jesus's ministry, this feeding happened second.
This feeding is mentioned by all four Gospel writers (Matthew 14:13–21; Mark 6:31–44; Luke 9:11–17; John 6:1–13).	This feeding is mentioned by only two Gospel writers (Matthew 15:32–39; Mark 8:1–10).
The people had not eaten all day (Mark 6:35).	The people had not eaten for up to three days (Matthew 15:32).
Jesus rested before teaching and feeding the crowd (Mark 6:31).	Jesus healed thousands for three days before feeding the crowd (Matthew 15:30).
Jesus looked upon the Jewish crowd with compassion (Matthew 14:14).	Jesus looked upon the Gentile crowd with compassion (Matthew 15:32).
The disciples had no idea how they were going to feed such a huge crowd (John 6:9).	The disciples still had no idea how they were going to feed such a huge crowd (Matthew 15:33).
Jesus tested the faith of his disciples (Matthew 14:16).	Jesus once again tested the faith of his disciples (Matthew 15:32).
Surprise! Surprise! The disciples failed the test (Matthew 14:17).	Surprise! Surprise! The disciples once again failed the test (Matthew 15:33).
Jesus started with five loaves and two small fish (Matthew 14:17).	Jesus started with seven loaves and a few small fish (Matthew 15:34).
Everyone ate and was satisfied (Matthew 14:20).	Everyone ate and was satisfied (Matthew 15:37).
The disciples filled twelve small wicker baskets[9] with the leftovers (Matthew 14:20).	The disciples filled seven large, hamper-type, man-sized baskets[10] with the leftovers (Matthew 15:37; Acts 9:25).

Clearly, the feeding of the five thousand and the feeding of the four thousand are similar miracles performed in front of two totally different groups of people in different settings in response to different circumstances for two different reasons. The five thousand men plus women and children Jesus fed were Jewish. Jesus broke bread with the Jews. Through that symbolic act, rich with cultural significance, Jesus expressed to his people his desire to enter into a relationship with them.

The four thousand were Gentiles. Here, Jesus expressed to the non-Jews of the world that he equally longed to enjoy reconciliation and establish a relationship with them. His emphasis was indeed shifting from presenting himself as the King of the Jews to the Savior of the world, a shift-of-emphasis that will become increasingly pronounced in the next chapter.

Chapter Wrap-Up

- Religious leaders traveled all the way from Jerusalem to confront Jesus about his disciples' failure to observe their man-made traditions. (Matthew 15:1–2)

- Jesus turned the tables on them and confronted them about their failure to obey a clear command of God. (Matthew 15:4–7)

- Jesus exposed the religious leaders for what they were—hypocrites. (Matthew 15:7)

- Jesus explained that he is interested in the inward character of the heart infinitely more than he is about holding to outward traditions. (Matthew 15:16–20)

- Jesus traveled out of the country and ministered to a Gentile woman's daughter who was demon-possessed. (Matthew 15:21–22)

- Jesus praised the Gentile woman as a woman of great faith. (Matthew 15:28)

- Just as Jesus miraculously fed a Jewish multitude in Matthew 14, he feeds a Gentile multitude in Matthew 15. (Matthew 15:32–39)

Study Questions

1. How did the Pharisees bypass God's command to honor fathers and mothers?

2. How did Isaiah describe this behavior?

3. Contrast what the Pharisees thought with what Jesus taught.

4. What is a similar danger for us today?

5. Why did Jesus answer the Canaanite woman the way that he did?

6. What is the subtle change of emphasis in Jesus's ministry between the feeding of the five thousand and the feeding of the four thousand?

7. What was so stunning about the feeding of the four thousand in contrast to the feeding of the five thousand?

Matthew 16:1–21: From That Time On

Chapter Highlights:
- A Whale of a Request
- Hypocrisy Exposed
- A Losing Proposition
- The Key Question
- Death Watch

Let's Get Started

The word *church* is without a doubt one of the most significant nouns in the Bible. From the Greek word *ékklesia*, this landmark term refers to us—that's right, you and me, and everyone else who loves Jesus Christ—as the "called-out" people of God.

In an instant of time, many exciting things happened to you and me when we invited Jesus into our lives. We were <u>forgiven</u> of our sins, indwelt by the Holy <u>Spirit</u>, blessed with more <u>blessings</u> than we can imagine, given <u>everything</u> we need to live a godly life, placed securely in Jesus's <u>hands</u>, and became a part of a wonderful worldwide community of very special people known throughout the New Testament as the <u>church</u>.

Is the church near and dear to God's heart? The New Testament writers referred to the church a heart-stopping seventy-nine times in seventeen of the twenty-seven New Testament books. The first mention of the word is in this chapter.

go to

forgiven
Romans 4:7

Spirit
Romans 8:9

blessings
Ephesians 1:3

everything
2 Peter 1:3

hands
John 10:28

church
1 Corinthians 12:27–28

Sadducees
Matthew 3:7

A Whale of a Request

The Pharisees seemed positively determined to negatively neutralize their own Messiah. What drove their hatred? What activated their insatiable appetite to search and destroy? Jealousy, because of Jesus's popularity? Greed, because Jesus's austere lifestyle seemed a silent rebuke of their showy way of life? Fear, because they sensed they were losing control of the people? Bitterness, because Jesus exposed their sin of hypocrisy? Yes, yes, and yes. And probably other reasons buried deep down in the dark crevasses of their sin-sick minds.

When you thought it couldn't get any worse, yet another sinister gathering of equally blind guides thrust themselves on center stage. Remember the <u>Sadducees</u> from chapter 3?

Ironically, the Sadducees were the bitter enemies of the Pharisees. An old adage unique to the Middle East that was as true in biblical times as it is today goes like this: The enemy of my enemy is my friend. Yet, since both the legalistic Pharisees and the rationalistic Sadducees regarded Jesus as Enemy #1, they decided to bury the hatchet, for the time being anyway, and to form a bizarre alliance, a conspiracy of hate, as they sought to do away with Jesus once and for all.

The Pharisees, Sadducees, Zealots, Essenes, and Herodians figured prominently in the life of Jesus, as the following chart shows.

Jewish Religious and Political Groups in New Testament Times

Who They Were	Where They Are First Mentioned	What They Did	What They Believed
Pharisees	Matthew 3:7	*Pharisee* means "separated ones." Demanded strict obedience to every Jewish law and tradition. Very influential in Jewish religious life. Closely related to "teachers of the law" (1 Timothy 1:7 NKJV), the professional interpreters of the Law.	*Religious conservatives:* The essence of hypocrisy, they held the people to a religious standard that God never demanded, an outrageous list of rules that they themselves failed to observe. They proclaimed themselves godly while disobeying God. Soundly rejected Jesus's claim to be the Messiah because he associated with notoriously wicked people and did not follow all of their traditions. Deserved and received Jesus's stern rebuke.
Sadducees	Matthew 3:7	Wealthy, upper class Jewish priestly party. *Chief Priest* and *Sadducee* almost synonymous, though they cared little for anything religious. Rejected the authority of the Bible beyond the Torah—the five books of Moses. Hated the Pharisees, and only united with them in their hatred of Jesus (Matthew 21:15).	*Religious liberals:* Denied the supernatural including miracles, angels, and the resurrection of the body. Thought of the Temple primarily as a place to conduct business. Lived only for the present, taking what they could, when they could, from whomever they could.
Zealots	Luke 6:15	A fiercely dedicated group of Jewish patriots who hated Rome and all that it stood for. Determined to end Roman rule in Israel through military means. Simon, one of Jesus's disciples, was a zealot.	*Religious militants:* Believed that the Messiah must be a political leader who would deliver Israel from Roman occupation.
Essenes	Not mentioned directly in the Bible	Jewish monastic group living in isolation, practicing ritual and ceremonial purity as well as personal holiness, and spending much time copying the Old Testament and their other religious books. Responsible for the Dead Sea Scrolls. John the Baptist might have been raised in an Essene community.	*Religious separatists:* Emphasized celibacy, purity, the apocalyptic end of the age, a righteousness based upon religious ritual and strict self-denial. John the Baptist's tone and theme sound similar to the writings of the Essenes.

Jewish Religious and Political Groups in New Testament Times (cont'd)

Who They Were	Where They Are First Mentioned	What They Did	What They Believed
Herodians	Matthew 22:16	A party of the Jews who supported the Herodian Dynasty. As their name suggests (Herod), they had the full backing of Rome. The Pharisees hated anything having to do with Rome, and therefore hated the Herodians. That they would join forces to plot the execution of Jesus shows just how desperate these two groups were.	The Herodians were not a religious party; they were a secular political party deeply loyal to Rome. They took their name from Herod Antipas, one of Herod the Great's notorious sons, a puppet of Rome, and the one who imprisoned and then beheaded John the Baptist.

The Mother of All Signs

MATTHEW 16:1–4 *Then the Pharisees and Sadducees came, and testing Him asked that He would show them a sign from heaven. He answered and said to them, "When it is evening you say, 'It will be fair weather, for the sky is red'; and in the morning, 'It will be foul weather today, for the sky is red and threatening.' Hypocrites! You know how to discern the face of the sky, but you cannot discern the signs of the times. A wicked and adulterous generation seeks after a sign, and no sign shall be given to it except the sign of the prophet Jonah." And He left them and departed.* (NKJV)

Do you remember when Jesus healed every person in the large multitudes that approached him right before the Sermon on the Mount? Remember when Jesus healed a man with leprosy? Remember when Jesus healed the centurion's servant? Remember when Jesus calmed the storm? Remember when Jesus raised a girl from the dead? When the Pharisees and Sadducees rushed up to Jesus to test him, to embarrass him, to discredit him, what question did they ask?

If you can believe it, they had the audacity, the unmitigated gall, to ask him to show them yet another sign from heaven to prove to them who he was. If they had just taken the time to open their blinded eyes and survey the landscape, they had plenty of signs. Yet still they wanted more.

Whenever Jesus's enemies sought a sign, they were not offering him an opportunity to prove who he was. They were trying to trip him up in their vain attempt to disprove who he was. Jesus knew that. So he nailed them to the wall.

go to

multitudes
Matthew 4:25

leprosy
Matthew 8:2

servant
Matthew 8:6

storm
Matthew 8:24

dead
Matthew 9:18

whale
Jonah 1:17

hypocrisy
Luke 12:1

Jesus nailed them to the wall when he declared, "A wicked and adulterous generation seeks after a sign" (Matthew 16:4 NKJV). He refused to dance to their tune. If these Pharisees wanted a sign, Jesus would give them a sign. One they would never forget. One they could never explain away. One that they could never discredit. One that they could never deny. The same sign he offered to them in Matthew 12:39. The ultimate sign. The mother of all signs. In fact, a whale of a sign. "The sign of Jonah" sign.

At the behest of these same religious leaders, the mobs would demand that Jesus be killed. Just as Jonah was "buried" in the belly of a <u>whale</u> and lived to tell about it, Jesus would walk out of his tomb alive, and the whole world would hear about it.

Hypocrisy Exposed

> MATTHEW 16:5–7 *Now when His disciples had come to the other side, they had forgotten to take bread. Then Jesus said to them, "Take heed and beware of the leaven of the Pharisees and the Sadducees." And they reasoned among themselves, saying, "It is because we have taken no bread."* (NKJV)

Given his recent confrontations with both the Pharisees and Sadducees, Jesus seized upon the disciples' forgetfulness to teach them an object lesson. To understand his meaning, we must first understand the meaning of the word *leaven*. When placed in dough, the leaven permeates the dough and causes it to rise. The leaven's ability to permeate, penetrate, and saturate the dough is what gives rise (no pun intended) to its significant meaning.

In Matthew 13:33 when Jesus compared the kingdom of heaven to yeast ("leaven" [NKJV]), he used yeast in a positive way. Here, in Matthew 16, when Jesus warned the disciples to avoid an aspect of his archenemies that had the ability to permeate their lives, he used yeast in a negative way. We learn from Luke's account that Jesus told the disciples the yeast represented "<u>hypocrisy</u>." Jesus warned his men not to fall under the permeating pronouncements of these self-serving Pharisees and Sadduccees. Yet all the while, the disciples just didn't get it. They thought Jesus was talking about bread.

what others say
Larry Crabb Jr. Citizens of this world live with two objectives: 1) to find some way to make their present lives happier, and 2) to influence the people and materials in their world to cooperate. Beneath their every act of altruism, benevolence, and sacrifice lies the motive of self-service that destroys its moral value.[1]

strength
1 Samuel 30:6

past
Psalm 40:1–4

Remember Not to Forget

MATTHEW 16:8–12 *But Jesus, being aware of it, said to them, "O you of little faith, why do you reason among yourselves because you have brought no bread? Do you not yet understand, or remember the five loaves of the five thousand and how many baskets you took up? Nor the seven loaves of the four thousand and how many large baskets you took up? How is it you do not understand that I did not speak to you concerning bread?—but to beware of the leaven of the Pharisees and Sadducees." Then they understood that He did not tell them to beware of the leaven of bread, but of the doctrine of the Pharisees and Sadducees. (NKJV)*

The disciples were shaking in their sandals because they thought Jesus was upset with them for forgetting to bring bread. Well, Jesus didn't get ticked off at such inconsequential things. But hadn't Jesus twice, mind you, created bread on the spot, enough to feed five thousand men, and then four thousand men, plus women and children?

The disciples once again lived up to their customary title, "You of little faith." Hardly had the toast popped out of the toaster, as it were, before they completely forgot about these two stunning miracles.

How much unnecessary anxiety do we suffer because we forget many of the marvelous things that God has recently done in our lives? Check out David's psalms, for example. We might want to think of them as entries in David's prayer journal. When David was upset by circumstances that seemed hopeless, he found new reservoirs of <u>strength</u> in the Lord by recounting the things that God had faithfully done for him in his <u>past</u>. We can do the same.

go to

Caesarea
Acts 25:4

ill-fated
Acts 27:44

executed
2 Timothy 4:6

A Losing Proposition

Do you play any sports? If so, have you ever faced an opponent whom you knew in your bones that, barring some sort of divine intervention, you could not beat? As you walked onto the field or court, or jumped into the pool, or entered the arena, you might have felt as though you were walking to your own execution. It's an empty and hopeless feeling, isn't it? The disciples are about to feel the same thing.

Let's set the scene. The New Testament mentions two significant cities radically different from each other, except for their names: <u>Caesarea</u> and Caesarea Philippi. The former was a port city built by Herod the Great on the coast of the Mediterranean. It would be from this Caesarea that the apostle Paul would sail on his <u>ill-fated</u> and final journey to Rome, where he was eventually <u>executed</u> as a martyr for his faith.

The latter lay at the base of the mighty Mount Hermon, twenty-five miles to the north of the Sea of Galilee. Having inherited the city from his father, the not-so-great Herod Philip crowned the city the capital of his territory.[3] Because there were lots of towns named Caesarea in those days, the Caesarea in Philip's territory was called Caesarea Philippi, named after the Caesar in Rome, and not so humbly named after himself. Jesus purposefully took the disciples on a field trip to this northern city to make a point they would never forget.

The Key Question

MATTHEW 16:13–17 *When Jesus came into the region of Caesarea Philippi, He asked His disciples, saying, "Who do men say that I, the Son of Man, am?" So they said, "Some say John the Baptist, some Elijah, and others Jeremiah or one of the prophets." He said to them, "But who do you say that I am?" Simon Peter answered and said, "You are the Christ, the Son of the living God." Jesus answered and said to him, "Blessed are you, Simon Bar-Jonah, for flesh and blood has not revealed this to you, but My Father who is in heaven. (NKJV)*

"Who do men say that I, the Son of Man, am?" That's they key question, isn't it? Every one of us must confront this question at some point in our lives. Who is Jesus? Teacher? Charismatic leader? Cult hero? Good man? Delusional egotist? Moralist? Fraud? Friend? Foe? Or is he truly God Almighty incarnate in a human body?

The jury was still out in many people's minds. Among the population-at-large, the answers ranged from John the Baptist (neat trick since Antipas had already beheaded him), to Elijah (good guess since he never <u>died</u>), Jeremiah (evidently because Jeremiah's message and <u>manner</u> mirrored that of Jesus), or take your pick of any of the other prophets.

Chalk one up for the disciples. Finally, thankfully, they were about to get one right. When Jesus asked them, "But who do you say that I am?" (Matthew 16:15 NKJV), anyone within sight of this scene could feel the rumbles reverberate through the Twelve. Peter plowed his way past the other eleven and blurted out for the world to hear, "You are the Christ, the Son of the living God" (Matthew 16:16 NKJV).

Bravo, Peter! This was Peter's moment in the sun. Or should we say, Son? This declaration was Peter's high-water mark as a disciple. But as you might suspect, Peter's stellar moment would be short-lived. We'll get to that in a minute.

died
2 Kings 2:11

manner
Jeremiah 1:10

proclaimed
Matthew 11:2–5

countless
John 21:25

megalomania
feelings of unlimited power and importance

> ## what others say
>
> ### Clark H. Pinnock
>
> The dilemma of Christ's identity will not be easily sidestepped. The most sensible solution is to bow to the force of the evidence for His divinity. Jesus is either guilty of criminal **megalomania**, or actually the person He claims to be. Once a non-Christian has faced the issue this way, he will not be easily able to shake off his responsibility to decide the issue once and for all.[4]

Think about this: Jesus <u>proclaimed</u> himself as the long-awaited Jewish Messiah. He performed <u>countless</u> miracles to validate that claim. Yet, scores of people, most notably the Pharisees and Sadducees, rejected his claims outright and sought to kill him. Does

go to

plotted
Matthew 12:14

uneducated
Acts 4:13

Spirit
1 Corinthians 2:14

persuading
2 Corinthians 5:21

spokespersons
Romans 10:14

draws
John 6:44

that trouble you? Why would these educated men who knew the Old Testament better than anyone conclude that Jesus was a fraud, so much so that they <u>plotted</u> to kill him?

On the other side of the ledger, why did a group of simple, unsophisticated, <u>uneducated</u> men become so convinced that Jesus was authentic that they willingly walked away from their businesses, homes, families, and friends to follow him? Here we have two groups of people, basically exposed to the same evidence, coming to two opposite conclusions. How do we explain this?

It all comes down to the Holy Spirit. Remember our discussion of Jesus's words about the unforgivable sin, the "blasphemy against the Spirit" (Matthew 12:31 NKJV)? When the Holy Spirit convinces someone of the truth about Jesus, that person must make a choice to accept or reject that truth. As Paul wrote, "For the wrath of God is revealed from heaven against all ungodliness and unrighteousness of men, who suppress the truth in unrighteousness" (Romans 1:18 NKJV). The word translated *suppress* speaks of extinguishing a flame by putting a lid on it. Imagine someone putting a lid on the truth so that it no longer pricks his or her conscience. That's the difference between these two groups. The religious leaders didn't receive the truth about Christ because they didn't want to.

When Peter acknowledged that Jesus was "the Christ, the Son of the living God" (Matthew 16:16 NKJV), Jesus dulled a wee bit of Peter's luster by saying (my paraphrases), "Ahem, Peter, before you start strutting your stuff, keep this in mind. You didn't reach that conclusion on your own. God the Father revealed it to you."

We can argue with people about Jesus until we are blue in the face, tossing at them every proof, bit of evidence, and argument we can muster. But unless and until the <u>Spirit</u> of God opens their hearts and minds to the truth, our words are just that—words.

<u>Persuading</u> people to commit their lives to Jesus Christ is a human-divine partnership. God uses us as his <u>spokespersons</u> to share the good news of the gospel with others. As we do, his Spirit convicts them of sin and <u>draws</u> them to himself. It's then up to the individual to receive or resist that drawing.

John F. Walvoord

Apart from the work of the Holy Spirit in bestowing grace, there seems to be no natural stirring in the human heart toward God. Man is spiritually dead and does not originate in himself a movement toward God and spiritual life.

Spiritual renewal begins when man is prompted by the Spirit of God, brought under conviction of need, and made aware of the provision of salvation in Christ (John 16:7–11).[5]

A Chip off the Old Block

MATTHEW 16:18 *And I also say to you that you are Peter, and on this rock I will build My church, and the gates of Hades shall not prevail against it.* (NKJV)

We now come to one of the most misunderstood, contentious, controversial, and yet significant passages in the Bible. Over the years the following few verses have proven themselves a tough theological nut for Bible scholars to crack.

Jesus used a play on words to make his point—a point commonly misunderstood today. You can stare at the words in English all you want and you will never see the play on words that Jesus purposely intended. To see it, you have to know a little Greek. The two words in question are *Peter* and *rock*.

Peter comes from the Greek word *Petros*, which means a small stone or pebble. But the word Jesus used for *rock*, *petra*, refers to a huge, unshakable, foundational boulder, like the Rock of Gibraltar. Plug those meanings back into the verse, and it will come out sounding something like this: "And I also say that you, Peter, are a small stone. But what you just declared about me—that I am the promised, long-awaited Messiah, and the Son of the living God—that is a huge, unshakable, <u>foundational</u> boulder. And it is upon the foundation of your statement about me that I will build my church. And the gates of Hades will not overcome it."

Alan Redpath

Most of us, God forgive us, are too big for God to use. We are too full of our own schemes and of our own way of doing things. God has to humble us and break us and empty us. So

boundary
Judges 20:1;
1 Chronicles 21:2

execution
Matthew 16:21

low, indeed, must God make us that we need every word of encouragement from heaven to enable us to take on the job and dare to go forward in the will of God. The world speaks about the survival of the fittest, but God gives power to the faint and He gives might to those who have no strength.[6]

Jesus never did anything randomly. It was more than mere coincidence that Jesus chose Caesarea Philippi as the place where he would grill the disciples about his true identity. Consider the location of Caesarea Philippi:

1. Located some twenty-five miles due north of Capernaum, the city rested at the headwaters of the Jordan River, right next door to Dan, the northernmost <u>boundary</u> of the Promised Land. This scenic resort city, with its lush landscape and cool refreshing waters, offered travelers welcome relief from the hot Galilean lowlands. But because of its close proximity to the border, this city became susceptible to the pagan influences of its neighbors to the north.

2. Towering some nine thousand feet above the city stood the highest mountain in the Middle East, the mighty Mount Hermon.

3. Originally named Panias (today, the name has been slightly corrupted into Banyas), the city boasted a huge temple built by Herod the Great to the Greek god Pan, who, according to pagan mythology, was born in a nearby cave. Devotees of this god made pilgrimages to this shrine, built right into the base of Mount Hermon.

Just imagine Jesus and his twelve disciples walking into this thoroughly pagan, Roman city. They would have been awed, stunned into an ominous silence, as they gazed for the first time upon the unbelievable spectacle of literally thousands of worshipers paying homage to their god.

They were just twelve simple men whose leader was dropping hints of his imminent <u>execution</u>. From all outward appearances, theirs was a movement in serious decline. All the while, the Pan religion gave every appearance of a living, thriving, robust religion of enormous power and immense influence. Pan had the resources. Pan had the buildings. Pan had the loyalty of thousands of devoted followers. Pan's power could not be broken.

It becomes clear, doesn't it, why Jesus chose this location to ask his disciples, "Who do men say that I, the Son of Man, am?" You can almost see Jesus bending down and picking up a small rock as he says, "You are Peter." But then see his upward gesture as his hands sweep the vastness of the mighty Mount Hermon towering above them when he announces, "And on this rock I will build My church." Peter's declaration was an unshakable Mount Hermon of truth upon which Jesus would build his church. And Jesus assured the disciples at this place that the "gates of Hades" (Matthew 16:18 NKJV) would never prevail against his church.

what others say

Ray C. Stedman

Twentieth-century Christians confront a thoroughly secularized and pagan world, just as the first-century Christians did. . . .

At a time like this nothing could be more helpful to the church than to review again the record of the early church's rise and growth. The same principles which produced explosive growth then will do so today. The same pattern of leadership which prevailed then must prevail again in the twentieth century. The same remarkable power which accounted for the church's success then can and must be found today, for Christ's promise has never changed: "I will build my church, and the gates of hell shall not prevail against it."[7]

Today Caesarea Philippi lies in ruins. The temple is gone. You can look in every cave and crevasse in the place in the place and you will not find one single, solitary worshiper of the mythological Pan. They have been replaced by pilgrim followers of Jesus Christ, people like you and me, who take pictures, dabble their toes in the Jordan, read Matthew 16 to one another, and meditate on the fact that two thousand years later, the seemingly impotent band of Jesus and his men has grown into an invincible, worldwide movement of millions who today would without hesitation give their lives for Jesus, and consider it their greatest honor and highest calling to do so.

Matthew is the only one of the four gospel writers to record this event at Caesarea Philippi, indeed, the only gospel writer to refer to the church. Do you not find it intriguing that the Gospel written to Jews about their Jewish Messiah establishing a Jewish kingdom is the only Gospel to refer to a brand-new, never-heard-of-before entity called the church? From Matthew 12 on, ever since the Pharisees accused Jesus of healing a blind and mute man by the power of

identical
Matthew 18:18

thousand
Acts 2:41

rejected
Acts 7:54

Satan, things changed dramatically. Believe it or not, even more changes will be coming shortly.

The Keys to the Kingdom

> MATTHEW 16:19 *and I will give you the keys of the kingdom of heaven, and whatever you bind on earth will be bound in heaven, and whatever you loose on earth will be loosed in heaven." (NKJV)*

When added to Christ's "rock" statement, one could regard this "keys of the kingdom" reference as a further indication that Peter had been set apart by Jesus as the foundation of the church. Jesus gave to Peter "the keys of the kingdom of heaven," and he later made a nearly <u>identical</u> statement to all the disciples. Admittedly, this does get a tad confusing, because everyone, including you and me, who becomes a member of Christ's church is also a citizen of the kingdom of heaven.

So just what did Jesus mean by this curious statement? We must first ask this key question: What, exactly, do keys do? Answer: Keys unlock doors. Peter and the other apostles were given the authority to unlock the door to the kingdom of heaven. Throughout Acts, the disciples proclaimed one singular, significant, authoritative message: Jesus is the Christ, the Son of the living God. Those who heard the message and responded to Christ as Lord were granted entrance into the "kingdom of heaven"; those who rejected Christ as Lord were by their own deliberate rebellion excluded from his kingdom.

Peter first used his "key" when he preached the gospel for the very first time in Acts 2. On that notable occasion, three <u>thousand</u> people repented of their sins, received Christ as their risen Savior and Lord, and entered the "kingdom of heaven" through that now unlocked door. The church was born!

However, when Stephen preached in Acts 7, the men who viciously <u>rejected</u> his message seriously risked their own willful exclusion from the kingdom. Peter used his "key" to unlock the door to the kingdom, while Stephen's "key" essentially bolted the door shut.

If you sense that Jesus is now using the words *kingdom* and *church* interchangeably, in a sense he is. A physical, tangible, earthly kingdom has been postponed indefinitely pending the second coming of

Christ to establish his earthly kingdom. Today, post-Pentecost (Acts 2), the citizens of Christ's heavenly kingdom are found in Christ's church. One day, all believers in Christ from all periods of human history will be together forever in our heavenly home. May that day come quickly.

Remember, as King, Jesus can delegate duties to his subjects. Today, every one of Jesus's followers possesses these same "keys." When we proclaim the good news about Jesus to others, we unlock the door to the kingdom for those who receive him and lock the door to those who reject him. God has entrusted us with a priceless privilege, a most valuable treasure, an awesome responsibility—one that we dare not take lightly or treat casually, but one that should be <u>protected</u> relentlessly and discharged faithfully.

Some people have used Christ's reference to binding and loosing as a biblical admonition for us to bind Satan. Yet, search the Scriptures and you will not find one single, solitary instance of anyone binding Satan. Nor are we ever commanded to do so. We are only commanded to <u>resist</u> the devil with the assurance that when we do, he must flee. Satan will be bound one day. On that day an <u>angel</u> will do the binding.

go to

protected
2 Timothy 1:14

resist
James 4:7

angel
Revelation 20:1–2

something to ponder

> **what others say**
>
> **Charles H. Spurgeon**
>
> If sinners will be damned, at least let them leap to hell over our bodies. And if they will perish, let them perish with our arms about their knees, imploring them to stay. If hell must be filled, at least let it be filled in the teeth of our exertions, and let not one go there unwarned and unprayed for.[8]

Don't Ask; Don't Tell

MATTHEW 16:20 *Then He commanded His disciples that they should tell no one that He was Jesus the Christ.* (NKJV)

We close out this section with Jesus making a strange request. Having just identified Jesus for who he truly was—"the Christ, the Son of the living God" (Matthew 16:16 NKJV)—Jesus warned his disciples not to tell anyone, but to keep it a deep, dark secret. Why? The next verse will tell us why.

go to

lights
Matthew 5:16

spread
Matthew 9:26

missions
Matthew 10:5

people
Matthew 12:23

fickleness
John 6:66

Death Watch

MATTHEW 16:21 *From that time Jesus began to show to His disciples that He must go to Jerusalem, and suffer many things from the elders and chief priests and scribes, and be killed, and be raised the third day. (NKJV)*

Previously, Jesus told his followers to let their <u>lights</u> shine in the world. He didn't raise a whimper of protest when news about him <u>spread</u> everywhere. He even sent his disciples on a <u>missions</u> trip during which they told everyone they met about Jesus. He stood in the most public of places, in full view of hoards of <u>people</u>, and raised his voice to deafening decibels when teaching the masses.

Why would he now suddenly, randomly it seems, switch gears completely, totally change his modus operandi, and tell his disciples to tell no one about him? The answer lies buried in the ominous words "From that time Jesus began to show to His disciples that He must go to Jerusalem, and suffer . . ." Jesus knew that he was going to be killed, executed like a common criminal. That now consumed his thoughts as he looked toward Jerusalem and contemplated his cross.

The Pharisees sought to kill Jesus before; now the momentum of the Let's-do-Jesus-in movement would build like a snowball rolling down a mountainside. The tide of public opinion, while always shaky at best given the <u>fickleness</u> of his followers, would turn against Jesus once and for all, culminating in a crescendo of cries demanding his crucifixion. These were dark days for Jesus. That's the reason for the silence. That's why Jesus wanted the disciples to keep his identity a secret. That's why he virtually disappeared from public view. From Matthew 16:21 on, Jesus prepared himself and his men for the unthinkable—the inevitable day when the very people he came to love would turn against him in hate and nail him to a cross. These days were getting darker by the minute.

Chapter Wrap-Up

- Yet again, the religious leaders demanded of Jesus a supernatural sign. (Matthew 16:1–4)

- Jesus warned the disciples about the danger of becoming hypocrites, just like the religious leaders had become.
(Matthew 16:12)

- Jesus took his disciples on a field trip to the northernmost border of the land in order to impress upon them a timeless truth.
(Matthew 16:13)

- People had different opinions as to who Jesus really was.
(Matthew 16:13–15)

- Peter declared the bedrock foundational truth of the church: that Jesus is the Messiah, the Son of the living God.
(Matthew 16:16)

Study Questions

1. What happens in the instant that we respond to Jesus's call?

2. What sign did Jesus give the Pharisees and Sadducees?

3. How did Jesus use the illustration of yeast both positively and negatively?

4. How do you explain the fact that two groups of people, exposed to essentially the same evidence, came to opposite conclusions?

5. What would the disciples have seen at the location of Caesarea Philippi, and what lesson did Jesus wish to teach in the place?

6. How do we know that Jesus did not confer upon Peter the distinction of being the first pope?

Matthew 16:22–18:35: Saying Good-Bye to Galilee

Let's Get Started

We ended the last chapter with this disturbing statement: "From that time Jesus began to show to His disciples that He must go to Jerusalem, and suffer..." (Matthew 16:21 NKJV). Nothing in Jesus's life or lesson will ever be the same "from that time" on. The arduous journey down the long and winding road leading to an old rugged cross begins right here.

The specter of Jesus's demise will now haunt him like a dark cloud. The morale of the disciples will plunge from the stellar heights of Peter's affirmative assertion, "You are the Christ" (Matthew 16:16 NKJV), to the bottomless pit of Judas's sinister signal: "Whomever I kiss, He is the One; seize Him" (Matthew 26:48 NKJV).

As Jesus's earthly existence begins to wind down, he begins to wind up his Galilean ministry. By the time we get to Matthew 19 in our next chapter, Jesus will have "departed from Galilee" as he heads into "the region of Judea" and travels up to Jerusalem to surrender to his cross (Matthew 19:1 NKJV). So with a lump in our throats and a heaviness in our hearts, we will consider together Jesus's final ministry in the north of the land, bracing ourselves for the moment when his mission goes south, both literally and figuratively.

Mere moments after Jesus conferred upon Peter his honorary doctorate in theology, Dr. Peter shot off his mouth one too many times, this time becoming the mouthpiece for—are you ready?—Satan. Dr. Jekyll and Mr. Hyde would have been proud.

Lest you be tempted, even for a split second, to think that Jesus overreacted to Peter's verbal indiscretion, let's remember that Jesus had been hinting at his coming crucifixion for quite some time. To put a pop-psychology spin on it, the disciples simply chose to live in blissful denial of the inevitable—their leader was going to die.

Our Jewish friends have a word that means guts, intestinal fortitude, or raw courage. Peter displayed a good measure of it here. They call it *chutzpah*. Just imagine Peter exploding in the face of

before
Matthew 16:16

redemptive
relating to ransom
for a price

Jesus, wagging his index finger before Jesus's sunbaked and sand-blown features, and rebuking him by forbidding him to go to the cross. If it wasn't so serious, it would be downright amusing.

Matthew chose a particular word, translated "rebuke," that is normally used by an official against someone under his jurisdiction. The tense of the verb suggests that Peter rebuked Jesus repeatedly.[1] We have here a classic example of a role reversal. Peter acted like the master by treating Jesus as his servant.

Sometimes force must be met by equal force, and that's exactly how Jesus reacted to Peter's rebuke. He threw it right back into Peter's face by pointing out the origin of Peter's attack. Unlike before, when Peter spoke the words of God the Father, this time Peter was duped into becoming the mouthpiece of Jesus's arch-enemy, Satan. The reality of what Jesus said had to shake Peter to the core of his being. Peter unwittingly became a tool in the hands of the devil to thwart God's **redemptive** plan. Somehow, Satan successfully prompted Peter to oppose God's will and to attempt to lure Jesus into disobeying his Father. Had Peter's rebuke resulted in persuading Jesus to forgo his painful destiny, the results would have been too devastating to contemplate.

Let's learn a lesson from Peter. Like the errant disciple, Christians can become unwitting dupes of the evil one. Satan scores a big victory when he gets the people of God to think that they are doing the work of God when in actuality they are opposing God's plans and purpose. Before we become critical of, gossip about, or in any other way verbally attack another Christian, we'd better make absolutely sure under whose influence we are truly talking—the Holy Spirit's influence or an evil spirit's influence.

Bearing One's Cross Before Wearing One's Crown

MATTHEW 16:22–27 *Then Peter took Him aside and began to rebuke Him, saying, "Far be it from You, Lord; this shall not happen to You!" But He turned and said to Peter, "Get behind Me, Satan! You are an offense to Me, for you are not mindful of the things of God, but the things of men." Then Jesus said to His disciples, "If anyone desires to come after Me, let him deny himself, and take up his cross, and follow Me. For whoever desires to save his life will lose it, but whoever loses his life for My sake will find it. For what profit is it to a man if he gains the whole world, and loses his own soul? or what will a man give in exchange for his soul? For the Son of Man will come in the glory of His Father with His angels, and then He will reward each according to his works. (NKJV)*

go to

brother
Galatians 1:19

Don't be surprised if these words sound familiar. You might hear the faint echo of Matthew 10:38. Like any good preacher who's got a killer sermon in his arsenal of messages, Jesus often repeated some of his best.

The point of Matthew 16:24–27 is perspective. Too many people today make choices and conduct their daily affairs solely on the basis of this world rather than the world to come. James learned well from his half <u>brother</u> Jesus. He evidently took this passage to heart and paraphrased it in James 1:9–11. He understood something about the brevity of life, especially when compared to an endless eternity. In the face of his coming death, Jesus assured the disciples that ultimately they would not be disappointed if they exchanged the temporal for the eternal. All but one followed his advice. Eleven of the Twelve died for their faith.

what others say

Vance Havner

Our Lord never put discipleship in fine print in the contract. He called on us to forsake all, take up our cross, deny self, love him more than anything else. We are not our own, we are bought with a price, the personal property of Jesus Christ with no right to do anything. "Love so amazing, so divine, demands my soul, my life, my all."[2]

Coming Attractions

MATTHEW 16:28 *Assuredly, I say to you, there are some standing here who shall not taste death till they see the Son of Man coming in His kingdom." (NKJV)*

The final verse of this chapter perfectly sets up the next one. While Matthew 16:28 is tough to translate, once the use of the word *kingdom* is properly understood, the whole thing snaps into crystal clear focus. Taken at face value, Jesus's statement makes little sense since, as we just mentioned, each of the disciples did "taste death" and the kingdom still has not yet come.

go to

martyr
Acts 12:2

transfigured
dramatically
changed in
appearance

martyr
someone killed for
his or her faith

Epistle
New Testament
letter

The term Matthew chose, *basileia*, is an abstract[3] rather than a concrete term, meaning that it often refers to a concept more than an actual physical kingdom. So the verse could read like this—"I say to you, there are some standing here who shall not taste death till they see the Son of Man *coming in* His royal majesty, His kingly sovereignty, His reigning glory, His ruling authority" (emphasis mine).

With this one statement, Jesus set the table for one of the most unusual occurrences in all of the Bible, something so stunning, so memorable that, as you'll see, both Peter and John wrote about it years after the fact. In just six short days, Jesus and his inner circle of Peter, James, and John would ascend the mighty Mount Hermon and Jesus would be **transfigured** right before their wide and wondering eyes.

A Regal Reunion

Matthew 17 opens with a common reference to three guys who, along with Andrew, formed Jesus's inner circle: "Peter, James, and John" (Matthew 17:1 NKJV). Among their many accomplishments, Peter and John eventually became significant New Testament writers with a grand total of seven New Testament books to their credit.

James wrote nothing so far as we know. (The book of James was written by a different James—Jesus's half brother.) He died at a relatively young age, becoming the first Christian **martyr** during the early years of the church's infancy. We've alluded to the writing careers of both Peter and John because so great was the impact of this one event that years later they were still making reference to it in their works.

Our friend Peter made this rather intriguing statement in his second **Epistle**: "He received from God the Father honor and glory when such a voice came to Him from the Excellent Glory: 'This is My beloved Son, in whom I am well pleased'" (2 Peter 1:17 NKJV).

John made an equally fascinating admission in the first chapter of his landmark Gospel: "The Word became flesh and dwelt among us, and we beheld His glory, the glory as of the only begotten of the Father, full of grace and truth" (John 1:14 NKJV).

Both Peter and John saw Christ's "glory" manifested, unveiled, revealed, and were never the same again. James saw it, too, but didn't live long enough to tell us about it. When did this event take place?

What exactly did they see? What could possibly have been so unusual, so unprecedented, so unexpected that it left them awestruck, so much so that they wrote of its wonder so many years later? Let's find out together.

Word
John 1:14

Shine, Jesus, Shine

Word
Jesus–the living expression of God

> MATTHEW 17:1–8 *Now after six days Jesus took Peter, James, and John his brother, led them up on a high mountain by themselves; and He was transfigured before them. His face shone like the sun, and His clothes became as white as the light. And behold, Moses and Elijah appeared to them, talking with Him. Then Peter answered and said to Jesus, "Lord, it is good for us to be here; if You wish, let us make here three tabernacles: one for You, one for Moses, and one for Elijah." While he was still speaking, behold, a bright cloud overshadowed them; and suddenly a voice came out of the cloud, saying, "This is My beloved Son, in whom I am well pleased. Hear Him!" And when the disciples heard it, they fell on their faces and were greatly afraid. But Jesus came and touched them and said, "Arise, and do not be afraid." When they had lifted up their eyes, they saw no one but Jesus only. (NKJV)*

It should have come as no surprise to the disciples that something big was about to happen. Jesus had told the Twelve that "some standing here" (Matthew 16:28 NKJV) would see a manifestation of his kingly authority. It makes perfect sense that his inner circle would be the beneficiaries of such a promise.

Both Peter and John looked upon the Transfiguration as a defining moment in their time as Christ's disciples. They, along with James, were among the precious few mentioned in the Bible who saw an actual manifestation of the glory of God. With such a memory indelibly seared into their minds, we can appreciate the passion and conviction with which Peter and John affirmed Christ's deity, as when they referred respectively to Jesus Christ as "our God and Savior" (2 Peter 1:1 NKJV), and "The **Word** was God" (John 1:1 NKJV).

At the beginning of Jesus's ministry, God the Father pronounced his blessing upon Jesus with the words, "This is My beloved Son, in whom I am well pleased" (Matthew 3:17 NKJV). Now, near the end of his ministry, God the Father offers the same endorsement by

Law
Matthew 7:12

ineffable
indescribable,
unspeakable

declaring in the hearing of Peter, James, John, Moses (the giver of the <u>Law</u>), and Elijah (the first of Israel's powerful prophets), "This is My beloved Son, in whom I am well pleased. Hear Him!" (Matthew 17:5 NKJV).

To what was God referring when he exhorted these men to listen to Jesus? The answer is offered by the context. This exhortation is sandwiched right in the middle of Jesus explaining how he must die, and once again reminding his men that he must suffer at the hands of the religious leaders. Since the disciples were obviously and understandably resistant to the notion that Jesus must die like a common criminal on a Roman cross, God the Father had to give to Jesus's disciples his approval of the death of his Son.

Scholars debate the location of the Transfiguration. We have two options from which to choose. It could have happened somewhere on the majestic Mount Hermon, directly above Caesarea Philippi, the place of Peter's proclamation. Or it might have happened on Mount Tabor just to the east of Nazareth and adjacent to the Jezreel Valley, future site of the Battle of Armageddon.

This is one of those stories where the *what* of what happened is far more significant than the *where* of what happened. Those who argue in favor of Mount Hermon point out that in the chronology of events, the Transfiguration occurs after Peter's proclamation; it makes sense, so the argument goes, that both events happened in close proximity to one another. Those who cast their vote in the direction of Mount Tabor point out the time line. The Transfiguration took place "six days" after Peter's proclamation, allowing Jesus and the disciples enough time to make the southbound journey to Tabor. Since neither Matthew (17:1–8), Mark (9:2–8), nor Luke (9:28–36) considered the location significant enough to identify, neither will we.

---

what others say

J. Oswald Sanders

Here is a sample of heavenly conversation. The two great representatives of Judaism—of the Law and the Prophets—officially surrendered the seals of office to the Lamb of God. Their work was accomplished and they conversed about the mystery of the cross, its majesty, its **ineffable** glory.[4]

go to

defiance
Numbers 20:12

die
Deuteronomy 34:5

suicidal
1 Kings 19:4

heaven
2 Kings 2:11

what others say

J. Dwight Pentecost

It is possible to make a man's garments and his countenance shine by focusing a floodlight on him. But the transfiguration was a revelation of the essential glory of the Father that belonged to Jesus Christ. The source of the illumination was internal, not external. The clothing of Christ as well as His countenance became dazzlingly brilliant because of the brightness of the glory that belonged to Jesus Christ and that shone from within. Heb. 1:3 says that He is the radiance of the Father's glory.[5]

That Jesus chose Moses and Elijah to share in this majestic moment certainly makes sense. Aside from representing "the Law and the Prophets" (Matthew 7:12 NKJV), a common reference to the Old Testament, there were other compelling reasons for Jesus to include these two men on the mountaintop that day.

Moses yearned to enter the Promised Land. But tragically, in one unguarded moment, through one desperate act of willful <u>defiance</u>, Moses threw away the privilege. Or did he? Moses did <u>die</u> without setting foot in the Holy Land, the longing of his life left unfulfilled. But the longing of his heart was satisfied in a way so glorious that in his wildest dreams he never imagined it could happen. He entered the land all right, and stood on its most majestic mountain peak, this at the invitation of and in the presence of the glorified Christ.

Elijah longed to live to see righteousness reign in the land. So distraught over the wickedness that permeated God's people, this powerful prophet became <u>suicidal</u> and begged God to strike him dead. He resigned himself to never seeing his dream realized. Or would he? Elijah went to <u>heaven</u> with his desperate longing unfulfilled. But that was not the end of the story. Elijah came back. He came back in a way he never expected. Just imagine what went through his mind as he stood in the Promised Land side by side with "Jesus Christ the righteous" (1 John 2:1 NKJV). God granted to Moses and Elijah the longings of their hearts; as we delight ourselves in him, God promises he will do the same for us.

Think of it: Moses, Elijah, Peter, James, John, and Jesus sharing with one another this memorable moment. A regal reunion indeed!

Will the Real John the Baptist Please Stand Up!

MATTHEW 17:9–13 *Now as they came down from the mountain, Jesus commanded them, saying, "Tell the vision to no one until the Son of Man is risen from the dead." And His disciples asked Him, saying, "Why then do the scribes say that Elijah must come first?" Jesus answered and said to them, "Indeed, Elijah is coming first and will restore all things. But I say to you that Elijah has come already, and they did not know him but did to him whatever they wished. Likewise the Son of Man is also about to suffer at their hands." Then the disciples understood that He spoke to them of John the Baptist. (NKJV)*

Back in Matthew 1:18 when Mary "was found with child of the Holy Spirit" (NKJV), four hundred years of God's silence were suddenly shattered. For four centuries no new **revelation** had been given by God through prophets, angels, or any other messenger. Just before God stopped "talking" as it were, he left Israel with this prediction: "Behold, I will send you Elijah the prophet before the coming of the great and dreadful day of the LORD" (Malachi 4:5 NKJV). Naturally, Elijah's appearance on the Mount of Transfiguration reminded the disciples of this somewhat confusing prophecy. Understandably, they asked Jesus to explain to them its meaning.

Jesus affirmed the prediction that Malachi made concerning the return of Elijah. Do you remember our comparison of the ministry of Elijah with that of John the Baptist in chapter 3? Elijah had indeed returned—metaphorically—in the person of John the Baptist. The disciples witnessed the fulfillment of that four-hundred-year-old prophecy. Sadly, the religious leaders failed to understand who John was, as did the Romans who executed him. So, too, the religious leaders failed to understand who Jesus was, as did the Romans who would soon execute him.

Bible scholars differ as to whether or not John the Baptist completely fulfilled Malachi's prophecy concerning the coming of Elijah or whether there is yet to come a future appearance of Elijah. Those who hold to the latter view believe that Elijah will be one of the two unnamed witnesses mentioned in Revelation 11. Based on Jesus's answer to his disciples' question, John the Baptist clearly fulfilled at least part of the prophecy. As to whether or not Elijah returns as one of the two witnesses, only time will tell.

prophecy

A Homesick Savior

Talk about going from the pinnacle to the pit. Jesus left the glorious heights of his mountaintop encounter with Moses, Elijah, and God his Father. He then climbed down into the dismal depths of the valley below where he was forced to face a mood-shattering reminder of the faithlessness of the very people he came to save. We have no doubt that were we to have personally witnessed this particular episode of Jesus's ministry, we would have seen one crestfallen Messiah. Our hearts ought to go out to Jesus as he gives us one of those rare, personal glimpses into the state of his own soul.

terror
Luke 8:25

No Rest for the Weary

MATTHEW 17:14–18 and when they had come to the multitude, a man came to Him, kneeling down to Him and saying, "Lord, have mercy on my son, for he is an epileptic and suffers severely; for he often falls into the fire and often into the water. So I brought him to Your disciples, but they could not cure him." Then Jesus answered and said, "O faithless and perverse generation, how long shall I be with you? How long shall I bear with you? Bring him here to Me." And Jesus rebuked the demon, and it came out of him; and the child was cured from that very hour. (NKJV)

A desperate dad brought his seriously sick son to Jesus in the hopes of receiving a healing touch for his tormented boy. Suffering from seizures, it became immediately apparent to Jesus that the little lad's infirmity was induced by a demon. But his father faced some significant challenges. It seems that the entire contingent of disciples could not cast the demon out of the child. What was this dad to do?

Jesus erupted with a gut-wrenching cry of deep emotion, no doubt the accumulated frustration of his dizzying days since the formal rejection of his messiahship in Matthew 12, and all that followed in its wake. He spoke the words of a homesick Savior whose emotional needle had hit empty. His was one volcanic reaction that must have stunned the crowds and brought <u>terror</u> to the ears of the disciples, who were themselves members of this "faithless" and "perverse" generation (Matthew 17:17 NKJV), men who lacked the faith to heal the boy.

Different Strokes

Some of Jesus's responses sound surprisingly severe. He didn't always make life comfortable for those around him. Part of the problem in understanding Jesus's harshness is cultural. People in the Middle East, both then and now, often speak with a directness and forthrightness that might take us aback, given our distinctly Western, politically correct, crazed culture.

For example, back in Matthew 8 the disciples were holding on for dear life as their fishing boat was tossed hither and yon by a ferocious storm on the sea. We might expect Jesus to respond to their cries with gentle, compassionate, and comforting words. But he didn't. Before rebuking the storm, he rebuked them. "Why are you fearful, O you of little faith?" he asked (Matthew 8:26 NKJV).

On another occasion, Mary and Jesus joined their friends at a wedding reception. When they ran out of wine, Mary asked her son to do something to save the situation. He sharply responded, "Woman, what does your concern have to do with Me? My hour has not yet come" (John 2:4 NKJV). A bit brusque, wouldn't you say?

Here, the disciples could not cast the demon out of the little boy. When they turned to Jesus for help, he spoke with stunning severity, and made no apology for it, for that is what the situation demanded.

Jesus's Mighty Mountain Men

MATTHEW 17:19–21 *Then the disciples came to Jesus privately and said, "Why could we not cast it out?" So Jesus said to them, "Because of your unbelief; for assuredly, I say to you, if you have faith as a mustard seed, you will say to this mountain, 'Move from here to there,' and it will move; and nothing will be impossible for you. However, this kind does not go out except by prayer and fasting."* (NKJV)

Ah, the faith to move mountains. We have heard it referred to so many times. Did Jesus intend to imply that if we have enough faith, we should be able to move any and every mountain that we face in our lives? Mountains of doubt, fear, insecurity, financial need, cancer? Just what did Jesus mean?

Peter died a martyr's death on a cross, being <u>crucified</u> upside down. Peter was certainly a man of faith. Why couldn't he move that mountain? James, as we previously noted, became the first Christian martyr, having been killed by the <u>sword</u>. Why couldn't he move that mountain? John was exiled to the island of <u>Patmos</u> and left there to die. Why couldn't he move that mountain?

The disciples had just seen one of the greatest miracles imagined— they had in essence seen a mountain move. On the Mount of Transfiguration, heaven intersected the earth. Moses and Elijah "appeared in glory" (Luke 9:31 NKJV); the appearance of Jesus's face was "altered, and His robe became white and glistening" (Luke 9:29 NKJV); God's voice thundered from peak to peak, and the disciples quaked in fear. You can bet they saw more than a mountain move! Yet when confronted by the powers of darkness as manifested in a little boy, their faith crumbled.

The disciples could not understand their failure to cast the demon out of the little boy, something they had earlier been <u>empowered</u> to do. Jesus told them, "This kind [of demon] does not go out except by prayer and fasting" (Matthew 17:21 NKJV). Clearly, the disciples entered into this contest with the forces of evil in a cavalier manner, totally underestimating the demonic power that held this boy in bondage. Perhaps remembering their earlier <u>successes</u>, the disciples evidently placed their faith in their power, thinking that they could wield it at will like a magic wand, sending demons to flight. They failed to place their faith in God and seek his will in the situation. Indeed, they didn't even pray before jumping into the fray. How then could they possible discern God's <u>will</u> in this situation?

With the memory of their mountaintop experience still fresh in their minds, Jesus took full advantage of this teachable moment to bolster the beleaguered belief of his battered band. He assured them that he would honor their faith no matter how small so long as their faith was in God, and they prayed and acted according to his will. God posts his requirements for faith on the door of his previous demonstrations of power.

go to

crucified
John 21:18–19

sword
Acts 12:2

Patmos
Revelation 1:9

empowered
Matthew 10:6–8

successes
Luke 9:10

will
Matthew 6:10;
1 John 5:14

office
Matthew 9:9

tax
Exodus 30:13–14

go to

what others say

A. W. Tozer

True faith rests upon the character of God and asks no further proof than the moral perfections of the One who cannot lie. It is enough that God said it, and if the statement should contradict every one of the five senses and all the conclusions of logic as well, still the believer continues to believe. "Let God be true, but every man a liar," is the language of true faith. Heaven approves such faith because it rises above mere proofs and rests in the bosom of God.[7]

On Death and Taxes

MATTHEW 17:22–27 *Now while they were staying in Galilee, Jesus said to them, "The Son of Man is about to be betrayed into the hands of men, and they will kill Him, and the third day He will be raised up." And they were exceedingly sorrowful.*

When they had come to Capernaum, those who received the temple tax came to Peter and said, "Does your Teacher not pay the temple tax?" He said, "Yes." And when he had come into the house, Jesus anticipated him, saying, "What do you think, Simon? From whom do the kings of the earth take customs or taxes, from their sons or from strangers?" Peter said to Him, "From strangers." Jesus said to him, "Then the sons are free. Nevertheless, lest we offend them, go to the sea, cast in a hook, and take the fish that comes up first. And when you have opened its mouth, you will find a piece of money; take that and give it to them for Me and you." (NKJV)

You may not be able to tell from these verses, but we have entered into a most poignant moment in the life and ministry of Jesus. After so many months, so many memories, so many momentous encounters, this will be Jesus's final visit to his adopted hometown of Capernaum. Wouldn't you know it? The last Capernaum miracle that Matthew records involved taxes.

As a major national thoroughfare, Capernaum boasted its own tax collector and tax collection <u>office</u>. You've got to wonder if Matthew felt a twang of guilt or a flashback of how things used to be when he plied his trade as a loathsome tax collector from this very place. Maybe, just maybe, the collectors who approached Peter about Jesus's oversight in paying the temple <u>tax</u> were former colleagues of our beloved author. At any rate, isn't it comforting to know that Jesus didn't like to pay his taxes any more than we do?

You might think that the miracle basically involved Peter finding a fish that had money in its mouth. However, the main type of fish that lives in the Sea of Galilee is a mouthbreeder. They spawn their young in their mouths. To feed their offspring, they will often swim near the shoreline where the water is warmer and shallower, and opening their mouths wide, scoop up some of the soil that has accumulated there, rich with minerals and much organic matter, as well as any other small item that may have been lost in the lake. These "St. Peter's Fish," as they are commonly called today, often have strange things in their mouths—coins, rings, etc. The miracle was not that the fish had money in its mouth; the miracle lay in the fact that the very first fish Peter caught had a coin in his mouth, exactly the right amount to pay the tax (see Illustration #6).

what others say

R. T. France

An annual half-shekel tax . . . was paid for the upkeep of worship in the temple by most adult male Jews, whether resident in Palestine or not. Unlike the Roman tax, . . . it was a matter of patriotic pride. It was, however, also a matter of controversy, as the Sadducees disapproved of the tax, and the men of **Qumran** paid it only once in a lifetime. So what was Jesus' attitude? Would he in this, as in other matters, take an independent line, and thus alienate the majority of patriotic Jews? The answer is characteristically . . . independent without being offensive—Jesus asserts that he is not obliged to pay it, but is prepared to do so to avoid "scandal" which might unnecessarily prejudice his mission. . . .[8]

Leaving Galilee for Good

MATTHEW 18:1–9 *At that time the disciples came to Jesus, saying, "Who then is greatest in the kingdom of heaven?" Then Jesus called a little child to Him, set him in the midst of them, and said, "Assuredly, I say to you, unless you are converted and become as little children, you will by no means enter the kingdom of heaven. Therefore whoever humbles himself as this little child is the greatest in the kingdom of heaven. Whoever receives one little child like this in My name receives Me.*

"But whoever causes one of these little ones who believe in Me to sin, it would be better for him if a millstone were hung around his neck, and he were drowned in the depth of the sea. Woe to the world because of offenses! For offenses must come, but

Jerusalem
Luke 9:51

Children
Matthew 19:14

woe to that man by whom the offense comes! If your hand or foot causes you to sin, cut it off and cast it from you. It is better for you to enter into life lame or maimed, rather than having two hands or two feet, to be cast into the everlasting fire. And if your eye causes you to sin, pluck it out and cast it from you. It is better for you to enter into life with one eye, rather than having two eyes, to be cast into hell fire. (NKJV)

As Jesus prepared to journey to <u>Jerusalem</u> to die, a troublesome issue threatened to crack the camaraderie enjoyed by his men. They actually got into a bit of a row about which one of them was the greatest disciple, and who of them deserved the privileged positions of power in the soon-to-come (so they thought) Jesus administration.

Jesus responded in fine fashion by placing a child in their midst. <u>Children</u> loved Jesus and flocked to him, no doubt because they sensed in him a genuine love and concern. He certainly did love kids, and this toddler was no outsider to his affection. He heaped praise upon the infant when he told the disciples that instead of trying to be high and mighty, they needed to humble themselves by becoming just like this trusting child—totally dependent upon their heavenly Father, totally accepting of his truth, totally sold out in love to him.

Illustration #6
Half-Shekel—A silver half-shekel coin such as the one depicted here was the amount Jews needed to pay the yearly temple tax. The coin was worth about two day's wages.

The Sea of Galilee boasts a bumper crop of black basalt volcanic rock, rough and porous.[9] Consequently, one of its primary industries was the manufacture and distribution of millstones. A typical millstone measured some four or five feet in diameter, was several inches thick, and required the strength of animals to roll it (see Illustration #7). Tie one of these around someone's neck, cast him into the sea, and, well, you get the picture. Using this classic case of hyperbole to make his point, Jesus chose this common cultural reference in order to underscore the seriousness of someone causing his children to stumble in their faith.

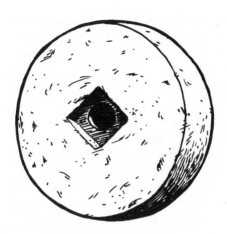

The Lord Is My Shepherd

MATTHEW 18:10–14 *"Take heed that you do not despise one of these little ones, for I say to you that in heaven their angels always see the face of My Father who is in heaven. For the Son of Man has come to save that which was lost. What do you think? If a man has a hundred sheep, and one of them goes astray, does he not leave the ninety-nine and go to the mountains to seek the one that is straying? And if he should find it, assuredly, I say to you, he rejoices more over that sheep than over the ninety-nine that did not go astray. Even so it is not the will of your Father who is in heaven that one of these little ones should perish. (NKJV)*

People who possess personal power, charismatic or dynamic personalities, don't necessarily impress our Savior; certainly not for those reasons. Aren't you glad that you don't have to be high and <u>mighty</u> to be noticed by God? When we simply and humbly place our faith in our heavenly Father in exactly the same way a small child instinctively places his or her faith in his earthly parents, we are closer to the kingdom of heaven than at any other time in our lives.

So great is the Father's love for us that he likens himself to a shepherd who, upon discovering that one of his precious sheep is missing, leaves the herd to rescue the one. He even dispatches angels to minister to us during times of distress. God loves you; he really, really loves you. He loves you, just the way you are.

People often ask about "guardian <u>angels</u>." Are there such things? The closest we come in Scripture to such a notion is Jesus's reference to "their angels" in verse 10. It's not that each child has one angel

mighty
1 Corinthians
1:26–29

angels
Daniel 3:28

send
Daniel 10:11

serve
Hebrews 1:14

forbearance
Ephesians 4:2

gentle
Galatians 6:1

forbearance
patient acceptance

assigned to him or her. Rather, the angels as a whole stand before the face of God, always at the ready for him to <u>send</u> them to help his children in times of need. How serious it is, then, to mistreat other Christians in front of the watching angels who care for and <u>serve</u> them.

Church Discipline: A Solemn Duty

MATTHEW 18:15–20 *"Moreover if your brother sins against you, go and tell him his fault between you and him alone. If he hears you, you have gained your brother. But if he will not hear, take with you one or two more, that 'by the mouth of two or three witnesses every word may be established.' And if he refuses to hear them, tell it to the church. But if he refuses even to hear the church, let him be to you like a heathen and a tax collector. Assuredly, I say to you, whatever you bind on earth will be bound in heaven, and whatever you loose on earth will be loosed in heaven. Again I say to you that if two of you agree on earth concerning anything that they ask, it will be done for them by My Father in heaven. For where two or three are gathered together in My name, I am there in the midst of them." (NKJV)*

Speaking of people causing Christians to stumble in their faith, what do we do when a Christian causes another Christian to stumble?

If we observe a Christian brother or sister committing a sin, the four-step process we are to follow is straightforward enough. Before we get into the specific steps, please note that Jesus here is talking about a brother who "sins." He is clearly referring to someone who violates a biblical absolute—breaks a clear-cut commandment of Scripture. We are not talking about someone who violates our preferences. We might not like their music. We might not adopt someone's style of dress as our own. But in those instances, we are commanded to show the individual **forbearance**. We do not confront someone in that type of instance. When an individual breaks a commandment right in front of us, that's another matter.

Paul suggests the attitude with which we follow Jesus's four-point plan: <u>gentle</u> humility. Gentle, because the goal is always to restore a sinning person; humility, because we are just as capable of sinning as the person we are seeking to restore.

Here's the plan:

Step One: Go to the person, gently and humbly. No one, *no one* need know about the incident except "you and him alone" (Matthew 18:15 NKJV). This is not a time for gossip. Note Jesus's hopeful words: "If he hears you, you have gained your brother" (18:15 NKJV). Restoration is always the goal.

forgives
1 John 1:9

forgets
Jeremiah 31:34

Step Two: If he or she refuses to listen to you, next approach the individual with two or three persons who have also witnessed the same sinful behavior. Coming from three or more independent sources, the individual will be hard put to deny these corroborating observations. Once again, if he listens, repents, and changes his behavior, that's the end of it. God <u>forgives</u> him; we forgive him. God <u>forgets</u>; we forget.

Step Three: Report the ongoing sin to the church leaders. If he or she repents at this point, all is well and restoration has been achieved. But if not, go to step four.

Step Four: Treat the individual as an unbeliever. Sound harsh? When a person purposes to set himself or herself in opposition to the will of God, he or she forfeits the benefits of being a vital part of a local body of believers. In truth, the sinning believer is making the choice to break fellowship with obedient believers, not the other way around. When repentance backed up by a change in lifestyle occurs, we are to receive the broken brother or sister back into fellowship with open arms.

The Four Solemn Steps of Church Discipline
(Matthew 18:15–17 NKJV)

The Four Steps	Four Steps Explained	Two Possible Outcomes
Step 1: **Private Confrontation**	If you see someone committing a sin (a clear violation of a biblical absolute), go to him or her in private, in a spirit of gentleness and humility (Galatians 6:1), and "tell him his fault between you and him alone" (18:15).	1. He will receive your words with gratitude and repent. "You have gained your brother." The process of discipline has worked. It stops right here. 2. He will reject your words and continue in his sin. This leads to Step 2.
Step 2: **One or Two Witnesses**	Go back to the individual with one or two others who have witnessed the same sin. This is in keeping with the biblical admonition: "By the mouth of two or three witnesses every word may be established" (18:16).	1. He will receive your words with gratitude and repent. "You have gained your brother." The process of discipline has worked. It stops right here. 2. He will refuse to listen and continue in his sin. This leads to Step 3.

go to

head
Ephesians 5:23

The Four Solemn Steps of Church Discipline
(Matthew 18:15–17 NKJV) (cont'd)

The Four Steps	Four Steps Explained	Two Possible Outcomes
Step 3: **Church Leadership**	Report the ongoing sin to the church leadership. They should then follow up by meeting with the individual and seeking to bring him to repentance.	1. He will receive their words with gratitude and repent. If so, the leaders forgive him and the matter is settled, never to be brought up again.
		2. He refuses to listen to the church leaders and continues in his sin. This leads to Step 4.
Step 4: **Removal from the Membership**	"If he refuses even to hear the church [leaders], let him be to you like a heathen and a tax collector" (18:17). In other words, treat him as an unbeliever. He is put out of the church membership at this point, and loses the privilege of fellowship with other believers. This is the equivalent of "[delivering] such a one to Satan for the destruction of the flesh, that his spirit may be saved in the day of the Lord Jesus" (1 Corinthians 5:5 NKJV; 1 Timothy 1:20).	1. He will repent. If so, he is restored to membership of and fellowship with the church. 2. He will continue in his sin. At that point, he is in God's hands. His sin is no longer between him and the church, but between him and God directly.

When Jesus talked about binding and loosing, he was not talking about prayer meetings; he was talking about church leaders making tough, sometimes gut-wrenching church discipline decisions following the pattern just mentioned. Jesus never meant to suggest that whenever three people ask God to make them rich, send rain, or heal a loved one, he is somehow obligated to give them whatever they want just because they agree together.

Believers not only hold in their hands the "keys of the kingdom" (Matthew 16:19 NKJV), but church leaders hold in their hands the keys to the church. The way they wield that responsibility will affect the one being disciplined, the offended church, and the watching world. Jesus assures these leaders that he adds his endorsement to their disciplining process. It is of paramount importance that in those rare instances when church discipline must be carried to the extreme, it is only done so under the watchful eye of Jesus, the <u>head</u> of his church.

To Err Is Human; to Forgive, Divine

the big picture

Matthew 18:21-35

Peter came to Jesus and asked how many times he should forgive his brother. He guessed that seven times should be enough. Jesus said he should forgive seventy-seven times.

Then Jesus shared a parable, the essence of which follows: A king had a servant who owed him a huge sum of money. When the servant begged the king's forgiveness, the king graciously dismissed the debt. This same servant found a fellow servant who owed him a paltry sum. When the second servant begged forgiveness, the forgiven servant refused and had him thrown into prison. When the king learned of this, he exploded. A man who was shown such grace should of all people be gracious to others. Because of his unforgiving spirit, the king threw the first servant into jail to be tortured until he could repay the original debt.

Jesus concluded the story by saying that his heavenly Father would treat each of them in the same way unless they learned to forgive their brother from their heart.

As we approach the end of this chapter, note the progression of thought. The disciples argued among themselves to determine who was greatest in the now-postponed kingdom. This prompted Jesus to give them a short lesson on humility, using a little child as his audiovisual aid.

Speaking of children, Jesus continued to speak of God the Father's love for us—his children—and uttered a strong word of warning to those who cause his people to stumble. Tragically, sometimes the offending person is a fellow Christian. So, Jesus gives us step-by-step instructions as to how to deal with sinning believers. Church discipline helps to keep the church as pure as earthly possible.

This caused Peter to blurt out, "Lord, how often shall my brother sin against me, and I forgive him?" (Matthew 18:21 NKJV). Notice that we are still speaking in the context of sin. A Christian hurts another Christian by actually breaking one of God's clear commandments. How many times must we forgive that person?

Jesus gave a classic answer. Not seven times, as Peter suggested, but seventy times seven, another of Jesus's purposeful exaggerations to make his point. We never stop forgiving. Why? Because the moment we stop forgiving, we start destroying. And the one whom we are destroying is ourselves.

The opposite of forgiveness is bitterness. Bitterness is to the soul what poison is to the body. When God formed us, he did not create within us the capacity to hate. Hate is an intruder, a rogue emotion that poisons hate-filled individuals and those unfortunate enough to be around them. So in response to Peter's question, Jesus responded with the principle of forgiveness.

In the parable, here was a man who was just forgiven of an enormous debt. We'll place the figure at ten million dollars. He turned right around and refused to forgive someone of a paltry sum of money, reckoned by some to be around eighteen dollars.

The point of the parable should be clear. God has forgiven us of an enormous debt, a ten-million-dollar debt. When someone sins against us, that by comparison is a very small debt. It's one thing for a person to strike out against and hurt God. It's quite another thing for a person to hurt another person. Since God has erased our incomprehensible debt, ought we not forgive the relatively small debts of those who sin against us? Should not we, the recipients of God's grace, dispense his grace to others?

This is precisely the reason we are warned in Hebrews 12:15 not to allow a root of bitterness to spring up in our hearts. For if we do, we defile ourselves and everyone around us.

what others say

Charles R. Swindoll

Did you hear what he said? He said that we who refuse to forgive—we who live in the gall of bitterness—will become victims of torture meaning intense inner torment. If we nurture feelings of bitterness we are little better than inmates of an internal concentration camp. We lock ourselves in a lonely isolation chamber, walled in by our own refusal to forgive.[10]

Chapter Wrap-Up

- Peter rebuked Jesus for suggesting that he was destined to die on a Roman cross. (Matthew 16:22)

- Jesus alluded to his second coming, when he will return "in the glory of His Father with His angels." (Matthew 16:27 NKJV)

- Jesus was "transfigured," or transformed into a blazing brilliance of God's glory, before the awestruck disciples. (Matthew 17:1–2)

- Two men appeared with Jesus on the Mount of Trans-figuration—Moses and Elijah. (Matthew 17:3)

- Jesus cast a demon out a boy from whom the disciples were unable to cast it out. (Matthew 17:18)

- Jesus again warned the disciples that he would be killed and raised from the dead. (Matthew 17:22–23)

- Jesus paid the Temple tax with a coin discovered in the mouth of a fish from the sea. (Matthew 17:27)

- Jesus warned the disciples about causing a child to stumble in his or her faith. (Matthew 18:10–11)

- Jesus established the pattern that churches are to follow today in dealing with a sinning member. (Matthew 18:15–17)

- Jesus taught a parable, the point of which is that we should never stop forgiving, just as God never stops forgiving us. (Matthew 18:21–22)

Study Questions

1. For what did Jesus rebuke Peter?

2. What might be the cost of following Jesus?

3. How do you explain Matthew 16:28 in light of the fact that all of the disciples have died and Christ's kingdom has not yet come?

4. How did God give Moses and Elijah the desires of their hearts?

5. What does the reference to "moving mountains" have to do with our faith?

6. What is the four-step plan for restoring a sinning brother to full fellowship?

7. How should we respond when someone sins against us?

Matthew 19-20: Green Mile

Let's Get Started

Before we consider the text, allow us to point out four important, introductory considerations. Stephen King, master of the macabre, coined a rather gruesome phrase that became the title of his runaway best-seller and blockbuster movie *The Green Mile*. In the movie, Tom Hanks portrays a jailhouse guard who, in the aftermath of the Great Depression, finds himself assigned to death row. There, he keeps watch over some of the country's most notorious criminals who have been sentenced to die by electrocution. The green linoleum floor that leads to the death chamber, and down which the convicted criminal must walk to his impending execution, is called the "Green Mile." No one wanted to walk the Green Mile, a somber stroll from which no one returned.

In a sense, in Matthew 19–20, we readers accompany Jesus on his walk down the Green Mile. In the book-turned-movie, the central figure, John Coffey, committed no crime. Falsely accused, unfairly tried, wrongly convicted, and unjustly sentenced, John Coffey resigned himself to his fate and willingly walked down the Green Mile and to the chair. A compassionate, caring man tormented by the pain of the people whom he loved, desperate to fix things he couldn't fix, heal those he couldn't heal, John Coffey was ready to die.

"I'm rightly tired of the pain I hear and feel, boss," he confessed to his executioner. "I'm tired of bein' on the road, lonely as a robin in the rain. . . . I'm tired of people bein' ugly to each other. It feels like pieces of glass in my head. I'm tired of all the times I've wanted to help and couldn't. . . . Mostly it's the pain. There's too much. If I could end it, I would. But I can't."[1]

Shortly thereafter, the warden threw the switch, the jailhouse lights dimmed, John Coffey uttered a muffled cry, and finally, gratefully, mercifully, he felt the pieces of glass in his head no more. Death became a blessing to this big, bald, lovable, and loving man. Jesus committed no crime. As we will witness in a future chapter, he will be falsely accused, unfairly tried, wrongly convicted, and unjustly sentenced. We'll leave that for later. For now, we will watch Jesus metaphorically meander down his own version of the Green Mile, encountering along the way six distinct groups of people:

1. His disciples, who will remain clueless as to their master's fate and impending doom

2. The ever-present needy, who want his healing touch

3. The relentless accusers, who will pepper him with questions aimed at discrediting his character and claims

4. The few who truly admire him

5. One who will ask him a sincere question and receive a disappointing answer

6. You and I, who, via Matthew's quill and parchment, can vicariously join Jesus on his final journey to Jerusalem to die

Test Question

Before we consider the text, allow us to point out four important, introductory considerations. First, Jesus did not speak his words in a vacuum. He responded to a question posed to him by his enemies, a feeble attempt (as it will turn out) on their parts to mire him in the quicksand of controversy. Second, we make a grave mistake if we attempt to interpret Jesus's words apart from the context in which they appear, and the intent with which Jesus said them. Third, while gallons of ink have been splashed on reams of paper (the work of Bible scholars trying for decades to make sense out of Jesus's statements), the passage we will now consider still contains a few surprises that not many commentators have chosen to address. Fourth, we know that this is a most tender and intensely personal subject. We will approach it with the utmost of caution and compassion for all who continue to bear the scars of a painful divorce. So with that much of a heads-up, let's dive in and enjoy the water as we paddle around this particular pond of puzzlement.

The Mathematics of Marriage: When One Plus One Equals One

MATTHEW 19:1–6 *Now it came to pass, when Jesus had finished these sayings, that He departed from Galilee and came to the region of Judea beyond the Jordan. And great multitudes followed Him, and He healed them there. The Pharisees also came to Him, testing Him, and saying to Him, "Is it lawful for a man to divorce his wife for just any reason?" And He answered and said to them, "Have you not read that He who made them at the beginning 'made them male and female,' and said, 'For this reason a man shall leave his father and mother and be joined to his wife, and the two shall become one flesh'? So then, they are no longer two but one flesh. Therefore what God has joined together, let not man separate." (NKJV)*

go to

quoted
Genesis 1:27; 2:24

hates
Malachi 2:16

death
Romans 7:2

live
Romans 7:3

axiom
statement generally
accepted as true

Solomon, wise man that he was, offered a profound observation in Ecclesiastes 1:9 when he wrote: "That which has been is what will be, that which is done is what will be done, and there is nothing new under the sun" (NKJV). This **axiom** certainly applies to any discussion of divorce and remarriage.

In Jesus's day, two schools of Jewish thought prevailed regarding this issue: (1) the followers of Rabbi Shammai took the narrow, strict, conservative view that God permits divorce only when one's wife is sexually unfaithful to her husband; and (2) Rabbi Hillel's disciples adopted an opposite and extreme standard that a man may "divorce his wife for any and every reason."

The conniving Pharisees sought to catapult Jesus right into the middle of this heated debate, seeking to hang him helplessly on the horns of this particular dilemma. If you thought Houdini was good at getting out of sticky situations, Jesus came into his own as a world-class theological escape artist. He simply did what he did best—quoted the Old Testament where God defined marriage.

Jesus's conclusion befuddled his enemies. Paraphrased, he said, "One man plus one woman equals one family under God, indivisible." From God's point of view, the so-called biblical divorce, a divorce of which God approves, is a myth, a mirage. God hates divorce. There is no such thing as a divorce of which God approves. His will, his design for marriage, is that one man and one woman commit themselves to one another "until death do us part," "for as long as we both shall live."

wrote
1 Corinthians 7:1,
10–16

divorce
Deuteronomy
24:1–4

tacit
implied although
not stated

God designed and defined marriage as a lifelong commitment between two people, a commitment that expires only upon the death of one's spouse, not divorce. A "biblical divorce" exists only as a fantasy, never as an actuality.

We are, of course, speaking here in the most idealistic of terms. Simply stated, God wills that one man and one woman commit themselves to one another for a lifetime. Unfortunately, we do not live in an ideal world. We live in a realistic world of imperfect people who make imperfect choices. Jesus categorically stated the ideal from God's frame of reference. But did he say anything about the real world where divorces and remarriages have become all-too-commonplace? Didn't Jesus allow divorce for certain reasons? And if so, don't divorces for those reasons qualify as a "biblical divorce"? As you are about to discover, the Pharisees wondered the same thing.

The church in biblical times struggled with this same subject, and even <u>wrote</u> the apostle Paul in hopes of receiving an authoritative answer. The modern-day church has inherited this same issue. Most congregations include many church members who have divorced their mates "for any and every reason," others who languish for years in dead marriages because they don't believe that it is ever right to divorce, and others still who hold every other conceivable viewpoint that appears on the divorce-remarriage spectrum.

The Division of Divorce: When One Divided by One Equals Two

MATTHEW 19:7–9 *They said to Him, "Why then did Moses command to give a certificate of divorce, and to put her away?" He said to them, "Moses, because of the hardness of your hearts, permitted you to divorce your wives, but from the beginning it was not so. And I say to you, whoever divorces his wife, except for sexual immorality, and marries another, commits adultery; and whoever marries her who is divorced commits adultery." (NKJV)*

The Pharisees correctly alluded to the fact that Moses permitted <u>divorce</u> in some instances. Didn't that serve as God's **tacit** approval of any divorce that "qualified" according to Moses's instructions? The Pharisees might have thought so, but Jesus didn't.

Jesus corrected them. Moses never *commanded* divorce; he admittedly *allowed* divorce in some instances, but only as a concession to those who were married to spouses who engaged in hard-hearted, unrepentant immorality. God certainly never willed divorces to happen. He does not approve of divorce when it does. But many things happen of which God does not approve. When Moses allowed divorce in some circumstances, he only did so as a concession to the hard-hearted sinfulness of willfully disobedient people.

go to

defined
Genesis 2:24

Exception Clause

So far so good, as far as Jesus's answer to the Pharisees is concerned. But, boy, did he open one heck of a Pandora's box with his next statement—the so-called exception clause. His words "except for sexual immorality" (Matthew 19:9 NKJV) have stirred up a hornet's nest of controversy. What exactly did he mean?

God <u>defined</u> marriage as a man and a woman becoming united together in one flesh. Paul used this principle to admonish his readers to avoid sexual intercourse with those to whom they were not married when he said, "Do you not know that he who is joined to a harlot is one body with her? for 'the two,' He says, 'shall become one flesh' . . . Flee sexual immorality" (1 Corinthians 6:16, 18 NKJV).

Jesus recognized (note my carefully chosen word here—*recognized*, not *approved of, allowed, endorsed in the case of,* or any other rendering that may denote approval of any kind) that when a husband or a wife is sexually "joined to" someone to whom he or she is not married, they have by that very act shattered their union with their wife or husband as they literally become one flesh with that other person. Divorce merely does *legally* what the adulterer has already done *physically*. Jesus is simply pointing out that if in that situation the nonadulterer decides to divorce his or her spouse, and then remarries someone else, he or she has not become an adulterer.

The adultery has already taken place. The marriage vow, and the physical union that symbolizes that vow, has been broken by the adulterous partner. And the violated spouse has chosen to respond to that breaking of the marriage vow by breaking up the marriage.

Thus, we are right back where we started. God does not approve of divorce under any circumstances. There is no such thing as a "bib-

go to

responsibility
Galatians 6:1–2

lical divorce." But marriage vows do get broken. Divorces do take place. This is where the church as a whole, and we as individuals, have a golden opportunity and a God-given <u>responsibility</u> to become lovingly and compassionately redemptive in the lives of the broken people who suffer through the agonies of an affair and/or a divorce.

No one can come through an affair or a divorce without suffering significant scars. May the church not add to their shame by branding them with a scarlet "A" or "D." Marital unfaithfulness is a sin to be sure, but it surely is not an unforgivable sin. Marital unfaithfulness affects many people, including any children in the home. These precious, broken people do not need to have their Christian brothers and sisters judge them. They need to have us love them. By gently and humbly moving them toward repentance for the regrettable choices that they have made, we can help them to receive God's forgiveness, his healing of their broken or bitter hearts, and his grace to begin to rebuild their lives. We are never more Christlike than when we play a redemptive role in someone's life, just as others have played a redemptive role in ours.

---

what others say

Larry Crabb Jr.

If we believe that the Lord is able to work on our behalf in all circumstances, then no collection of marital setbacks will prompt us to seriously consider divorce or withdrawal. If God is really as powerful as He claims to be, then the path of obedience will always lead to His intended circumstances. The hope (better, the certainty) that God is at work to accomplish His plan even in the most difficult of marriages must remain firmly rooted in our awareness of His powerful grace.[2]

To Marry, or Not to Marry, That Is the Question

MATTHEW 19:10–12 *His disciples said to Him, "If such is the case of the man with his wife, it is better not to marry."*

But He said to them, "All cannot accept this saying, but only those to whom it has been given: for there are eunuchs who were born thus from their mother's womb, and there are eunuchs who were made eunuchs by men, and there are eunuchs who have made themselves eunuchs for the kingdom of heaven's sake. He who is able to accept it, let him accept it." (NKJV)

eunuchs
men physically
unable to have sex

Getting back to Jesus's original premise (that there is no such thing as a biblical divorce), for once the disciples understood exactly what Jesus was saying. No wonder they responded with a gasp. Jesus's curious reference to **eunuchs** was his way of saying to his men, "Not so fast. It's not that easy to be married, but it's not that easy not to be married. Not everyone can handle a celibate life."

The biblical standard for marriage before God is sky-high—two people committing themselves to one another for "as long as they both shall live." That is a worthy standard for which we strive. It should not scare us, as it did the disciples, from entering into the bliss and blessing of a God-ordained institution. But let us be quick to acknowledge that even the best people fail to live up to the ideal. While we purpose before God to honor our marriage vows for life. Again, if the unthinkable occurs, the church should shine its brightest as a hospital offering healing for the hurting.

Jesus Loves the Little Children

MATTHEW 19:13–15 *Then little children were brought to Him that He might put His hands on them and pray, but the disciples rebuked them. But Jesus said, "Let the little children come to Me, and do not forbid them; for of such is the kingdom of heaven." And He laid His hands on them and departed from there. (NKJV)*

While this particular passage may seem out of place in the flow of the chapter, perhaps this is really the best place for it. We might wonder why Matthew chose to include this little aside in his Gospel. It doesn't seem to advance the narrative or support his theme. Yet, I cannot help but think that as Matthew finished the section dealing with divorce, his mind went immediately to those who suffer the most from the breakup of a family—the children.

Jesus loved (and loves) the little children, and they loved him. The disciples didn't want to be bothered by a bunch of kids, not an untypical response of many adults concerning the little ones running around the church. But Jesus overruled his insensitive men and invited the children to come. He then turned this encounter into

go to

accountable
Romans 2:5–6

accounts
Mark 10:17–30;
Luke 18:18–30

another of his teachable moments when he made the observation, "of such is the kingdom of heaven" (Matthew 19:14 NKJV).

There are two prevalent views—the metaphorical and the literal—as to what Jesus meant by that statement. The metaphorical view is the notion that just as a child enters the world with a precious innocence, and tends to trust his or her mommy and daddy with a total dependence, so we approach our new life in Christ with a precious innocence and total dependence upon our heavenly Father.

The literal view states that young children who sadly die go immediately into the presence of Jesus Christ. Some refer to an "age of accountability," a point at which a child knows right from wrong, can make obedient or rebellious choices, and therefore becomes accountable for his or her choices. Of course, there is no specific age when every child reaches that point; it's unique to each individual. But the thought here is that any child who dies before reaching the "age of accountability" goes immediately to heaven.

Both of these views are true. Saving faith is a childlike dependence upon our heavenly Father. Young children who die before reaching an age of accountability will immediately go to heaven. Having said that, Matthew's intended purpose in penning these verses was to give us a keen insight into the character of Jesus, who both loved and was loved by children.

Threading the Needle

MATTHEW **19:16–20** *Now behold, one came and said to Him, "Good Teacher, what good thing shall I do that I may have eternal life?" So He said to him, "Why do you call Me good? No one is good but One, that is, God. But if you want to enter into life, keep the commandments." He said to Him, "Which ones?" Jesus said, "'You shall not murder,' 'You shall not commit adultery,' 'You shall not steal,' 'You shall not bear false witness,' 'Honor your father and your mother,' and, 'You shall love your neighbor as yourself.'" The young man said to Him, "All these things I have kept from my youth. What do I still lack?"* (NKJV)

The title with which the young man greeted Jesus is most telling. According to Mark's and Luke's accounts, he approached Jesus with the words "Good Teacher." These words show that he recognized Jesus as a man of keen insight, but nothing more.

Jesus responded with a curious reply. Fact is, there is no good thing that we can do to earn or inherit eternal life. The Scriptures clearly teach that no one can be saved from their sins by observing Old Testament **Law**. The law condemns us as sinners since we each—you, me, and this rich young ruler—break God's law every day. And that's just the point! Here came this respectable young man approaching the Holy God of the universe while actually believing that his lifestyle was in perfect harmony with the Ten Commandments.

Hearken back to Matthew 5 for a moment and recall Jesus's opening line to the Sermon on the Mount: "Blessed are the poor in spirit, for *theirs* is the kingdom of heaven" (Matthew 5:3 NKJV, emphasis mine). This guy was anything but "poor in spirit." He came to Jesus proud in spirit, boldly declaring his self-righteousness when he basically said, "I have kept all these commandments since I was a boy!" This guy actually claimed perfection from his childhood through adulthood. Talk about a holier-than-thou attitude!

Jesus quoted several of the Ten Commandments to transform the man from a proud seeker to a humble sinner. When that failed, Jesus zeroed in on the bull's-eye of the man's heart—his money.

Poor Little Rich Man

MATTHEW 19:21–22 *Jesus said to him, "If you want to be perfect, go, sell what you have and give to the poor, and you will have treasure in heaven; and come, follow Me." But when the young man heard that saying, he went away sorrowful, for he had great possessions. (NKJV)*

Compare, if you will, the young man's proud proclamation of his own perfection to the humble confessions of Isaiah (Isaiah 6:5), Peter (Luke 5:8), or John (Revelation 1:17). Jesus did not condemn the man for being wealthy. The problem with the young man was not his money; the problem was that his money had become his god. How blessed is the one who masters his resources to help those in need; how cursed is the one whose money masters him.

Law
Galatians 2:16

Law
first five books of the Bible, summarized in the Ten Commandments

Abraham
Genesis 12:5

Job
Job 1:3

Paul
Philippians 4:12

love
1 Timothy 6:10

draws
John 6:44

grace
undeserved leniency

The man who honestly believed that he broke no commandment in actuality shattered the very first one; it reads, "You shall have no other gods before Me" (Exodus 20:3 NKJV).

The accumulation of wealth is not evil in and of itself. Many godly people enjoyed a bountiful supply of money, including <u>Abraham</u>, <u>Job</u>, and even, on occasion, <u>Paul</u>. Speaking of Paul, he did not teach that money is the root of all evil, as some people allege. The root of all evil is the <u>love</u> of money.

Jesus does not command rich people to give away all their money. He does demand that they be willing to if he should ask them to. For if Jesus is not Lord of every aspect of someone's life, including his money, in reality he is not Lord at all.

Mission Impossible

MATTHEW 19:23–26 *Then Jesus said to His disciples, "Assuredly, I say to you that it is hard for a rich man to enter the kingdom of heaven. And again I say to you, it is easier for a camel to go through the eye of a needle than for a rich man to enter the kingdom of God." When His disciples heard it, they were greatly astonished, saying, "Who then can be saved?" But Jesus looked at them and said to them, "With men this is impossible, but with God all things are possible." (NKJV)*

This is another of those rare occurrences when the disciples actually understood something that Jesus said. They asked the right question. Understanding the irresistible nature of money, they in essence blurted out, "Since money is so tantalizing and the desire for money so all-consuming, who in and of themselves can possibly deny his or her greed and enter the kingdom of heaven?"

Jesus's answer, as usual, was simple, concise, and to the point: A person can be saved only when God first does a work of **grace** in his heart and <u>draws</u> him to himself.

What did Jesus mean when he said, "It is easier for a camel to go through the eye of a needle than for a rich man to enter the kingdom of God" (Matthew 19:24 NKJV)? During biblical times, cities were fortified with walls. The entrances to the cities were called gates. At night, for the protection of its citizens, the people were brought into the city from the outlying fields in which they farmed and the gates were locked shut. These gates were big enough to allow men, horses, equipment, even chariots to enter the city. A conquering army would have no trouble storming the gates unless they were secured.

In case an individual didn't make it back in time and needed to be let in, a small doorway was cut into the gate, the width of which was just enough to allow him to enter the city. This small doorway was called "the eye of a needle."

Now here's the point: A man and his camel could enter the eye of a needle—a tight squeeze to be sure, but doable nonetheless—unless the camel was loaded with stuff. That stuff hanging off the sides of the camel made it too wide to enter. The stuff became a barrier to entry. For a person to enter the city, he must first unpack from the camel all of his stuff. Get the point? Because of our human tendency to love money, many an otherwise good person has sold their souls, families, friendships, or whatever in the raw pursuit of wealth.

Jerusalem or Bust

Matthew 20 is the final chapter before Jesus formally enters Jerusalem and is greeted by his fickle following as their long-awaited Messiah. As Jesus makes his final ascent to Jerusalem, he must tie up a few loose ends:

1. In response to Peter's arrogant assertion, "We have left all and followed You" (Matthew 19:27 NKJV), Jesus will teach the Twelve something about justice versus fairness.

2. In response to a mother's outrageous request, Jesus will remind his men of his mission.

3. In response to two men's desperate plea, Jesus will perform yet another miracle of mercy.

4. And then the fickle finger of fate turns against him one last time.

First Things First

MATTHEW 19:27–30 *Then Peter answered and said to Him, "See, we have left all and followed You. Therefore what shall we have?" So Jesus said to them, "Assuredly I say to you, that in the*

go to

Millennium
Revelation 20:1–6

regeneration, when the Son of Man sits on the throne of His glory, you who have followed Me will also sit on twelve thrones, judging the twelve tribes of Israel. And everyone who has left houses or brothers or sisters or father or mother or wife or children or lands, for My name's sake, shall receive a hundredfold, and inherit eternal life. But many who are first will be last, and the last first." (NKJV)

In fairness to the disciples, they did give up a lot to follow Jesus. As we noted earlier, Peter was quite well-off when he left the family fishing business at Jesus's call. Taking nothing for granted, Peter thought he would offer Jesus a not-so-subtle reminder that he and his friends had basically done what Jesus told the rich young ruler to do.

Jesus promised them that they would be justly rewarded for their sacrifices, as will every believer, including us, who must give up much to serve the Savior. Lest Peter get too big for his britches, Jesus immediately followed his promise with this subtle word of warning, "But many who are first will be last, and the last first" (Matthew 19:30 NKJV). So stunning a revelation was his statement that it required a lengthy story to explain its meaning.

Isn't it interesting that Jesus once again made reference to his kingdom, only this time in the future tense. Here he referred to his now-postponed kingdom, commonly referred to today as the prophesied <u>Millennium</u>, or the thousand-year reign of Christ. His assurances were carefully crafted and timed, coming as they did within days of his crucifixion. He promised them that no matter what might happen in Jerusalem, their future in his coming kingdom would be assured.

Prophecy

That's Just Not Fair!

day, the owner handed out the wages, giving every worker the same amount—one **denarius**. the first workers cried, "Unfair!"

"Friend," the owner explained, "I am doing you no wrong. Did you not agree with me for a denarius? . . . Or is your eye evil because I am good?" (Matthew 20:13, 15 NKJV). Jesus ended the story by affirming again that the last would be first and the first would be last.

prize
Matthew 19:27

death
John 21:19

thief
Luke 23:43

denarius
silver coin equal to a day's wage for a Roman soldier

Peter had this thing about fairness. When he reminded Jesus that he had given up much to become a disciple, Peter made it clear that he wanted his fair share of the <u>prize</u>. Jesus seized upon this teachable moment and taught Peter and the others a lesson about fairness using one of his favorite teaching techniques, a parable. The story was straightforward enough, simple in its meaning, profound in its implications.

The implications of this parable are far-reaching. Peter left everything to follow Jesus. He faithfully served Christ for decades and died a martyr's <u>death</u> of crucifixion exactly as Jesus told him he would. He deserves, and will receive, great rewards. But so will the <u>thief</u> on the cross, who became a believer in Jesus with his dying breath. When it comes to our rewards, length of service is not the issue. Faithfulness to God's will is.

<u>Paying the Ultimate Price</u>

MATTHEW 20:17–19 *Now Jesus, going up to Jerusalem, took the twelve disciples aside on the road and said to them, "Behold, we are going up to Jerusalem, and the Son of Man will be betrayed to the chief priests and to the scribes; and they will condemn Him to death, and deliver Him to the Gentiles to mock and to scourge and to crucify. And the third day He will rise again." (NKJV)*

Jesus then offered this caveat: If Peter and the others thought that they had given up a lot for the cause, Jesus would sacrifice so much more, infinitely more. He reminded them that they were walking up to Jerusalem for the last time. He would soon be condemned, mocked, flogged, and crucified. As we will soon see, Jesus would die a death more excruciating, more hideous, more unthinkable, more torturous than any other human being has before or since. Peter and the others had nothing about which to complain.

Be Careful What You Ask for

Herod
Acts 12:2

Patmos
Revelation 1:9

MATTHEW 20:20–23 *Then the mother of Zebedee's sons came to Him with her sons, kneeling down and asking something from Him. And He said to her, "What do you wish?" She said to Him, "Grant that these two sons of mine may sit, one on Your right hand and the other on the left, in Your kingdom." But Jesus answered and said, "You do not know what you ask. Are you able to drink the cup that I am about to drink, and be baptized with the baptism that I am baptized with?" They said to Him, "We are able." So He said to them, "You will indeed drink My cup, and be baptized with the baptism that I am baptized with; but to sit on My right hand and on My left is not Mine to give, but it is for those for whom it is prepared by My Father." (NKJV)*

The disciples just didn't get it. Reread Matthew 20:17–19 and 20–23 without a break, as one continuous narrative. Jesus had just reaffirmed to his men that he would meet his untimely demise at the hands of the Romans in Jerusalem. Yet, brothers James and John still attempted to maneuver into position to sit in the places of prominence when Jesus launched his military coup d'état, overthrowing Rome and establishing his kingdom in the process. Jesus must have been beside himself in utter disbelief. To make matters worse, these "men" had their mommy do the dirty deed for them. The word *baptidzo*, translated "baptism," means "to immerse," as a cloth might be immersed in a liquid dye solution. Jesus warned James and John to consider carefully their requests, because the long, dark shadow of suffering had been cast upon his path. It's the old story: Be careful what you ask for; you might just get it. James became the first Christian martyr; he was beheaded by <u>Herod</u>. John was banished like a common criminal to the penal colony on <u>Patmos</u> where he suffered a miserable existence among the caves that formed that desolate island rock. They did indeed drink from the cup of Jesus's suffering; they were indeed immersed into the cup of Jesus's death.

what others say

Josh McDowell

One can detect in the New Testament the apostles' attitude toward Christ: their expectation of a reigning Messiah. After Jesus told his disciples that he had to go to Jerusalem and suffer, James and John asked him to promise that in his kingdom they could sit on his right and left hands. . . . What type

At Your Service

MATTHEW 20:24–28 *And when the ten heard it, they were greatly displeased with the two brothers. But Jesus called them to Himself and said, "You know that the rulers of the Gentiles lord it over them, and those who are great exercise authority over them. Yet it shall not be so among you; but whoever desires to become great among you, let him be your servant. And whoever desires to be first among you, let him be your slave—just as the Son of Man did not come to be served, but to serve, and to give His life a ransom for many." (NKJV)*

The other ten disciples became furious at James and John—not because of the request, but because James and John got to Jesus before they did! Their collective response exposed the nasty little secret that they each harbored in their sin-sick hearts; they, too, sought places of prominence in the kingdom.

Blind ambition has destroyed far too many of Christ's choice servants. If, after three years of walking, talking, and watching Jesus, the disciples fell prey to prideful ambition, let us be forewarned. We, too, are susceptible to this cancer of the soul.

apply it

what others say

C. S. Lewis

Whenever we find that our religious life is making us feel that we are good above all, that we are better than someone else—I think that we may be sure that we are being acted on, not by God, but by the devil. The real test of being in the presence of God is that you either forget about yourself altogether or see yourself as a small, dirty object. It is better to forget about yourself altogether.[4]

The Blind Leading the Blind

MATTHEW 20:29–34 *Now as they went out of Jericho, a great multitude followed Him. And behold, two blind men sitting by*

Jericho
Joshua 6:1

the road, when they heard that Jesus was passing by, cried out, saying, "Have mercy on us, O Lord, Son of David!" Then the multitude warned them that they should be quiet; but they cried out all the more, saying, "Have mercy on us, O Lord, Son of David!" So Jesus stood still and called them, and said, "What do you want Me to do for you?" They said to Him, "Lord, that our eyes may be opened." So Jesus had compassion and touched their eyes. And immediately their eyes received sight, and they followed Him. (NKJV)

On the surface of things, the healing of the two blind men appears to be just another garden-variety miracle. Two men sat on a road, heard the commotion as Jesus and his entourage passed by, ignored the rebuke of the crowd, cried out to him a desperate request to be healed, and Jesus compassionately touched their eyes and healed them.

When the story continues, Jesus and the Twelve have climbed nearly four thousand feet in elevation and stand on the eastern side of the Mount of Olives, anticipating their entry into Jerusalem and the beginning of Jesus's final week. The healing of the blind men was a momentous miracle in that it served as the bridge into the final events of Jesus's life.

One troublesome discrepancy might cause a casual reader a bit of unnecessary concern. Matthew states that Jesus met the blind men as he and the disciples "went out of Jericho" (Matthew 20:29 NKJV), while Luke records that this encounter took place as Jesus "was coming near Jericho" (Luke 18:35 NKJV). Is this a contradiction?

The archaeologist's spade comes to our rescue. At the time of the New Testament, there were two Jerichos: Joshua's <u>Jericho</u>, whose walls "came a-tumblin' down," and a New Testament Jericho that included Herod's winter palace, built just to the southwest of the Old Testament Jericho, also referred to by the same name. Matthew's and Luke's accounts are both accurate. Jesus was obviously leaving the one while entering the other.

One or Two?

One other small detail might unnecessarily become a stumbling block to someone's confidence in the accuracy of the Bible. Matthew categorically states, "Two blind men [were] sitting by the road"

(Matthew 20:30 NKJV), while Mark and Luke refer to one blind man (Mark 10:46; Luke 18:35). So which is it, one or two? The answer is a definite two.

These two accounts are not contradictory, but rather are complementary. That is, each writer is accurate, but neither biblical writer is required to be complete regarding the details of any story. The two accounts complement each other in that when we read them side by side we get the full flavor of what was going on. Like any newspaper reporter today, the biblical writers were permitted to exercise editorial control over what they wrote. Matthew told a more complete version of the story, while Mark and Luke chose to zero in on just one of the two men, <u>Bartimaeus</u>.

If Mark or Luke had said, "Only one blind man sat beside the road," we'd have a problem. By referencing a blind man and then proceeding to tell his story, Matthew exercised his writer's discretion to include only those facts pertinent to his purpose.

With the healing of these blind men, the stage was now set for Jesus's final week to begin. As we'll see in the next chapter, it began with quite a loud bang.

go to

Bartimaeus
Mark 10:46

Chapter Wrap-Up

- In answer to the Pharisees attempt to trap Jesus, he tackled the controversial and intensely personal issue of divorce and remarriage.
- When a rich young ruler came to Jesus with a question, he did not receive the answer that he sought.
- Jesus assured his disciples that they would be justly rewarded for their many sacrifices in following Jesus.
- Jesus used yet another parable, this time about a landowner, to illustrate an important spiritual principle.
- Jesus warned his disciples about the dangers of blind ambition.
- Jesus healed a blind man just before walking up to Jerusalem for the last time before his death.
- The stage was now set for the last week of Jesus's life to begin.

Study Questions

1. What is God's definition of marriage?

2. How do we know that Jesus's definition of marriage is applicable to us today?

3. What is the meaning of the "exception clause" regarding divorce and remarriage?

4. Why was the rich man's response to Jesus so inappropriate?

5. How did Jesus respond to Peter's pressure about "receiving his fair share"?

6. Of what did Jesus warn James and John when they asked him for places of prominence next to Jesus in his kingdom?

7. What did Jesus mean when he told James and John that they would "drink My cup"?

8. What was Jesus's mission statement?

Matthew 21–23: Eight Days a Week

Chapter Highlights:
- **The King Is Coming!**
- **Perfectly Angry**
- **Desperate Men Make Desperate Moves**
- **The Weeping Prophet**

Let's Get Started

If we could portray the events of Matthew 21–23 as a movie, ominous music would start playing in the background during the scene in which Jesus and his disciples approach Jerusalem. This is Jesus's final week before his crucifixion.

Jesus was a man <u>born</u> to <u>die</u>. Jesus was born by the light of a star, a star whose light also cast upon him the shadow of his torturous death. At the onset of Matthew 21, Jesus is a mere five days away from his impending execution.

God gave us a picture of how it would feel to sacrifice an only son when he told Abraham to sacrifice his son Isaac. A brisk ten-minute walk from the place where Abraham "bound Isaac his son and laid him on the altar, upon the wood" (Genesis 22:9 NKJV), Jesus was nailed to the rough wood of an "Old Rugged Cross." Such was the price he paid to **redeem** you and me from the penalty of our many sins.

born
Galatians 4:4

die
John 3:16

redeem
Galatians 4:5

redeem
to ransom, free, or rescue by paying a price

The King Is Coming!

MATTHEW 21:1–7 *Now when they drew near Jerusalem, and came to Bethphage, at the Mount of Olives, then Jesus sent two disciples, saying to them, "Go into the village opposite you, and immediately you will find a donkey tied, and a colt with her. Loose them and bring them to Me. And if anyone says anything to you, you shall say, 'The Lord has need of them,' and immediately he will send them." All this was done that it might be fulfilled which was spoken by the prophet, saying:*
"Tell the daughter of Zion,
'Behold, your King is coming to you,
Lowly, and sitting on a donkey,
A colt, the foal of a donkey.'"
So the disciples went and did as Jesus commanded them. They brought the donkey and the colt, laid their clothes on them, and set Him on them. (NKJV)

Passover
Matthew 26:2

suffered
Exodus 1:11–14;
5:6–9

Messianic
relating to a military
or political leader
to overthrow
oppression

Jesus's final week actually consisted of eight very full days. In today's reckoning, we call the two Sundays that bookended the week Palm Sunday and Easter Sunday respectively. A lot transpired between those two Sundays. Some of it was good; much of it was not so good, at least as far as the disciples were concerned.

Messianic hopes were at an all-time high. In homes throughout Roman-occupied Israel, families were diligently making preparations for their upcoming <u>Passover</u> observance. The streets of Jerusalem were beginning to swell as pilgrims traveled from far and wide to be present on the temple grounds for this most important feast. Passover commemorated God's miraculous deliverance of the Israelites from the torment they <u>suffered</u> in Egypt under the ironfisted bondage of a tyrannical Pharaoh. As patriotic fervor flows in the streets and explodes in the skies in the United States during its Independence Day celebrations, so in Israel the memory of freedom from Egypt and a passion for freedom from Rome burned brighter at this time of year than at any other.

During this final week of Jesus's life, the people of Israel gathered en masse in the Holy City with the expectation that at any moment, seemingly out of nowhere, their long-awaited Messiah would miraculously appear and kick the oppressors out of their homeland. Peace would at long last descend upon the City of Peace!

Almost every move Jesus and the people made was predicted by the prophets centuries before. Zechariah 9:9 and Isaiah 62:11 both predicted that Jesus would enter Jerusalem, not in the grand and pompous style of a conquering king with his military escorts, fine thoroughbreds, and imposing chariots. No, Jesus would ride alone into the city—humbly, unarmed, on the back of a common donkey.

When pilgrims journeyed "up to Jerusalem," making the almost-four-thousand-foot climb from the ancient city of Jericho deep within the Jordan Rift, they would crest the Mount of Olives in eager anticipation of their first glimpses of Jerusalem in general and their beloved Temple in particular. Even today, nothing rivals the spectacular view as one looks upon this singular place where God touched the earth.

In Jesus's day, a dark shadow fell over the Temple, dimming the joy of each pilgrim, a stark and dark reminder to every Jew that they were not a free people. Just to the northwest of the Temple arose a place of greater height than the Temple—the Roman fortress known as the Antonia. It was named in honor of Herod the Great's patron, Mark Antony.

When Herod enlarged the Temple and its supporting platform, a project that took <u>forty-six</u> years to complete, he constructed the Antonia Fortress with two purposes in mind. His primary, practical purpose was to provide a base of operations from which Roman soldiers could keep a watchful eye on the Temple and surrounding courtyard. His secondary, symbolic purpose was to send a subliminal message that Caesar was more powerful than the ancient, "impotent" God of the Hebrews.

go to

forty-six
John 2:20

blessing
Psalm 118:26

Hosanna
Psalm 118:25

Pomp and Circumstance

MATTHEW 21:8–11 *And a very great multitude spread their clothes on the road; others cut down branches from the trees and spread them on the road. Then the multitudes who went before and those who followed cried out, saying:*
"Hosanna to the Son of David!
'Blessed is He who comes in the name of the LORD!'
Hosanna in the highest!"
And when He had come into Jerusalem, all the city was moved, saying, "Who is this?" So the multitudes said, "This is Jesus, the prophet from Nazareth of Galilee." (NKJV)

The people's collective cry of greeting was written word perfect hundreds of years before this event. Their enthusiastic and heartfelt proclamation of <u>blessing</u> came right out of Psalm 118. "<u>Hosanna</u>" literally means, "Save us now." Not in the eternal-life, salvation-from-hell sense, but rather in a purely political sense. "Save us now" from Rome's oppression was their cry.

Once Jesus entered the city gate, the entire populace trembled in anticipation of what was to come. They hailed and honored "the Prophet" promised and predicted in Deuteronomy 18:15–18, who had at last arrived. Their King had come! As messianic fervor climaxed in an all-time crescendo of national euphoria, the future seemed bright indeed.

Zechariah, Isaiah, and the unnamed writer of Psalm 118 lived in eager anticipation of this glorious day.

Prophecy

first
John 2:15

R. C. Sproul

At the very moment that the crowds are hailing Him as the one who comes from God, Jesus is aware that they did not really understand who He was or what His mission involved. He understood that His redemptive task was still hidden from their eyes. They celebrated peace but knew nothing of the meaning of peace. For the ultimate peace to be established Jesus had to die as an atonement for His people's sins.[1]

Spring Cleaning

MATTHEW 21:12–17 *Then Jesus went into the temple of God and drove out all those who bought and sold in the temple, and overturned the tables of the money changers and the seats of those who sold doves. And He said to them, "It is written, 'My house shall be called a house of prayer,' but you have made it a 'den of thieves.'" Then the blind and the lame came to Him in the temple, and He healed them. But when the chief priests and scribes saw the wonderful things that He did, and the children crying out in the temple and saying, "Hosanna to the Son of David!" they were indignant and said to Him, "Do You hear what these are saying?" And Jesus said to them, "Yes. Have you never read,*
   'Out of the mouth of babes and nursing infants
   You have perfected praise'?"
   Then He left them and went out of the city to Bethany, and He lodged there. (NKJV)

To say that Jesus entered Jerusalem with a bang would be the understatement of the millennium. He stormed through the temple courtyard like a whirlwind. Make no mistake about it—Jesus was angry.

If the guys who manned the money-changing and animals-for-sacrifice concessions felt a bit of déjà vu, they did so for good reason. This wasn't the <u>first</u> time Jesus went on a rampage in the temple area. Jesus made a whip and chased out the money changers at the beginning of his ministry; here he did it again at the end of his ministry. Both times this occurred during Passover. Both times he generated the same result—he enflamed the ire of his enemies.

Perfectly Angry

Jesus got angry for good reason. Jews traveled by foot or by camel, a several-days-journey, spent enormous sums of money, and endured much danger and discomfort, all in a self-sacrificing effort to arrive in town in time for the big day. These committed people could not possibly bring an animal for the Passover sacrifice, especially when you consider that they would have had to keep it in a pristine, <u>unblemished</u> condition. These travelers had to purchase their animals once they arrived at the Temple. Since many Jews traveled far and wide to Jerusalem, they needed to change their money to the local currency.

Long before Jesus entered the temple area, unscrupulous vendors had set up their shops, and licked their chops in anticipation of these needy worshipers coming into town. They happily sold them animals for the sacrifices at obscenely inflated prices. Then, they added to their profits when they resold the same animals to other weary, unsuspecting travelers. Not to be outdone, the money changers exchanged the people's money all right, but at grossly unfair exchange rates.

unblemished
Leviticus 22:21

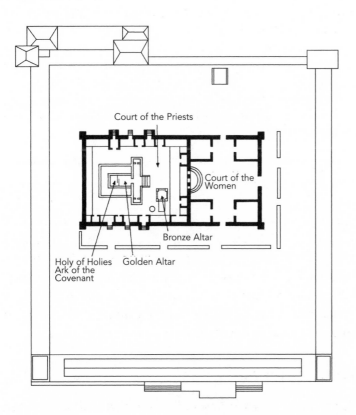

Court of the Priests

Court of the Women

Bronze Altar

Holy of Holies
Ark of the Covenant

Golden Altar

Illustration #8
Temple Diagram—
The Court of the Gentiles was a gathering place for much activity. The stalls of money changers and merchants were under the porches that surrounded the court. Religious leaders also held schools and debates there.

The Symbolism Is the Substance

go to

Lazarus
John 11:1

in
Matthew 20:21

fig
Hosea 9:10;
Joel 1:7

judgment
Jeremiah 8:13;
Joel 1:12

MATTHEW 21:18–20 *Now in the morning, as He returned to the city, He was hungry. And seeing a fig tree by the road, He came to it and found nothing on it but leaves, and said to it, "Let no fruit grow on you ever again." Immediately the fig tree withered away. And when the disciples saw it, they marveled, saying, "How did the fig tree wither away so soon?"* (NKJV)

After an eventful Sunday, Jesus awoke early Monday morning, rounded up his dozen disciples, and headed from Bethany, home of his close friend Lazarus, on the eastern slope of the Mount of Olives, up over the crest of the hill, down the steep western side of this most famous of mountain ranges, across the Kidron Valley, into Jerusalem. He made one notable stop along the way. He killed a fig tree.

Why did Jesus kill a fig tree? While this might seem kind of harsh, we have to understand the significance of the symbolism. The disciples "marveled" at what happened to the tree and why it happened.

Let's remember that up until the bitter end the disciples fully anticipated that by the week's end, Rome would be out and they would be in. The notion that Jesus would not be sending Israel's oppressors back to Rome, licking their wounds all the way, had not entered the disciples' minds. It never crossed their minds that these torturous tyrants would actually hang Jesus from a cross and leave him there to die. How could Jesus get through to his men that plans had changed? How could he convince them that they were in for some tough and challenging times? Enter one fig tree.

The fig tree (see Illustration #9) often symbolizes the nation of Israel, since figs are a sweet fruit of God's bountiful blessing in the land, as is an obedient Israel a sweet fruit of God's bountiful blessing in the earth. A barren fig tree often represents God's judgment on a fruitless Israel that failed to live up to its many spiritual advantages.

Illustration #9
Figs—Figs grow on trees and were a favorite in Galilee. They are still plentiful today.

The nation regarded Jesus's offer of his kingdom with contempt, and for its trouble became a fruitless people. As the fig tree withered so quickly, so divine judgment would soon fall upon the land. Less than forty years after Jesus cursed the fig tree, Rome cursed and crushed the country, burned Jerusalem, and leveled the Temple. Israel ceased to exist—from AD 70 until its miraculous resurrection from the ashes of the Holocaust, May 14, 1948. No wonder the disciples marveled.

what others say

Charles H. Spurgeon

The first Adam came to the fig tree for leaves, but the second Adam [Jesus] looks for figs. He searches our character through and through to see whether there is any true faith, any true love, and living hope, and joy which is the fruit of the Spirit, any patience, any self-denial, any fervor in prayer, any walking with God, any indwelling of the Holy Spirit. And if he does not see these things, he is not satisfied with churchgoing, prayer meetings, communions, sermons, and Bible readings, for all these things may be no more than leafage.[2]

Mountain Moving

MATTHEW 21:21–22 *So Jesus answered and said to them, "Assuredly, I say to you, if you have faith and do not doubt, you will not only do what was done to the fig tree, but also if you say to this mountain, 'Be removed and be cast into the sea,' it will be done. And whatever things you ask in prayer, believing, you will receive." (NKJV)*

Many sincere believers have mistakenly interpreted Jesus's mountain-moving words to mean that if they have enough faith God is somehow obligated to move "mountains" in their lives—be they mountains of debt, disease, discouragement, depression, disobedient children, etc. Jesus meant nothing of the kind.

When Jesus spoke of moving by faith "this mountain," he was beckoning the disciples not to lose hope even though they would soon face seemingly insurmountable challenges.

1. They would watch in horror as Rome killed their leader.

2. At least one of them (John) would live to see the destruction of Israel.

3. The others would be hounded, harassed, and perhaps even killed at the hands of the Romans.

Rome, symbolized by "this mountain," would one day metaphorically be thrown into the sea. In spite of its imperial power, the Roman Empire would be crushed, and the soldiers who marched throughout the land would one day flee to their ships and sail across the Mediterranean Sea back to their homeland, never to dominate the Holy Land again. So long as the thing requested is actually God's will, you can receive "whatever things you ask in prayer" (Matthew 21:22 NKJV).

To which mountain did Jesus here refer? The most obvious answer is the Mount of Olives, since they were standing on it. But the Mount of Olives is not a stand-alone mountain; it is a mountain range. Jesus wasn't talking about the Mount of Olives. He had something else in mind.

From the road where Jesus spoke of "this mountain" there was a singular mountain that dominated the skyline—the infamous Herodium (see Illustration #10). Located just south of Jerusalem, a citadel of a palace complex had been built on a conspicuous peak by Herod the Great as one of several fortresses within which he could barricade himself from his enemies. Lavishly ordained with marble and gold, this landmark boasted two reinforced circular walls and four spectacularly tall watchtowers. In its heyday it literally gleamed like some ancient diamond in the desert.

Clearly visible from both Jerusalem and Bethlehem, it came to symbolize Roman dominance over the countryside. But get this! Herod erected his palace on top of a *man-moved* mountain. Jesus said that faith can move a mountain, but so can fresh supplies of slaves. Herod found a mound that served as a suitable location for his palace, and then commanded his slaves literally to take down a nearby hill, bucketful of dirt by bucketful, transport it to his chosen site, and build up this mound to a staggering height, erecting his fortress inside and on top of this man-moved, man-made mountain.

Today Herod's palace is an empty cone of dirt, long ago stripped of its marble and gold, plundered of its vast resource of riches. Herodium gives mute testimony to the fact that Jesus was right after all. Rome was indeed thrown into the sea.

Desperate Men Make Desperate Moves

MATTHEW 21:23–27 *Now when He came into the temple, the chief priests and the elders of the people confronted Him as He was teaching, and said, "By what authority are You doing these things? And who gave You this authority?" But Jesus answered and said to them, "I also will ask you one thing, which if you tell Me, I likewise will tell you by what authority I do these things: The baptism of John—where was it from? From heaven or from men?" And they reasoned among themselves, saying, "If we say, 'From heaven,' He will say to us, 'Why then did you not believe him?' But if we say, 'From men,' we fear the multitude, for all count John as a prophet." So they answered Jesus and said, "We do not know." And He said to them, "Neither will I tell you by what authority I do these things.* (NKJV)*

blasphemy
John 5:18–23;
10:18, 31–33

blasphemy
to speak against God

The chief priests and elders thought that by asking Jesus by whose authority he did what he did, they would force Jesus to say, "from God," allowing them to accuse him of **blasphemy** and to kill him for the offense. But the best-laid plans of mice, and men, and religious leaders didn't exactly turn out the way they had hoped. Jesus played by his own rules. He quickly turned the tables on them and answered their question with a question of his own.

Illustration #10
Herodium Today—
Herod used slaves to build this mountain where he placed a fortress. Today a dirt heap is all that remains.

Talk about a catch-22! When Jesus asked these self-righteous leaders about the legitimacy of John the Baptist's ministry, Jesus put them on the defensive. If they affirmed John's ministry, they would thereby condemn themselves; if they denied it, they would suffer the wrath and reactions of the people who still revered John and all that he stood for. They *could* not answer, so Jesus *did* not answer.

go to

rejects
1 Corinthians
1:26–29

Do As I Say, Not As I Do

MATTHEW 21:28–32 *"But what do you think? A man had two sons, and he came to the first and said, 'Son, go, work today in my vineyard.' He answered and said, 'I will not,' but afterward he regretted it and went. Then he came to the second and said likewise. And he answered and said, 'I go, sir,' but he did not go. Which of the two did the will of his father?" They said to Him, "The first." Jesus said to them, "Assuredly, I say to you that tax collectors and harlots enter the kingdom of God before you. For John came to you in the way of righteousness, and you did not believe him; but tax collectors and harlots believed him; and when you saw it, you did not afterward relent and believe him.* (NKJV)

Jesus put these guys in their place, but he wasn't through—not by a long shot. With his execution just days away, Jesus had had enough. He had the religious leaders on the ropes, and he went for the knockout. He pummeled them with three penetrating parables. With each story, Jesus held up a mirror and forced these leaders to take a long, hard look at themselves. They didn't like what they saw.

The unmistakable symbolism of the first story stung the religious leaders to the core. They represented the second son. They had all of the privileges, all of the advantages of God's personal attention and communication. They, of all people, should have joyfully responded to the invitation of the father to be involved in his work. At first they appeared to acquiesce, but later shunned and ignored his offer. The scum of society—prostitutes and tax collectors, of whom Matthew was one—were represented by the first son, who initially showed no interest. Yet, it would be the humble <u>rejects</u> and castoffs, not the proud and prominent, whom God would allow to participate in his work.

what others say

Warren Wiersbe

Now is a good time to point out a truth about Christian service that for some reason we overlook: God is as concerned about the servant as He is the service. If all God wanted to do was get the work done, He could send His angels and they would do it better and faster. But He not only wants to do something through us, He also wants to do something in us.[3]

Temper, Temper

stone
Psalm 118:22

MATTHEW 21:33–41 *"Hear another parable: There was a certain landowner who planted a vineyard and set a hedge around it, dug a winepress in it and built a tower. And he leased it to vinedressers and went into a far country. Now when vintage-time drew near, he sent his servants to the vinedressers, that they might receive its fruit. And the vinedressers took his servants, beat one, killed one, and stoned another. Again he sent other servants, more than the first, and they did likewise to them. Then last of all he sent his son to them, saying, 'They will respect my son.' But when the vinedressers saw the son, they said among themselves, 'This is the heir. Come, let us kill him and seize his inheritance.' So they took him and cast him out of the vineyard and killed him. Therefore, when the owner of the vineyard comes, what will he do to those vinedressers?" They said to Him, "He will destroy those wicked men miserably, and lease his vineyard to other vinedressers who will render to him the fruits in their seasons." (NKJV)*

The Pharisees joined the chief priests as they listened indignantly to this second parable. There was a landowner who had a piece of property that was important to him. In it he had planted a vineyard which he personally cared for and tended with special attention. When he set off on a journey, he trusted certain men to mind his pet project. But when he sent his servants to collect the fruit, the workers beat them, stoned them, and killed them. Finally the owner sent his son. The workers mercilessly murdered him as well, thinking that they would then inherit the vineyard. When the owner returned, he "[destroyed] those wicked men miserably" (Matthew 21:41 NKJV).

Stone-Cold Fury

MATTHEW 21:42–46 *Jesus said to them, "Have you never read in the Scriptures:*

'The <u>stone</u> which the builders rejected
Has become the chief cornerstone.
This was the LORD's doing,
And it is marvelous in our eyes'?
"Therefore I say to you, the kingdom of God will be taken from you and given to a nation bearing the fruits of it. And whoever falls on this stone will be broken; but on whomever it falls, it will grind him to powder." Now when the chief priests

and Pharisees heard His parables, they perceived that He was speaking of them. But when they sought to lay hands on Him, they feared the multitudes, because they took Him for a prophet. (NKJV)

The symbolism of this parable could not be missed. The vineyard was Israel. The workers were the religious leaders. The murdered servants were the Old Testament prophets. The son of the landowner was the Son of God. The religious leaders got the point all right.

How did these "wicked" religious leaders respond to the parable? They sought all the more to arrest Jesus and have him killed, just like Jesus told them they would. How ironic!

Here Comes the Bride

MATTHEW 22:1–10 *And Jesus answered and spoke to them again by parables and said: "The kingdom of heaven is like a certain king who arranged a marriage for his son, and sent out his servants to call those who were invited to the wedding; and they were not willing to come. Again, he sent out other servants, saying, 'Tell those who are invited, "See, I have prepared my dinner; my oxen and fatted cattle are killed, and all things are ready. Come to the wedding."' But they made light of it and went their ways, one to his own farm, another to his business. And the rest seized his servants, treated them spitefully, and killed them. But when the king heard about it, he was furious. And he sent out his armies, destroyed those murderers, and burned up their city. Then he said to his servants, 'The wedding is ready, but those who were invited were not worthy. Therefore go into the highways, and as many as you find, invite to the wedding.' So those servants went out into the highways and gathered together all whom they found, both bad and good. And the wedding hall was filled with guests. (NKJV)*

Jesus rounded out his trio of tales by describing a lavish wedding in which the king, the father of the groom, spared no expense. As in the previous parable, the servants were mistreated, abused, and killed. The king became enraged, sent in his army, destroyed the murderers, and burned their city. He then sent other servants into the highways to invite anyone they could find.

Designer Dress

MATTHEW 22:11–15 *But when the king came in to see the guests, he saw a man there who did not have on a wedding garment. So he said to him, 'Friend, how did you come in here without a wedding garment?' And he was speechless. Then the king said to the servants, 'Bind him hand and foot, take him away, and cast him into outer darkness; there will be weeping and gnashing of teeth.' For many are called, but few are chosen."*

Then the Pharisees went and plotted how they might entangle Him in His talk. (NKJV)

There is some debate as to the significance of the wedding garments. The most plausible interpretation is that the garments refer to our being clothed with Christ's righteousness. The prophet Isaiah put it this way: "All our righteousnesses are like filthy rags" (Isaiah 64:6 NKJV). Even the good things we do are tainted by sin. None of us act out of absolutely pure motives 100 percent of the time. As Jeremiah reminds us, "The heart is deceitful above all things, and desperately wicked; who can know it?" (Jeremiah 17:9 NKJV). We need to change our clothes! Or as Paul wrote, "Put off . . . the old man which grows corrupt according to the deceitful lusts . . . [and] put on the new man which was created according to God, in true righteousness and holiness" (Ephesians 4:22, 24 NKJV).

The religious leaders came to the party dressed in the clothing of their own self-righteousness. They didn't think they needed Christ's forgiveness. They rejected his grace. They came on their own merit, and that with tragic results.

With this final story, Jesus drove the dagger of truth deep into their souls. The chief priests and Pharisees were the murderers. They had killed the prophets and were about to kill God's Son. They would ultimately be destroyed. Their city would ultimately be burned.

go to

Exodus
Exodus 3:6

Herodians
Jewish sect loyal
to the Herodian
dynasty

The religious leaders could not stomach any more. Rather than respond with humble repentance, they set themselves once and for all to destroy their King with a murderous rage they could no longer contain.

Knockout Punch

> **the big picture**
>
> ### Matthew 22:16–46
>
> The Pharisees, Sadducees, and Herodians got together to make one last desperate attempt to defeat and destroy Jesus. They bombarded him with a barrage of questions that they thought would trip him up and cause him to discredit himself before the crowds. They asked him questions about paying taxes, life after death, and the greatest commandment. Boy, were they in for a surprise. Jesus once again turned the tables on them, as he so often did, by countering their questions with one of his own. With that one question, he silenced his critics once and for all.

"The enemy of my enemy is my friend." We've heard it before. How true in this case. The Pharisees hated the Sadducees who hated the Herodians who hated the Pharisees. Yet they each hated Jesus even more. United by their common hatred, they let loose with a barrage of questions in yet another attempt to trap Jesus with his own words.

Question #1: "Is it lawful to pay taxes to Caesar?" (Matthew 22:17 NKJV). If Jesus said yes, the Pharisees would have accused him of selling out to Rome. If he said no, the **Herodians** would have said, "Gotcha." Jesus refused to step into the trap. He calmly asked for a coin, pointed out that Caesar's image was stamped on the coin, and answered, "Render therefore to Caesar the things that are Caesar's, and to God the things that are God's" (Matthew 22:21 NKJV).

Question #2: The Sadducees, who deny life after death, concocted a ridiculously strange story about some woman who married and subsequently buried seven brothers. They asked, "In the resurrection, whose wife of the seven will she be?" (Matthew 22:28 NKJV). Jesus skillfully wiggled out of this noose by pointing out that in heaven marriage will be irrelevant. Jesus referred to angels, whose existence the Sadducees denied, and quoted from Exodus since they only believed in the first five books of the Bible. No wonder the crowds "were astonished at His teaching" (Matthew 22:33 NKJV).

Question #3: The Pharisees returned to the ring and tried to pin down Jesus by making him single out "the great commandment" (Matthew 22:36 NKJV). He answered, "'Love the LORD your God with all your heart, with all your soul, and with all your mind.' . . . 'Love your neighbor as yourself'" (Matthew 22:37, 39 NKJV). Jesus summed up the underlying moral ethic of the entire Bible: Love God, love others. Everything else is just commentary.

Question #4: This time Jesus did the asking. "What do you think about the Christ? Whose Son is He?" (Matthew 22:42 NKJV). After getting the Pharisees to admit that the Messiah was "the son of David" (Matthew 22:42 NKJV), Jesus quoted Psalm 110:1, in which King David refers to the Messiah as his Lord. How could his son be his Lord, Jesus asked. Implied answer: He can't. Unless he is also God come in the <u>flesh</u>.

By so affirming his humanity (the son of <u>David</u>) and his deity (the Son of <u>God</u>), Jesus left his accusers scratching their heads in frustration. The good news is that they dared not ask him any more questions; the bad news is that by so silencing his enemies, Jesus effectively signed his own death warrant. Less than seventy-two hours later, they would kill him.

go to

flesh
John 1:14

David
Matthew 1:1

God
Matthew 8:29

phylacteries
Exodus 13:9–10

tassels
Deuteronomy 22:12

phylacteries
small leather boxes containing Scripture

tassels
strings tied at the corners of their prayer shawls

The Blind Leading the Blind

the big picture

Matthew 23:1–12

Jesus talked plainly to the people about the sins of the Pharisees and teachers of the law.

Right in front of the crowds and his disciples, Jesus stripped these leaders bare, and exposed them for what they really were—"blind," a term he will use five times in this chapter (Matthew 23:16, 17, 19, 24, 26).

Jesus began by addressing the crowds. He lamented the fact that these dear people had been intimidated by their leaders into obeying them and doing "whatever they tell you" (Matthew 23:3 NKJV). But these hypocrites were not worthy of such honor and respect. They clearly did not "practice what they preached." They wore large **phylacteries** and long **tassels** to impress the people with their spirituality. And in so doing, they set in motion a basic life principle as

go to

gnat
Leviticus 11:23

gnat
the smallest
unclean animal

binding in the spiritual realm as the law of gravity in the physical realm: "Whoever exalts himself will be humbled, and he who humbles himself will be exalted" (Matthew 23:12 NKJV).

what others say

Curtis C. Mitchell

Now, the only difference between the Pharisees and many Christians today is that our do's and don'ts are different. The same basic philosophy is there. To become ever more proficient at your do's and don'ts, and become like a trained seal going through your little routine each week, is not authentic New Testament Christianity, but legalism.[5]

Woe to You!

the big picture

Matthew 23:13–36

Jesus pronounces seven woes against the Jewish leaders.

If you think of words as bullets, then Jesus fired an automatic weapon, hitting his targets with pinpoint precision. Seven times he justly condemned the Jewish religious leaders for their blatant hypocrisy. Here's our paraphrase:

Woe to the Pharisees

The Seven Woes	Meaning of Each Woe
Woe #1 (23:13–14)	You have so obscured God's truth that you make it impossible for the people you lead to enter the kingdom of heaven. And just for the record, you're not going to enter it either.
Woe #2 (23:15)	The people you influence are farther away from heaven than they would have been if you had left them alone.
Woe #3 (23:16–22)	By making ridiculous and arbitrary distinctions between swearing by the gold in the Temple and by the Temple itself, you justify lying with impunity. Who do you think you are? You of all people should be trusted under God to tell the truth.
Woe #4 (23:23–24)	You who are so focused on such external things that don't matter, such as straining your drinks so that you don't swallow a **gnat**, totally neglect the internal things that do matter, such as justice, mercy, and faithfulness.
Woe #5 (23:25–26)	Your lives are like a cup that has been cleaned on the outside but is filthy and not fit for use on the inside.

Woe to the Pharisees (cont'd)

The Seven Woes	Meaning of Each Woe
Woe #6 (23:27–28)	You try to look so good on the outside, but are rotten on the inside. You pretend to be so holy, when you are actually so wicked.
Woe #7 (23:29–32)	You say that you would not have killed the <u>prophets</u> the way your forefathers did; yet you are plotting to <u>murder</u> your Messiah!

prophets
Acts 7:51–52

murder
John 11:47–53

glory
1 Kings 8:11

God
Matthew 22:32

western wall
closest accessible point to the site of the ancient Temple

Jesus finished his discussion with a synopsis of what would happen to those who fit the above characterization. Jesus promised that both these "serpents" (Matthew 23:33 NKJV) and "this generation" (Matthew 23:36 NKJV) would suffer greatly. They would ultimately pay a hefty price for their shedding of "righteous blood," Jesus's righteous blood.

The Weeping Prophet

MATTHEW 23:37–39 *"O Jerusalem, Jerusalem, the one who kills the prophets and stones those who are sent to her! How often I wanted to gather your children together, as a hen gathers her chicks under her wings, but you were not willing! See! Your house is left to you desolate; for I say to you, you shall see Me no more till you say, 'Blessed is He who comes in the name of the LORD!'" (NKJV)*

As he sat on the Mount of Olives, looking over Jerusalem and viewing it through the lens of prophecy, Jesus clearly saw what was coming to his beloved city. People would be killed. The city would be burned. The Temple would be destroyed. And so, Jesus wept.

Stand with us atop the Mount of Olives, look to the west, and notice what you cannot see—nearly two thousand years later no Temple exists. Then notice what you can see—glistening in the sunlight shines the golden dome of the Muslim shrine that sits over the sacred spot where God's <u>glory</u> once flamed and flashed. Allah is now praised where the <u>God</u> of Abraham, Isaac, and Jacob once touched the earth. No wonder Jews now wail at the **western wall**. So have we.

Chapter Wrap-Up

- Jesus entered the city of Jerusalem on Palm Sunday, thus beginning his final week before his crucifixion. (Matthew 21:1–11)

- Just as he did at the beginning of his ministry, Jesus cleansed the Temple at the end of his ministry. (Matthew 21:12; John 2:15)

- Jesus cursed a fig tree, symbolic of the fruitlessness of God's people who were given so much but did so little with God's bountiful blessings. (Matthew 21:18–22)

- Jesus had conflicts with the Pharisees, Sadducees, and Herodians who hounded him relentlessly and plotted together to get rid of him. (Matthew 22:15–33)

- Jesus taught the greatest commandment—to love God and to love others. (Matthew 22:37–39)

- Jesus pronounced several "woes" on the Pharisees for their blatant hypocrisy. (Matthew 23:13–36)

- Jesus wept over the city of Jerusalem. (Matthew 23:37–39)

Study Questions

1. What kind of a Messiah did the people believe they were welcoming into Jerusalem with palm branches and joyful cries?

2. How did the cries of the crowd betray their faulty perspective?

3. Why did Jesus kill a fig tree?

4. What strategy did Jesus use to deflect the attempts of the Jewish leaders to trap him with trivial questions?

5. What did Jesus say was the greatest commandment?

6. What were the "woes" that Jesus pronounced on the religious leaders?

7. Is it possible that any of his condemnations could hit home with us?

8. What did Jesus do when he viewed Jerusalem from the Mount of Olives?

Matthew 24-25: Prophetic Powwow

Let's Get Started

The disciples were finally starting to get it. Drop by drop, the ice-cold water of reality began to trickle into their clouded minds. Their anticipation for, and their participation in, a coming kingdom would have to be put on hold indefinitely. Week's end was fast approaching. Passover was almost here. Yet the Twelve could detect no trace, not even a hint in Jesus's external demeanor that he was about to overthrow the Romans and set up shop in Jerusalem as the capital of his kingdom.

Rather than talking revolt, Jesus uncorked a shocker of a statement. Pointing out the beautiful buildings of the temple complex, Jesus mentioned that they would be so completely destroyed that "not one stone shall be left here upon another, that shall not be thrown down" (Matthew 24:2 NKJV). That must have generated some interesting conversation among the disciples.

As they sat upon the Mount of Olives overlooking the Temple and its courtyard, some of the braver souls among them slithered up to Jesus privately and essentially whispered in his ears, "You've got to be kidding. When's this going to happen?" Matthew 24 and 25, the Olivet **Discourse**, all ninety-four verses of it, comprise his startling answer to their question.

Discourse
formal and extended conversation

Confusion and Concern

MATTHEW 24:1–3 *Then Jesus went out and departed from the temple, and His disciples came up to show Him the buildings of the temple. And Jesus said to them, "Do you not see all these things? Assuredly, I say to you, not one stone shall be left here upon another, that shall not be thrown down."*

Now as He sat on the Mount of Olives, the disciples came to Him privately, saying, "Tell us, when will these things be? And what will be the sign of Your coming, and of the end of the age?" (NKJV)

two
Matthew 26:2

The disciples, still reeling from the object lesson of the cursed fig tree, had no doubt overheard Jesus lament over Jerusalem, "See! Your house is left to you desolate" (Matthew 23:38 NKJV). His men knew that Jesus referred to the Temple when he said that. They could not fathom that this massive structure—boasting stones that measured forty by twelve by twelve feet, gleaming with white marble and solid gold plates that reflected the rising sun and made the building look positively luminescent, as if it were exploding into flames, sitting on a Temple Mount platform equaling the size of six football fields—could possibly be laid waste and made desolate.

Confusion was in no short supply on the Mount of Olives just <u>two</u> days before Jesus's execution. The disciples desperately needed to know what was going to happen and when. In response to their questions, Jesus spoke to them in the frankest of terms as he explained how to interpret the signs of the times.

The Signs of the Times

> MATTHEW 24:4–14 *And Jesus answered and said to them: "Take heed that no one deceives you. For many will come in My name, saying, 'I am the Christ,' and will deceive many. And you will hear of wars and rumors of wars. See that you are not troubled; for all these things must come to pass, but the end is not yet. For nation will rise against nation, and kingdom against kingdom. And there will be famines, pestilences, and earthquakes in various places. All these are the beginning of sorrows. Then they will deliver you up to tribulation and kill you, and you will be hated by all nations for My name's sake. And then many will be offended, will betray one another, and will hate one another. Then many false prophets will rise up and deceive many. And because lawlessness will abound, the love of many will grow cold. But he who endures to the end shall be saved. And this gospel of the kingdom will be preached in all the world as a witness to all the nations, and then the end will come. (NKJV)*

Jesus gave his disciples a series of signs to look for as indications that his "coming, and...the end of the age" (Matthew 24:3 NKJV) were near at hand. The key that unlocks our understanding of these signs is found in Jesus's words in verse 8: "All these are the beginning of sorrows" (NKJV). As we list the various series of signs for you, you will note that these types of things have always been present in the world. But any mother will tell you, as the anticipated moment of the birth of her baby approaches, her contractions increase dramatically in frequency and intensity. So, too, the second coming of Jesus will be preceded by a dramatic increase in the frequency and intensity of the signs of his coming at the end of the age.

The first series of signs consists of a dramatic and disturbing increase in the following:

Olives
Zechariah 14:4

week
Daniel 9:24

- False religious teachers who will deceive many (Matthew 24:5, 11);
- Wars and rumors of wars (verse 6);
- Natural disasters, including famines and earthquakes (verse 7);
- Persecutions and executions of Christians worldwide (verse 9);
- Christians turning away from their faith, even to the point of betraying their former brothers and sisters in Christ (verse 10);
- Self-absorbed people who do deeds of wickedness against each other, rather than acts of love (verse 12).

Obviously, the frequency and intensity of these signs are increasing dramatically in our day. But Jesus clearly said this is only "the beginning."

Rapture vs. Second Coming

There is much debate among commentators as to whether Jesus was referring to the rapture of the church or his second coming in these verses. Let's first briefly distinguish between these two events.

The Rapture refers to that event described in 1 Thessalonians 4:16–18 during which Jesus appears in the clouds and his followers are suddenly removed from the earth and meet him in the air. The second coming of Christ is exactly that—a coming. Described for us in Revelation 19:11–16, Jesus literally comes back to the earth, setting foot on the Mount of <u>Olives</u>, from which he will finally, as promised, establish his kingdom and rule the earth for a thousand years.

Things get a bit dicey, however, when we try to pin down with some certainty the timing of these two events in relation to a seven-year period commonly known as the Tribulation or the seventieth <u>week</u> of Daniel. For this discussion, we'll narrow the playing field to a trio of the most commonly held viewpoints.

Tribulation
Matthew 24:21;
Revelation 7:14

holding
2 Thessalonians 2:7

beast
Revelation 13:1

destined
1 Thessalonians
1:10; 5:9

Tribulation
unprecedented
suffering on the
earth

1. *Pre-Tribulation Rapture:* The Rapture occurs before the **Tribulation**. In this scenario, the church is currently acting as a restraining influence, <u>holding</u> back the full manifestation of evil in the world. When the church is removed in the Rapture, a Satan-controlled individual named the <u>beast</u>, sometimes referred to as the Antichrist, bursts on the scene out of the chaos created by the sudden disappearance of millions of Christians worldwide. He negotiates a peace treaty guaranteeing the security of Israel for seven years, thus beginning the countdown to the climax of history, the second coming of Christ at the end of the Tribulation.

2. *Mid-Tribulation or Pre-Wrath Rapture:* The Rapture occurs some time during the Tribulation, perhaps halfway through the Tribulation, but certainly before God pours his wrath out upon the earth. The church is removed because God has not <u>destined</u> believers to experience his wrath, either in this life or in the life to come.

3. *Post-Tribulation Rapture:* The Rapture occurs during the second coming of Christ, essentially combining these two occurrences into one grand event. The church will be taken out of the earth, meet the Lord in the air, and come right back with him as he sets his foot on the Mount of Olives and subsequently sets up his kingdom.

While many sincere Christians earnestly and passionately debate this controversy, God's timetable will not be affected.

If either View #1 or #2 is correct, then the "signs of the times" referred to by Jesus in the Olivet Discourse do not refer to the Rapture, but rather to the Second Coming. However, since the Rapture will be at most a little over seven years before the Second Coming, as the time of the Second Coming approaches, so does the time of the Rapture.

The Abomination of Desolation

MATTHEW 24:15–16 *"Therefore when you see the 'abomination of desolation,' spoken of by Daniel the prophet, standing in the holy place"* (whoever reads, let him understand), *"then let those who are in Judea flee to the mountains.* (NKJV)

Believe it or not, this singular passage of Scripture defines and describes the fullest possible manifestation of evil in the world. Jesus clearly alluded to an unprecedented event first predicted in the book of Daniel. In summary, "the <u>abomination</u> of desolation" refers to that moment, halfway through the Tribulation, when the beast blatantly walks into the "holy place," the holiest portion of the newly constructed Temple, defiantly sets up an image presumably of himself, and pompously proclaims himself to be God. People will <u>worship</u> him.

abomination
Daniel 9:27

worship
Revelation 13:8

plan
Isaiah 14:14

"The abomination of desolation" (Matthew 24:15 NKJV) is Satan's best attempt at pulling off his <u>plan</u> and obtaining that which he has wanted all along—to be worshiped as God.

Naturally, this act of utter defiance cannot go unanswered. No sooner will Satan desecrate the Temple—the "Father's house" (John 2:16 NKJV)—than God will speak. Like his Son before him, God the Father will launch his own cleansing of the Temple as he commands his angels to "pour out the bowls of the wrath of God on the earth" (Revelation 16:1 NKJV).

Run for Your Life!

MATTHEW 24:17–25 *Let him who is on the housetop not go down to take anything out of his house. And let him who is in the field not go back to get his clothes. But woe to those who are pregnant and to those who are nursing babies in those days! And pray that your flight may not be in winter or on the Sabbath. For then there will be great tribulation, such as has not been since the beginning of the world until this time, no, nor ever shall be. And unless those days were shortened, no flesh would be saved; but for the elect's sake those days will be shortened. Then if anyone says to you, 'Look, here is the Christ!' or 'There!' do not believe it. For false christs and false prophets will rise and show great signs and wonders to deceive, if possible, even the elect. See, I have told you beforehand. (NKJV)*

While Revelation 16 gives us a glimpse into what will take place from heaven's point of view, Jesus allows us to view these awful events from earth's point of view. His basic but urgent warning can be summed up in one word: "Flee!"

Matthew 24:16–25 reads like the pages of a script from a

En Gedi
1 Samuel 23:29

Hollywood disaster movie. Jesus's dire warnings of impending doom include the following:

- Do travel light; don't grab stuff from inside your house (24:17).

- Do travel fast; don't even go back to get your jacket (verse 18).

- Do hope that you are not pregnant or nursing an infant (verse 19).

- Do hope that this will not happen during the winter (verse 20).

- Do hope that this will not happen on the Sabbath, lest your travel cause you to have a conflict of conscience—about breaking the Sabbath—to add to your distress (verse 20).

- Don't believe the false claims of anyone who says to you that he is the Messiah (verse 23).

When Jesus warned "those who are in Judea [to] flee to the mountains" (Matthew 24:16 NKJV), he might have been referring to the region southeast of Jerusalem, particularly around the Dead Sea, where many caves offer people places of refuge and hiding. David hid from Saul in this area in a place called <u>En Gedi</u>. This could also include the hills of Moab and Edom, located in modern-day Jordan, just the other side of the Dead Sea. This particular warning might even refer to the enchanted city of Petra. Petra's reddish rock caves make for perfect hiding places. Since one can only enter Petra on camel or horseback down an extremely long and narrow canyon, Petra can be easily defended by a small group of men with a modest cache of weapons.

The Climax of History

MATTHEW 24:26–31 *Therefore if they say to you, 'Look, He is in the desert!' do not go out; or 'Look, He is in the inner rooms!' do not believe it. For as the lightning comes from the east and flashes to the west, so also will the coming of the Son of Man be. For wherever the carcass is, there the eagles will be gathered together.*

"Immediately after the tribulation of those days the sun will be darkened, and the moon will not give its light; the stars will fall from heaven, and the powers of the heavens will be shaken. Then the sign of the Son of Man will appear in heaven, and then all the tribes of the earth will mourn, and they will see the Son of Man coming on the clouds of heaven with power and great

glory. And He will send His angels with a great sound of a trumpet, and they will gather together His elect from the four winds, from one end of heaven to the other. (NKJV)

Suddenly, unexpectedly, spectacularly, and without warning, Jesus will return. His second coming will be likened to the bright flashes of lightning that shoot across the sky. As eagles can see a carcass from their soaring heights, so "the coming of the Son of Man" (Matthew 24:27 NKJV) will be seen from both near and far by everyone.

Finally, the nations will know. The truth will come crashing down around the people of the planet. The ice-cold water of reality will shock them senseless as they are made to understand that they have rejected and rebelled against their God. Israel in particular will <u>mourn</u> over her rejection of her own Messiah.

Human history as we know it will reach its crescendo when God's angels gather his **elect**, including those in heaven and those on the <u>earth</u>. These will be assembled before Christ, and together they will usher in the Millennium and reign with Christ for one <u>thousand</u> years.

Nature will react in dramatic fashion, fulfilling a myriad of Old Testament prophecies such as Isaiah 13:9–10; 34:4; Ezekiel 32:7–8; Joel 2:10, 31; Amos 8:9; and Zephaniah 1:15. These events precisely parallel descriptions given in Revelation 6:12–13; 8:12; and 19:11–21. Given the fact that these prophecies have yet to be fulfilled, the similarities of descriptions among the different biblical writers are compelling.

Like a Thief in the Night

MATTHEW 24:32–39 *"Now learn this parable from the fig tree: When its branch has already become tender and puts forth leaves, you know that summer is near. So you also, when you see all these things, know that it is near—at the doors! Assuredly, I say to you, this generation will by no means pass away till all these things take place. Heaven and earth will pass away, but My words will by no means pass away.*

"But of that day and hour no one knows, not even the angels of heaven, but My Father only. But as the days of Noah were, so also will the coming of the Son of Man be. For as in the days before the flood, they were eating and drinking, marrying and giving in marriage, until the day that Noah entered the ark,

mourn
Zechariah 12:10–14

elect
Matthew 24:22

earth
Matthew 25:32

thousand
Revelation 20:4

elect
chosen ones

Noah
2 Peter 2:5

years
Genesis 6:3

and did not know until the flood came and took them all away, so also will the coming of the Son of Man be. (NKJV)

The end will come as one great big, unexpected surprise. When people least expect it, Jesus will return. The exact timing of this event has got to be one of heaven's best-kept secrets. Consider this: Even Jesus did not know the exact day or hour.

You might be thinking. "If it comes at the end of the Tribulation, can't anybody with a calendar and calculator determine the time of his return? And if so, how can it possibly be that big of a surprise?" The answer to the first question is a definite, "Well, yes and no!" The answer to the second flows logically out of the first. Let me explain.

First, while it's true that no one can know the "day and hour" of Christ's coming, we can know the season. That's precisely the point of the fig tree illustration in Matthew 24:32. So when the afore-mentioned "signs of the times" occur with great frequency and intensity, "this generation" that witnesses these things will know that Jesus's coming "is near—at the doors!" (24:33 NKJV) and will live to see the climax of history.

Second, his coming will catch people by surprise much as the Flood in Noah's day startled everybody even though Noah had been warning them for a shocking one hundred twenty years. Just as "the flood came and took them all way" (Matthew 24:39 NKJV), so our Lord will come with a heart-stopping suddenness.

Coming Judgment

MATTHEW 24:40–44 *Then two men will be in the field: one will be taken and the other left. Two women will be grinding at the mill: one will be taken and the other left. Watch therefore, for you do not know what hour your Lord is coming. But know this, that if the master of the house had known what hour the thief would come, he would have watched and not allowed his house to be broken into. Therefore you also be ready, for the Son of Man is coming at an hour you do not expect. (NKJV)*

If two people are out in a field, one will be taken away into judgment; the other will remain to be gathered by the angels and enter the Millennium with Jesus. Two women will be grinding at a mill. One will be swept away into judgment; the other will be left to enter the Millennium. So just as a thief comes when a homeowner least expects it, so "the Son of Man is coming at an hour you do not expect" (Matthew 24:44 NKJV).

Some people are confused by the references to two men or two women with one suddenly taken and one left behind. That description sounds an awful lot like the Rapture where Christians who are alive will be "caught up together . . . to meet the Lord in the air" (1 Thessalonians 4:17 NKJV). How can we know for sure that the man and woman who are taken in Matthew 24:40–41 are actually unbelievers who are taken away in judgment, rather than Christians who are caught up to meet the Lord in the air? We know this for two compelling reasons.

First, when the apostle Paul describes the Rapture in 1 Corinthians 15:51, he prefaces his remarks with this mouthwatering little tease: "Behold, I tell you a mystery" (NKJV). The word translated "mystery" is a precise term that refers to new truth never before revealed.[1] Obviously, if Jesus had already revealed the truth about the Rapture, Paul would be giving his readers old news and not a mystery. Therefore, the reference here in Matthew must be describing the Second Coming.

Second, just as in the days of Noah, the time of Christ's second coming will be a time of judgment on the earth. Of those who are "taken," Matthew uses the exact same word that John used when Pilate "delivered [Jesus] to them to be crucified. So they took Jesus and led Him away" (John 19:16 NKJV) to be crucified. It is a word that speaks of being handed over to the authorities for judgment, just as in Noah's day, "the flood [God's judgment] came and took them all away" (Matthew 24:39 NKJV)).

Since Jesus is fully God, how could he not know the day and hour of his return? Doesn't his admission in Matthew 24:36 contradict his **omniscience**? It would appear so, until we dig deeper into what actually happened during Jesus's **incarnation**.

There were times when Jesus put his omniscience on display, such as his encounter with <u>Nathanael</u> and his interview with the <u>woman</u> at the well. In both instances he obviously knew private and personal details about each of these individuals that he couldn't possibly know apart from divine omniscience. At other times his omniscience seemed to fail him. How can that be?

Nathanael
John 1:48

woman
John 4:18

omniscience
having an infinite knowledge of everything

incarnation
God becoming a man

earth
John 17:4–5

attributes
characteristics

The apostle Paul rushes to our rescue in his explanation of the "Kenosis," or self-emptying of Christ described in Philippians 2:5–11. When Jesus, "who, being in the form of God . . . made Himself of no reputation" (Philippians 2:6–7 NKJV), he temporarily and voluntarily set aside the independent use of his divine **attributes** and submitted the exercise of his attributes to the will of his Father. Sure, Jesus could have known the day and hour of his return, but chose not to. He yielded his right to know to the will of his Father.

This self-emptying lasted only as long as Jesus lived here on earth. The independent use of all his attributes has been restored. You can be sure that today he is well aware of both the day and the hour of his glorious return!

Having just couched his coming in the context of a sudden surprise that will catch many off-guard, and exhorted his hearers to be watching and waiting for his return, Jesus then illustrated his point with three parables. They each underscored this same warning: "Watch therefore, for you know neither the day nor the hour in which the Son of Man is coming" (Matthew 25:13 NKJV)). Make it burn indeed!

Keep It Simple

MATTHEW 24:45–51 *"Who then is a faithful and wise servant, whom his master made ruler over his household, to give them food in due season? Blessed is that servant whom his master, when he comes, will find so doing. Assuredly, I say to you that he will make him ruler over all his goods. But if that evil servant says in his heart, 'My master is delaying his coming,' and begins to beat his fellow servants, and to eat and drink with the drunkards, the master of that servant will come on a day when he is not looking for him and at an hour that he is not aware of, and will cut him in two and appoint him his portion with the hypocrites. There shall be weeping and gnashing of teeth." (NKJV)*

The first parable contrasts a "faithful and wise servant" with one who is evil. The wise servant goes about his tasks faithfully, motivated by a desire to please his master. The evil servant thinks, "When the cat's away the mice will play," and goes for the gusto, only to be caught boozing and beating the other servants when the master returns.

Jesus adds a bit of gusto himself when he points out, "The master of that servant will come on a day when he is not looking for him and at an hour that he is not aware of" (Matthew 24:50 NKJV). What could be simpler than that?

Jesus's words must have made an indelible impact upon his disciples. They were sitting on the Mount of Olives, don't forget. They had a commanding view of the Temple. Jesus had told them that soon the entire complex would be torn down as a judgment against God's people. Why? Because Israel should have been watching for the first appearance of their Messiah. They should have recognized Jesus the moment he began his ministry. The Old Testament Scriptures had painted a detailed and compelling portrait of the One who was coming.

Instead, they rejected their Messiah. Indeed, within hours of these predictions, they killed him.

betrothal
Matthew 1:18

Say It Often

MATTHEW 25:1–13 *"Then the kingdom of heaven shall be likened to ten virgins who took their lamps and went out to meet the bridegroom. Now five of them were wise, and five were foolish. Those who were foolish took their lamps and took no oil with them, but the wise took oil in their vessels with their lamps. But while the bridegroom was delayed, they all slumbered and slept. And at midnight a cry was heard: 'Behold, the bridegroom is coming; go out to meet him!' Then all those virgins arose and trimmed their lamps. And the foolish said to the wise, 'Give us some of your oil, for our lamps are going out.' But the wise answered, saying, 'No, lest there should not be enough for us and you; but go rather to those who sell, and buy for yourselves.'*

And while they went to buy, the bridegroom came, and those who were ready went in with him to the wedding; and the door was shut. Afterward the other virgins came also, saying, 'Lord, Lord, open to us!' But he answered and said, 'Assuredly, I say to you, I do not know you.' Watch therefore, for you know neither the day nor the hour in which the Son of Man is coming. (NKJV)

The type of wedding to which Jesus referred typically included three distinct stages:

1. The legal marriage arranged by the parents of the bride and bridegroom, called <u>betrothal</u>

2. The ceremony during which the bridegroom, along with his friends, would proceed from his home to the dwelling of his bride where he would claim her as his own

3. The marriage processional from the bride's home to the home of the bridegroom, wherein the couple would celebrate their union with their friends and a lavish marriage banquet[2]

The bride in Jesus's story had selected ten "virgins" or bridesmaids to participate with her in the festivities. The bridesmaids waited with the bride in eager anticipation of the groom's arrival. In the event that he came at night, each carried her own olive oil lamp for the long procession. Five of the virgins came prepared with jars of olive oil for a longer-than-expected period of watching and waiting. The other five foolishly presumed that the bridegroom would come quickly, failed to bring extra oil, and were unprepared to watch and wait in the event of his delay.

Well, the groom was delayed in coming. The five prepared bridesmaids had plenty of oil to last throughout the entire processional and happily entered into the banquet to celebrate the marriage. The foolish virgins ran out of oil on the way. By the time they arrived at the banquet the door had been shut. They had been shut out.

Being the master teacher that he was, Jesus understood the importance of repetition in his teaching. He kept his point simple in the first story: Jesus will come back on a day and at an hour when people least expect him. He said it often by repeating his point in the second story: You'd better be watching and waiting so that you are not caught unprepared.

Now let's see if he makes it burn.

Make It Burn

the big picture

Matthew 25:14–30

Jesus told a parable about a man who went on a journey and left his possessions in the care of three of his servants. While he was gone, two of his servants doubled his money (talents), while a third buried what he had been entrusted with and did nothing to increase its value.

When the nobleman returned, he called upon his servants to give him a report. The two who had doubled their master's money were commended and regarded by their master as "good and faithful" (Matthew 25:21, 23 NKJV). The third, however, shamefully offered his master a lame excuse and braced for his rebuke. His master denounced him as a "wicked and lazy servant" (25:26 NKJV). The money that had been given to him was taken away and conferred on one of the others, and then he himself was summarily thrown into "The outer darkness. There will be weeping [from sorrow] and gnashing of teeth [in rage]" (25:30 NKJV).

This parable has nothing to do with our talents (such as singing, painting, playing the piano, etc.); it has everything to do with our talents (i.e., our money). In biblical times, a talent was a large sum of money, weighing anywhere from fifty-eight to eighty pounds and varying in value depending upon whether it was gold or silver.[3] We're talking here about cold, hard cash.

Why did the third servant come to such a humiliating end? In reality, he acted as if he believed his master would never return. He wasted the privilege of serving him and squandered the opportunity that had been entrusted to his care. All he had left in the end was a silly excuse and an attempt to shuffle off his responsibility. He actually tried to blame the master for his own lack of work and vigilance. His doom came swiftly and justly. "Keep it simple, say it often, and make it burn." It was sizzling!

what others say

Jay Kesler

One amazing element in the story is the low estimate the man with the talent had of his master. He thought of him as one who "reaped where he didn't sow" and "gathered where he scattered no seed." The master rebuked the servant, indicating that if he indeed thought him greedy, he should have at least put the money in the bank so it would have earned a little interest.[4]

The Great Divide

MATTHEW 25:31–40 *"When the Son of Man comes in His glory, and all the holy angels with Him, then He will sit on the throne of His glory. All the nations will be gathered before Him, and*

Great White Throne
Revelation 20:11–15

He will separate them one from another, as a shepherd divides his sheep from the goats. And He will set the sheep on His right hand, but the goats on the left. Then the King will say to those on His right hand, 'Come, you blessed of My Father, inherit the kingdom prepared for you from the foundation of the world: for I was hungry and you gave Me food; I was thirsty and you gave Me drink; I was a stranger and you took Me in; I was naked and you clothed Me; I was sick and you visited Me; I was in prison and you came to Me.' Then the righteous will answer Him, saying, 'Lord, when did we see You hungry and feed You, or thirsty and give You drink? When did we see You a stranger and take You in, or naked and clothe You? Or when did we see You sick, or in prison, and come to You?' And the King will answer and say to them, 'Assuredly, I say to you, inasmuch as you did it to one of the least of these My brethren, you did it to Me.' (NKJV)

Jesus brought his Mount of Olives discourse to a rousing, if frightful, conclusion with yet another graphic image portraying a somber event yet to take place at the end of the age.

The image that Jesus chose to illustrate this particular judgment is that of a shepherd who separates his sheep from goats. You'll want to remember for the sake of this discussion, that sheep are good and goats are bad.

This judgment is not to be confused with the <u>Great White Throne</u> judgment. The judgment mentioned here of the sheep and goats precedes Christ's thousand-year reign and seems to be limited to only those people who survive the seven-year Tribulation and are alive during Christ's second coming. The Great White Throne judgment is the final judgment of all other unbelievers, living and dead, at the conclusion of the Millennium.

When Jesus returns he will establish his throne in Jerusalem, and all of the people from all of the nations of the world who are alive will be gathered before him.

Rewards and Punishments

MATTHEW 25:41–46 *Then He will also say to those on the left hand, 'Depart from Me, you cursed, into the everlasting fire prepared for the devil and his angels: for I was hungry and you gave Me no food; I was thirsty and you gave Me no drink; I was a stranger and you did not take Me in, naked and you did not clothe Me, sick and in prison and you did not visit Me.' Then they also will answer Him, saying, 'Lord, when did we see You hungry or thirsty or a stranger or naked or sick or in prison, and did not minister to You?' Then He will answer them, saying, 'Assuredly, I say to you, inasmuch as you did not do it to one of the least of these, you did not do it to Me.' And these will go away into everlasting punishment, but the righteous into eternal life."* (NKJV)

The basis of Jesus's judgment has to do with how Gentiles, the people of "all the nations," will treat the Jews, "the least of these My brethren," during the Tribulation (Matthew 25:32, 40 NKJV). During the abomination of desolation, the beast or Antichrist will declare all-out war against the Jews and seek their total annihilation.

There will be some Gentiles who love Christ and love his people. They will literally put their lives on the line and risk losing everything to help the Jews. These people will give the Jews something to eat or drink, invite them into the homes, clothe them, care for their sick, and even visit them in prison. Individuals who did these sorts of things during the Holocaust are to this day referred to by Jews as "righteous Gentiles." Such self-sacrificing acts toward Jesus's *brothers* during the Tribulation will give undeniable evidence that these Gentiles genuinely love Jesus and are truly his followers. God rewards people to practice the love of Jesus and longs to find those whose faith is accompanied by action.

> ## what others say
>
> ### John White
>
> We may be bothered by the idea of an angry God because we know what our own anger is like. The matter may be complicated because we were taught that anger is innately evil. Certainly our human anger can be a vicious, evil, ugly thing. It's inconceivable to think of God as having that same guilt-provoking rage. But there we go again creating God in our own image. We read into God's anger what we experience of our own. Yet God's anger is altogether unlike ours—His anger is against evil. All evil. Everywhere. Always. My anger is often about trivia.[5]

Is it not remarkable that even after Israel's complete rejection of Jesus as her Messiah, he still loves his people, the Jews, embraces them as his "brothers," and rewards or curses Gentiles based upon their treatment of his chosen people? Truly his love is unconditional. He loves his own, and he will love them to the end.

Chapter Wrap-Up

- Jesus indicated that the day was coming when the Temple in Jerusalem would be destroyed. (Matthew 24:2)

- Jesus told the disciples to be watching for certain signs that would indicate that his coming is drawing near. (Matthew 24:3–26)

- Jesus said that the days immediately preceding his coming would be like the days of Noah when people were eating and drinking with no thought about God. (Matthew 24:36–44)

- Jesus used parables to encourage his disciples to be ready for his coming, and not to be caught unprepared. (Matthew 25:13)

- A judgment day is coming when people will be held accountable for their sins. (Matthew 25:31)

Study Questions

1. What prompted the disciples to ask Jesus about end-time events?

2. What is the difference between the Rapture and the Second Coming?

3. How will people know that the coming of Christ is getting closer?

4. If the Second Coming occurs at the end of the Tribulation, how can it be a surprise?

5. What is the mutual point of the three parables that Jesus related?

6. How should these affect or impact our lives?

7. Is the separation of the sheep and the goats the same thing as the Great White Throne judgment?

Matthew 26:1–27:26: Countdown to Crucifixion

Chapter Highlights:
- Conspiracy Theory
- The Last Supper
- Garden of Glory, Garden of Grief
- Trial of the Centuries

Let's Get Started

Jesus was now just two short days away from being executed at the hands of the Romans, at the insistence of the Jews, at the behest of the religious leaders. Finally, the Pharisees, Sadducees, chief priests, and teachers of the law would be rid of him—or so they thought. Jesus warned his disciples that events would now begin to spin quickly out of control.

This would not be the first time Jesus's enemies plotted to <u>kill</u> him. He had always slipped through their fingers; his <u>time</u> had not yet come. This time, however, Jesus faced his date with destiny.

go to

kill
Luke 4:29–30;
John 5:18; 10:39

time
John 7:6

surreptitiously
secretly, stealthily

Conspiracy Theory

> **MATTHEW 26:1–5** *Now it came to pass, when Jesus had finished all these sayings, that He said to His disciples, "You know that after two days is the Passover, and the Son of Man will be delivered up to be crucified." Then the chief priests, the scribes, and the elders of the people assembled at the palace of the high priest, who was called Caiaphas, and plotted to take Jesus by trickery and kill Him. But they said, "Not during the feast, lest there be an uproar among the people." (NKJV)*

It's Wednesday of Jesus's last week, two days before the Passover. While Jesus was sitting on the Mount of Olives, looking out over Jerusalem and warning the disciples that his crucifixion was but forty-eight hours away, the not-so-holy chief priests and elders of the people were **surreptitiously** gathering somewhere in the Holy City to plot Jesus's execution. This committee of killers decided that they should act prudently and await the end of the Passover until after the masses of pilgrims would have exited the city. That way they could avoid an uprising, as this would surely catch the attention of the Romans and force them into the fray. Among the planners and plotters was the corrupt Jewish high priest-turned-puppet of Rome, Caiaphas.

deadly
John 11:50

Annas
Luke 3:2

Josephus
Jewish historian

Caiaphas served as the Jewish high priest from AD 18 to AD 36, a remarkably long tenure for that particular office. This little detail might give us some insight into the character of this man; he no doubt enjoyed a close relationship both with Rome and the various Herods who ruled the roost in Jerusalem.

As high priest Caiaphas had jurisdiction over the Temple, and probably profited personally from the corruption to which Jesus so violently reacted on the previous Sunday, a mere three days prior to this meeting of murderous minds. If so, this would indicate that Caiaphas's <u>deadly</u> hatred for Jesus went beyond the political; it became as personal as his pocketbook. No wonder every time Caiaphas is mentioned in the Gospels he is seeking Jesus's destruction.

In 1990, while constructing a water park in Jerusalem's Peace Forest, a workman stumbled upon an ancient cave, which contained a dozen bone boxes, or ossuaries, the designs of which indicate that they are from the time of Jesus. The cave yielded evidence that it was the burial site of a small family.

"The tomb was found just where we might expect to find the cave-tomb of a priestly family; it lies near a well-known group of highly decorated cave-tombs of prominent families dating to this same period. This kind of burial was not for everyone. It was reserved for the Temple aristocracy. (Incidentally, the Temple could be seen from this tomb.)"[1]

Now get this: Two of the ossuaries had the name "Caiaphas" inscribed on them, indicating that this was the burial cave of the Caiaphas clan or family! It gets even better. The most elaborate, exquisitely decorated of these ossuaries bore on its side this breath-taking inscription: "Joseph, son of Caiaphas." Inside the box, excavators discovered the bones of six different people: four young people, an adult woman, and a man about sixty years of age.

Now here's the punch line: "<u>Annas</u>, who served as high priest from AD 6–15, had five sons as well as a son-in-law, all of whom served as high priest at one time or another. Annas's son-in-law was none other than the high priest Caiaphas, who presided at Jesus's trial (Matthew 26:57). **Josephus** refers to him as 'Joseph who was called Caiaphas of the high priesthood'"![2]

Given the location of the cave, the intricate patterns that adorned the most elaborate of the boxes, coupled with the testimony of

Josephus, can there be any doubt that the remains of the sixty-year-old man are those of Caiaphas, "the high priest described in the New Testament as having interrogated Jesus before delivering him to the Roman authorities"?[3]

Selling Out His Savior

MATTHEW 26:6–16 *And when Jesus was in Bethany at the house of Simon the leper, a woman came to Him having an alabaster flask of very costly fragrant oil, and she poured it on His head as He sat at the table. But when His disciples saw it, they were indignant, saying, "Why this waste? For this fragrant oil might have been sold for much and given to the poor." But when Jesus was aware of it, He said to them, "Why do you trouble the woman? For she has done a good work for Me. For you have the poor with you always, but Me you do not have always. For in pouring this fragrant oil on My body, she did it for My burial. Assuredly, I say to you, wherever this gospel is preached in the whole world, what this woman has done will also be told as a memorial to her."*

Then one of the twelve, called Judas Iscariot, went to the chief priests and said, "What are you willing to give me if I deliver Him to you?" And they counted out to him thirty pieces of silver. So from that time he sought opportunity to betray Him. (NKJV)

What made Judas sell out his Savior to his enemies? The answer lies in this short vignette that includes a leprous man, an awestruck woman, a conniving thief, and some expensive perfume.

We are indebted to Mark and John for many of the details of this story, details that Matthew chose to omit. Basically, we know that Jesus dined in the home of Simon the Leper, along with his friends Mary, Martha, and their brother, Lazarus.

Jesus had recently <u>raised</u> Lazarus from the dead, so both Mary and Martha must have been filled with a profound sense of awe. So grateful was Mary that she took an **alabaster** jar of costly oil of **spikenard** (see Illustration #11), <u>broke</u> the flask, and anointed Jesus's head and <u>feet</u> with the oil. Mark indicates that the value of the oil exceeded a year's <u>wages</u>, and this does not include the price of the shattered jar.

go to

raised
John 11:7–44

broke
Mark 14:3

feet
John 12:3

wages
Mark 14:5

alabaster
fine marble, quarried in Egypt

spikenard
fragrant oil extracted from the root of a plant

poor
John 12:5–6

slave
Exodus 21:32

Some of the disciples, led by Judas, vehemently protested such a flagrant waste of money. Judas pretended to be motivated by a sincere concern for the <u>poor</u>, but that was nothing more than a sham, a lie, a pretense, a cover. Jesus addressed the disciples' concerns by pointing out that Mary anointed him for his coming burial, for it was customary to anoint the dead with expensive perfume to cover the smell of decay. It is doubtful that Mary understood it that way; if the disciples didn't expect Jesus to be killed, she probably didn't either. Hers was the sacrificial and heartfelt act of a most grateful and devoted woman. Jesus commended Mary and he assured her that the memory of her sacrifice would never be forgotten.

Well, Jesus's response was too much for Judas to stomach. He quickly consorted with the chief priests and ended up selling the life of his friend and master for thirty silver coins, the paltry price of a common <u>slave</u>. Once Judas defected and joined their ranks, the chief priests could not resist this once-in-a-lifetime opportunity. They vetoed their original plan to wait until after the Passover to do Jesus in. They decided to seize the day and take him out now.

By the way, it might interest you to note that of the four Gospel writers, only Matthew specifically states that Judas was paid "thirty pieces of silver" (Matthew 26:15 NKJV). Leave it to the tax collector to know the exact amount that Judas was paid.

We enter something of a chronological quagmire with the story of the woman with the alabaster jar, because while Matthew does not mention the timing of this event, John specifically states that it comes a full "six days before the Passover" (John 12:1 NKJV), placing it even before the Triumphal Entry. There is no contradiction here, as Matthew does not state, nor even imply, that he intended to place this story in its proper sequence. Matthew apparently placed it here because Jesus's praise of the woman who poured the perfume on his head was the straw that broke Judas's back. From this moment on, Judas sought a way to betray him. Thus, Matthew chooses to place this story in close proximity to verse 25 where Jesus will unmask Judas as his betrayer.

Perfect Preparations

MATTHEW 26:17–19 *Now on the first day of the Feast of Unleavened Bread the disciples came to Jesus, saying to Him,*

"Where do You want us to prepare for You to eat the Passover?"
And He said, "Go into the city to a certain man, and say to him,
'The Teacher says, "My time is at hand; I will keep the Passover
at your house with My disciples."'" So the disciples did as Jesus
had directed them; and they prepared the Passover. (NKJV)

Illustration #11
Spikenard—Mary's perfume was made from the spikenard plant. The plant had to be imported at great expense from India, making the perfume expensive.

Peter
Luke 22:8

water
Luke 22:10

Even though from the disciples' point of view events may have been spinning out of control, Jesus was in complete control. This is evident in the unfolding story of the Last Supper.

The time of the Passover had finally arrived, the day "when the Passover must be killed" (Luke 22:7 NKJV). Since the Jews reckoned the beginning of a day at sundown, Jesus planned to eat the Passover meal with his disciples on Thursday night, knowing that he would be sacrificed the next day, what we call today "Good Friday," as "the Lamb of God who takes away the sin of the world" (John 1:29 NKJV).

Jesus sent <u>Peter</u> and John into Jerusalem to find a man carrying a jar of <u>water</u>. That man would lead them to the predetermined location that Jesus had chosen for their meal. (One wonders if perhaps Jesus kept the location a secret until the last moment in order to prevent Judas from getting a heads-up and plotting to have him arrested there.)

At any rate, the man was spotted, the Upper Room was readied, and that evening Jesus and his men shared their final meal together. The fact that just the right man was spotted at just the right time, and that just the right disciples, Peter and John, found him defies

death
Luke 23:46

broke bread
Acts 2:46

coincidence. Jesus clearly exercised sovereign control over these details, as well as many other aspects of the Crucifixion, even to the point of determining the precise time of his <u>death</u>.

The man carrying the jar of water stood out to Peter and John because—let us put this as delicately as we can—in biblical times, carrying water was women's work. At the time of the Gospels, the Essene quarter of Jerusalem was located in the southwest corner of the city. The "Essene Gate" has been excavated. Given the Essenes' commitment to celibacy, only men lived in this quarter. Some have speculated that Jesus and his disciples shared their Passover meal in an upper room of a home in the Essene quarter. This might explain why a man and not a woman would be carrying the water. Today, the traditional site of the Upper Room is located in what would have been the Essene quarter of Jesus's day.

The Last Supper

MATTHEW 26:20–30 *When evening had come, He sat down with the twelve. Now as they were eating, He said, "Assuredly, I say to you, one of you will betray Me." And they were exceedingly sorrowful, and each of them began to say to Him, "Lord, is it I?" He answered and said, "He who dipped his hand with Me in the dish will betray Me. The Son of Man indeed goes just as it is written of Him, but woe to that man by whom the Son of Man is betrayed! It would have been good for that man if he had not been born." Then Judas, who was betraying Him, answered and said, "Rabbi, is it I?" He said to him, "You have said it."*

And as they were eating, Jesus took bread, blessed and broke it, and gave it to the disciples and said, "Take, eat; this is My body." Then He took the cup, and gave thanks, and gave it to them, saying, "Drink from it, all of you. For this is My blood of the new covenant, which is shed for many for the remission of sins. But I say to you, I will not drink of this fruit of the vine from now on until that day when I drink it new with you in My Father's kingdom." And when they had sung a hymn, they went out to the Mount of Olives. (NKJV)

During the meal, Jesus exercised more sovereign control when he exposed Judas as his betrayer. The moment of truth was especially poignant given the aforementioned significance of bread in that culture. When two people <u>broke bread</u> together, that meaningful act symbolized the deep bond of love, commitment, and fellowship that existed between them as they shared with one another the sustenance of life.

When we add that bit of knowledge into the mix, Jesus's words take on a much more profound meaning when he said, "He who eats bread with Me has lifted up his heel against Me. . . . Most assuredly, I say to you, one of you will betray Me . . . It is he to whom I shall give a piece of bread" (John 13:18, 21, 26 NKJV). At that exact moment, when Jesus broke a piece of bread and handed it to Judas, given the cultural significance that would have been attached to his receiving and eating the bread, "[Judas] then went out immediately" (John 13:30 NKJV). He could not bring himself to break bread with the one he would soon betray. As if to add insult to injury, Judas later betrayed Jesus with a <u>kiss</u>.

kiss
Matthew 26:48

primeval
ancient, primitive

> ## what others say
>
> ### W. A. Criswell
>
> But our Lord did not create a monument out of marble to bring to us the memory of our Savior's suffering in our behalf. In fact, this memorial is not in the form of any kind of structure. He did it in a **primeval**, fundamental, and basic way—by eating and drinking—and this simple memorial is to be repeated again and again and again. The broken bread recalls for us His torn body, and the crimson of the cup reminds us of the blood poured out upon the earth for the remission of sins.[4]

From Betrayal to Denial

MATTHEW 26:31–35 *Then Jesus said to them, "All of you will be made to stumble because of Me this night, for it is written:*
'I will strike the Shepherd,
And the sheep of the flock will be scattered.'
"But after I have been raised, I will go before you to Galilee." Peter answered and said to Him, "Even if all are made to stumble because of You, I will never be made to stumble." Jesus said to him, "Assuredly, I say to you that this night, before the rooster crows, you will deny Me three times." Peter said to Him, "Even if I have to die with You, I will not deny You!" and so said all the disciples. (NKJV)

Peter was in fine form this night. If ever he was up for an occasion, it was now. As Jesus and his men made their way to the Garden of

fire
Luke 22:55

wept
Matthew 26:75

olives
John 8:1

often
John 18:2

usual
Luke 22:39

Gethsemane, Jesus gave them a glimpse of what they were in for. He told them that before the Middle Eastern sun rose in the sky, they would each fall away from him.

In typical fashion Peter jumped in front of the others and declared his loyalty to Jesus, a loyalty to the death. But Jesus sobered his sanguine disciple with this stinging indictment: Before that night was over, Peter would deny Jesus three times. "Not so!" Peter retorted. But let the record show that Jesus's prediction came true. After warming himself by a <u>fire</u>, heating his hands with Jesus's executioners, and swearing with an oath, "I do not know the Man!" Peter went out and <u>wept</u> bitter tears.

Garden of Glory, Garden of Grief

MATTHEW 26:36–38 *Then Jesus came with them to a place called Gethsemane, and said to the disciples, "Sit here while I go and pray over there." And He took with Him Peter and the two sons of Zebedee, and He began to be sorrowful and deeply distressed. Then He said to them, "My soul is exceedingly sorrowful, even to death. Stay here and watch with Me." (NKJV)*

The name Gethsemane means "oil press." This garden, at the bottom of the Mount of Olives, is so named because in biblical times, in a large cave, there sat a rather large oil press, placed there to squeeze the oil out of the abundance of <u>olives</u> that grew on the hillside. As Jesus knelt praying in the garden, he was "pressed" or "squeezed" by the sheer weight of his woeful anticipation and sorrowful contemplation of his fate come morning.

Jesus was no stranger to the Garden of Gethsemane. He and his disciples went there <u>often</u>, transforming an otherwise ordinary garden into a garden of glory. On this fateful evening Judas naturally assumed that Jesus and his men would gather once again in this place that had become for Jesus an island of solitude, reflection, and contemplation. Sure that Jesus would follow his <u>usual</u> routine, Judas planned to betray Jesus there.

This was without a doubt the most emotionally distressful moment in Jesus's entire earthly life up to this point. True, this was but a taste of what was to come in the next several hours, but as Jesus knelt by a tree to pray, he became "exceedingly sorrowful, even to death" (Matthew 26:38 NKJV). So great was his agony that Luke records that Jesus sweat drops of <u>blood</u>, a condition known as hematidrosis, or the effusion of blood into one's perspiration, caused by extreme anguish. For Jesus, the prospect of bearing the sins of the whole world literally pressed his life's blood right out of him.

blood
Luke 22:44

cup
Isaiah 51:17;
Jeremiah 25:15–17;
27–29

what others say

Mary Alice Chrnalogar

Jesus was so troubled and full of anxiety and sorrow in the Garden of Gethsemane that he cried out, "My soul is sorrowful unto death" (Matthew 26:38 Douay). Jesus was genuinely troubled because of those who rejected him and were not saved, and because of the agonizing death he knew he would suffer. Still Jesus had perfect faith.

So you can have faith and be troubled, perplexed, or have fears. We wouldn't say Jesus sinned, yet often disciples who have worry, doubt, or fear can be told they "lack trust in God" and, therefore, they are in sin. Jesus was able to pray more earnestly because he fell into a great agony (Luke 22:44).[5]

Jesus's Unanswered Prayer

MATTHEW 26:39–46 *He went a little farther and fell on His face, and prayed, saying, "O My Father, if it is possible, let this cup pass from Me; nevertheless, not as I will, but as You will." Then He came to the disciples and found them sleeping, and said to Peter, "What! Could you not watch with Me one hour? Watch and pray, lest you enter into temptation. The spirit indeed is willing, but the flesh is weak." Again, a second time, He went away and prayed, saying, "O My Father, if this cup cannot pass away from Me unless I drink it, Your will be done." And He came and found them asleep again, for their eyes were heavy. So He left them, went away again, and prayed the third time, saying the same words. Then He came to His disciples and said to them, "Are you still sleeping and resting? Behold, the hour is at hand, and the Son of Man is being betrayed into the hands of sinners. Rise, let us be going. See, My betrayer is at hand." (NKJV)*

Three times Jesus prayed that if possible, God the Father would spare him the agony of the "<u>cup</u>" of God's wrath. Three times, just when he needed them the most, his disciples fell asleep, leaving him to face his agony alone. Yet each time he prayed, Jesus yielded to the will of his Father. As we learned in our discussion of the Kenosis,

weapons
John 18:3

Satan
John 13:27

Jesus did indeed become "obedient to the point of death, even the death of the cross" (Philippians 2:8 NKJV).

The Serpent Strikes

MATTHEW 26:47–56 *And while He was still speaking, behold, Judas, one of the twelve, with a great multitude with swords and clubs, came from the chief priests and elders of the people. Now His betrayer had given them a sign, saying, "Whomever I kiss, He is the One; seize Him." Immediately he went up to Jesus and said, "Greetings, Rabbi!" and kissed Him. But Jesus said to him, "Friend, why have you come?" Then they came and laid hands on Jesus and took Him. And suddenly, one of those who were with Jesus stretched out his hand and drew his sword, struck the servant of the high priest, and cut off his ear. But Jesus said to him, "Put your sword in its place, for all who take the sword will perish by the sword. Or do you think that I cannot now pray to My Father, and He will provide Me with more than twelve legions of angels? How then could the Scriptures be fulfilled, that it must happen thus?" In that hour Jesus said to the multitudes, "Have you come out, as against a robber, with swords and clubs to take Me? I sat daily with you, teaching in the temple, and you did not seize Me. But all this was done that the Scriptures of the prophets might be fulfilled." Then all the disciples forsook Him and fled. (NKJV)*

Judas was a pawn, a stooge, an asset to be used and thrown away. Sure, Judas was in the garden, accompanied by a murderous mob outfitted with lanterns, torches, and <u>weapons</u>. But someone, or should we say "something" else was in the garden with them. <u>Satan</u> needed a stooge and he found a willing accomplice in Judas.

Having planned and plotted for just the right moment, "that serpent of old, called the Devil and Satan" (Revelation 12:9 NKJV) saw his opportunity and struck with full fury. "Kill Jesus," he reasoned, "and heaven and earth will be mine to mold into whatever image I choose." So Judas, the unwitting servant of Satan, led the bloodthirsty gang into the garden, planted his kiss of death on the cheek of his <u>friend</u>, and slid into the shadows to watch them lead Jesus away in chains.

friend
Matthew 26:50

healed
Luke 22:51

Of course, Peter was not about to be silent. His moment had come. A military coup was in the offing. So he instinctively grabbed his sword, turned toward the first target he could find, swung squarely for his head, and promptly missed. Give him an A for effort. He tried to split the servant of the high priest's head wide open like a watermelon, but managed only to cut off his ear. Wouldn't you love to know what Peter was thinking when Jesus rebuked him, touched the servant, and <u>healed</u> his ear? We can make a guess. Peter will not speak up again until he denies Jesus with the oath, "I do not know the Man!" (Matthew 26:72 NKJV).

Peter wouldn't be the only one to struggle with his thoughts and emotions on this seminal night. Matthew ends this section of his story with the enormously sad confession, "Then all the disciples forsook Him [Jesus] and fled" (26:56 NKJV). How painful it must have been for him to pen those words. Let us not forget that among the disciples was one man whose name was Matthew. Yes, it's true. No doubt for the rest of his life, the writer of this Gospel lived with the knowledge that at the moment when Jesus needed him the most, he fled in fear like all of the rest, leaving Jesus to face his fate alone. If the disciples deserted Jesus, we should be on guard because we could do the same.

Trial of the Centuries

MATTHEW 26:57–63a *And those who had laid hold of Jesus led Him away to Caiaphas the high priest, where the scribes and the elders were assembled. But Peter followed Him at a distance to the high priest's courtyard. And he went in and sat with the servants to see the end. Now the chief priests, the elders, and all the council sought false testimony against Jesus to put Him to death, but found none. Even though many false witnesses came forward, they found none. But at last two false witnesses came for-*

go to

judge
Psalm 98:8–9

misquote
Mark 14:58

Temple
John 2:19–21

ward and said, "This fellow said, 'I am able to destroy the temple of God and to build it in three days.'" And the high priest arose and said to Him, "Do You answer nothing? What is it these men testify against You?" But Jesus kept silent. (NKJV)

Jesus will one day <u>judge</u> the world, but not before the world judges him—the Jewish and Roman worlds at least.

After his betrayal in the garden, Jesus was led away to be tried—not once, but twice. The Jewish court would be the first to take their swings. Then the Romans would enter the fray.

The hours before the Crucifixion were dark for Jesus, both literally and figuratively. He faced a Jewish jury in the dark of the night, spent the wee hours of the morning agonizing in isolation in a dark and dank pit, only to be passed back and forth from Jewish leader to Roman official, eventually to wind up in front of the crowds as they chanted in unison for his crucifixion.

High Priest Caiaphas reenters the narrative at this point. Matthew, in his abbreviated account of Jesus's arrest and subsequent trials, chooses to begin his story line with the interrogation by Caiaphas.

We know from John's written record that Jesus first faced Annas, the former high priest and father-in-law to Caiaphas. Matthew offers his readers a leaner and meaner account, focusing on his main point—that Jesus was accused, tried, and condemned illegally before the first-century equivalent of Jewish and Roman kangaroo courts. By the time these upholders of injustice got hold of him, Jesus didn't stand a chance.

Jesus faced two trials—one Jewish and religious, the other Roman and political. The religious leaders knew that in order to get Jesus killed, he had to be handed over to the Roman authorities since they alone could sentence a man to die by crucifixion. So Matthew's first stop is at the home of the high priest where the Sanhedrin, the justices of the Jewish Supreme Court, seventy-one in all, waited eagerly to sink their venom-dripping fangs into Jesus's jugular vein. How embarrassing it must have been for the members of the court to realize that they had no basis upon which to condemn Jesus to die! They had to recruit two false witnesses to <u>misquote</u> and misinterpret Jesus's words about building the <u>Temple</u> in three days, a clear distortion of what he really said.

Vengeful Verdict

go to

Son of Man
Daniel 7:13

right hand
Psalm 110:1

MATTHEW 26:63b–68 *And the high priest answered and said to Him, "I put You under oath by the living God: Tell us if You are the Christ, the Son of God!" Jesus said to him, "It is as you said. Nevertheless, I say to you, hereafter you will see the <u>Son of Man</u> sitting at the <u>right hand</u> of the Power, and coming on the clouds of heaven." Then the high priest tore his clothes, saying, "He has spoken blasphemy! What further need do we have of witnesses? Look, now you have heard His blasphemy! What do you think?" They answered and said, "He is deserving of death." Then they spat in His face and beat Him; and others struck Him with the palms of their hands, saying, "Prophesy to us, Christ! Who is the one who struck You?" (NKJV)*

When Caiaphas tried to force Jesus to respond to these absurd accusations, he became incensed at Jesus's silence. Finally, when Jesus alluded to Psalm 110:1 and Daniel 7:13, clearly claiming to be "the Christ, the Son of God," the high priest lost control of his volcanic rage, tore his clothes as a sign of his unbridled fury at hearing what was to his self-righteous ears such unbelievably wretched words, and shouted, "Blasphemy!" a capital offense.

The Sanhedrin, the Jewish Supreme Court, decreed with one voice that Jesus deserved to die. In their bones they knew Jesus to be an innocent man. They knew that the entire proceeding was illegal under their own laws. They knew that the charges against Jesus were trumped up. "All the council sought *false* testimony against Jesus to put Him to death" (Matthew 26:59 NKJV, emphasis mine). Yes, they knew. And yet, these men of such high moral character stooped so low as to play a little guessing game with Jesus as they covered his eyes, repeatedly slapped him in the face, and taunted him to tell them who hit him.

The Rooster Crows

MATTHEW 26:69–75 *Now Peter sat outside in the courtyard. And a servant girl came to him, saying, "You also were with Jesus of Galilee." But he denied it before them all, saying, "I do not know what you are saying." And when he had gone out to the gateway, another girl saw him and said to those who were there, "This fellow also was with Jesus of Nazareth." But again he denied with an oath, "I do not know the Man!" And a little*

Peter
Luke 22:61

flagellation
to punish by
whipping

aperture
opening, hole

later those who stood by came up and said to Peter, "Surely you also are one of them, for your speech betrays you." Then he began to curse and swear, saying, "I do not know the Man!" Immediately a rooster crowed. And Peter remembered the word of Jesus who had said to him, "Before the rooster crows, you will deny Me three times." So he went out and wept bitterly. (NKJV)

There is a time gap in the record between the time the Sanhedrin sentenced Jesus to die in the late evening and his trial before Pilate in the "morning" (Matthew 27:1 NKJV). During the gap, a couple of notable events took place.

First, Peter, who had been following the proceedings from afar, joined Jesus's accusers in the courtyard outside of the high priest's home. It was there that Peter was asked three times if he was one of Jesus's disciples, and three times out of three Peter vehemently denied even knowing him.

Second, Jesus had to be held somewhere for the night before facing Pilate in the morning. It is interesting to note that the trial before the Sanhedrin was patently illegal. Capital cases required public trials during the day at the Temple. But when you're killing the Son of God, who cares about trivial details of the law? So the Jewish court condemned Jesus to die at night, and then had to figure out where to hold him in custody until the morning. Where did they put him? Once again, we can thank the archaeologist's spade for the answer.

The high priest's house has been excavated, including the courtyard where Peter sat in cozy and close proximity to Jesus's judges and jury, warming himself with those self-righteous and self-serving men. You'll never believe what they found under the house—a prison!

"The rock-hewn chambers were the prison associated with that palace. The upper chamber, it is suggested, was a guard chamber and the rings in the walls were used to tie prisoners for **flagellation**; the lower pit was the place of incarceration and the **aperture** in the wall allowed the guards to watch those below. That Christ himself was confined here during the night of his trial before Caiaphas is then also surmised."[7]

Through that opening Jesus could easily have heard the rooster crow for the third time, stared into the eyes of <u>Peter</u>, and watched him rush away as he went out to weep bitter tears, having just denied and disowned the one he swore to defend, even to the death.

And Then There Were Eleven

MATTHEW 27:1–10 *When morning came, all the chief priests and elders of the people plotted against Jesus to put Him to death. And when they had bound Him, they led Him away and delivered Him to Pontius Pilate the governor. Then Judas, His betrayer, seeing that He had been condemned, was remorseful and brought back the thirty pieces of silver to the chief priests and elders, saying, "I have sinned by betraying innocent blood." And they said, "What is that to us? You see to it!" Then he threw down the pieces of silver in the temple and departed, and went and hanged himself. But the chief priests took the silver pieces and said, "It is not lawful to put them into the treasury, because they are the price of blood." And they consulted together and bought with them the potter's field, to bury strangers in. Therefore that field has been called the Field of Blood to this day. Then was fulfilled what was spoken by Jeremiah the prophet, saying, "And they took the thirty pieces of silver, the value of Him who was priced, whom they of the children of Israel priced, and gave them for the potter's field, as the LORD directed me." (NKJV)*

"(Judas) went and hanged himself." Why did someone who began his ministry so hopefully, so excitedly—enjoying such promise, so many privileges, such close proximity to Jesus—end his life so hopelessly, so tragically? We will never know.

It's now early on Friday morning. After spending a long and lonely night in what can only be described as a hand-hewn pit under Caiaphas's house, Jesus was hoisted by rope out of his hole, bound, and led to Pilate, the Roman governor whose jurisdiction included Jerusalem. Jesus had endured the mockery of the Jewish trial the night before; now it was the Romans' turn to have at him.

go to

Pilate
Matthew 27:2–14

Herod
Luke 23:6–12

sentencing
Matthew 27:15–26

humiliating
Luke 23:11

Pilate's headquarters were located in the seaport city of Caesarea Maritima. But given the volatile nature of the Passover feast, he made his way up to Jerusalem for the weekend. Christ was brought before <u>Pilate</u>, interrogated by <u>Herod</u>, and then brought back to Pilate for a final hearing and subsequent <u>sentencing</u>.

As Judas watched Jesus being shuttled from one end of Jerusalem to the other and back again, viewing the <u>humiliating</u> treatment that he had to endure, something in his psyche snapped. He could bear his guilt no longer. Judas was so "remorseful" that he went back to the chief priests, threw his blood money away, found a tree, and hanged himself.

Judas's money was used to buy a field, known as the "potter's field" (Matthew 27:7 NKJV). This field is located just south of Jerusalem at the place where the Kidron Valley on the eastern side and the Valley of Hinnom on the western side of the city intersect. The soil there is especially good for making pottery. Thus, it was known as the potter's field. But after that field soaked up Judas's blood, and given that it was purchased with blood money, its name was changed to the now-more-fitting Field of Blood.

Zechariah predicted the exact amount of the price paid to Judas for betraying Jesus, as well as the name of the field in which he would be buried (Zechariah 11:12–13).

Judas's suicide is recorded only in Matthew's Gospel and in the book of Acts. The Acts account reads quite a bit differently from Matthew. Once again we have an example of two different statements being complementary not contradictory.

According to Matthew, Judas hanged himself. Yet Luke, writing in Acts 1:18, states categorically that in the field purchased with his money, Judas fell "headlong, he burst open in the middle and all his entrails gushed out" (NKJV). So which is it? You can't have it both ways. Or can you?

Question: Recognizing that Judas fell from something high enough that he hit the ground below with such force that he burst open and spilled his intestines, from what could he possibly have fallen?

Answer: How about a tree? This particular field is surrounded by several rocky cliffs, out of which grow a number of trees. Given the shallowness of their roots, and their brittleness since water is in short supply, it is quite conceivable that Judas hung himself from a tree whose branches hung over one of these cliffs. A probable scenario would have the branch breaking under Judas's weight, causing his body to fall to and shatter on the rocks below, creating the gruesome scene described in Acts 1:18.

Judas's description of Jesus is quite remarkable. Judas cried out in remorse, "I have sinned by betraying innocent blood" (Matthew 27:4 NKJV). He would not be the last of Jesus's enemies to make statements about Jesus's innocence:

- Pilate said: "Behold, I am bringing Him out to you, that you may know that I find no fault in Him" (John 19:4 NKJV).
- Mrs. Pilate said: "Have nothing to do with that just Man" (Matthew 27:19 NKJV).
- The thief on the cross said: "This Man has done nothing wrong" (Luke 23:41 NKJV).
- The Roman centurion said: "Certainly this was a righteous Man!" (Luke 23:47 NKJV).

Even Christ's enemies gave testimony that Jesus died an innocent man.

Between a Rock and a Hard Place

MATTHEW 27:11–23 *Now Jesus stood before the governor. And the governor asked Him, saying, "Are You the King of the Jews?" Jesus said to him, "It is as you say." And while He was being accused by the chief priests and elders, He answered nothing. Then Pilate said to Him, "Do You not hear how many things they testify against You?" But He answered him not one word, so that the governor marveled greatly.*

Now at the feast the governor was accustomed to releasing to the multitude one prisoner whom they wished. And at that time they had a notorious prisoner called Barabbas. Therefore, when they had gathered together, Pilate said to them, "Whom do you want me to release to you? Barabbas, or Jesus who is called Christ?" For he knew that they had handed Him over because of envy. While he was sitting on the judgment seat, his wife sent to him, saying, "Have nothing to do with that just Man, for I have suffered many things today in a dream because of Him." But the chief priests and elders persuaded the multitudes that they should ask for Barabbas and destroy Jesus. The governor

innocent
John 19:4

envy
Matthew 27:18

answered and said to them, "Which of the two do you want me to release to you?" They said, "Barabbas!" Pilate said to them, "What then shall I do with Jesus who is called Christ?" They all said to him, "Let Him be crucified!" Then the governor said, "Why, what evil has He done?" But they cried out all the more, saying, "Let Him be crucified!" (NKJV)

Pilate knew that Jesus was innocent. He even said that Jesus was <u>innocent</u>. He recognized that the Jewish leaders were motivated only by their own <u>envy</u> of this innocent man. His wife even told him to have nothing to do with Jesus. Although he was the ruler in charge, he found it difficult to lead.

> **what others say**
>
> ### Max Lucado
>
> Pilate's question is yours. "What will I do with this man, Jesus?"
>
> You have two choices.
>
> You can reject him. That is an option. You can, as have many, decide that the idea of God becoming a carpenter is too bizarre—and walk away.
>
> Or you can accept him. You can journey with him. You can listen for his voice amidst the hundreds of voices and follow him. Pilate could have. He heard many voices that day—he could have heard Christ's. Had Pilate chosen to respond to this bruised Messiah, his story would have been different.[9]

The Moment of Truth

MATTHEW 27:24–26 *When Pilate saw that he could not prevail at all, but rather that a tumult was rising, he took water and washed his hands before the multitude, saying, "I am innocent of the blood of this just Person. You see to it." And all the people answered and said, "His blood be on us and on our children." Then he released Barabbas to them; and when he had scourged Jesus, he delivered Him to be crucified.* (NKJV)

Pilate could have let Jesus go, but he didn't. This pathetic, spineless Roman governor caved in to the pressure of the people. He understood that Jesus's execution would constitute a gross injustice. And yet, even when Pilate's own custom of releasing a prisoner at Passover gave him an easy out, he still ordered Jesus beaten and handed him over to be crucified.

Illustration #12
Roman Scourge—
The soldiers expertly
wielded a whip of
this type to flog
Jesus near to the
point of death.

Let's consider an oft-overlooked word used by Matthew to describe some of the suffering endured by Jesus. Pilate had Jesus "scourged." This scourging, sometimes called flogging, of a prisoner involved the use of a whip consisting of several strands of leather attached to the end of a wooden handle. Each strand had bits of bone, metal, or stone attached to its end (see Illustration #12).

The victim was typically stripped naked from the waist up, bound to a post by the wrists fastened high over his head in order to stretch the skin of the back to its maximum, and whipped mercilessly and repeatedly by a Roman soldier especially expert at wielding the whip. The flesh would be torn from the back as muscles were ripped and vital organs exposed. Flogging could be fatal, but the intent was not to kill the victim. The goal was to beat the victim to within an inch of his life.

If Pilate had hoped that by having Jesus scourged he would satisfy the blood lust of the crowds and thereby avert his having to render an undeserved death sentence, he was sadly mistaken. They demanded Christ be crucified. So crucified, he would be.

Chapter Wrap-Up

- The religious leaders plotted to kill Jesus, and found in Judas, one of his own disciples, a willing accomplice. (Matthew 26:14–16)

- Jesus and the disciples celebrated the Passover together, and Jesus instituted the "Last Supper." (Matthew 26:26–29)

- Jesus predicted that Peter would deny Jesus three times, something he would die with him first. (Matthew 26:30–35)

- As Jesus prayed in the Garden of Gethsemane, the religious leaders led by Judas came and arrested Jesus and took Him away. (Matthew 26:47–49)

- False witnesses testified against Jesus at an illegal trial, prompting Caiaphas to denounce him as a blasphemer. (Matthew 26:59–65)

- Pilate could have chosen to release Jesus according to a long-standing custom, but gave into the demands of the crowd and released Barabbas instead. (Matthew 27:15–25)

Study Questions

1. Describe the character of Caiaphas and his role in the arrest and subsequent trial of Jesus.

2. Describe the character of Judas and his motivation in the betrayal of Christ.

3. Describe the character of Peter and how he could have denied the Lord so vehemently.

4. Describe the character of Pilate and speculate why he acted with such weakness of character.

5. What is the origin of what we celebrate today as "Communion," "the Lord's Supper," or the Eucharist?

6. How many times did Jesus pray in the Garden of Gethsemane, and for what did he pray?

7. Did Peter merely deny Jesus, or was there more to it than that?

8. Did Pilate believe that Jesus deserved to die?

Matthew 27:27–28:20: Crucified, Raised, and Praised

Let's Get Started

To say that the events that preceded, accompanied, and immediately followed the Crucifixion were remarkable would be the essence of understatement. We guarantee that neither you nor I have ever witnessed or experienced anything like them. No one ever has, except for the people who were alive and present in Jerusalem on the day that will truly live on in infamy—the day religious hypocrisy teamed up with Roman brutality in a vain attempt to kill the Son of God.

Forsaken, Not Forgotten

MATTHEW 27:27–31 *Then the soldiers of the governor took Jesus into the Praetorium and gathered the whole garrison around Him. And they stripped Him and put a scarlet robe on Him. When they had twisted a crown of thorns, they put it on His head, and a reed in His right hand. And they bowed the knee before Him and mocked Him, saying, "Hail, King of the Jews!" Then they spat on Him, and took the reed and struck Him on the head. And when they had mocked Him, they took the robe off Him, put His own clothes on Him, and led Him away to be crucified.* (NKJV)

Matthew described the humiliation that preceded the Crucifixion. Most any reader can understand the basics of what Jesus had to endure. The author assumed, however, that his original readers would comprehend some of the culturally specific references that he made, the significance of which we might miss. So we'll fill in some of the blanks as far as Matthew's written imagery is concerned.

Praetorium: This was Pilate's residence in Jerusalem. The most likely location is the Antonia Fortress, adjacent to the northwest corner of the temple complex, from where the Roman soldiers had a commanding bird's-eye view of all of the goings-on around the Temple.

go to

purple
Mark 15:17;
John 19:2

face
John 19:3

The whole garrison: This group of the governor's soldiers numbered some six hundred men who were assigned to serve and protect Pilate during his stay in Jerusalem.

A scarlet robe: Mark and John described the color of the robe as "purple," indicating that its true color was something between what we might call "royal blue" and red. The robe was most likely a military cloak belonging to one of the soldiers, something hastily obtained in the heat of the moment to be used to mock Jesus's claim that he was the king of the Jews. They placed the robe upon him soon after he was beaten. The blood from his many wounds no doubt coagulated among the fibers of the robe, sending excruciating pain coursing through his body when they later ripped the robe from him.

A crown of thorns: Of course a king needs a crown. The Romans chose to crown him with thorns. The thorns to which Matthew refers measured—if you can imagine this!—several inches in length. The crown was woven from the strands and spikes of the date palm. These would have cut deeply into Jesus's scalp, causing profuse bleeding and unimaginable pain.

A reed: To imitate a king's scepter, the soldiers chose a long stick or reed. The merciless soldiers made a crude game out of their abuse. According to the record they taunted him, spat upon him, repeatedly struck him on the head and in the face with his staff as they knocked those spikelike thorns deeper and deeper into his scalp.

Every one of their moves was calculated to inflict the maximum amount of pain and ridicule on Jesus. They achieved their goal. When they got done with him, he didn't even look human. From a purely human perspective, God was losing ground and the good guys were getting hammered.

Isaiah predicted that by the time the soldiers got done with him, Jesus's "visage was marred more than any man, and His form more than the sons of men" (Isaiah 52:14 NKJV). Now we know why.

prophecy

what others say

Mark R. Littleton

Have you ever told God He's making a mistake? Not in so many words, perhaps, but by implication. Sometimes I find myself saying when evil strikes or problems explode, "Why are you letting this happen, Lord?" . . .

> By seeing God for who He is—all-knowing, wise, and therefore perfectly capable of running the universe without our advice—the Christian can give thanks when evil seems to have the winning edge. He knows God has everything well in hand.[1]

This Is Jesus, the King of the Jews

MATTHEW 27:32–44 *Now as they came out, they found a man of Cyrene, Simon by name. Him they compelled to bear His cross. And when they had come to a place called Golgotha, that is to say, Place of a Skull, they gave Him sour wine mingled with gall to drink. But when He had tasted it, He would not drink. Then they crucified Him, and divided His garments, casting lots, that it might be fulfilled which was spoken by the prophet:*

"They divided My garments among them,
And for My clothing they cast lots."

Sitting down, they kept watch over Him there. And they put up over His head the accusation written against Him:

THIS IS JESUS
THE KING OF THE JEWS.

Then two robbers were crucified with Him, one on the right and another on the left. And those who passed by blasphemed Him, wagging their heads and saying, "You who destroy the temple and build it in three days, save Yourself! If You are the Son of God, come down from the cross." Likewise the chief priests also, mocking with the scribes and elders, said, "He saved others; Himself He cannot save. If He is the King of Israel, let Him now come down from the cross, and we will believe Him. He trusted in God; let Him deliver Him now if He will have Him; for He said, 'I am the Son of God.'" Even the robbers who were crucified with Him reviled Him with the same thing. (NKJV)

The Romans had perfected the art of crucifixion, designing it to inflict upon the victim the maximum amount of torture for the longest amount of time. Some victims even lived long enough to be eaten alive by birds or wild beasts. The doom of death could literally last for days, as the victim slowly expired from a combination of exhaustion, dehydration, high fever, and suffocation.

History tells us that the Romans crucified many Jews during their occupation of the land. They even crucified as many as two thousand in one day![2] All the trees lining the roads to and from Jerusalem became places for crucifixions.

tree
Deuteronomy 21:23

myrrh
Mark 15:23

mother
John 19:27

thief
Luke 23:43

Cyrene
city in North Africa

Crosses were most often rooted olive trees, the predominant tree in the Jerusalem area. Thus, Paul's brief reference to crucifixion is quite literal when he writes, "Cursed is everyone who hangs on a tree" (Galatians 3:13 NKJV). This might also explain the religious leaders' insistence that Jesus be crucified. All notions of Jesus being the Messiah would die a cursed death with him.

When Matthew wrote that a man from **Cyrene** helped to carry the cross, what he actually carried was the crossbeam that would be attached to the tree. Jesus, of course, tried but could not carry his own cross; his back muscles were no doubt destroyed by his scourging. To add to the humiliation, the crimes of the individual were printed on a placard and hung around his neck. Later it would be attached to the cross above the prisoner's head.

The victim's hands would be nailed through the wrists so that the nail would not pull through the skin of the hand. The feet usually would be nailed together using one spike through the instep or Achilles' tendon. Then he would be left there to burn in the noonday Middle Eastern sun or freeze during a Jerusalem snowfall, his life ebbing away as the seconds dragged on for minutes, which turned to hours, which became days of unspeakable torture.

Christ was crucified at a place of Roman execution known as Golgotha, or Calvary, the place of a skull. Golgotha was so named most likely because it was a skull-shaped hill or because skulls accumulated there as a result of the many executions in that place, or both.

As an act of mercy, a soldier offered Jesus some wine mixed with gall. Gall usually refers to something bitter. With his eye for detail, Mark identified it as myrrh, a substance which, when mixed with wine, produced a pain-deadening medication, the same kind of myrrh brought by the wise men as a gift for the Christ child. Jesus refused it because he knew that he had to keep his wits about him. He had much to do in the final hours of his life, including providing for the care of his mother and saving the thief on the cross.

An inscription listing his "crimes" was placed over his head. He hung there in agony, refusing to defend himself against the outrageous verbal assaults leveled against him, both by passersby and the two thieves who were crucified with him.

Jesus's garments were divided, as foretold in Psalm 22:18.

There is some concern over the discrepancies among the four Gospel accounts of the <u>inscription</u> placed on the cross over Jesus's head. Each of the writers quotes the inscription—the list of crimes that Jesus committed. But each account is different from the others. How do we explain this?

Two explanations account for these discrepancies. First, both Luke and John point out that the inscription was printed in Greek, Latin, and Hebrew; the varying accounts may simply reflect this variation in language. Second, each of the writers exercised his editorial prerogative in recording the substance of the inscription and emphasizing the portion of the inscription he deemed most significant. Using our tried-and-true principle of "complementary, not contradictory," the full inscription reads, "THIS IS JESUS OF NAZARETH, THE KING OF THE JEWS."

go to

inscription
Mark 15:26;
Luke 23:38;
John 19:19

third
Mark 15:25

The Ultimate Price—Paid in Full!

MATTHEW 27:45–50 *Now from the sixth hour until the ninth hour there was darkness over all the land. And about the ninth hour Jesus cried out with a loud voice, saying, "Eli, Eli, lama sabachthani?" that is, "My God, My God, why have You forsaken Me?" Some of those who stood there, when they heard that, said, "This Man is calling for Elijah!" Immediately one of them ran and took a sponge, filled it with sour wine and put it on a reed, and offered it to Him to drink. The rest said, "Let Him alone; let us see if Elijah will come to save Him." And Jesus cried out again with a loud voice, and yielded up His spirit. (NKJV)*

According to the Jewish reckoning of time, the soldiers nailed Jesus to the cross at the <u>third</u> hour, or 9:00 a.m. Something strange occurred at the sixth hour, or high noon—an eerie darkness enveloped the land. One gets the feeling that nature itself could not bear to look upon the perverse outrage that was occurring in the heart of the Holy City.

The darkness that settled over the land has mystified many people down through the centuries. What exactly was the cause? There is a type of soil in that part of the Middle East known as "loess" soil. When the prevailing winds hit the ground at just the right angle, that thick, gritty, almost chalklike dirt is blown high into the air. It can become so thick that it actually blots out the sun. If this is the cause

glory
Luke 2:8–9

account
Mark 15:36

willfully
John 19:30

of the darkness, it was a darkness that people not only saw but also felt. Isn't it ironic that when Jesus was born, God's <u>glory</u> lit the heavens with a pyrotechnic display of supernatural proportions; yet when he died, nature closed its eyes as it were and Jesus died in the dark?

At 3:00 p.m., when Jesus cried out to God, a flurry of activity followed. Some who heard this mistakenly thought that Jesus was calling on Elijah to help him. In response to Jesus's cry, others filled a sponge with wine vinegar and offered it to Jesus. This was a different drink than the wine mixed with gall mentioned earlier. This was a cheap wine commonly consumed by soldiers.

Mark's <u>account</u> gives us the best insight as to why someone did this; he hoped to prolong Jesus's life and suffering motivated by a perverse curiosity to see if Elijah would come to rescue Jesus from the cross. It didn't work, of course. Jesus had not called upon Elijah, bringing the Old Testament prophet back from the dead. Jesus also <u>willfully</u> died immediately afterward. The curiosity seekers who wanted some spectacular showing of Elijah must have felt disappointed, but not for long.

Jesus uttered this bloodcurdling cry, "My God, My God, why have You forsaken Me?" (Matthew 27:46 NKJV), which was a fulfillment of Psalm 22:1.

<u>Surely . . . the Son of God</u>

MATTHEW 27:51–56 *Then, behold, the veil of the temple was torn in two from top to bottom; and the earth quaked, and the rocks were split, and the graves were opened; and many bodies of the saints who had fallen asleep were raised; and coming out of the graves after His resurrection, they went into the holy city and appeared to many. So when the centurion and those with him, who were guarding Jesus, saw the earthquake and the things that had happened, they feared greatly, saying, "Truly this was the Son of God!" And many women who followed Jesus from Galilee, ministering to Him, were there looking on from afar, among whom were Mary Magdalene, Mary the mother of James and Joses, and the mother of Zebedee's sons. (NKJV)*

The moment of Jesus's death was marked by the most remarkable events yet recorded in Scripture. Here they come in rapid-fire succession:

- The curtain in the Temple that separated the **Holy** **Place** from the **Holy of Holies** was torn in two from top to bottom. The symbolism of this phenomenon must not be missed. Prior to this, one high priest could enter the Holy of Holies only once a year to offer a sacrifice for the sins of the people. The tearing of the veil signified that the way into God's presence was now open to everyone at any time through the <u>blood</u> Jesus shed on the cross. Matthew made a point of noting that the veil was torn, not from the bottom to the top by a human hand, but from top to bottom by God's hand.

- A devastating earthquake shook the entire region, splitting the rocks around the crucifixion site.

- Tombs opened, releasing the bodies of many holy people who had once died and were now raised.

- When a centurion and others who joined him in guarding Jesus felt the earthquake and saw all that happened, they exclaimed that Jesus surely was "the Son of God!" (Matthew 27:54 NKJV).

Only Matthew mentions the miracle of bodies being raised from the dead. Since they appeared to many people, ample eyewitnesses could testify to the validity of the miracle. But they are never mentioned again in Scripture. Perhaps after a short visit on earth they went to heaven as a foretaste of what will occur during the Rapture (1 Thessalonians 4:16).

go to

Holy
Exodus 26:33;
Hebrews 9:3

blood
Hebrews 10:19–22

Holy Place
inner room of
the Temple

Holy of Holies
innermost room
where God
manifested his
presence

> ## what others say
>
> ### Charles H. Spurgeon
>
> Sin abounded so much that it put out the light of the sun. So heavy was it that it cracked the solid earth and rent the rocks asunder and caused the graves to open, while the great veil of the temple was rent in two from the top to the bottom. Yet "where sin abounded, grace did much more abound" (Rom. 5:20).[3]

When Jesus hung on the cross, all of your sins and all of mine were placed on him. As the prophet described it, "The LORD has laid on Him the iniquity of us all" (Isaiah 53:6 NKJV). When Jesus cried out, "My God, My God, why have You forsaken Me?" (Matthew 27:46 NKJV), he was experiencing the agonizing abandonment of his Father, as God poured out upon his Son the white-hot lava of his wrath. Jesus once and for all paid the penalty for the sins of every sin-

go to

Sabbath
John 19:31

gnat
Matthew 23:24

died
John 19:33

Calvary
another name
for Golgotha

gle person who has ever lived (1 John 2:2). In that singular moment frozen in time, Jesus became the sin-bearer for you and for me.

Today in Jerusalem the Church of the Holy Sepulcher encompasses both the location of **Calvary** and the place of the tomb where Jesus was buried. The actual rock of Calvary is a huge thing, both in height and circumference. The amazing thing is this: The rock is split all the way through, as if something or someone grabbed it on both sides and broke it into two pieces. Could this be one of the rocks to which Matthew refers when he says, "The earth quaked, and the rocks were split" (Matthew 27:51 NKJV)?

Sealing His Fate

The other three Gospel accounts of Jesus's death fill in some of the details that Matthew chose to omit. One of these details has to do with the fact that Jesus's legs were not broken. John records that the Jews did not want to leave three men alive on crosses during the Sabbath (as if it would matter after crucifying their Messiah). You talk about straining out a gnat while swallowing a camel—we are left to marvel at the mental machinations of these woefully wicked religious leaders.

So at their behest, a soldier broke the legs of each of the two criminals who were hung on either side of Jesus. They did this in order to hasten death, as the victim would no longer be able to gulp in quick breaths of air by pushing up on the spike through his feet or ankles. With the legs broken, his body would sag, placing enormous strain on the muscles he used to breathe, thus hastening death by a combination of shock and asphyxiation. When the soldiers came to Jesus, they saw he had already died. They did not break his legs.

Because the soldiers did not mindlessly break Jesus's legs along with the others, they inadvertently fulfilled a most important directive of Scripture that requires the bones of the Passover lamb not be broken (Exodus 12:46; Numbers 9:12). Jesus was our Passover Lamb who takes away the sins of the world (1 Corinthians 5:7; 1 Peter 1:19). They likewise unknowingly fulfilled the prophecy of Psalm 34:20, "Not one of His bones shall be broken" (John 19:36 NKJV).

Tombstone

Council
Luke 23:50

good
Luke 23:50

decision
Luke 23:51

disciple
John 19:38

Nicodemus
John 3:1

demons
Luke 8:2

mother
Mark 15:40

James
Matthew 27:56

distance
Luke 23:49

Arimathea
town twenty miles
northwest of
Jerusalem

MATTHEW 27:57–61 *Now when evening had come, there came a rich man from Arimathea, named Joseph, who himself had also become a disciple of Jesus. This man went to Pilate and asked for the body of Jesus. Then Pilate commanded the body to be given to him. When Joseph had taken the body, he wrapped it in a clean linen cloth, and laid it in his new tomb which he had hewn out of the rock; and he rolled a large stone against the door of the tomb, and departed. And Mary Magdalene was there, and the other Mary, sitting opposite the tomb. (NKJV)*

Burial came quickly to the now-deceased Son of God. Joseph, a most interesting individual from **Arimathea**, offered his own family tomb for the burial of Jesus. Would you believe us if we told you that Joseph was a member of the Jewish <u>Council</u>, the Sanhedrin? He was. What if we added that Luke referred to him as a <u>good</u> and upright man? He did. Suppose you discovered that Joseph opposed the <u>decision</u> to have Jesus crucified? Indeed, he did! And can you imagine that Joseph was actually a <u>disciple</u> or follower of Jesus? Oh, yes, he was a disciple, although up to this point he had kept it a secret.

Joseph was soon joined by another prominent Jewish leader, <u>Nicodemus</u>, himself a Pharisee and member of the Jewish ruling council. Together, they buried Jesus in Joseph's new tomb, a dramatic and detailed fulfillment of Isaiah 53:9, which reads, "And they made His grave with the wicked—but with the rich at His death, because He had done no violence, nor was any deceit in His mouth" (NKJV).

A large rolling stone was fitted in front of the cavelike tomb. The men departed, leaving three women, Mary Magdalene, from whom Jesus had cast seven <u>demons</u>; and another Mary, the wife of Clopas and <u>mother</u> of James the younger; and Salome, the mother of <u>James</u> and John. This trio of women watched from a <u>distance</u>, unable to stomach from a closer vantage point the torture that Jesus endured.

We know from John's account that one more Mary sat in vigil in front of the cross—Mary, the mother of Jesus (John 19:26). As she watched her son die, she no doubt remembered the words Simeon spoke to her: "A sword will pierce through your own soul also" (Luke 2:35 NKJV). Mary felt the full force of that sword piercing her soul on this darkest of days.

go to

resurrection
John 2:22

locked
John 20:19

The Plot Thickens

MATTHEW 27:62–66 On the next day, which followed the Day of Preparation, the chief priests and Pharisees gathered together to Pilate, saying, "Sir, we remember, while He was still alive, how that deceiver said, 'After three days I will rise.' Therefore command that the tomb be made secure until the third day, lest His disciples come by night and steal Him away, and say to the people, 'He has risen from the dead.' So the last deception will be worse than the first." Pilate said to them, "You have a guard; go your way, make it as secure as you know how." So they went and made the tomb secure, sealing the stone and setting the guard. (NKJV)

Irony abounds in the biblical record of Jesus's life and death. Here is arguably the greatest irony of them all: for all of Jesus's warnings about his coming crucifixion and <u>resurrection</u>, the disciples never quite got it. But the chief priests and Pharisees understood him completely.

Jesus's executioners approached Pilate with the alarming news that Jesus claimed that after three days he would rise from the dead. Pilate responded to the religious leaders' concern by immediately implementing three measures guaranteed to keep a very dead Jesus inside the tomb.

1. Pilate ordered that his men secure the tomb for three days. This was to prevent the disciples from stealing the body and faking a resurrection. Apparently Pilate didn't realize that one of Jesus's own disciples had betrayed him; a second denied him; and the other ten fled in fear, leaving him to die alone. They were cowering in corners behind <u>locked</u> doors, understandably fearful that if the Romans put Jesus on a cross, his followers might each have a tree with their name on it too.

2. Pilate placed a guard at the tomb. Typically, a Roman guard consisted of four men, one to stand as a sentinel to watch over the other three in order to ensure that they were alert and ready to respond to any crisis. They "were not allowed to sit down, much less to sleep. The captain of the guard saw that every man was alert, chastising (a soldier) if found asleep at his post, and sometimes even punishing him by burning his shirt upon him, as a warning to (the others)."[4]

3. Pilate ordered the tomb sealed, presumably with wax and a cord, making any tampering with the large stone in front of the tomb immediately apparent. The seal probably included the official Roman stamp pressed into the wax, thus letting anyone know that if they broke that seal, they would answer to Rome.[5] And we know what that could mean!

I Serve a Risen Savior

Clopas
John 19:25

James
Matthew 27:56

spices
Luke 24:1

feet
John 13:5

> MATTHEW 28:1–4 *Now after the Sabbath, as the first day of the week began to dawn, Mary Magdalene and the other Mary came to see the tomb. And behold, there was a great earthquake; for an angel of the Lord descended from heaven, and came and rolled back the stone from the door, and sat on it. His countenance was like lightning, and his clothing as white as snow. And the guards shook for fear of him, and became like dead men.* (NKJV)

Two women are front and center as we move now to Sunday morning, one week to the day after Jesus's triumphal entry into Jerusalem. What a week it was!

Mary Magdalene, along with Mary, the wife of Clopas and mother of James the younger, approached Jesus's tomb with the intention of anointing his body with spices. If washing someone's filthy feet constituted an act of selfless love, how much more was this unenviable task? Bodies were anointed postmortem for one reason: to mask the stench of decay. Were these women in for a surprise!

Once again, the earth growled and the region shook to its core as a violent earthquake rumbled through the area. Only this one wasn't caused by the slippage of subterranean tectonic plates. This earthquake was caused by an angel descending from heaven and rolling the stone from the entrance of the tomb. Make no mistake about it. The angel did not open the tomb to let Jesus out; he opened the tomb to let the women in!

The elite, heavily armed, highly trained, invincible Roman guardsmen now shook with fear and fainted at the sight of an angel and the seismic eruption that heralded his arrival. As the men dove for cover, the women watched and listened with awe and wonder.

He Is Not Here; He Has Risen Indeed!

MATTHEW 28:5–10 *But the angel answered and said to the women, "Do not be afraid, for I know that you seek Jesus who was crucified. He is not here; for He is risen, as He said. Come, see the place where the Lord lay. And go quickly and tell His disciples that He is risen from the dead, and indeed He is going before you into Galilee; there you will see Him. Behold, I have told you." So they went out quickly from the tomb with fear and great joy, and ran to bring His disciples word.*

And as they went to tell His disciples, behold, Jesus met them, saying, "Rejoice!" So they came and held Him by the feet and worshiped Him. Then Jesus said to them, "Do not be afraid. Go and tell My brethren to go to Galilee, and there they will see Me." (NKJV)

Assured by the angel that they had nothing to fear, the women were also told that—would you believe it?—the body that they came to anoint was gone! The tomb was empty. Jesus was not there.

The angel gave the women a message to deliver to the disciples (if they could possibly get past the locked doors and find those men quaking in fear underneath tables and beds). The message was a personal one from Jesus. He would meet them up north in Galilee and talk with them there.

As these ladies dutifully and excitedly ran to deliver their message, Jesus suddenly appeared to them with the comment, "Rejoice!" The women, understandably overcome with emotion, fell at his feet, and worshiped their risen Lord and Savior.

what others say

Richard F. Lovelace

In Jesus's death and resurrection, all the "dynamics of spiritual death" were disarmed and destroyed. Our distance from God and apathy toward him, our compulsive egoism, our selfish manipulation of others, our crippling attitudes and habits, all the shackles of our flesh are dissolved and released.[6]

Cover-Up

MATTHEW 28:11–15 *Now while they were going, behold, some of the guard came into the city and reported to the chief priests all the things that had happened. When they had assembled with the elders and consulted together, they gave a large sum of money to the soldiers, saying, "Tell them, 'His disciples came at night and stole Him away while we slept.' And if this comes to the governor's ears, we will appease him and make you secure." So they took the money and did as they were instructed; and this saying is commonly reported among the Jews until this day. (NKJV)*

Fearful of the impact of the news of the Resurrection, the religious leaders financed a cover-up with a sizable bribe paid to the soldiers to spread the news that the disciples stole Jesus's body. Wait a minute! Isn't this what the leaders were afraid of in the first place? That the disciples would indeed steal the body?

The telling of this lie required a large sum of money because if word got back to Pilate that the disciples had in fact jacked the body, the soldiers who guarded the tomb would have been executed for dereliction of duty.

The chief priests had to add to the money the promise that if Pilate heard about this, they would personally appease him. Note that they were so determined not to believe in Jesus that they even were willing to pay some Romans a chariotful of money and put their own lives on the line to defend their lie.

The cover-up might have worked except for one thing: Jesus was seen alive in too many places by too many people for too long a period of time. At the very least, Jesus appeared to these people in the following chart.

Post-Resurrection Appearances of Christ

Person/People	Scripture
Mary Magdalene at the tomb	Mark 16:9
The women on their way to tell the disciples	Matthew 28:9–10
Two of the disciples (unnamed) on the road to Emmaus	Luke 24:13–22
Peter	Luke 24:34
Ten of the eleven disciples, Thomas being absent	Luke 24:36–43
The eleven disciples, Thomas being present	John 20:26–31
Seven disciples (named in the text) by the Sea of Galilee	John 21:1–25
More than 500 people at one time, many of whom were still alive at the time Paul wrote the Corinthian church	1 Corinthians 15:6
James	1 Corinthians 15:7
The apostles, when Jesus ascended into heaven	Acts 1:3–11
Paul, on the road to Damascus	1 Corinthians 15:8; Acts 9:1–6

go to

met
1 Corinthians 15:6

King to the End

MATTHEW 28:16–18 *Then the eleven disciples went away into Galilee, to the mountain which Jesus had appointed for them. When they saw Him, they worshiped Him; but some doubted. And Jesus came and spoke to them, saying, "All authority has been given to Me in heaven and on earth. (NKJV)*

In obedience to the words of the angel and Jesus himself, the disciples, now numbering eleven, traveled north to Galilee and <u>met</u> Jesus there. Understandably, some of the disciples doubted that the unimaginable had really occurred. Just a few dark days before, it seemed that there leader was dead and all hope was lost. Now, he appeared to them very much alive.

Someone has said, "Kill a monarch and his rule ends; kill a martyr and his rule begins." That was certainly the case with Jesus. Jesus was born the "King of the Jews" (Matthew 2:2 NKJV), killed for being the "King of the Jews" (Matthew 27:37 NKJV), and is now resurrected as the "King of kings and Lord of lords" (Revelation 19:16 NKJV), to whom "all authority has been given . . . in heaven and on earth" (Matthew 28:18 NKJV), the strongest possible affirmation of his deity.

Alone, but Never Alone

MATTHEW 28:19–20 *Go therefore and make disciples of all the nations, baptizing them in the name of the Father and of the Son and of the Holy Spirit, teaching them to observe all things that I have commanded you; and lo, I am with you always, even to the end of the age." Amen. (NKJV)*

On the basis of the authority given to him by God, Jesus commissioned his followers—those who were present, and every disciple who follows him today, including us—to make disciples of all nations. This is the church's Great Commission, spoken by the King concerning his kingdom. The church will fulfill her commission, for we read of a day yet future when we all shall sing to his praise, "You were slain, and have redeemed us to God by Your blood out of every tribe and tongue and people and nation" (Revelation 5:9 NKJV).

Finally, Matthew brings us full circle. He began his Gospel with an angel appearing to Joseph and assuring him that his beloved bride-to-be was still a virgin, that she would bear him a son, and that his name would be "'Immanuel,' which is translated, 'God with us'" (Matthew 1:23 NKJV). Now he ends with that same promise, "I am with you always, even to the end of the age" (Matthew 28:20 NKJV).

God is indeed with us. He is with us always.

Chapter Wrap-Up

- The crowds mocked Jesus even as he was being beaten and carrying his own cross to the place of his execution. (Matthew 27:29–30)
- The mocking continued as Jesus hung on a cross in between two thieves. (Matthew 27:38–40)
- Jesus cried out in agony when God the Father punished his own Son in your place and mine for our sins. (Matthew 27:46)
- Several remarkable signs occurred at the moment of Jesus's death. (Matthew 27:51–54)
- Jesus was buried in a borrowed tomb. A Roman guard was placed there to make the grave secure and prevent the disciples from stealing the body. (Matthew 27:57–66)
- When women went to the tomb, they found the tomb empty. (Matthew 27:1–8)
- Jesus appeared to his disciples and told them (and us) to make disciples of all nations. (Matthew 28:19–20)

Study Questions

1. How was the prophecy of Isaiah 52:14 fulfilled?

2. What list of crimes were posted on the cross of which Jesus was guilty?

3. At what moment did Jesus's suffering become extreme beyond description?

4. Why did the curtain between the Holy Place and the Holy of Holies need to be torn?

5. What did the centurion say when Jesus died?

6. Look up and list the various appearances of Jesus after he arose from the dead. How did these nullify the efforts of the Jewish and Roman leaders to cover up Jesus's resurrection?

7. What did the Roman officials do when they heard about the Resurrection?

8. What promise of God did Matthew suggest at the beginning of his book and then restate in the closing verses? What assurance does it offer to us as well?

Appendix A—Map of Israel in Jesus's Day

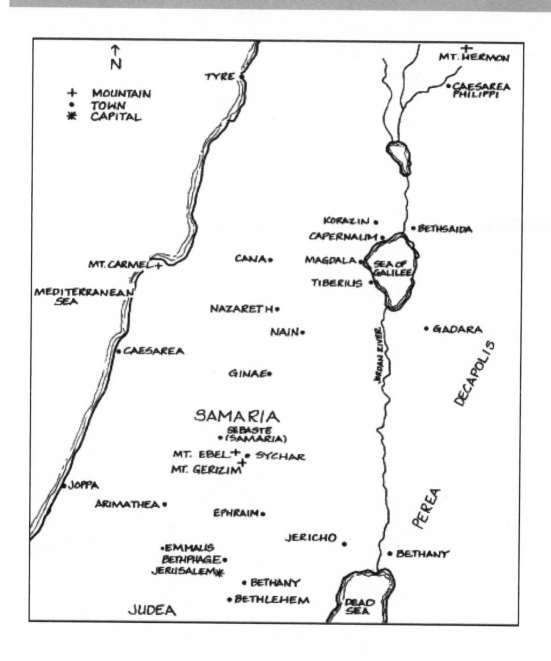

Appendix B—The Answers

Chapter 1: Matthew 1—Virgin-Born Savior-King

1. Jesus is the Jewish Messiah (in fulfillment of the biblical requirements). (Matthew 1:1; 2 Samuel 7:16; Luke 1:30–32)

2. Very important. Matters of property ownership and inheritance issues were determined by one's genealogy. In Jesus's case, his genealogy establishes the fact that he is Jewish and is rightfully the King of the Jews.

3. The genealogy proves that Jesus is qualified to fulfill both the Abrahamic and Davidic covenants. (Matthew 1:1–17; Genesis 12:1–3; 2 Samuel 7:5–16)

4. Abrahamic and Davidic covenants (Genesis 12:1–3; 2 Samuel 7:5–16)

5. Because Joseph knew that he was not the human father of Jesus. (Matthew 1:18)

6. Mary's incredulity (Luke 1:34); Joseph's reaction to Mary's pregnancy (Matthew 1:19–25); the fact that no father was ever identified (John 8:41); Jesus's works proved he was supernatural in his nature (Matthew 14:35–36, John 21:25).

7. Matthew's arguments were based on the fulfillment of scores of predictions about the coming Messiah, quoted from Israel's own prophets. (Matthew 1:22–23; John 6:14)

8. Savior, the One who will save his people from their sins. (Matthew 1:21)

Chapter 2: Matthew 2—Child Born King

1. The wise men were most likely individuals schooled in the knowledge of astronomy, astrology, agriculture, mathematics, history, and the occult who traveled from Persia or Babylon to pay their respects to Jesus a year or two after his birth.

2. Some two years passed between the birth of Jesus and the arrival of the Magi. We know this because: Herod ordered the execution of all the boys in Bethlehem who were two years and under (Matthew 2:16); Jesus's family had moved

from a stable (Luke 2:7) to a house (Matthew 2:11); Jesus was described in the passage as a child (Matthew 2:11).

3. Gold emphasized Christ's royalty, frankincense his deity, and myrrh his humanity and mortality. (Matthew 2:11)

4. "I would rather be Herod's pig than his son."

5. Herod was not a descendant of David and therefore had no regal right to hold that title, nor was he a descendant of Abraham and therefore had no legal right to that title.

6. Herod was a man both hated and hunted. He needed to be able to barricade himself against those who sought to kill him.

7. The chief priests were religious leaders who served in the Jewish temple; the teachers of the law were scholars who taught the Old Testament.

8. Bethlehem means, "House of Bread." The "breaking of bread" in biblical times signified a bond of friendship and fellowship between two people.

9. Rachel epitomized the heartfelt desire of every young Jewish woman to bear children of her own. She thus graphically symbolizes the anguish of the mothers who lost their children to Herod's Holocaust. (Matthew 2:16–18; Jeremiah 31:15)

Chapter 3: Matthew 3—King's Herald

1. This title has nothing to do with John's denominational affiliation. He is called "the Baptist" because of his ministry of baptism. (Matthew 3:6)

2. The Essenes, at a community called Qumran by the Dead Sea. John was certainly a son of the desert. His preaching sounds similar themes to that of the writings of the Essenes.

3. Repent means to change one's mind or purpose concerning sin and to have a complete change of

attitude (spiritual and moral) toward God. (Matthew 3:2)

4. There are several significant and striking parallels between John the Baptist and Elijah. John was not a reincarnation of Elijah, but a carbon-copy of this mighty prophet.

5. His diet and clothing were perfectly suited to the harsh desert climate in which he lived. (Matthew 3:4)

6. The Holy Spirit would be poured out on his people, cleansing them and putting a new spirit within them. The other side involves God's judgment on those who demand to live in rebellion against him. (Matthew 3:11–12; Ezekiel 36:25–26; Isaiah 63:10)

7. The wheat are those who have sincerely repented of their sins and received Christ in their lives; chaff are religious imposters. (Matthew 3:12)

8. Immediately after Jesus's baptism, God the Father spoke on behalf of his Son and sent the Holy Spirit to descend like a dove on his Son. (Matthew 3:16–17)

9. He didn't. But Jesus's baptism allowed him to identify with the sins of his people, validate John's ministry to the crowds, mark the beginning of Jesus's public ministry, align him with the humble masses who were repentant, and symbolize his death, burial, and resurrection. (Matthew 3:13–17)

Chapter 4: Matthew 4—Testing of the King

1. Angels are mentioned in one-half, or thirty-three of the sixty-six books of the Bible.

2. He is called Satan, the Tempter, Destroyer, Evil One, Liar, Deceiver, a Roaring Lion, and twenty other descriptive names.

3. Lucifer said "I will ascend to heaven, I will raise my throne above the stars of God, I will sit enthroned on the mount of assembly, I will ascend above the tops of the clouds, I will make myself like the Most High." (Matthew 4:1; Isaiah 14:12–14)

4. The Lust of the Flesh, Lust of the Eyes, and Pride of Life. (1 John 2:16)

5. He quoted Scripture that was appropriate to each temptation. (Matthew 4:4, 7, 10)

6. Capernaum was situated along a major trade route. It positioned Jesus in a place of profound influence, so that what he taught and did would be spread throughout the then-known world.

7. James and John left a family fishing franchise to follow Jesus. Their father, Zebedee, was able to afford hired help. Peter owned his own fishing

boat, and his mother-in-law owned a prime piece of real estate right near the water's edge on the Sea of Galilee.

8. Jesus's establishment in the Galilee region was predicted seven hundred years before his birth, and Jesus deliberately settled in that place so as to make common sinners the focus of his ministry. (Matthew 4:12–17; Isaiah 9:1–2; Matthew 9:12)

9. Jesus's ministry style was marked by teaching, preaching, and healing. (Matthew 4:23–25)

Chapter 5: Matthew 5—Sermon on the Mount, Part One

1. He begins by defining eight essential characteristics or attitudes that should characterize a true citizen of Christ's kingdom. (Matthew 5:1–10)

2. The common people were oppressed by the control of the religious leaders and the imperial power of Rome. Jesus said it was not the religiously self-righteous but the "poor in spirit" who would inherit the kingdom. Jesus also said that it was not the militarily mighty but the "meek" who would inherit the earth. (Matthew 5:3, 5)

3. The opposite of being proud in spirit, to be poor in spirit means that we come to God empty-handed, humble, in desperate need of his mercy and forgiveness. (Matthew 5:3; Luke 18:13)

4. No. In fact, they are polar opposites. Meekness is a power under control.

5. The recipient of God's mercy (the poor in heart) ought to be the first to dispense it; those who mourn, admit their sins, confess them, and experience the cleansing of the "pure in heart"; only the meek (those who put God's agenda ahead of their own) can truly be at peace with their fellowmen; individuals who truly hunger after a lifestyle of righteousness will often suffer persecution. (Matthew 5:3–10)

6. Salt acts as a preservative, retarding the rate of decay in meat. In the same way, Christ's true followers retard the rate of moral and spiritual decay in society. (Matthew 5:13–16)

7. The belief that in the original writings the Bible contains no errors. (Matthew 5:18)

8. Jesus said that if we harbor hatred or lust in our hearts, it's as if we are guilty of murder and adultery. (Matthew 5:22, 28)

9. *No one* can attain the perfection of God. However, that is why Jesus came to die on the cross. So we can come empty-handed to plea for his mercy and he will grant us the righteousness of Christ and the ability to do what is pleasing to him. (Matthew 5:48; Romans 3:10–11; 4:5–8; Ephesians 2:8–10)

Chapter 6: Matthew 6–7—Sermon on the Mount, Part Two

1. Jesus is looking for quiet devotion. He longs to find people who go about the business of performing good deeds as a natural and normal part of their lives. (Matthew 6:1–4)

2. Do not use prayer as a forum to display your spirituality; do not use meaningless repetition, do use Jesus's example for prayer as a guide; do approach God intimately and respectfully. (Matthew 6:5–15)

3. The proper motivation is that God's name be lifted up as holy through my life and in my world. It is important because James warned that if we pray with the wrong motives, our prayers will go unanswered. (Matthew 6:9)

4. When people recognize that Jesus is the King of kings and Lord of lords, and submit their lives to him, they become citizens of his heavenly kingdom. (Matthew 6:10)

5. When Jesus prayed in the Garden of Gethsemane on the night before his crucifixion, he understandably asked his Father to spare him the cup of suffering that he would suffer on the cross. Yet, he submitted to the will of his Father when he prayed, "Not my will, but Yours be done." (Matthew 26:39)

6. Bread is the basic staple of life. The point here is that we live in daily dependence upon God to meet our every need, but not necessarily our every want. (Matthew 6:11)

7. Not at all. A wise person does indeed save money "for a rainy day." It is wrong, however, for a Christian to serve money. Money is a wonderful servant, but a terrible master. (Matthew 6:24)

8. God will do his part if we do ours: love God (give him first place in our lives) and obey God (live as he wants us to). (Matthew 6:33–34)

9. The speck and the plank are the same thing, just a different perspective. Hold a speck up to your eye, and it looks like a plank. The point is that we should not be too quick to judge another, because we tend to judge others for what is actually true about ourselves. (Matthew 7:3)

10. We can receive or reject him. As Matthew says, we can choose the wide road to destruction, or the narrow road to life (7:13–14). We can put on a religious act, or bear the true fruit of righteousness (7:15–23). We can build our lives on an unstable foundation, or the solid footing that Jesus offers (7:24–27).

Chapter 7: Matthew 8:1–9:34—Credentials of the King

1. A leper was socially banished by Old Testament law to prevent the spread of the disease. For Jesus to touch him was unthinkable in light of this and his own personal danger. Yet, not only did this man need healing of body but a healing of heart, so the touch communicated acceptance. (Matthew 8:1–4; Leviticus 13:45–46)

2. Jesus's words communicated that admission into Christ's kingdom was not a matter of pedigree, but Christ's authority and our willing response. (Matthew 8:5–13; John 3:16)

3. In the first three miracles Jesus reached out to the rejects of that society: a leper, a Gentile and his servant, and a woman. (Matthew 8:1–14)

4. In the next three he demonstrated his authority over the natural, supernatural, and moral realms. (Matthew 8:23–9:8)

5. Yes. They occur when the prevailing winds collide at just the right angle over the sea. In a matter of minutes, the sea can go from calm to waves reaching several feet in height that could indeed sink a boat caught in the middle of the lake during such a storm. (Matthew 8:23–27)

6. The pig farmers pleaded with Jesus to leave their region, quite possibly because they were angry that Jesus had essentially wrecked the economy of the region, some might have been terrified by what they had just witnessed, still others didn't want anything to do with the Son of God. (Matthew 8:34)

7. Demon possession is indicated by specific, remarkable, and obvious characteristics such as uncontrollable violence, homicidal and suicidal tendencies, phenomenal strength, loud and disturbing cries, nakedness, an obsession with the dead, a recognition of Jesus as God, and a fear of their final destiny. (Matthew 8:28; Mark 5:4–5; Luke 8:27–28)

8. As Jesus's popularity grew, the Pharisees circulated the rumor that Jesus did not get his power from God at all—it came from Satan. Now the people had to decide—would they believe Jesus's claims that he was God, or would they reject him as an imposter? We have the same choice today. (Matthew 9:34; John 8:48–50; Acts 16:30–31)

Chapter 8: Matthew 9:35–10:42—Mark These Men

1. Jesus was a man of sorrow, familiar with suffering. His heart was broken over the harassed and downtrodden people he came to save. (Isaiah 53:3–4, Matthew 9:35–38)

2. Jesus's inner circle was made up of Peter, James, John, and Andrew. Peter and Andrew were brothers, as were James and John.

downtrodden people he came to save. (Isaiah 53:3–4; Matthew 9:35–38)

2. Jesus's inner circle was made up of Peter, James, John, and Andrew. Peter and Andrew were brothers, as were James and John. (Matthew 10:2)

3. Peter spoke more often and got reproved more often. He affirmed Jesus boldly and denied Jesus strongly. He received praise from Christ and yet had to be rebuked by him. He displayed great humility and struggled with great arrogance. Peter, as did the rest of Jesus's disciples, showed that God can use flawed people (like us) to do God's work. (Matthew 10:1–4; 1 Corinthians 1:26–31)

4. James and John. (Mark 3:17)

5. Andrew, the soft-spoken disciple who, even though he was part of the inner circle, remains almost anonymous in that very little is said about him by the Gospel writers.

6. Nathanael. He raised the question, "Can anything good come out of Nazareth?" (John 1:46)

7. Jesus warned them that they would be arrested, flogged, persecuted, and hated—the exact same things that would happen to Jesus. (Matthew 10:17–25)

8. The majority of the people the disciples were sent out to help would reject them and their message, so they needed to decide they would rather be right than popular. (Matthew 10:11–28)

9. Jesus gave his followers the reassurance that God cares about every detail of their lives. He also reminds them that the real death to be concerned about is not physical—it is spiritual, and God will honor those who honor him. (Matthew 10:26–33)

Chapter 9: Matthew 11—Turning Tide

1. Satan is a deceitful schemer and we can see examples of his mental trickery from Eve to Jesus himself. He is the father of all lies. We need to remember that faith holds on to what reason has accepted in spite of our changing moods, and not allow doubts to master us. (Matthew 11:2–3; Ephesians 6:11–13; Genesis 3:1; Matthew 4:1–11; John 8:44)

2. Herod Antipas stole his brother's wife. When John confronted him about his illicit affair, Herod had him imprisoned. (Matthew 14:3–5)

3. Jesus affirmed to John the Baptist the things that he did—healing the blind, lame, lepers, etc. These miracles authenticated Jesus as the King of the Jews and the Jewish Messiah. At no time did Jesus denounce John for having his doubts. (Matthew 11:4–6)

4. Jesus praised John in glowing terms for not being taken in by the trappings of the rich, and walking in the power and spirit of the prophets. He sparked the spiritual conflict in which we are still involved to this day. In contrast, "this generation" was involved in child's play, refusing to see and accept Jesus for who he was, making excuses for non-involvement, and justifying their rejection of the truth. (Matthew 11:7–19)

5. Jesus often visited, and performed many miracles in these three towns. The more we are given, the more we are held accountable. God will judge us based on what we have done with what we have been given. (Matthew 11:20–24; Luke 12:48; Romans 2:5–6)

6. In the context of what was happening to Jesus and his disciples, the faith of Jesus's forerunner was failing. Public opinion was turning against Jesus. Jesus had just pronounced a curse on three towns, one of which was his adopted hometown. Jesus desired to offer hope to his followers. It was important to give them the confidence that he was in control of circumstances that must have seemed to the disciples as if they were spinning out of control. (Matthew 11:25–30)

7. Jesus offered those who were weighted down by the unrealistic demands of their religious leaders and the oppression and cruelty they suffered at the hands of the Romans. Jesus offered to them much needed compassion, rest, and hope. (Matthew 11:28–30)

Chapter 10: Matthew 12—D-Day

1. Before Matthew 12, Jesus addressed crowds, used miracles to publicly display God's power, spoke of the kingdom in the present tense, focused on his mission and message, spoke in a simple and straightforward manner, and presented his message to Israel alone. After Matthew 12, Jesus huddled with his disciples, performed miracles as private acts of compassion, spoke of the church in the future tense, focused on his crucifixion and resurrection, taught in parables, and turned his message toward the nations. Jesus had no choice but to make this shift as Israel made a formal and final rejection of him as their Messiah. (Matthew 12:1–21)

2. Everyone in town personally knew the man in question, so when he was healed it was obviously more than a magician's trick. Isaiah prophesied that the Messiah would perform miracles of this kind. This act had to be from God as Satan would not act against himself. (Matthew 12:22–32; Isaiah 35:5–6)

3. The unforgivable sin is the blasphemy of the Holy Spirit—a complete, total, and final rejection of the Holy Spirit's witness that Jesus Christ is the Savior of sinners.

4. Opinions may differ as to whether this sin can be committed today, but Hebrews 4:4–6 and Hebrews 10:26–27 seem to indicate that this level of rejection is still possible, if, having been convicted by the Holy Spirit of the validity of Christ and his claims, an individual willfully turns away and rejects what he knows to be the truth. (Matthew 12:30–32)

5. Jesus's point was that empty religion, where a person is trying to get his act together on his own, will meet a disastrous end. True Christianity is not external and cold, but an internal, genuine relationship with Jesus Christ. (Matthew 12:43–50)

6. Genuine believers, those who do the will of God, are Jesus's mother and brothers. (Matthew 12:50)

Chapter 11: Matthew 13—I Love to Tell the Story

1. A parable is a carefully crafted story comparing an unknown concept to a known one in order to communicate a basic idea or principle in life. (Matthew 13:1–2)

2. The preaching of the gospel does not determine the condition of a person's heart; it reveals it. Even today, many people come to Christ for the wrong reasons. Many just want answers to prayers, help in trouble, a novelty religion, or fire insurance. The only correct way to come is empty-handed, with a poverty-stricken spirit. (Matthew 13:3–9, 18–23)

3. God doesn't waste words. He expects us to act on what we have been told. If we treat the truth with contempt, we may forfeit the privilege of receiving any more truth. (Matthew 13:10–17)

4. Great things can come from small beginnings. A straggling group of twelve men would swell to a worldwide movement. (Matthew 13:31–35)

5. The true followers of Jesus and the sons of the wicked one will exist together until the coming judgment at the end of the age.

6. In Jesus's first visit to Nazareth, the townspeople tried to throw him off a cliff. In his second visit, they pointed out his humble origins and local relatives in derision. Their lack of faith limited the ministry he could have among them. (Matthew 13:44–58)

Chapter 12: Matthew 14—Day in the Life

1. Herod Antipas's father was Herod the Great (who murdered all the boy babies in Matthew 2). Herod Antipas's brothers (Archelaus and Philip II) ruled the surrounding lands of Judea, Samaria, Idumea, and to the north of Galilee. Herod Antipas himself terrorized Galilee and Perea, murdering John the Baptist and examining Christ before his crucifixion. (Matthew 14:1–11)

2. Jesus retreated to a private place for a time of private reflection (on the death of his cousin) and rest (from the clamor of the crowds). (Matthew 14:13)

3. People-people can also get peopled out. The Old Testament principle of the Sabbath was designed to give us the rest that our minds and bodies need. (Matthew 14:13, Exodus 20:8–11)

4. The differences: Matthew depicts Jesus as a king providing for his subjects (Matthew 14:15–21). Mark emphasizes an exhausted Jesus serving those in need (Mark 6:32–44). Luke shows a human Jesus as if he were presiding over a family meal (Luke 9:10–17). John records Jesus's "bread of life" sermon (John 6:1–13).

5. All show Jesus as a man of compassion, a teacher, and a miracle-worker. All picture his followers participating in service with him, and all provide a pattern for what he longs to do in our own lives.

6. The disciples declared with one voice, "Truly You are the Son of God!"

7. We also should respond to any display of Christ's power in our own lives with a reaffirmation of his lordship. (Matthew 14:22–33)

Chapter 13: Matthew 15—Lessons on Legalism

1. The Pharisees declared their money and property as "Corban" (a word that means "set apart for sacred purposes"), thus preventing their resources to be used to assist their parents. (Matthew 15:3–9; Exodus 20:12; Numbers 30:2; Mark 7:11)

2. Isaiah declared that they honored God with their lips but their hearts were far from him. (Isaiah 29:13)

3. The Pharisees were obsessed with religious ritual, had a fascination with outward matters (like food), judged others for their behavior, emphasized man-made customs, worried about short-term consequences, and centered themselves around ceremony. Jesus concerned himself with inward purity, sought after character, looked upon people with compassion, emphasized inward compliance to God's commands, warned about long-term consequences, and taught concerning the substance of the soul. (Matthew 15:10–20)

4. We are in danger of being just like the Pharisees when we judge the spiritual conditions of people by our own preferences or "traditions," holding them to a higher standard than God's. When this happens, our own spiritual vitality comes into doubt.

5. Jesus was exhausted and trying to grab a moment's rest and peace. He also had a clear understanding of the precise nature of his mission. Despite how they sound in our English translations, his words were not derogatory, but compassionate. He granted her request and praised her highly for her faith. (Matthew 15:21–28)

6. The Jewish leaders were trying to kill him. His plans to establish a kingdom were now aborted, and his manner and message altered in anticipation of the cross. His identity was no longer simply the "King of the Jews," but the "Savior of the World." (Matthew 15:29–39; John 5:18, Matthew 13:11; Luke 9:51; Luke 19:10)

7. In the feeding of the five thousand, Jesus "broke bread" with Jews. In the feeding of the four thousand, he now broke bread with Gentiles. (Matthew 15:32)

Chapter 14: Matthew 16:1–21—From That Time On

1. We are forgiven of our sins, indwelt by the Holy Spirit, blessed with unimaginable blessings, given all we need to live a godly life, placed securely in Jesus's hands, and made a part of the church. (Romans 4:7; 8:9; Ephesians 1:3; 2 Peter 1:3; John 10:28; 1 Corinthians 12:27–28)

2. Jesus gave the sign of Jonah—that is, he would die and be buried. But just like Jonah was "buried" in the belly of the big fish and lived to tell about it, Jesus would walk out of the tomb alive and the whole world would hear about it. (Matthew 12:39–40; 16:4)

3. In Matthew 13:33, when Jesus compared the kingdom of heaven to yeast, he was referring to the Gospel's influence and its ability to permeate society. In Matthew 16, Jesus was warning that the yeast of "hypocrisy" could permeate and penetrate the disciples' lives if they did guard themselves against that. (Matthew 16:5–12)

4. Unless the Spirit of God opens a person's mind and heart to the truth, he cannot see or accept the truth. (Matthew 16:15–17; 1 Corinthians 2:14–16)

5. Caesarea Philippi boasted a huge temple to the Greek god of Pan. Thousands of worshipers would be swarming around this edifice to pay homage to their god. Jesus assured his disciples that although this religion appeared thriving and invincible, Christ's church would prevail and nothing would ever overcome it. (Matthew 16:18)

6. Jesus used a play on words in the original language. He stated that Peter was a small stone, but Peter's declaration that Jesus is the Christ, the Son of the living God, was a huge rock, not unlike the mighty Mount Hermon towering above them, the foundation upon which Christ would build his Church. (Matthew 16:18)

Chapter 15: Matthew 16:22–18:35—Saying Good-Bye to Galilee

1. Jesus rebuked Peter for forbidding Jesus to go to the cross. (Matthew 16:23)

2. Following Jesus might result in us losing our lives. (Matthew 16:24–26)

3. A more literal translation of verse 28 would read, "I tell you the truth, some who are standing here will not taste death before they see the Son of Man manifesting his royal majesty" (kingly sovereignty, reigning glory, ruling authority). (Matthew 16:28)

4. Moses longed to enter the land that God had promised to his people; Elijah desired to see righteousness reign in Israel. In the Transfiguration, both saw their highest dreams fulfilled. (Numbers 20:12; 1 Kings 19:4, 14; 1 John 2:1; Matthew 17:1–8)

5. The disciples had witnessed "heaven moving earth" on the Mount of Transfiguration, an event that should have bolstered their faith and given them the courage to face any situation over which Christ had control with absolute victory (such as the demon-possessed boy). Based on God's demonstrations of power in the Scriptures and in our own lives, we too can have faith that whatever God has promised he will fulfill. He is completely sufficient for any circumstance or challenge he allows to enter our lives. (Matthew 17:20; 1 Corinthians 10:13; 2 Corinthians 12:9)

6. First, go to the person and discuss the problem one on one. Next, approach the individual with two or three people who have witnessed the same sinful behavior. Then, report the sin to the church leaders for them to deal with. Finally, treat the person as an unbeliever. Any one of these steps can be the last if the sinning believer repents and turns from error. (Matthew 18:15–17)

7. We should forgive others, just as God forgives us. In the parable, Jesus painted the picture of how we have been forgiven of an enormous debt

of sin. No one will ever sin against us to the degree that we have sinned against God. If he forgave us, we should forgive others. (Matthew 18:21–35)

Chapter 16: Matthew 19–20—Green Mile

1. One man plus one woman together for as long as they both shall live. (Matthew 19:5)

2. We know this definition is binding upon us today because Jesus went all the way back to Adam and Eve. Thus, his definition transcends time and culture. (Genesis 2:24)

3. When a marriage partner unites himself or herself with someone to whom he or she is not married, they have by that act shattered the God-ordained union with their husband or wife. Divorce merely does *legally* what the adulterer has already done *physically*. Jesus is simply pointing out that for the non-adulterer to divorce and remarry there is no sin, for the adulterer was the one to break up the marriage by his or her act of adultery. (Matthew 19:7–9; Genesis 2:24; 1 Corinthians 6:16, 18)

4. When a mere mortal encounters something immortal, he had better be afraid. Unlike Peter, Isaiah, John, and others who came face-to-face with God and at once recognized their own shortcomings, this man declared that he was perfect. The fact was that he had broken the first commandment by making money his god. (Matthew 19:16–22; Luke 5:8; Isaiah 6:5; Revelation 1:17; Exodus 20:3; 1 Timothy 6:10)

5. When it comes to our rewards, length of service is not the issue. Faithfulness to God's will is. Whether we are martyred like Peter or become a believer with our dying breath, our rewards will be the same because our Master is generous with his servants. (Matthew 20:1–16; Luke 23:43; 2 Corinthians 11:23–28; 2 Timothy 4:8)

6. In order to attain a place of prominence in Christ's kingdom, one must be ready to participate in his suffering in the lowly rank of a servant. Christ gave us an accurate example of what that would entail in his own life. (Matthew 20:20–28; Philippians 2:5–11)

7. He meant that the disciples would indeed drink of the cup of suffering. Every one of the disciples died for their faith with the exception of John, who was banished to the Island of Patmos. (Matthew 19:23)

8. Jesus's mission statement is as follows: "The Son of Man did not come to be served, but to serve, and to give His life a ransom for many" (Mark 10:45; Matthew 19:28 NKJV).

Chapter 17: Matthew 21–23—Eight Days a Week

1. The people were looking for a political ruler to deliver them from the oppression of Rome. (Matthew 21:9)

2. When they shouted "Hosanna" they were really saying "Save us now from the tyranny of Rome." When Jesus failed to fulfill their misguided expectations, they turned on him. (Matthew 21:1–11; John 19:15)

3. The fig tree often symbolizes the nation of Israel, since figs are a sweet fruit of God's bountiful blessing in the Land, as is an obedient Israel a sweet fruit of God's bountiful blessing in the earth. A barren fig tree often represents God's judgment on a fruitless Israel that fails to live up to its many spiritual advantages. (Matthew 21:18–22; Hosea 9:10; Joel 1:7, 12; Jeremiah 8:13)

4. Jesus turned the tables and answered their questions with questions of his own. They could not give an answer to either query that was both politically correct and would appease the populace, so they had to swallow their pride and remain silent. (Matthew 21:24–27; 22:41–46)

5. Jesus said that the greatest commandment was to love God and to love others. (Matthew 22:37–39)

6. Jesus pronounced his curse of "Woe" to those who obscured God's truth; led people astray; distorted God's Word and thus spoke lies; focused on externals; refused to allow God to cleanse them for his use; appeared different on the outside than they were on the inside; tried to hinder God's messengers. (Matthew 23:13–36)

7. Each of these same compromises can be true of any of us today. Let us take heed that they never are.

8. He wept over Jerusalem because he knew of the suffering that was going to befall the Holy City. (Matthew 23:37–39)

Chapter 18: Matthew 24–25—Prophetic Powwow

1. Jesus told the disciples that not one stone of the magnificent Temple would be left standing. (Matthew 24:2)

2. The Rapture is an event during which Jesus appears in the clouds and his followers are suddenly removed from the earth to meet him in the air. The Second Coming describes the time when Jesus will actually set foot on the Mount of Olives and establish his kingdom, ruling for one thousand years. (Matthew 24:30–31; 1 Thessalonians 4:16–18; Matthew 24:36–41; Zechariah 14:4; Revelation 19:11–16)

3. Jesus indicated several "signs of the times" that indicate that his coming is drawing near. (Matthew 24:4–26)

4. An individual cannot know the day or the hour, but he can be aware of the season. And even though Jesus's coming is predicted, people will not be paying attention to the signs any more than they did in the days of Noah. (Matthew 24:32–33, 36–39)

5. The point of the three parables is that we should wait with anticipation, watch with diligence, and serve with industry until the Lord returns. (Matthew 24:45–25:30)

6. This perspective should effect every aspect of our lives. (1 Thessalonians 5:5–6; Revelation 3:11)

7. The judgment of the sheep and goats precedes Christ's thousand-year reign and seems to be limited to people who survive the seven-year Tribulation and live through Jesus's second coming. The Great White Throne judgment will pronounce the final sentence on all other unbelievers, both living and dead, at the conclusion of the Millennium. (Matthew 25:31–46; Revelation 20:11–15)

Chapter 19—Matthew 26:1–27:26: Countdown to Crucifixion

1. Caiaphas was a priest-politician-puppet figure serving in that capacity from AD 18 to AD 36, catering to both the Jews and the Romans. He was a major contributor to the corruption of the temple, and hated Jesus for his stand against it. He was Jesus's first interrogator in the mock Jewish trial before Jesus was turned over to the Romans. (Matthew 26:3–5, 57–68)

2. Judas was a hypocrite who pretended to be concerned about providing for the poor while covertly dipping his hand into the money he kept for the disciples. He broke bread with and kissed our Lord—both signs of intimate friendship—all the while seeking to sell him for the price of a common slave. His motivation was greed, but in the end he regretted his actions and committed suicide. (Matthew 26:8–16, 25–26, 48–50; 27:1–10; John 12:6)

3. Peter was both impulsive and proud. Ready to defend his Lord with a sword in the garden, he denied him vehemently only a few short hours later. Defined as a "sanguine" by temperament, he fits the profile of "weak character" and "all mouth." However, later in his life, God transforms him into a mighty man of God. The problem was that he was committed to Christ but not to his program. (Matthew 26:33–35, 51–53, 69–75)

4. Pilate was a spineless Roman governor who recognized Jesus's innocence but caved into the pressure of the Jewish leaders in order to preserve his own office. He could have chosen to respond to Jesus but valued the prominence of his political office more than the integrity of his own character. (Matthew 27:11–26)

5. Jesus and the disciples celebrated a Passover Seder together, with an added significance. Jesus used the broken bread and the cup of wine as symbols of his coming death characterized by his body being broken and blood shed as payment for our sins. (Matthew 26:26–31)

6. Three times Jesus prayed in the Garden that the cup of God's wrath could pass from him. Yet, he submitted his will to the will of his Father and went to the cross for us. (Matthew 26:36–46)

7. Peter disowned Jesus, swearing with an oath that he didn't even know the man. (Matthew 26:72)

8. Pilate wanted desperately to release Jesus because, as he himself declared, "I am innocent of the blood of this just person." (Matthew 27:24)

Chapter 20: Matthew 27:27–28:20: Crucified, Raised, and Praised

1. The soldiers who held Jesus made a cruel game out of their abuse. After being scourged within an inch of his life, Jesus was taunted, spat upon, and repeatedly struck with his staff upon the head driving the thorns of his crown deeper into his scalp. By the time they were done, he did not even look human. (Matthew 27:27–31)

2. "This is Jesus the King of the Jews." Jesus was killed for being who he really is. (Matthew 27:37)

3. When Jesus cried out, "My God, My God, why have You forsaken Me?" In that awful moment, God the Father poured out upon his Son all of the hellish torment that we deserve because of our sins. Jesus truly died alone. (Matthew 27:46)

4. Before the crucifixion of Jesus, only one priest could enter the Holy of Holies once a year to offer sacrifice for the sins of the people. After Jesus made atonement for our sins on the cross, the way into God's presence was opened to everyone at any time. God himself tore the veil from the top to the bottom. (Matthew 27:51; Exodus 26:33; Hebrews 9:3; 10:19–22)

5. "Truly this was the Son of God." (Matthew 27:54)

6. Mary Magdalene (Mark 16:9), women on the road (Matthew 28:9–10), disciples on the road (Luke 24:13–22), Peter (Luke 24:34), ten disci-

ples (Luke 24:36–43), eleven disciples (John 20:26–31), seven disciples (John 21:1–25), more than five-hundred (1 Corinthians 15:6), James (1 Corinthians 15:7), apostles at the ascension (Acts 1:3–11) Paul (1 Corinthians 15:8). Jesus was seen alive in too many places, by too many people, for too long a time.

7. They paid off some people to spread the lie that the disciples stole the body. (Matthew 27:11–15)

8. At the beginning of Matthew, an angel announced to Joseph that Jesus would be called "Immanuel," meaning "God with us." At the end of Matthew, Jesus reassured his disciples that he would always be with them. We may some-times feel alone, but we will never be alone— even until the end of time. (Matthew 1:23; 28:20; Hebrews 13:5)

Appendix C—The Experts

Arthur, Kay—Well-known Bible teacher and best-selling author, cofounder of Precept Ministries.

Barclay, William—Professor of divinity and biblical criticism at Glasgow University, best-selling author, broadcaster on radio and television, regular contributor to widely circulated newspapers.

Boa, Kenneth—President of Reflections Ministries and Trinity House Publishers, and the author or coauthor of numerous books about the Bible and spiritual formation.

Boice, James Montgomery—Author, pastor of Tenth Presbyterian Church in Philadelphia, chairman of the International Council on Biblical Inerrancy, and speaker on the worldwide radio program, *The Bible Study Hour.*

Bonhoeffer, Dietrich—Lecturer in systematic theology at Berlin University, a writer whose works have been translated into several languages; he was incarcerated by the Nazis and martyred for his faith.

Briscoe, Stuart—Pastor of Elmbrook Church in Waukesha, Wisconsin, director of Telling the Truth tape ministry, and author of many books.

Bruce, F. F.—Former Rylands Professor of Biblical Criticism and Exegesis at Manchester University, England, and author of numerous books and commentaries.

Calvin, John—Theologian and Reformer, most famous for the *Institutes of the Christian Religion*, a work summarizing the basis of evangelical teaching.

Campolo, Tony—Pastor, author, professor of sociology, founder of the Evangelical Association for the Promotion of Education, which furthers inner-city schools for kids with learning disabilities.

Chadwick, Samuel—Fiery and outspoken member of the Methodist revival during the latter part of the nineteenth century. Later he became principal of Cliff College, a school for Methodist pastors, and the author of *The Way to Pentecost.*

Chafer, Lewis Sperry—Founder and first president of Dallas Theological Seminary. His books on systematic theology are considered classics.

Chambers, Oswald—Itinerant evangelist and Bible college teacher. Most of his works were compiled posthumously after 1917 by his wife.

Chrnalogar, Mary Alice—Respected international consultant in the field of cult education, rescuing the victims of destructive and abusive churches.

Cloud, Henry—Clinical psychologist, codirector of the Minerth-Meier Clinic West, author, popular speaker, and host of a daily radio broadcast.

Colson, Charles "Chuck"—Former presidential adviser who went to prison during the Watergate era, currently founder of Prison Fellowship, a worldwide ministry.

Crabb, Larry (Lawrence J.), Jr.—Psychologist, professor at Colorado Christian University, popular conference speaker, and author.

Criswell, W. A.—Pastor emeritus of the First Baptist Church of Dallas, Texas, and author of more than thirty books.

DeHaan, Richard W.—Teacher of the *Radio Bible Class*, contributor to Our Daily Bread devotional series, and author.

Dobson, James C.—Psychologist, best-selling author, and founder of Focus on the Family Ministries.

Drummond, Henry—Popular lecturer during the late 1800s, particularly among students; pastor; and author of numerous books.

Elliot, Elisabeth—Well-known speaker, author, and widow of martyred missionary Jim Elliot.

Emery, Allan—President of the Billy Graham Evangelistic Association.

Falwell, Jerry—Founder and chief spokesman for the Moral Majority, television preacher, and pastor of the Thomas Road Baptist Church.

Ferrin, Howard W.—President of Providence Bible Institute.

Fleming, Jim—Founder and president of Biblical Resources in London.

Flynn, Leslie B.—Senior pastor of Grace Conservative Baptist Church in Nanuet, New York, and a prolific author.

France, R. T.—Vice-principal and senior lecturer in New Testament Studies at London Bible College.

Getz, Gene—Professor of practical theology at Dallas Theological Seminary, and founding pastor of Fellowship Bible Church in Dallas, Texas.

Gothard, Bill—Speaker and founder of the seminar series Institute of Basic Youth Conflicts.

Gromacki, Robert—Professor of Bible and Theology at Cedarville Bible College.

Guthrie, Donald—Lecturer, vice-principal, and registrar at the London Bible College, and a prolific author.

Halley, Henry H.—Author of a highly acclaimed handbook on biblical subjects.

Hanegraaff, Hank—President of Christian Research Institute.

Havner, Vance—Beloved evangelist, country preacher, and author.

Hession, Roy—Internationally beloved evangelist and Bible teacher, author whose works have been translated into more than forty languages.

Huffman, John A., Jr.—Author, senior minister of the historic First Presbyterian Church of Pittsburgh, and host of a prime-time TV interview show on a local NBC affiliate.

Hughes, R. Kent—Writer of numerous books, and pastor of College Church in Wheaton, Illinois.

Huizenga, L. S.—Expert on public health and the author of a book on leprosy entitled *Unclean! Unclean!*

Hunter, John—Associated full-time with the Torchbearers, Capernwray, and Major Ian Thomas.

Hybels, Bill—Pastor of Willow Creek Community Church in South Barrington, Illinois, and an author of Gold Medallion–winning books.

Ironside, H. A.—Pastor of Moody Memorial Church in Chicago for many years, an internationally loved Bible teacher and preacher, and writer on all the New Testament books.

Johnston, Russ—Former regional director for the Navigators, lecturer on college campuses for World Outreach for Christ, and seminar speaker on "How to Live by Faith."

Keiper, Ralph L.—Former associate professor in English Bible at Conservative Baptist Theological Seminary, associate editor of *Eternity* magazine, and lecturer at conferences and universities across America.

Keller, W. Phillip—Internationally known and loved for his moving and insight-filled devotional studies on the Bible.

Kesler, Jay—Former president of Youth for Christ International, pulpit pastor at the First Baptist Church in Geneva, Illinois, and an author.

LaHaye, Tim—Best-selling author, founder and president of Family Life Seminars.

Lenski, R. C. H.—Noted Bible scholar and commentator.

Lewis, C. S.—Teacher of English Literature and Language, Professor of Medieval and Renaissance English Literature at Cambridge, and best-selling author.

Lindsey, Hal—Author of best-selling books, frequent speaker on Christian cable television about end-time events.

Littleton, Mark R.—Former pastor and youth pastor, currently a businessman in Millersville, Maryland.

Lloyd-Jones, D. Martyn—Author, physician, and minister at Westminster Chapel in London.

Lockyer, Herbert—Pastor in Scotland and England for twenty-five years, lecturer for the Moody Bible Institute, and conference speaker throughout the United States and Canada.

Lovelace, Richard F.—Professor of church history at Gordon-Conwell Theological Seminary, and regular columnist for *Charisma* magazine.

Lucado, Max—Minister at the Oak Hills Church in San Antonio, writer, speaker, and the voice of *Upwards*, a daily radio program.

Luther, Martin—Father of the Protestant Reformation in the early 1500s, who promoted the concept that salvation was by faith alone; he nailed his thesis of 95 statements on the door of the Wittenberg Church in Germany.

MacArthur, John F., Jr.—Pastor of Grace Community Church in Sun Valley, California, president of the Master's College, best-selling author and radio preacher.

MacDonald, Gordon—Author, conference speaker, and consultant for churches and business groups.

McDowell, Josh—Author of many best-selling books, traveling staff member for Campus Crusade for Christ, speaker at more than 580 universities in fifty-seven countries.

McGee, J. Vernon—Bible teacher of the radio program, *Thru the Bible*, pastor, and college lecturer.

Miller, D. Larry—Police lieutenant, frequent speaker, and best-selling author.

Miller, Keith—Episcopalian layman, lecturer, counselor, business consultant, and articulate writer on personal and church renewal, psychology, faith, and relationships.

Mitchell, Curtis C.—Professor of Biblical Studies at Bola University, well-known speaker at churches and conferences.

Moody, D. L.—Premier evangelist and soul-winner of the late 1800s in Great Britain and the U.S., founder of Moody Bible Institute.

Morgan, G. Campbell—Prolific writer of theology and devotional works, popular lecturer at Christian conferences in the early 1900s.

Morris, Leon—Retired principal of Ridley College in Melbourne, Australia, and author of more than forty books, including various commentaries.

Nee, Watchman—A Chinese evangelist in the mid-1900s whose gifted preaching brought far-reaching results even to a persecuted church.

Ogilvie, Lloyd John—Chaplain of the U.S. Senate, former pastor, author of numerous books and articles, speaker on radio and television.

Ortlund, Raymond C.—Senior pastor of Lake Avenue Congregational Church in Pasadena, California, popular conference speaker, and author.

Palau, Luis—International evangelist to over three million people in thirty-seven nations (170 million more through radio and television broadcasts).

Pentecost, J. Dwight—Professor of Bible exposition at Dallas Theological Seminary, pastor, and author of over a dozen books.

Pinnock, Clark H.—Professor of theology at Trinity Evangelical Divinity School.

Pope John Paul II—Elected head of the Catholic Church, an advocate for moral and theological conservatism, and the author of numerous best-selling books, many dedicated to his personal mission of spreading "The single truth"—God's Word.

Redpath, Alan—Formerly the senior minister at Moody Memorial Church in Chicago, more recently a pastor in Edinburgh, Scotland.

Richards, Larry (Lawrence O.)—Writer of nearly one hundred books, including textbooks used in Bible colleges and seminaries, and a Bible teacher to all age groups.

Ridenour, Fritz—Former youth editor for Gospel Light Publications and best-selling author.

Robertson, Pat—Founder and chairman of the Christian Broadcasting Network (CBN) and host of the *700 Club*, a popular news talk program.

Ryrie, Charles Caldwell—Professor of Systematic Theology at Dallas Theological Seminary and the author of numerous books on the Bible and Christian living.

Sanders, J. Oswald—Former director of Overseas Missionary Fellowship, principal of New Zealand Bible Training Institute, and author of many books.

Sproul, R. C.—Professor of Systematic Theology at Reformed Theological Seminary; director emeritus of Prison Fellowship, Inc.; minister; teacher; and chairman of the board of Ligonier Ministries.

Spurgeon, Charles H.—Called the "prince of preachers," his sermons held throngs spellbound at the Metropolitan Tabernacle in London in the nineteenth century and now in written form.

Stanley, Charles—Senior pastor of the twelve thousand-member First Baptist Church of Atlanta and popular speaker for *In Touch*, a national television and radio program.

Stearns, Bill—An experienced youth pastor and author of teaching material for youth curriculum.

Stedman, Ray C.—Nationally recognized expositor, author of several well-known books, and a pastor.

Steele, Les L.—Author, former pastor, currently teaching Christian Education at Seattle Pacific University.

Strauss, Lehman—Popular Bible expositor and author of many books on Bible topics and related issues.

Swenson, Richard A., M.D.—Practicing physician and associate professor at the University of Wisconsin Medical School.

Swindoll, Charles R.—President of Dallas Theological Seminary, host of the nationally syndicated radio program *Insight for Living*, and author of many books.

Tada, Joni Eareckson—Artist, speaker, and author of over twenty books, president of Joni and Friends Ministries, which advances Christ's kingdom among the disabled.

ten Boom, Corrie—Helped her family hide Jews and members of the Dutch underground during WWII, and later spent ten months in concentration camps. Her story is told in her books *The Hiding Place* and *Tramp for the Lord*.

Thomas, Gary—Writer and the founder and director of the Center for Evangelical Spirituality.

Thomas, Gary—Writer and the founder and director of the Center for Evangelical Spirituality.

Tippit, Sammy—Founder and president of God's Love in Action, evangelist in the United States and Europe (particularly in the former Eastern bloc countries).

Townsend, John—Clinical psychologist, codirector of the Minerth-Meier Clinic West, author, popular speaker, and host of a daily radio broadcast.

Tozer, A. W.—Pastor, longtime editor of what is now called *Alliance Life*, the official magazine of the Christian and Missionary Alliance church, and author of many books.

Walvoord, John F.—Chancellor of Dallas Theological Seminary, former president of that institution for thirty-four years, author, and co-editor of *The Bible Knowledge Commentary*.

Watson, Thomas—Preacher in the Puritan era, best known for his sound doctrine and practical wisdom, most of his works were published posthumously.

White, John—Best-selling author, who works with Vineyard Christian Fellowship in Vancouver and has a worldwide ministry that has taken him to every continent.

Wiersbe, Warren—One of the evangelical world's most respected Bible teachers, author of more than one hundred books, former director of Back to the Bible, a radio ministry, and former pastor of Moody Memorial Church in Chicago.

Wilkinson, Bruce—President of Walk Thru the Bible ministries, author of several books, including the best-seller *The Prayer of Jabez*.

Willard, Dallas—Professor at the University of Southern California's School of Philosophy; visiting professor at the University of Colorado.

Endnotes

Introduction

1. Jerome Murphy-O'Connor, *The Holy Land* (New York: Oxford Press, 1998), 288.

2. Bruce Wilkinson and Kenneth Boa, *Talk Thru the Bible* (Nashville, TN: Thomas Nelson, 1983), 308.

Matthew 1: Virgin-Born Savior-King

1. Ronald A. Beers, gen. ed., *The Life Application Bible* (Wheaton: Tyndale House, 1988), 1319.

2. John F. MacArthur Jr., *The MacArthur Study Bible* (Nashville, TN: Word, 1997), 1518.

3. Adapted from *Nelson's Complete Book of Bible Maps and Charts* (Nashville, TN: Thomas Nelson, 1993).

4. J. Oswald Sanders, *The Incomparable Christ* (Chicago: Moody, 1971), 14.

5. Peter Trutza, *Zondervan Pictorial Encyclopedia of the Bible*, vol. 4 (Grand Rapids, MI: Zondervan, 1975), 96.

6. J. Dwight Pentecost, *The Words and Works of Jesus Christ* (Grand Rapids, MI: Zondervan, 1981), 357–58.

7. W. E. Vine, *Vine's Expository Dictionary of New Testament Words*, vol. 2 (Old Tappan, NJ: Fleming H. Revell, 1966), 274.

8. Herbert Lockyer, *All the Messianic Prophecies of the Bible* (Grand Rapids, MI: Zondervan, 1973), 62.

9. Josh McDowell, *Evidence That Demands a Verdict* (San Bernardino, CA: Campus Crusade for Christ, 1972), 147.

Matthew 2: Child Born King

1. William Hendrickson, *Exposition of the Gospel According to Matthew, New Testament Commentary* (Grand Rapids, MI: Baker, 1973), 152.

2. MacArthur, *The MacArthur New Testament Commentary, Matthew 1–7*, 22.

3. Henry H. Halley, *Halley's Bible Handbook* (Grand Rapids, MI: Zondervan, 1965), 419.

4. William Shakespeare, *The Tragedy of Julius Caesar* (New York: Airmont, 1965), 59.

5. Peter Connolly, *Living in the Time of Jesus of Nazareth* (Tel Aviv, Israel: Steimatzky Ltd., 1983), 20.

6. Archibald Thomas Robertson, *Word Pictures in the New Testament*, vol. 1 (Grand Rapids, MI: Baker, 1930), 17.

7. Jim Fleming, *Survey of the Life of Jesus* (Jerusalem: Biblical Resources), 12–13.

8. J. Vernon McGee, *Matthew*, vol. 1 (Pasadena, CA: Thru the Bible Books, 1973), 17–18.

9. Miriam Feinberg Vamosh, "Caesarea: Queen of the Coast," *ERETZ Magazine* (Jerusalem, Israel: Ha-Tzvi, 1996): 2.

10. Vine, *Vine's Expository Dictionary of New Testament Words*, vol. 2, 130, 163; vol. 3, 96.

11. Josephus, *Wars of the Jews*, bk. 1, trans. William Whiston (Grand Rapids, MI: Kregel Publications, 1966), chapter 33, section 5, 469.

12. Peter Connolly, *Living in the Time of Jesus of Nazareth*, 44.

Matthew 3: King's Herald

1. Kaari Ward, ed., *Jesus and His Times* (Pleasantville, NY: Reader's Digest, 1987), 200.

2. G. Campbell Morgan, quoted by J. Oswald Sanders, *Bible Men of Faith* (Chicago: Moody, 1965), 173.

3. Jack Finegan, *The Archelolgy of the New Testament* (Princeton, NJ: Princeton University, 1992), 6.

4. Spiros Zodhiates, *The Hebrew-Greek Key Study Bible* (Grand Rapids, MI: Baker, 1984), 1139.

6. Stanley Tussaint, *Behold the King* (Portland, OR: Multnomah, 1980), 60.

7. Warren Wiersbe, *Meet Your King* (Wheaton, IL: Victor, 1980), 23.

8. J. Dwight Pentecost, *The Words and Works of Jesus Christ* (Grand Rapids, MI: Zondervan, 1981), 85.

9. F. F. Bruce, *Answers to Questions* (Grand Rapids, MI: Zondervan, 1972), 221.

10. D. Larry Miller, *Men of the Bible—The Smart Guide to the Bible*™ (Nashville, TN: Thomas Nelson, 2007).

11. Lehman Strauss, *Be Filled with the Spirit* (Grand Rapids, MI: Zondervan, 1976), 102.

12. Gordon MacDonald, *Ordering Your Private World* (Nashville, TN: Thomas Nelson, 1984), quoted by Max Lucado, *The Inspirational Bible* (Nashville, TN: Word, 1995), 1166.

13. Vine, *Vine's Expository of New Testament Words*, vol. 2, 97.

14. Lewis Sperry Chafer, quoted in *Systematic Theology*, vol. 1, abridged edition, John F. Walvoord, ed. (Wheaton, IL: Victor, 1988), 179.

Matthew 4: Testing of the King

1. William Barclay, *The Gospel of Matthew*, vol. 1 (Philadelphia: Westminster, 1975), 63.

2. Pope John Paul II, "Pontiff Addresses Satan in Sermons," *Nashville Banner*, September 11, 1986, A12.

3. C. S. Lewis, *The Screwtape Letters*, quoted by Robert J. Morgan, *Nelson's Complete Book of Stories, Illustrations, and Quotes* (Nashville, TN: Thomas Nelson, 2000), 681.

4. Max Lucado, *The Inspirational Bible* (Nashville, TN: Word, 1995), 624B.

5. Larry Richards, *The Servant King* (Elgin, IL: David C. Cook, 1976), 47.

6. Yadin Roman, "Jesus of Galilee," *ERETZ Magazine* (Jerusalem, Israel: Ha-Tzvi, 1998): 14.

7. Murphy-O'Connor, *The Holy Land*, 217.

8. R. C. H. Lenski, *The Interpretation of St. Matthew's Gospel* (Minneapolis: Augsburg, 1964), 168.

9. Josephus, *The Wars of the Jews*, bk. 3 (Grand Rapids, MI: Kregel Publications, 1966), chapter 3, section 2.

10. Dallas Willard, "Discipleship: For Super Christians Only?" *Christianity Today*, October 10, 1980, 24.

11. Murphy-O'Connor, *The Holy Land*, 218–20.

12. B. B. Warfield, quoted in MacArthur, *The MacArthur New Testament Commentary, Matthew 1–7*, 128.

13. Joni Eareckson and Steve Estes, *A Step Further* (Grand Rapids, MI: Zondervan, 1982), 127.

Matthew 5: Sermon on the Mount, Part One

1. Randy Smith, lecture, "The Life and Followers of Jesus," May 1997.

2. G. Campbell Morgan, *The Gospel According to Matthew* (New York: Fleming H. Revell, 1929), 42.

3. Ibid., 42

4. Fritz Rienecker, *Linguistic Key to the Greek New Testament* (Grand Rapids, MI: Zondervan, 1980), 307.

5. Kay Arthur, *How Can I Be Blessed* (Old Tappan, NJ: Fleming H. Revell, 1985), 96.

6. W. E. Vine, *Vine's Expository Dictionary of New Testament Terms*, vol. 3 (Old Tappan, NJ: Fleming H. Revell, 1940), 231.

7. Colson, *Who Speaks for God?* 68.

8. Oswald Chambers, *Studies in the Sermon on the Mount* (London: Marshall, Morgan, and Scott, 1960), 20.

9. Spurgeon, quoted by Carter, *Spurgeon at His Best*, 23.

10. MacArthur, *The MacArthur New Testament Commentary, Matthew 1–7*, 295.

11. J. Oswald Sanders, *A Spiritual Clinic* (Chicago: Moody, 1961), 20.

12. Vance Havner, *Pleasant Paths* (Grand Rapids, MI: Baker, 1945), 72.

13. Lucado, *The Inspirational Bible*, 1429.

Matthew 6–7: Sermon on the Mount, Part Two

1. Chambers, *Studies in the Sermon on the Mount*, 87.

2. Treblinka Nazi Concentration Camp survivor, quoted by Julius Segal, *Winning Life's Toughest Battles* (New York: Ivy Books, 1986), 105.

3. Samuel Chadwick, quoted by Cameron V. Thompson, *Master Secrets of Prayer* (Lincoln, NE: Back to the Bible, 1959).

4. Rienecker, *Linguistic Key to the Greek New Testament*, 17–18.

5. Corrie ten Boom, *Each New Day* (Old Tappan, NJ: Fleming H. Revell, 1977), March 8.

6. Chambers, *Studies in the Sermon on the Mount*, 58.

Endnotes

7. Jerry Falwell, ed., *Liberty Commentary on the New Testament* (Lynchburg, VA: Liberty Press, 1978), 31.

8. D. Martyn Lloyd-Jones, *Studies in the Sermon on the Mount* (Grand Rapids, MI: Wm. B. Eerdmans, 1960), 72.

9. H. A. Ironside, *Matthew* (Neptune, NJ: Loizeaux Brothers Inc., 1984), 65–66.

10. Allan C. Emery, *A Turtle on a Fencepost* (Waco, TX: Word, 1979), 34–35.

11. D. Martyn Lloyd-Jones, *Studies in the Sermon on the Mount*, 131.

12. John Calvin, quoted in William J. Bouwsma, *John Calvin, A Sixteenth-Century Portrait* (New York: Oxford University, 1988), 37.

13. Wiersbe, *Meet Your King*, 51.

14. Arthur, *How Can I Be Blessed*, 265.

Matthew 8:1–9:34: Credentials of the King

1. C. S. Lewis, *Miracles* (New York: Macmillan, 1947), 174.

2. L. S. Huizenga, *Unclean! Unclean!* (Grand Rapids, MI: Wm. B. Eerdmans, 1927), 149.

3. Charles Swindoll, *Come Before Winter* (Portland, OR: Multnomah, 1985), 202.

4. Charles Caldwell Ryrie, *The Miracles of Our Lord* (Neptune, NJ: Loizeaux Brothers, 1984), 21.

5. Tim LaHaye, *Jesus: Who Is He?* (Sisters, OR: Multnomah, 1996), 137, 151.

6. James F. Strange and Hershel Shanks, "Has the House Where Jesus Stayed in Capernaum Been Found?" *Biblical Archeology Review*, November/December 1982 (Washington, DC: Biblical Archeology Society), 26–37.

7. *MacArthur Study Bible*, 1406.

8. Barclay, *The Gospel of Matthew*, 321.

9. Alfred Edersheim, *The Life and Times of Jesus the Messiah*, bk. 3 (Grand Rapids, MI: Wm. B. Eerdmans, 1971), 609.

10. LaHaye, *Jesus: Who Is He?* 302.

Matthew 9:35–10:42: Mark These Men

1. Max Lucado, *The Applause of Heaven*, quoted in *The Inspirational Bible*, 1099.

2. Howard W. Ferrin, *Twelve Portraits* (published by the author in 1949), 20.

3. Herbert Lockyer, *All the Apostles of the Bible* (Grand Rapids, MI: Zondervan, 1972), 61.

4. Angelique L'Amour, *A Trail of Memories* (New York: Bantam, 1988), 198.

5. Rienecker, *Linguistic Key to the Greek New Testament*, 31.

6. Tippit, *Fire in Your Heart*, 111.

7. Dietrich Bonhoeffer, quoted by Erwin W. Lutzer, *Hitler's Cross* (Chicago: Moody, 1995), 182.

Matthew 11: Turning Tide

1. Wilkinson and Boa, *Talk Thru the Bible*, 347.

2. Lenski, *The Interpretation of St. Matthew's Gospel*, 425.

3. C. S. Lewis, *Mere Christianity* (New York: Macmillan, 1952), 109.

4. D. Martyn Lloyd-Jones, *Spiritual Depression* (Grand Rapids, MI: Wm. B. Eerdmans, 1965), 154.

5. Josephus, *Antiquities of the Jews*, bk. 2, chapter 18, section 5, trans. William Whiston (Grand Rapids, MI: Kregel Publications, 1966), 382.

6. Henry Drummond, quoted by Warren Wiersbe, *Listening to the Giants* (Grand Rapids, MI: Baker, 1980), 115–16.

7. Barclay, *The Gospel of Matthew*, vol. 2, 10.

8. C. S. Lewis, *Mere Christianity* (New York: MacmillanCollier, 1960), 55–56.

Matthew 12: D-Day

1. Lenski, *The Interpretation of St. Matthew's Gospel*, 461.

2. Charles Swindoll, *The Quest for Character* (Portland, OR: Multnomah, 1987), 45.

3. A. W. Tozer, *The Best of A. W. Tozer*, Warren Wiersbe, comp. (Harrisburg, PA: Christian Publications, 1978), 89.

Matthew 13: I Love to Tell the Story

1. Wilkinson and Boa, *Talk Thru the Bible*, 310.

2. Stuart Briscoe, *Patterns for Power* (Glendale, CA: Regal, 1979), 5.

3. Richards, *The Servant King*, 105–6.

4. Dietrich Bonhoeffer, *The Cost of Discipleship* (New York: Macmillan, 1966), 43.

5. Gleason Archer, ed., *Zondervan Pictorial Dictionary*, vol. 5 (Grand Rapids, MI: Zondervan, 1977), 596.

6. MacArthur, *The MacArthur New Testament Commentary, Matthew 8–15* (Chicago: Moody, 1987), 378.

7. Edersheim, *The Life and Times of Jesus the Messiah*, bk. 3 (Grand Rapids, MI: Wm. B. Eerdmans, 1972), 592–93.

9. John F. Walvoord, *Matthew: Thy Kingdom Come* (Chicago: Moody, 1974), 103.

8. John F. Walvoord, *Matthew: Thy Kingdom Come* (Chicago: Moody, 1974), 103.

9. Lenski, *The Interpretation of Matthew's Gospel*, 528.

10. A. W. Tozer, *The Knowledge of the Holy* (New York: Harper and Row, 1961), 95.

Matthew 14: Day in the Life

1. Lenski, *The Interpretation of St. Matthew's Gospel*, 555–57.

2. Josephus, *Antiquities of the Jews,* bk. 18 (Grand Rapids, MI: Kregel Publications, 1966), chapter 5, paragraph 2, 382.

3. Jack Finegan, *The Archeology of the New Testament* (Princeton, NJ: Princeton University, 1992), 17.

4. Alfred Edersheim, *The Life and Times of Jesus the Messiah,* bk. 3, 660.

5. Joni Eareckson Tada, *Secret Strength* (Portland, OR: Multnomah, 1988), 302.

6. Richard W. DeHaan, *Good News for Bad Times* (Wheaton, IL: Victor, 1975), 122.

7. W. E. Vine, *Vine's Expository Dictionary of New Testament Words,* vol. 1 (Old Tappan, NJ: Revell, 1966), 183.

8. Matthew Henry, *Matthew Henry's Commentary,* vol. 5 (Old Tappan, NJ: Fleming H. Revell, n.d.), 199.

9. J. Oswald Sanders, *Bible Men of Faith* (Chicago: Moody, 1974), 182.

10. MacArthur, *MacArthur New Testament Commentary, Matthew 8–15,* 421.

11. Bargil Pixner, *With Jesus Through Galilee According to the Fifth Gospel* (Jerusalem: Corazin, 1992), 69.

12. Henry Cloud and John Townsend, *Boundaries* (Grand Rapids, MI: Zondervan, 1992), 105.

13. Richard A. Swenson, M.D., *Margin* (Colorado Springs, CO: NavPress, 1992), 77.

14. Johnston M. Cheney, *The Life of Christ in Stereo* (Portland, OR: Western Baptist Seminary Press, 1969), 74–75.

15. Edersheim, *The Life and Times of Jesus the Messiah,* bk. 1 (Grand Rapids, MI: Wm. B. Eerdmans, 1972), 678.

16. Herschel Shanks, ed., *Archaeology and the Bible: The Best of BAR* (Washington, DC: Biblical Archaeology Society, 1990), 209.

17. Elisabeth Elliot, *Keep a Quiet Heart* (Ann Arbor, MI: Vine, 1995), 41.

18. James C. Dobson, *Emotions, Can You Trust Them?* (Ventura, CA: Regal, 1982), 118–19, 131.

Matthew 15: Lessons on Legalism

1. Gene A. Getz, *Building Up One Another* (Wheaton, IL: Victor, 1978), 43.

2. Lloyd John Ogilvie, *Autobiography of God* (Ventura, CA: Regal, 1979), 193–94.

3. Gary Thomas, *Sacred Pathways* (Grand Rapids, MI: Zondervan, 2000), 14.

4. Swenson, *Margin,* 106.

5. Barclay, *The Gospel of Matthew,* vol. 2, 134.

6. MacArthur, *The MacArthur New Testament Commentary, Matthew 8–15,* 469.

7. Charles H. Spurgeon, *Faith's Checkbook* (Chicago: Moody, n.d.), iii.

8. W. Phillip Keller, *Salt for Society* (Waco, TX: Word, 1981), 117.

9. Vine, *Vine's Expository Dictionary of New Testament Words,* vol. 1, 99.

10. Ibid.

Matthew 16:1–21: From That Time On

1. Larry Crabb Jr., *Finding God* (Grand Rapids, MI: Zondervan, 1993), 45.

2. R. Kent Hughes, *Living on the Cutting Edge* (Westchester, IL: Crossway, 1989), 58.

3. Jerome Murphy-O'Connor, *The Holy Land* (New York: Oxford University, 1998), 174.

4. Clark H. Pinnock, *Set Forth Your Case* (Chicago: Moody, 1974), 91.

5. John F. Walvoord, *The Holy Spirit at Work Today* (Lincoln, NE: Back to the Bible Broadcast, 1973), 18.

6. Alan Redpath, *Victorious Christian Living* (Grand Rapids, MI: Fleming H. Revell, 1994), 27.

7. Ray C. Stedman, *Birth of the Body* (Santa Ana, CA: Vision House, 1974), 9–10.

8. Spurgeon, quoted by Carter, *Spurgeon at His Best,* 67.

Matthew 16:22–18:35: Saying Good-Bye to Galilee

1. MacArthur, *The MacArthur New Testament Commentary, Matthew 16–23* (Chicago: Moody Press, 1988), 40.

2. Vance Havner, *Playing Marbles with Diamonds* (Grand Rapids, MI: Baker, 1985), 18.

3. Vine, *Vine's Expository Dictionary of New Testament Words,* vol. 2, 294.

4. Sanders, *Bible Men of Faith,* 137.

5. J. Dwight Pentecost, *The Glory of God* (Portland, OR: Multnomah, 1978), 76.

6. Watchman Nee, *The Release of the Spirit*

(Indianapolis: Sure Foundation, 1965), 9.

7. A. W. Tozer, quoted by Wiersbe, *The Best of A. W. Tozer*, 169.

8. R. T. France, *Matthew* (Leicester, England: InterVarsity, 1995), 267.

9. Merrill C. Tenney, ed., *The Zondervan Pictorial Encyclopedia of the Bible*, vol. 4 (Grand Rapids, MI: Zondervan, 1975), 227.

10. Charles Swindoll, *Seasons of Life* (Portland, OR: Multnomah, 1984), 167.

Matthew 19–20: Green Mile

1. Stephen King, *The Green Mile* (New York: Pocket, 1996), 491.

2. Larry Crabb Jr., *The Marriage Builder* (Grand Rapids, MI: Zondervan, 1982), 111.

3. Josh McDowell, *More Than a Carpenter* (Wheaton, IL: Tyndale, 1981), 75.

4. Lewis, *The Joyful Christian*, 166.

Matthew 21–23: Eight Days a Week

1. R. C. Sproul, *The Glory of Christ* (Wheaton, IL: Tyndale, 1990), 133.

2. Spurgeon, quoted by Carter, *Spurgeon at His Best*, 269.

3. Warren Wiersbe, *On Being a Servant of God* (Nashville, TN: Thomas Nelson, 1993), 16.

4. Charles Stanley, *Confronting Casual Christianity* (Nashville, TN: Broadman, 1985), 44.

5. Curtis C. Mitchell, *Let's Live!* (Old Tappan, NJ: Fleming H. Revell, 1960), 19.

Matthew 24–25: Prophetic Powwow

1. John F. Walvoord and Roy B. Zuck, eds., *The Bible Knowledge Commentary, New Testament Edition* (Wheaton, IL: Victor, 1988), 545.

2. John F. Walvoord, *Matthew: Thy Kingdom Come* (Chicago: Moody, 1974), 193.

3. W. F. Arndt and F. W. Gingrich, *A Greek-English Lexicon of the New Testament* (Chicago: University of Chicago, 1957), 811.

4. Jay Kesler, *The Strong Weak People* (Wheaton, IL: Victor, 1978), 44.

5. John White, *Greater Than Riches* (Downers Grove, IL: InterVarsity, 1992), 62–63.

Matthew 26:1–27:26: Countdown to Crucifixion

1. Hershel Shanks, *In the Temple of Solomon and the Tomb of Caiaphas* (Washington, DC: Biblical Archaeology Society, 1993), 35–38.

2. Hershel Shanks, *Jerusalem: An Archaeological Biography* (New York: Random House, 1995), 187.

3. Ibid., 35.

4. W. A. Criswell, *Great Doctrines of the Bible*, vol. 3 (Grand Rapids, MI: Zondervan, 1983), 83.

5. Mary Alice Chrnalogar, *Twisted Scriptures* (Grand Rapids, MI: Zondervan, 2000), 129.

6. Tim LaHaye, *Finding the Will of God in a Crazy Mixed-Up World* (Grand Rapids, MI: Zondervan, 2001), 122.

Matthew 27:27–28:20: Crucified, Raised, and Praised

1. Mark R. Littleton, *A Place to Stand* (Portland, OR: Multnomah, 1986), 144.

2. Jim Fleming, *The World of the Bible Gardens* (Jerusalem: Biblical Resources, 1999), 44.

3. Spurgeon, quoted by Carter, *Spurgeon at His Best*, 272–73.

4. McDowell, *Evidence That Demands a Verdict*, 224.

5. Walvoord, *The Bible Knowledge Commentary*, 92.

6. Richard F. Lovelace, *Renewal as a Way of Life* (Downers Grove, IL: InterVarsity, 1985), 126–27.

Index

original audience, vi
presents Jesus as King of
Jews, vii–viii
records events at Caesarea,
215–16
treatment of parables, 166
treatment of Sermon on
Mount, 66
truthfulness, vii
when written, vi
See also book of Matthew,
structure
book of Matthew, structure,
116
arranged thematically, 66
opens with genealogy, 3–8
shifts to teachings on
church, 176
turning point, 139
bread, 209
as basic needs, 94–95
in biblical times, 22
breaking bread, 300–301
See also leaven
broad way to destruction, 100
brood of vipers, 37–38, 159–60
brothers of Jesus, 162
bruised reed, 153, 155

C

Caesar Augustus, 17
Caesarea Philippi, 27, 214–16
vs. other Caesarea, 210
Caiaphas, 295–97, 307
trying Jesus, 305–7
Cain, 3
calf, as Mark emblem, v
Calvary, 320, 324
Calvin, John
on worry, 99
camel's hair, 36–37
camel through needle's eye,
252–53
Canaanites, 5, 55
Capernaum, 54–55, 115, 144,
145

Jesus's last visit, 232–33
as Jesus's ministry
headquarters, 55–56, 109
name's significance, 56
Casper, 17
casting lots for garments,
319–20
causing little ones to stumble,
233–34
celibacy, 248–49
centurion
asks Jesus's help, 109–10
at cross, 311, 322–323
Chadwick, Samuel
on power of prayer, 90
Chafer, Lewis Sperry
on Trinity, 44
chaff, as sinners, 41
Chambers, Oswald
on humility and holiness, 90
on motives for prayer, 93
charity, 89–90
cherub, 48, 49
See also angel, angels
chief priests, 21, 22, 264–65,
326
bribe guards, 328–29
confront Jesus, 269–77
See also Caiaphas; Pharisees;
Sadducees
children
assured place in heaven,
249–50
child and kingdom, 233–36
children praise Jesus, 264
children of Abraham, 37–38
Chorazin, 144, 145
Christians
as light of world, 77–78
as salt of earth, 75–76
See also disciples of Jesus
Christmas star, 19–20, 23
Christ, the Christ. *See* Jesus
Chrnalogar, Mary Alice
on Christians in agony, 303
church, vii, 176, 217

times mentioned in New
Testament, 205
church discipline, 236–38
Church of the Holy Sepulcher,
324
Cloud, Henry
on setting limits, 185
Coffey, John, 243–44
coin in fish's mouth, 231–33
Colson, Charles
on witness, 77
confessing Jesus, 132
corban, 196
covenants in the Bible, 4
Crabb, Larry, Jr.
on self-seeking, 209
on troubled marriages, 248
Criswell, W. A.
on Last Supper, 301
crown of thorns, 53, 317, 318
cut off hand, foot, 234

D

damned, 172
See also hades; hell
Dan, 214
Daniel, 42, 72, 73
darkness at Jesus's death,
321–22
David, 4–5, 69, 151–52, 209,
284
Davidic Covenant, 4, 156
Dead Sea Scrolls, 32–33, 206
Decapolis, 60
DeHaan, Richard W.
on God's knowledge of
suffering, 182
"Deliver us from the evil one,"
96
demon, demons, 47, 229–32
following Jesus, 155–57
Jesus casting out demons,
59–61
See also demon possession;
devil
demon possession, 60, 110,

See also sin
Fortress Antonia, 262–63
four living creatures, v
France, R. T.
  on temple tax, 233
frankincense, 23, 24

G

Gadarene. *See* Gergesenes
Galilee, 26, 27, 54–55, 60
  as spiritually weak, 54,
    55–56
Garden of Gethsemane,
  90–96, 301–5
genealogy, 4
  See also Jesus, genealogy
Genesis, v
Gennesaret, 191, 192
Gentiles, 130
  as birds, 173
  as dogs, 200
  evangelized after Jews, 129
  in God's plan, 153–55,
    160–61, 201–2
  in Jesus's genealogy, 6
  judgment of Gentiles, 291–94
Gergesenes, 113–15
Gethsemane. *See* Garden of
  Gethsemane
Getz, Gene A.
  on legalism, 194
"Give us this day our daily
  bread," 94–95
giving, 89–90
God (God the Father), vii, 71
  as Father, 91, 100, 146–49
  his wrath, 323–24
  as holy, 92–93
  speaks at Jesus's baptism,
    41–42
  at Transfiguration, 225–26
  See also Holy Spirit; Holy
    Trinity; Jesus
God's will, 93–94
God's Word. *See* Bible, as
  inerrant

gold, 23, 24
Golgotha, 319
graves open, 322–23
Great White Throne
  judgment, 292
Greeks wanting to see Jesus,
  126
Green Mile, 243
guards at Jesus's tomb, 327–28

H

hades, 66, 144, 213, 215
  See also hell
hairs numbered, 132
Halley, Henry H.
  on wise men visiting Jesus,
    18
"Hallowed be your name,"
  92–93
harmless as doves, 130
harvest, 123
Havner, Vance
  on cost of discipleship, 223
  on mind as battleground, 83
healing, 60
  See also Jesus, healing
heaven, vii
  See also salvation
Heli, 7
hell, vii, 131–32, 171–72
Herod (the Great), 17–29,
  141, 180, 181, 214, 263,
  268–69
  death and aftermath, 26–29
  hears of Jesus's birth, 19–20
  as "King of the Jews," 18–19
  murders children of
    Bethlehem, 24–26
  plots to kill Jesus, 21–24
Herod Agrippa I, 28, 256
Herod Agrippa II, 28
Herod Antipas, 27, 28, 198,
  207, 211, 310
  beheads John, 180–84
  fears Jesus is John returned,
    180

  imprisons John the Baptizer,
    139–41
Herod Archelaus, 27, 28, 180
Herod Philip I, 28, 210
Herod Philip II, 27, 28, 180–81
Herodians, 207, 274
Herodias, 28, 180–81,
  183–84
Herodium, 268–69
high priest. *See* Caiaphas; chief
  priests
high priest's prison, 308
Hillel, 245
Holocaust, 267, 293
holy angels, 47
  See also angels
Holy of Holies, 323
Holy Spirit
  and conception of Jesus, 8–9
  convicts of sin, 159
  descends on Jesus at
    baptism, 41–45
  gives Christians testimony,
    131
  sin against Spirit, 157–60
  testifies to Jesus, 212
  See also baptism: with Holy
    Spirit; Holy Trinity
Holy Trinity, 42–44
honey, 37
honoring father, mother,
  195–96
Hosanna, 263, 264
Hosea, 24, 25
house on rock vs. sand, 101–2
householder, 176
Hughes, R. Kent
  on gratitude for God's care,
    210
Huizenga, L. S., 108
humility, 70–72, 236
hunger for God, 72–73
Hunter, John
  on commitment to Christ's
    program, 309
hyperbole, 234

hypocrisy, 208–10
   See also Pharisees

I

Idumea, 27
immaculate conception, 8
Immanuel, 331
inscription over cross, 320–21
Ironside, H. A.
  on fasting, 97
Isaac, 4, 261
Isaiah, on Jesus, 124
  See also Jesus, prophecies
    about Jesus
Ishmael, 4
Israel, 174–75, 267
  as rejecting Jesus, 155

J

Jacob (stepfather Joseph's
  father), 7
Jairus, 117–18
James (brother of Jesus), 177,
  224
  on care for others, 196
James (disciple of Jesus), 124,
  231, 302
  called by Jesus, 58–59
  as disciple, 125–26
  as martyr, 126
  at transfiguration, 224–27
  wants to reign with Jesus,
    256
  as well off, 59
James (son of Alphaeus), 124,
  128
Jeconiah, 7
Jeremiah, 24, 25, 210–11
Jericho, 6
  as two places, 258
Jerusalem, 262, 277
Jesus
  accused of blasphemy, 115
  accused of pact with devil,
    155–59

  agonizes in Gethsemane,
    302–4
  angel shows empty tomb,
    327–28
  arrested, tried, condemned,
    304–7
  baptism at Jordan, 41–45
  Beatitudes, 66–75
  begins preaching, 57
  blesses children, 249–50
  buried, 325–27
  calls all Christians family,
    162–63
  calls disciples, 57–59
  calls God Father, 146–48
  calls Matthew as disciple,
    115–16
  calls, sends out disciples,
    123–29
  casts out demons, 110
  challenges Pharisees, 193–98
  childhood in Nazareth, 27–29
  conceived via Holy Spirit, 8–9
  condemned by Pilate, 311–16
  confronts chief priests, 269–77
  confronts John's doubts,
    139–43
  counsels rich young man,
    250–53
  crucified with two thieves,
    319–20
  curses unripe fig tree, 266–68
  dedicated at Temple, 14
  dies on cross, 321–22, 324
  eats Passover with disciples,
    298–302
  enters Jerusalem on donkey,
    261–64
  finally rejected at Nazareth,
    177
  flight to Egypt, 14, 24
  forbids testimony he is
    Christ, 217–18
  genealogy, 3–8
  given name Jesus, 12, 14–15
  gives disciples Great

    Commission, 330–31
  hears of John's death, 182,
    184–85
  his brothers and sisters, 162
  Joseph's dream vindicates
    Mary, 11–12
  leaves Galilee for good, 245
  many abandon him, 188–89
  Mary and Joseph betrothed,
    10–11
  mocked by soldiers, 317–19
  moves to Capernaum, 54–55
  multiplies loaves, fishes,
    186–89
  Peter proclaims him Christ,
    210–13
  Pharisees call him
    demon-inspired, 119
  Pharisees plot to kill him,
    152–53
  post-resurrection
    appearances, 329
  preaches, heals in Galilee,
    59–61
  predicts death before
    Pharisees, 160–61
  prepares for death, 151
  priests plot to kill him, 295–97
  promises to faithful disciples,
    253–55
  rebukes Peter, 221–23
  rebukes unbelief, 143–47
  refuses Pharisees a sign,
    207–10
  risen Jesus greets women, 328
  Sermon on Mount, 65–105
  stills storm, 112–13
  strange phenomena at death,
    322–23
  tackles tough questions,
    245–49
  teaches mainly in parables,
    165–76
  tempted by devil, 50–54
  throws moneychangers from
    temple, 264–65

Q

Qumran, 32–33

R

Rachel, 25
  Rachel's tomb, 25–26
Rahab, 5, 6
Ramah, 24, 25, 26
Rapture, 281–82, 323
Redpath, Alan
  on God's ways vs. ours,
    213–4
reed, 317, 318
religion, empty religion,
    161–62
  See also faith
remarriage, 246–47
remnant, 146
repent, repentance, 34
  in Beatitudes, 66–70
  failure to repent, 144–47
  repentant thief, 73–74
resurrection, 327–29
Revelation
  four living creatures, v
  See also Olivet discourse
Richards, Larry, viii
  on Jesus's parables, 166
  on Word of God, 53–54
riches, 167, 168
  See also Jesus, teachings:
    money
rich young man, 250–53
righteousness
  examples in daily life, 96–98
  in Jesus's teaching, 79–80
Ruth, 5, 6
Ryrie, Charles Caldwell
  on faith, 110

S

Sabbath, 151–53, 185
Sadducees, 274
  characteristics, 205–7

and John the Baptizer,
    37–39
  and Pharisees, 205–7
  See also Pharisees
Salome, mother of James,
    John, 325
  See also mother of Zebedee's
    sons
salt of the earth, 75–76
salvation, 93
  and confessing Jesus,
    131–32
  and good works, 101
  and money, 250–53
  as narrow gate, 100
  and prayer, 93
  as presented in Matthew, vii
  as presented in parables,
    165–77
  See also faith
Samaria, 27
Samaritans, 130
Sanders, J. Oswald
  on John the Baptizer, 184
  on mind as battleground, 83
  on transfiguration, 226
  on virgin birth, 10
Sanhedrin, 19
  Jesus's trial as illegal, 307–8
  See also Caiaphas
Satan, 48, 143, 157, 283
  and Judas, 304–5
  offers Jesus compromised
    power, 53
  Peter as Satan, 221–23
  See also demon, demons;
    devil
Saul, 284
scarlet robe, 318
scourging, 313
scribes, 79–80, 112, 115, 193
  See also Pharisees; Sadducees
Scripture, Scriptures (*see* Bible)
Sea of Chinnereth, 56
Sea of Galilee, 27, 56
  as dangerous, 112–13

Sea of Tiberias, 56
second coming, 279–94
  natural disasters, 284–85
  only Father knows, 285,
    287–88
  signs, 280–81
  See also Olivet discourse
seeds, 167–70
self-righteousness, 251–52
Sermon on the Mount,
    65–105
  applications, 80–105
  Beatitudes, 66–75
  its effect, 65
  as King's Creed, 107
  "Righteousness from the
    Inside Out," 80
  structure, 78, 99
  use of "twos," 102
  where preached, 66
servant leadership, 256–57
seventieth week of Daniel,
    281–82
seventy times seven, 239–40
sexual immorality, 246–47
shake dust off feet, 130–31
Shammas, 245
Sheba, 160–61
sheep among wolves, 130
sheep from goats, 291–93
sheep without shepherd, 123
Shekinah, 20
Sidon, 144, 145, 198
sign from heaven, 207–8
sign of Jonah, 207–8
Simeon, 325
Simon (Jesus's brother), 177
Simon the Canaanite, 124
  See also Simon the Zealot
Simon of Cyrene, 319–20
Simon the leper, 297
Simon Peter, 124 *see* Peter
Simon the sorcerer, 101
Simon the Zealot, 129
  See also Simon the Canaanite
sin, vii

V

veil of Temple torn, 322–23
virgin birth, 8–14

W

walking on water, 189–91
Walvoord, John, 174
  on Holy Spirit, 213
washing hands, 312
wedding garments, 273
wheat, as righteous ones, 41,
  170–72
White, John
  on God's judgment, 293
wicked one, 167
  see also devil; Satan
Wiersbe, Warren
  on God's care for his
    servants, 270
  on hypocrisy, 99
  on repentance, 34
Wilkinson, Bruce, and
  Kenneth Boa
  on Christ's parables, 165
Willard, Dallas
  on "disciple" vs. "Christian,"
    58
wine mixed with gall, 319,
  320
  See also sponge of sour wine
wineskins, 116
winnowing fan, fork, 39, 41
wise man, 101–2
wise men (adoring Jesus), vi,
  17–24
  gifts to Jesus, 23–24
  gifts' significance (table), 24
  identity, number, 18
  what they saw in heavens,
    19–20
  when they saw Jesus, 18
wise as serpents, 130
witnesses, 236–37
woman of Canaan, 199–201
woman at well, 28
women, in Jesus's genealogy, 5
Word, Word of God (*see* Bible)
worry, 98–99

Y

yoke, 148
"Your kingdom come,"
  meaning, 93–94
"Your will be done," 93–94

Z

Zacharias, 31, 32
Zealots, 206
Zebedee, 58, 59
Zebulun, 54–56